I Still Can't Fly

Library of Congress Cataloging-in-Publication Data:
Carroll, Kevin
I Still Can't Fly : Confessions of a Lifelong Troublemaker
1. Sanitation worker—Nonfiction 2. New York City Department of Sanitation
3. Public Sector Union 4. Catholic School 5. Heroin addiction
6. Opioid addiction 7. Kevin Carroll.

Cover art by Anna Usacheva
Book design by Paco Salas Pérez
Set in Adobe Garamond Pro and Cabazon

Published by Hardball Press
Brooklyn, New York

ISBN 978-0-9991358-5-3
www.hardballpress.com

I Still Can't Fly

Confessions of a Lifelong Troublemaker

Kevin John Caroll

HARDBALL
PRESS

For my baby.

I still love ya a whole universe full.

1

How did I get here? An abandoned first-floor apartment in a dilapidated rat infested building in a filthy blighted neighborhood where a toll-free call for a car insurance rate quote comes with a free steering wheel lock. Criminals own the streets. Drug dealers own the criminals. I don't feel out of place.

A tiny flame beseeches an unlikely blessing as it flickers in the belly of Our Lady of Guadalupe on the kitchen counter. The rank smell of festering urine reminds me of my purpose: get in, get out. I've adjusted to the shadows like an anxious cat. February in New York inhibits my ability to manage my fingertips, while twenty-seven years of addiction strangles clarity of thought like a python squeezing life from its next meal. My body is heaving with anxiety. How did I get here?

The scrawny hooded lookout nervously paces the room and suddenly kicks a ratty old step stool. The sole piece of furniture in the garbage strewn apartment crashes against a wall. The pizza box lying on its top step scatters a clique of roaches that scurry to new digs under a hamburger roll. "Gimme my damn money, bitch." The tiny runt stated his gripe with conviction, but he had as much chance of collecting as I had of buying dope with Monopoly money. "Get outside, Flaco. We talk later." The black Puerto Rican, probably female pitcher (dealer) with the big round pock-marked face looked like a football lineman. Her bad attitude was apparently the byproduct of a disturbing reflection. "You gonna look real stupid wit my mother fuggin foot hanging out yo dumb ass, Flaco. I said get outside."

The young Spanish lookout resembled a short mop stick with a big coat. He stuffed his gloved hands deep in his pockets and glared at the woman with a hatred most criminals reserve for the police department.

Every ten bags of dope sold, the lookout gets a ten-dollar bill, and it appears the big dealer shorted Flaco ten bucks on the last bundle. We had a Mexican standoff. The lookout wasn't looking out. The pitcher wasn't pitching until she finally noticed the white junkie suffering silently on the cold radiator. "Whaddaya need, handsome?"

1

"Four."

"I only got two leff. If ya take 'em, I can go upstairs and re-up."(get more).

Flaco was still grumbling as I handed the big girl half of what I needed to get straight. "I'll be right back. And I ain't gonna tell you again, Flaco, get yo dumb, skinny ass outside before—"

CRASH! The sudden explosion of the front door was as startling as a Mike Tyson punch in the face. "Down on the fucking floor! Lemme see hands! Down! Down! On the fucking floor!"

How did I get here?

As I remember, it wasn't that difficult.

2

The sudden commotion out in the corridor warned of the approaching doom. The front door slammed, startling all, closing off my only prayer of escape. Fear of the unknown smothered the air like an atomic mushroom cloud. I was mad, confused, wondering why mom and dad sent me to this horrible place.

After peeling my nose off the window, away from the dream of freedom just beyond, I turned towards the blackboard and gazed in horror as a giant nun floated across the classroom floor like a witch. Sister Mary Monster hovered behind the big desk, hands on hips, dark piercing eyes squinting above crew cuts and ponytails at the only Christian recruit still standing.

My brain was already racing through almost six years of warnings. Wait till the NUNS get hold of you. You better not try THAT with the nuns. We'll see if you're still smiling when THEY get you in the first grade, wise guy. I always thought my mom was joking, but this isn't funny.

Quick action was obviously crucial for staying healthy. I was still pondering a move to take the last seat in the last row when she barked, "What is your name?" Already in fear for my mortal existence, I gazed down at my shiny new Buster Brown shoes and mumbled, "Kevin." The dark shadow slapped two heavy palms on the green blotter and leered down her pointed nose over rimless glasses. "What is your last name, Kevin!?" The intensity of the moment sucked the air from my lungs, but I still managed to squeak, "Carroll?" So far I got the first two questions right, but it was all uphill from here.

"Well, well," she mused, "you're in the right room, Mister Carroll, except your seat is right here." Sister pointed down with what looked like the massive finger of God at what became my permanent position at the head of the class, third isle, front seat, a short arm's length from a good smack in the head.

Seconds ago on this very first day of school, the room overflowed with giggles and smiling faces, all searching for a little seat next to a friend. In its place, dead silence shrouds the room as my young brain stumbles through what could only be described as an epiphany. I was about to get educated.

Like a convicted murderer en route to the electric chair, my steps toward the giant digit were painfully slow. Vise-like fingers suddenly snapped out like a cobra, grabbing hold of my ear—that appendage from here on to be regarded as the handle on the side of my head—as she rudely ushered me into my personal corner of hell. The carefree life I've known for almost six years officially ended that very same moment.

Sister Mary Monster was big. Seven foot, maybe eight. Okay, maybe not that big, but the giant nun seemed to grow a whole lot scarier when her needs required spontaneous adjustment activated by annoying young Christians. Her thick furry brow ran from one side of her face to the other on a big holy melon framed in starched white material, topped with a brown hood and a veil that cascaded down her back. When she walked, the rest of Sister's long brown habit flowed to the ground, covering her shoes, giving the illusion of elevation. Sister could float and she could float fast. Take away the giant rosary beads and long white Tarzan rope tied around her waist and Sister could've been mistaken for a medieval executioner.

As the unmercifully long days were dragging into a possible life sentence, my scattered brain actually found a way of avoiding the monster in front of the classroom. It was Sister's own voice that triggered my natural instincts. Her monotonous droning of spelling, phonics, religion and arithmetic sounded more like a lazy babbling brook, so it only took her a few minutes before she put me fast to sleep, sometimes three or four times a day. By the time Sister called on me to recite the next line, add two numbers or ask me what Jesus said, my brain was a million miles away.

THE DREAM

Unlike previous missions, this time I flew into enemy airspace well-fortified. I had everything: atom bombs, H-bombs, cherry bombs. You name it, I had it. Final count down. "Pilot to bombardier. Ten seconds to drop. Nine, eight... " The usual landmarks were whizzing past me in a blur of rainbow colors. "Seven, six... " The screaming turbo engines nearly sheared the giant oak tree that filled the sky above old Aunt Mae's house on O'Brien Avenue. Boom! A biblical thunderclap cracked the sky." Five, four…"

Red light! Red light! The cockpit panel lit up like a damn Christmas tree. To my right at three o'clock a screaming vapor trail is headed directly for me. I'm hit! My left wing incinerated before my eyes. The sky darkened to an eerie purple as thick black smoke obliterated the sun. Another missile. Ka-blewie! That one sheared off my tail section. I'm going down! This can't be happening again! Firepower is raining from the heavens with incomprehensible terror. "Mayday! Mayday!" Now my damn radio's out! "Eject! Eject!" Sonofabitch, this freaking button is stuck. Death is coming to get me as I watch all five and a half years of my life pass before my eyes faster than Superman. I was blown out of the sky and crashed back to earth in a fireball of hellish proportion.

"Mister Carroll, I said read the next line. Mister Carroll!"

There I was as usual, sitting at my little desk in the front row of the class with my eyes wide open, startled back to reality while still smack in the middle of my latest mission. "Mister Carroll!" Unfortunately, this one ended the exact same way as all the others. "Mister Carroll, I said read the next line."

The monolith of gloom slowly folded her hands into the large billowy sleeves of her habit. What is she looking for? Switchblade? Brass knuckles? Maybe even a two by four. Don't look up. Her evil eye is now burning through the top of my head. A quick prayer is my only way out. **Please, God. Please make Sister disappear.** It was my first meaningful plea for assistance and I was hardly awestruck by His obvious lack of concern. Left to my own devices, I nervously ran my finger down the page.

"Uhh… look, Jane… see… Spot." The dead silence behind me exploded into giggles. Sister quickly hushed the entire class with a sudden whack! in the back of my head. "Wrong page, Mister Carroll." Now we're both pissed off and it's not even ten a.m., lavatory time.

The eternity in hell that was only two and a half months in Holy Cross Grammar School didn't teach me enough arithmetic to make change of a quarter, but a good ear twisting did work on rare occasions, so it was up to my dad to finally drum one number into my thick skull: twenty-nine. November the 29th is my birthday, still six whole days away. It might as well have been six years.

Mom insisted and dad agreed that if I was a very good boy in school for just the next few days, they would let me have a birthday party, and they would buy me the greatest toy in history, the giant Mattel Bulldog

Tank. Or, I could do what comes natural and get zip. Zilch. If I'm lucky, maybe I'll get a Spalding or a leftover turkey sandwich for lunch. In fact, mom said I'd be real lucky just to turn six years old. What the hell kind of deal is that?

In order to survive a possible bypass of November the 29th I learned to quickly decipher mom's early morning warnings. Kevin, I don't want to see any notes today. That was easy, that simply meant, try not to do anything stupid enough that Sister would find a need to memorialize it on paper. Sister Mary Monster's favorite chore after smacking me around was writing down all the trouble that somebody got me into that day. To make certain her note went all the way home, she would summon my seven year old sister Kathleen and hand it over with strict instructions. But if mom said, now Kevin, you be a very good boy in school today, don't make sister mad at you, that means mom is learning to speak Chinese. Be a very good boy? I had a better chance of obtaining a Ph.D. in mathematics by Christmas morning. That is not going to happen. Not a chance Not even a little one.

Even after hearing the terms of the deal repeated a thousand times I still figured I could pull off a miracle. I'll be blowing Jap planes out of the sky with my Mattel Bulldog tank before you could say, "Hey boys and girls, what time is it?"

Monday morning. Crack-a-dawn. I am awake, but unfortunately mom wants me to go to school again. I'll just stay in bed with my eyes closed and fake it, hopefully until Saturday. I sure wish Grandma was here. Grandma knows God better than anybody. Grandma told me if I ever needed anything from the Lord, all I had to do is pray to the right saint, sit back, the saint talks to God, and bam! God takes care of the whole shootin' match. I hope the Lord doesn't mind me cutting out the middleman. **Dear God, I don't know the special saint's name for changing days back, but I need it to be Sunday again, real, real bad.**

Though my head was buried snuggly under my pillow, I still managed to hear my big sister Kathleen flush the toilet bowl. I can't believe it, it's really Monday morning and it's almost my turn. **You're killing me here.**

"Kathleen, let's go!"

Silence. Maybe my big sister fell asleep on the crapper?

"Kathleen, you out yet? Come on. Kevin's gotta get in there!" It's a damn good thing I was already awake, that high-pitched squeal mom calls a voice cut through the early morning calm like a good smack in the ear from Sister Mary Monster. "Momeeee, I'm out!" The torture is about to begin.

"Kevin! It's time to get movin'." This praying stuff doesn't seem to be working. Maybe if I rub my forehead real, real hard, it'll feel like a fever or a brain tumor or something. "Kevin, you up yet?" I got it. I'll just lie real still and breathe real slow through my nose, mom will think I'm dead.

"Ma, I don't feel too good. I got a earache."

"Kevin, something's gonna be wrong with your rear-end if I have to come in there." It was definitely time to panic. Chicken pops. I need chicken pops. Something believable. Something contagious.

"Mommee! He's still in bed!"

"Kevin, move it!" My excuse was dead and my big sister killed it.

At bedtime Kathleen and I slept together in the only bedroom in the house until mom and dad were ready for the sack, when Dad then carried us out and into the living room, where we dreamed undisturbed on the Castro convertible, until the crack of dawn, when my mom was suddenly screaming inside my brain. "Kevin, wash and brush right this instant!" Little Tommy slept on the hi-riser in the bedroom with the door closed.

The fear of my next encounter with the monster of Holy Cross was all consuming, like being awakened during brain surgery five days a week. "Let's go. I poured the milk."

I took a whiz, slowly brushed my teeth and shuffled back into the hallway. My dumb school shoes always managed to appear by the banister at the head of the staircase. Once again I prayed they'd disappear before mom was shaking clean socks under my nose.

Mom was in the kitchen standing at the ironing board putting the finishing touches on my stupid white shirt. "Don't just look at 'em, they're not gonna walk to school by themselves." Mom stood the hot iron upright and slid the shirt off the board. "See if you can manage to keep it clean for a few days." I grabbed my warm shirt, slipped it on and turned away. Defeated. Traumatized. "Come back here, mister." I looked over my shoulder as mom snatched my ugly Catholic school tie from a hook inside the hall closet door. "Don't look at me like that." Mom quickly tied the red plaid noose around my neck. "Ya have ta goda school."

"Why?"

"You have a lot of questions, wise guy, but mostly because I say so."

7

That was the dumbest answer to that question since last Friday. It also sounded like the only one she had. That means it's time for breakfast. You can't send a little kid into the valley of death on an empty stomach. First a big old bowl of Cheerios in my Lone Ranger bowl. Then some Bosco in my big old Howdy Doody glass. Grandpa says I should look like a little colored kid 'cause I drink so much Bosco.

"Ma, I'm goin'." My sister was standing at the mirror at the top of the staircase. Kathleen buttoned her plaid coat at the chin, then she cocked her matching beret until it was just right. "Gimme a kiss," insisted mom. I was already gazing into a bowl of yellow milk. **Please, God, can you fill this bowl one more time, please, like You did with the loaves and fishes?** It didn't work. Maybe I'm missing a magic word or something.

My big sister was holding the knob on the banister, leaning over sticking out her stupid tongue. "I'm gonna get you," I whispered. Kathleen spun around and hurried down the stairs. "Kevin, move your ass before ya late again!" Mom doesn't miss a trick. Ten minutes ago I was working on a performance worthy of an Academy Award. Now she's looking to push me out the door on my way to die. How come time doesn't move this fast when I'm sitting in front of Sister Mary Monster?

I grabbed the bottle of milk with two hands and quickly gulped down another glass of Bosco. Then I went into the hall closet and yanked my ugly blue corduroy coat by the sleeve off the hangar. I hate my ugly school coat. When I backed away from the door, mom appeared with the dumb schoolbag. Where's my guardian angel? Where's grandma? Where's my dad? I grabbed my school junk and shuffled towards the staircase. "Come back here, Mister." I turned in hopes of an eleventh hour stay of execution. "Here, take ya lunch box and gimme a kiss and tuck in that shirt." Not even the slightest hint of compassion. "It keeps comin' out."

"Well, if you stop running around here."

"Whaddaya want me to do, walk real slow like old Mister Mulligan?" Mom gave me, the look. "Don't be so nasty. Now, did ya brush 'n' go?" I nodded and mumbled as she spun me around, tucking the tail of my dumb shirt securely into my stupid pants. "Now gimme a kiss."

"I just did that."

"No you didn't. Do it again." Then she put one right on the kisser.

8

"I think you might need your raincoat for later," she predicted. "It looks like rain."

"What does rain look like when it's not raining?"

"Don't be so smart, I'll give ya a good smack." I looked her right in the eye and dared, "Go ahead, you don't hurt me." Mom tugged the lapel of my ugly school coat. "If it rains you better not get wet, mister. Now be a good boy, please?"

♧

I was the biggest troublemaker in the first grade, maybe the entire school, so if mom really expected me to be a good boy, she'd gag me, throw my skinny ass in the hall closet and eat the key. But she didn't do that. Not ever. Instead, she turned me loose on the world once again.

I slowly stepped into the frigid morning while mom prayed from the top of the staircase. "Please be a good boy today, Kevin. Stay out of trouble." My usual attempt to calm her anxiety was already an exhausting ritual. "Okaaaay." The effort was hardly worth the air that escaped from my little lungs.

3

My neighborhood is mostly Irish, German and Italian middle class families. I just happen to be Irish, German, Italian and middle class. I fit right in. Clason Point is bordered on the north by Bruckner Boulevard. The peninsula disappears into the East River a few hundred yards south of the Shore Haven Beach Club.

Dad talks about the old trolleys that no longer service our neighborhood, but the rails are still imbedded in the cobble stones along Soundview Avenue. White Plains Road boarders Clason point to the east and Rosedale Avenue the west. One and two-family homes dominate my tiny corner of the Bronx.

One long row of attached brick houses on one side of Taylor Avenue and one row on the other side of the street. According to mom, this single block is my entire authorized universe. My best friend Steven Guardino lives right next door on the second floor.

The secret code for calling Stevie was the same every day. I jab the doorbell, three short rings, three long rings and three more quick ones. My Uncle Johnny told me that means SOS, and THAT means trouble. He also told me to use that same signal whenever I go to somebody's house, especially grandma's house where he lives. Uncle Johnny says people should be warned of impending doom. I wasn't exactly sure what impending doom means, but Uncle Johnny says I bring it with me everywhere I go. So how come Uncle Johnny never answers the front door at grandma's house anymore?

"How did I know it was you, Kevin?" As usual, Steven's mom had little pin curls all over her head. "Morning, Missus Guardino," I said politely. "Good morning, Kevin. Go ahead up, Steven's running a little late."

Stevie's mom says we're like two peas in a pod. That means whenever Stevie got in trouble I got in trouble, and when I got in trouble he got in trouble. We don't plan it like that, it just happens. "Go sit on the couch and behave yourself. Carmine's watching Captain Kangaroo."

Stevie's dumb three-year old cousin Carmine lives downstairs. Dumb Carmine was always hanging around Stevie's house. My little brother

Tommy's annoying little friend was sitting Indian style on the rug, grabbing his hair with one fist and sucking his thumb on the other. On the television, Mister Greenjeans was pulling a white mouse from the upper chest pocket of his coveralls. Dumb Carmine was staring at the show, so I slowly crept up behind and smacked him in the head to let him know I was back. "Aunt Annie, Kevin Carroll hit me again and he said a bad word!" The next sound was like a flaming cattle prod jabbed into my ear. "KEVIN. WHAT DID YOU SAY TO HIM!?"

Stevie's mom was still busy in the kitchen, so I didn't actually see the bulging veins in her neck and that skinny finger wagging in my face, but that doesn't mean the picture wasn't perfectly clear in my head. "Nuthin', Missus Guardino." Carmine was giggling like a baby. "Kevin, you leave Carmine alone. He was nice and quiet before you got here. You hear me, Kevin?"

"Yeeees, Missus Guardino." Carmine was still trying to get even. "I hope Sister beats you up again, ya big stupid."

"I'll get you outside, Carmine. Ya big liar."

The bathroom door opened with a crash. I peeked into the hall. Stevie was still pulling up his zipper, shaking his head and snarling at the big black rubber galoshes awaiting him by the staircase. They snarled right back. "Steven, put on those boots." Stevie plopped down on the top step. "No, I'm not going anywhere." Stevie was wrong. We were minutes from walking the last mile into the valley of death, and one of us will surely be suited up for a chance of light drizzle—in New Jersey.

Stevie was still fastening the last few buckles when his mom reached for the doorknob on the hall closet. My best friend suddenly jumped up and barricaded the opening with his outstretched arms. "No!" I couldn't have said it better myself. Missus Guardino grabbed Stevie's collar and pulled his face right up to her nose. "I have a feeling it's gonna rain today mister, so you're wearing the rain coat whether you like it or not." Defeat filled Stevie's eyes as he looked towards me for a little help. I couldn't think of anything.

"It's not gonna rain today. Just ask Kevin."

"I don't care what Kevin thinks. The weatherman says it's gonna rain."

I slowly trudged down the stairs. Stevie stomped right along behind grumbling about removing his ugly yellow raincoat as soon as physically possible, which is usually about fifty yards, the range his agitated mom could no longer reach to give him a good swift hop in the ass.

Just up the block we could already see Mother Godzilla, the principal and chief executioner scanning the horizon for stragglers. As we dawdled along trying to stretch a block into the Yellow Brick Road, I thought, what could bring a smile to Stevie's face on another miserable morning faster than the prospect of a birthday party? Well, the sight of our school blown to smithereens by a Russian bomb in the next two seconds could do it too, but news of a birthday party, now that's big time. Real big. "Hey, Stevie, I'm havin' a birthday party this Saturday. Wanna come?" Stevie's eyes bugged out. He quickly displayed a matching smile. "Yeah," he gleamed, "whaddaya havin'?" The valley of death was suddenly a million miles away. "Everything. Chocolate cake, ice cream, taterchips, M&M's... Everything."

"No girls, right?" What the hell kind of question is that? "Hell no, you crazy? I ain't no sissy."

"Whaddaya gettin'?" Stevie wondered. "Whaddaya think? The Bulldog Tank," I boasted.

"Wow," he gushed, "that's neat." The Mattel Bulldog Tank is the greatest toy in history. The giant army tank will make me the envy of Taylor Avenue three weeks before Christmas.

As far as I was concerned everything I told Stevie was a done deal. "All I gotta do is be good in school till Wednesday." Stevie's smile disappeared and his eyes sank to the pavement. "You ain't havin' no party."

Stevie knew me better than anyone, so his lack of faith made me a little nervous. "Yes, I am. You'll see."

As we approached the end of our class line my second bestest friend hurried up behind us. "Hey, Kev. Hey, Stevie, what's up?" Steven merely shrugged his yellow shoulders, so Fat Tony Boy knew not to mention Stevie's dumb rain coat. "Hey, Tony Boy, I'm havin' a birthday party this Saturday. Wanna come?" The three of us were shivering in the cold. I was anxious for Fat Tony Boy's reply when stupid Bernadette McDogface, with her stupid red braids, put her finger to her lips. "Shhh, quiet. No talking in line." I quickly turned to give 'Burn-ta-death' my special evil eye for ugly, red-headed big mouth tattletales, but Sister Mary Monster's radar picked up the commotion and whistled a left-handed Pearl Harbor on the back of my melon. Smack!

"Ouch!" I spun, startled but already displaying my best look of confusion while rubbing the dead skin on the back of my head.

"Good morning, Mister Carroll," she bristled. "What's so important? We would all like to know."

13

"I wasn't talking again, Sister. I just got something stuck in my throat." Sister didn't want a smart answer, either, but considering she took me by surprise, this was an exceptional display of my art. Being annoying this early in the day is considered a rare gift, and so far my only reason for coming to school.

Sister stood tall enough to look over the building, arms folded, tapping one invisible foot hard enough to crack the sidewalk. "Wipe that stupid look off your face, Mister Carroll. You're starting the day off on the wrong foot again." Sister whipped around and floated back to the head of the line. It's spooky to see how she could do that. It must be something the Holy Ghost teaches in nun school. I wish the hell I could float.

We slowly filed into the valley of death the same way the Christians were led to slaughter into the Coliseum by the Romans, two at a time, in dead silence of course.

In spite of the fact that Stevie and the rest of my classmates laughed at everything I said, I couldn't get a smile out of Sister Mary Monster if I was the patron saint of laughter. Nuns weren't put on this earth to laugh and have a good time, they were here to keep professional troublemakers like me in line, and at Holy Cross Grammar School we were in lines all the time.

We lined up to go in and out of school and to pledge allegiance. We lined up for the lunchroom, the lavatory and for fire drills. We even lined up for the civil defense air raid drills in case the Russians attempted to bomb our little tiny school to smithereens. Every line that took me away from my front row seat came with a smile, except one: Sister Mary Monster's ass-whippin' line, and that line could be anywhere in the valley. "Get up and stand behind that door, Mister Carroll. Push your desk out into the corridor, Mister Carroll. Put yourself in the closet and close the door, Mister Carroll." Of course, I was in charge of the ass whippin' line and my best friend Steven Guardino was usually second in charge. We spent more time praying together on holy ass-whippen lines than we did doing actual school work. We never paid to get on the line. "I'll take care you later, Mister Carroll." We paid to get off.

I hung my ugly blue corduroy coat in the closet and barely started my shuffle up the isle towards my personal corner of hell when the darkness of the valley suddenly grew bleaker. A potential problem was rapidly taking on new meaning: potential disaster. That second glass of Bosco at breakfast was beginning to seek water level. I had to go and

I had to go now. My eyes were turning yellow and I was beginning to leak out of my ears. Ten AM lavatory time seemed as far away as my birthday.

Sister stood by the window under the flag blocking any prayer of the Lord's sunlight, raised arms, open palms. That meant stand. We stood as one and faced the stars and stripes. First we pledge allegiance, then we pray. I was praying for a Russian attack. It didn't happen, and this time I was praying my freaking ass off.

We sat as one and folded our hands while Sister floated next to my desk, my eyes transfixed on the gigantic crucifix that hung from her waist. Could I be next? Could Sister possibly do to me what the crazy Romans did to the little tiny Jesus? Maybe not, but another painful morning was already well under way.

We were in our seats but a few seconds when Sister instructed us to open our catechisms. Intent on impressing the Ten Commandments, she began to read. "God said thou shalt not take the Lord thy God's name in vain." My hand rose, slowly enough to be noticed, but hardly enough to embarrass myself, but distress was already surging with the full force of an open fire hydrant. All eyes found their way to the back of my head as the latest dilemma unfolded with un-godly speed.

Sister was already glaring a hole through my brain. Her ability to instill holy hell with a hard stare far surpassed the petrifying intensity in the eyes of any holy picture, but it wasn't just those dark piercing orbs making me nervous. My insides are about to blow. Still, I sat. But within two minutes my hand waving was by far exceeding the legal speed limit for first graders. "God said thou shalt not kill." Again, she's glaring straight into my eyes. Does she mean me?

From previous encounters Sister knew me to be fast on my feet. I sat within swatting distance in the place of honor for the star trouble-maker, third aisle, front desk. Escape would take an effort worthy of a world-class athlete. I was fast and about to get a whole lot faster.

Her constant look to intimidate was a factor, but no longer my primary concern. Not after the last time. Once was embarrassing, twice infuriating, and because Sister failed at her first two attempts to teach me proper bladder control, I figured my latest emergency was merely her next opportunity to correct my deficiency before the end of religion class. So my problem was no longer just my chocolate-milk bloated bladder. My problem as usual was the big angry bully who seemed to delight in the fact that she could enrage and humiliate me without fear of reprisal.

15

By the time we completed all Ten Commandments my little friend was totally uncooperative, sort of like we didn't know each other anymore. So while one hand was in the air the other was holding onto my little friend so we wouldn't have an accident before getting permission to go. I was hopping in my seat like a little tiny troublemaker strapped into the electric chair, but what bugged me most was that Sister Mary Monster seemed to think that this was all very funny. "Excuse me, Mister Carroll," she calmly queried. "Are you going to do a little dance for us right there in your seat?" I stated the obvious, rather sharply, "No. I have to go to the lavatory."

"Just sit there until I'm good and ready."

"But I hafta go bad."

"Be quiet and put ya hand down, Mister Carroll."

I was tightening every muscle, navel to knees, when I suddenly recalled dad's simple insight that he imparted after mom informed him that Sister was forcing me to whiz in my pants. "Luke," he consoled. My dad always calls me Luke when he's trying to make an important point stick inside my head. Actually, dad calls me Luke all the time, except when he's mad. "Luke, when ya gotta go, ya gotta go." Yep, my dad's pretty damn smart for an old guy.

I sprung up from my desk so fast Sister practically spun herself into the floor reaching for my ear. I was out the door blazing through the corridor with such a fear I could've zoomed past Superman racing a speeding locomotive, and who was following so close behind that I thought she had to go, too? Good old Muscles Mary floated behind me at God's speed, but God wasn't fast enough and neither was Sister. I crashed through the lavatory door.

My arrival wasn't a moment too soon, so I still had my dignity, though everything else was now in serious jeopardy. "Mister Carroll, when you get out here I'll teach you to disobey me." Intuition comes with the job title, so I quickly zipped up and ran into the last toilet stall by the window and locked the latch.

"Do you hear me, Mister Carroll?" Sister was hovering in the doorway, ranting and raving like a holy wrestler. I quickly settled onto the crapper, chin cradled in sweaty hands while playing piano with my fingers on the sides of my face. My first thought was that mom and dad would find out, and then it's no cartoons and maybe even no dinner for a year. Forget my birthday. This is serious pressure. BANG! The lavatory door suddenly crashed open. Sister quickly floated up to my stall. A holy woman in the boy's lavatory? There's never a cop around when you need one.

"Mister Carroll, if you don't open this door this second you will be a very sorry young man."

Well, she definitely gave me something to think about this time. I was already 'sorry' my mom didn't believe I was deaf and forced me into this hell on earth. How much 'sorry' does Sister think I'm capable of within a twenty-four-hour period?

"I'm not comin' out."

"Oh, we'll see about that you little hooligan." Her steely determination was unnerving, but I am a professional. Her reaction was hardly unexpected. "You're in a perilous situation, Mister Carroll. Get out here right this instant." The massive holy predator was peering down like King Kong, her big hairy knuckles violently shaking the door. "I'm losing my patience, Mister Carroll." I looked up in horror. "Go away. I said I'm not comin' out." She finally erupted. "GET OUT HERE... NOW! OPEN THIS DOOR!" Her startling explosion almost flushed me right down the crapper.

Sister was huffing and puffing and banging and clanging, trying to rip the entire stall door off the hinges. My fear was rapidly escalating towards anger and my anger quickly degenerating towards stupidity when "Shit!" slipped out of my mouth.

"What did you say to me you little HOOLIGAN?"

To say that Sister was mad doesn't quite tell the story, so with a brand new reference point for fear I quickly responded, "Nothing." Probably the smartest answer to make it out of my mouth since the first day of school. It will take some world class storytelling to get out of this one and I'm not sure how fast I'll be able to talk with a mouth full of rosary beads. Dad's not going to like this one bit. No sirree.

Sister floated back towards the door with biblical like purpose, her rosary beads cracking the dead silence as they jingled from her waist.

Confusion, hesitation and even fear loomed in my head. Could I possibly run fast enough under extreme pressure with a huge holy predator hot on my heels?

I frantically slid over to the lavatory door and peeked out like a burglar. I could still hear Sister hurrying up the stairs at the far end of the corridor. The principal's eight grade classroom is on the second floor.

Mother Godzilla does triple duty as eighth grade teacher, principal and chief executioner. Her big gigantic head and snarling teeth sit atop

17

broad shoulders that, put together, look like an arsenal small Christians should avoid by any means. So when Sister Mary Monster finally gets together with Mother Godzilla, escape would be damn near impossible to play out. But plan 'B' was already unfolding with the same sudden swiftness as a smack in the ear from behind.

Fat Tony Boy calls me a skinny bellink for the same reason everybody calls him Fat Tony Boy. It was obvious. He was fat, I was skinny. But I wasn't quite skinny enough. The lavatory window barely opened six inches. Unfortunately my head was just a hair over six inches fat. Another plan had to be formulated in a big fat hurry before holy people surrounded my position. Thinking on the run is something I was well adjusted to. Something will come to me. Something always does. Usually.

I pulled the door a crack and employed an anxious ear while muffled voices floated through the storm clouds in my brain. As the voices grew louder I could hardly distinguish Mother and Sister from the blood pounding in my head. Mother and Sister were imploring saints I don't think my Grandma ever heard of, and Grandma knew them all, from Saint Butch, patron saint of tiny troublemakers, to Saint Jude, patron saint of something from somewhere. Boy, I sure wish Grandma was here right now because I could definitely use a special prayer to somebody really special.

The next wave of terror brought another horrifying image. God was certain to be helping big old Mother down those stairs while whispering my next move in her ear before I could think of it myself. I slipped into the hallway and ran for my life. And coat. Well, I still can't fly, but I raced past Sister Clara Bell's open classroom door in world record speed for first graders. Then, I spotted it. It wasn't divine intervention, but the red blur of the fire alarm box suddenly brought into focus a plan that damn near borders on inspirational and the closest thing to genius to run through my brain all year.

I jumped as high as humanly possible for a rather puny troublemaker and pulled down the bright red handle that read, DO NOT TOUCH. The wail of a thousand pissed off holy women was suddenly screaming into both sides of my head. To my great relief, not a holy crusader saw me do it. Not a one, I think. At least I'm pretty sure.

Ding-ding-ding-ding-ding-ding-ding-ding-ding! The fire alarm was still ringing throughout the valley as I reached for the doorknob to re-enter my classroom when the door suddenly pulled away. Jesus!

18

Scared the living crap out of me. I thought it was the Holy Ghost or any number of holy dead spooks the nuns had conjured up for a sneak attack, but it wasn't. It was stupid Bernadette McDogface. We bumped right into each other.

"Oooh, you're in big trouble now, Kevin Carroll. Sister's gonna get you good." Bernadette actually paused in the middle of a potential burning inferno just to give me the bad news. One by one the entire class followed Bernadette into the corridor with the same calm swiftness we had practiced in the event of a real fire.

The last row of kids was still filing out the door as I scrambled towards the closet in the rear of the room. I quickly snatched my ugly winter coat off the hook and ran to the end of the line. I was still wiggling into my coat when Fat Tony Boy glanced over his shoulder. "What happened?" said Tony. Though pretty excited, I was still trying to catch my breath, but mostly I was mad. "She's gonna kick my ass." Fat Tony Boy was out the door, his new compact shadow hugging his rear-end like a wet diaper.

4

Little kids and bigger kids were moving with purpose as the nuns hurried through the middle of two columns of furious energy. In a precious few seconds I was either going to be a tiny flash of white vapor disappearing down Taylor Avenue or a skinny piece of dead meat impaled on the wrought iron fence. If grandma's intuition is anything like mom's, my Celtic Guardian Angel should be right outside the front door standing in the middle of the sidewalk. Nuns can't mess with grandma. Grandma knows God.

We called Sister Clara, Sister Clara Bell because of Clara-Bell the Clown on the Howdy Doody Show, but Sister Clara Bell wasn't funny. The big round nun entered the picture like a charging bull elephant, which means the rest of the picture just got entirely blotted out. Sister wasn't tall, but what she lacked in height she more than made up for in total mass, a short, fat boogeyman with a very, very long Tarzan rope tied around her middle. But it wasn't just that look that was frightening, because Sister handled tiny troublemakers the same way she handled a veal cutlet parmigiano hero: she inhaled them. Her presence at this particular moment could turn two killer nuns into a holy lynch mob.

The suffocating fear of an early morning thrashing was all consuming. So, unless I escape, the nuns will be lighting a fire under the holy ass-whippin' chair in Mother Godzilla's office. Hell in comparison would seem like an appropriate place to store ice cream.

I scurried behind Fat Tony Boy and peeked around his arm to see the front entrance a few yards away. Mother's voice was already blaring from just beyond the open doors, her rapid-fire words demanding absolute compliance. "Quickly children, move quickly." Sister Mary Monster clapped a steady beat to the movement of little feet. "Move along children. No talking. Stay together. Move quickly." I turned towards the gray frigid morning. The three holy predators gathered in a conspiratorial knot in the middle of the sidewalk, but it wasn't until Sister Clara-Bell blurted my name and 'fire alarm' in the same sentence that I knew I'd be sent home today with more than a damn note. Maybe even stitches.

Sneaking past this threatening brown wall of unholy retribution was suddenly taking on a whole new meaning: sudden death. How did I get here? I should've been out a window or a back door by now. And how come there's no helicopter hovering over the damn roof, dangling a long rope to pull me the hell out of here? My imagination could be counted on for lots of things, but this time, no freaking helicopter.

I was still close enough behind Fat Tony Boy to be his very thin shadow, but when I peeked around his shoulder sister suddenly yelled, "THERE!" Sister Mary somehow pointed me out through a passing line of two hundred little Christians that looked almost exactly like me, except I'm the only one wearing a nice warm ugly blue corduroy coat. Everyone else is wearing white shirts and frozen smiles.

The three angry nuns quickly joined hands and stretched out, feet pumping up and down in place like crazed football linebackers ready to pounce. I'll close my eyes for a split second. If they don't disappear I will. They didn't.

Go!

I grabbed the end of the fence and catapulted around and awaaaaay. Oh, nooooo, what's happened? I'm rolling all over the damn ground. This can't be happening. Holyeee s#*@, I've been tripped by a holy person. Illegal procedure, I want a do-over. How come I didn't hear a whistle? Where's the referee? Where's a damn cop? And look, my fancy gray pants are ripped and my knees are bleeding to death.

Mother was already hovering over my crumpled bleeding carcass like a vulture, her hostile stare focusing fiery intentions, but she was panting like a winded sprinter. Sister Clara-Bell's big face came down to greet me. "Well, Mister Carroll. I see you're in trouble once again. Just wait 'til we get you inside." Off in the distance the wail of a fire truck siren perked all ears to attention.

Sister Mary Monster stepped into the picture, which darkened considerably when she bent way over and glowered into my eyes. "God does not have time for this, Mister Carroll. Now you'll see what happens to little hooligans that curse and pull fire alarms."

I was still kneeling on the sidewalk when I spotted Stevie freezing his rear-end off like everybody else.

"Stevie, go get my mom." My voice was trembling and I was scared to death. I wasn't crying, tears of rage cascaded both cheeks unabated. Stevie's eyes were darting between Sister's and mine, his tiny Buster Brown shoes cemented to the pavement by fear. "If you want some of what he's gonna get," threatened Mother, "just try and move off that spot, Mister

Guardino."

In the freezing bleakness of a gray November morning the three spooky gigantic nuns stood there huffing and puffing in anger, while two hundred wide-eyed frozen Christian popsicles awaited more action. Mount Godzilla finally blew up all over me. "GET UP. NOW!" Her gigantic voice cracking the icy stillness. The entire student body stood there, stunned. Unlike me they were ready for more. I was ready to go.

I was still on my bloody knees in a desperate search through a forest of tiny legs for an opening to daylight. "And where exactly do you think you're going, Mister Carroll?" I was heading for daylight, ya holy bag of wind, but Sister grabbed the handle and hoisted me all the way up to my tippy toes. Sister Clara-Bell probably noticed that I was a tad off balance and decided to equal the tension from the other side. At this rate I'll definitely be flying home for Christmas. Dumbo the elephant won't have a damn thing on me by the time we strung the lights on the holiday tree.

The two nuns were still holding me aloft when the big red truck with its lights ablaze screeched to a stop. I felt an uncanny resemblance to a tiny cartoon character that just ran off the top of a mountain, feet spinning a thousand miles an hour, going nowhere, but down. The siren droned to eerie silence as they hustled me towards my reflection in the double glass doors that leads directly into the darkness of the valley of death.

They were still clamped onto both ears when they rushed me into Mother Godzilla's office on the ground floor. Sister Mary Monster suddenly administered a wicked slap to the back of my head. I tripped onto the holy ass whippin' chair, banged my mouth, bruising my top lip and almost knocked my little teeth down my throat. "Sit up! Sit up straight!" Trying to piss me off again failed without question because I was already free falling towards the abyss of deep hatred. My mind was set, she would get nothing but anger. I could've used a really good idea, but I couldn't think of one.

Mother was still huffing and puffing when she grabbed the back of her chair and slammed it back against the wall. The three angry nuns emitted so much smoke I thought the room would catch fire. Mother Godzilla plopped her enormous rear end onto her seat and gazed into my eyes like an enraged lunatic. I held her stare with the confidence of a four-hundred-pound wrestler. Mother then instructed Sister Clara Bell to indulge the forgiveness of the Fire Department. "Sister Clara, please inform the lieutenant that we had a little mishap by the name of Mister

23

Carroll." Sister Clara Bell rushed her enormousness out the door, while Mother squeezed the armrests like she was trying to rip them off to beat over my head. So far they were controlled fury, but so was I, and with good reason. At any moment either one of them could single-handedly beat the living crap out of me. A very special prayer was in order. I didn't have one. Not even a short one. **𝔓𝔩𝔢𝔞𝔰𝔢 𝔊𝔬𝔡. 𝔓𝔩𝔢𝔞𝔰𝔢 𝔪𝔞𝔨𝔢 𝔪𝔢 𝔡𝔦𝔰𝔞𝔭𝔭𝔢𝔞𝔯.** See what I mean? And I thought I sounded pretty sincere.

My teeth were clenched so tight they almost broke apart, and breath was only possible through nostrils flared with disdain. A raging anger was now in full control of my brain. I was resolute: no apology and absolutely no confession. Unfortunately there was still a lot of talking to do, and by the time I explain my morning to dad at five in the evening the only thing that'll be left inside my battered skull would be three pounds of brain mush paralyzed by eight more hours of fear.

Dad has more patience than anybody. To me, he's more religious than these three nuns put together. Unfortunately dad's gentle attempts to calm my fears were almost always ineffective because the nuns were that much better at inspiring terror.

Sister Mary Monster said my aggressive behavior was sinful. I figured her job was to keep beating that allegation through the back of my head until we were both on the same page. My silence at the dinner table was merely a form of protection. Lying to dad? My second best option.

My dad is the youngest of nine children. His twin sisters are thirteen months older, and because the three youngest Carroll's looked so much alike everybody called little 'Buddy' Carroll the triplet. Many years later and before dad entered the Army the twins entered the convent. After long months of very serious reflection, God bestowed on the twins exactly what they came for: floating instructions. God turned my dad's two sisters into identical twin Ursuline Nuns. Identical twin nuns? Who ever heard of something like this? I have nuns floating around my own family. Cursing at Nuns? Dad will never see this in a good light. I'll just spare him the ugly facts and lie through my teeth with as straight a face as a tiny Irish/German/Italian/Catholic Pope. Me, dad? I would never say a bad word, especially to a nun. That would be, uh, crazy, uhhh. Sister probably forgot to clean the potatoes out of her ears. Pull a fire alarm? Uhhh, aren't they the red boxes way, way, up on the telephone poles? I never left my desk, uh, except to take a whiz... . really. Besides, I don't even think I could reach it? Do you? No siree, dad, not me. Maybe you should ask Stevie what happened.

24

My imagination was getting way ahead of the current situation. For the moment my tiny ass was grass, and these big holy lawnmowers were taking on a full tank of fuel. Mother Godzilla slowly leaned her big angry mush into my tiny innocent face. "Who do you think you are, Mister Carroll? You little hooligan! Are you crazy? Do you think you're going to get away with this?" This is what's known in the biz as a multiple choice ass-whippin' test: three quick questions, bam, bam, bam, right in a row. My next answer had life and death written all over it.

So, who do I think I am? Well, I'm Kevin John Carroll, tiny terror of Taylor Avenue, the first grade, the corridor and now the principal's office. Am I crazy? I guess it depends on who you ask, but I wouldn't be asking any nuns. It's pretty obvious what they think. Do I think I'll get away with this? Well, it's not looking good. Mom will probably cancel my birthday party as soon as I walk through the front door. And forget the Mattel Bulldog Tank, I'll be lucky to turn six years old.

Mother's voice was still bouncing off the wall behind my melon. I sat motionless. Not so much as a blink. Forget dialogue. I'll be accepting my Ph.D. in mathematics from Albert Einstein in Hell before I open my mouth.

This type of anger takes a whole lot of concentration, and concentration is the one thing Sister Mary Monster said that I was severely lacking, so as my body sat rigid my brain took off on a new adventure.

There I was, driving my new Bulldog Tank all over the neighborhood with a smile as bright as the brilliant idea in my head, and just as I was aiming the cross hairs on the front of my school, somebody kicked the holy ass whippin' chair and startled me back to reality.

Mother jumped out of her seat and slammed her two big palms on the desk. "Mister Carroll! What do you think is so funny? What in God's name are you smiling about?" Sister Mary chimed, "Are you listening, Mister Carroll?" And I don't mean chimed like a bell. "Are you an idiot? What do you think is so funny, you little hooligan? We'll just see if your parents think it's funny when you get expelled." I didn't know expelled, so I wasn't sure if they were gonna hang me on a little cross Friday afternoon in my underwear or wash my mouth out with soap. Not a solitary muscle twitched in my face as the stone glare of a gargoyle stared her back, dead in the eye. Ouch! Expelled?

From just beyond the dark threatening clouds that hovered over the valley a familiar voice suddenly blossomed in my ears. "Hello, Mother." A friendly face magically appeared like a rainbow after a biblical thun-

25

derstorm. "Look at you, Joseph Pareti," greeted Sister Mary Monster. It was Uncle Joe, my mom's younger brother. Uncle Joe graduated from Holy Cross five years ago, super-duper cum laude. He was taught at one time or another by the present execution squad, including the absent avenger, Sister Clara Bell.

"Mother Beatrice, Sister Mary Grace," Uncle's shiny face gushed, "How have the two of you been?"

"Joseph Pareti, look at you all grown up and so handsome. Look at him Sister. How nice of you to come visit, Joseph." Sister Mary Monster cupped hands in prayer. "Joseph, we heard you done us proud at Cardinal Hayes." My brain quickly studied this transformation as the two nuns changed directions faster than a mouse fart in a hurricane. One second they were about to plug in my chair, the next, hallelujah, the prodigal son has returned.

Uncle Joe's face lit up like a freaking Christmas tree. "Yes, that's right. Thank you, Sister." Mother's voice droned on and on. And he's going to be President of the United States someday and blah blah blah... blah blah blah. Ten minutes turned into a thousand years while Uncle Joe, Mother and Sister took turns extolling the virtues of a good Catholic School education. "Mother, how is Sister Clara? I'd love to see her while I'm here." That-a-boy, Uncle Genius. I guess two killer holy women aren't enough in one room? Did you call the cops before you walked in here, too? Hey, is that a warrant sticking out of your back pocket? You know, now that I look around the room, there has to be at least one cubic millimeter of unused breathable air in this office. Sure, we can squeeze Sister Clara Bell's big fat ass in here. Why don't I just go look for her myself. Take a look around Uncle Joe, I'm right over here, I'm in the holy ass whippen' chair. We're related, so did you bring bail? Did you talk to the governor? Let's go already, they're gonna kill me this time for sure.

Uncle Joe finally spotted me behind the door. "What are you doing here, Kevin? You don't look so good." Didn't I say he was a genius? "Are you all right? Are you sick or something?" Uncle Joe, wake the hell up. Does this look like the nurse's office? "What happened to ya lip, Kevin? And what happened to ya pants? Ya mother's gonna kill ya when she sees those pants." Uncle Joe didn't know a whole lot, but he was obviously well acquainted with mom's violent tendencies.

The two nuns not only dressed alike, but now wore twin looks of amazement. The gold star graduate is somehow familiar with the tiny

26

terror of Holy Cross? "Mother, is my nephew in some kind of trouble?" Is this possible? The tiny terror is actually a blood relative to Joseph Pareti? What in God's name is this world coming to? Mother Godzilla motioned with a nod towards the window and Sister quickly floated along with Uncle clueless in tow.

Uncle Joe confirmed it alright, we're definitely related, but when Uncle Joe threw in the fact that my Dad's twin sisters are both Ursuline nuns and that my Godmother is Sister Regina Therese, my Aunt Jeannie, their jaws dropped right down to the floor, and who was right there to pick them up with a smile? Me, Kevin John Carroll, tiny terror of the holy ass whippen' chair.

Uncle Joe finally explained why he'd come to school in the first place and his appearance was probably coincidence, but you couldn't convince me that my grandma had nothing to do with this. Uncle Joe's mere presence completely extinguished the burning bush under the holy ass whippin' chair, but his actual purpose for coming along was much more down to earth. My Uncle Joe came by to ask Mother Godzilla if he could draw the nativity scene in colored chalk on the blackboard, the way he did when he was a student, sort of an early Christmas present for his favorite nuns.

Hugs and kisses and smiling faces filled the valley with joy, and when all the good-byes were said and done, Uncle Joe turned to the only somber expression in the room. "Come on, Kevin. I guess you're going home early today." Well, it's about freaking time.

As we walked into the light of day, Uncle Joe was already babbling the standard line of all good Christian soldiers. "Mother is giving you another chance, Kevin, so you have to change your ways and blah blah, blah... ..blah, blah, blah." Unfortunately for me and Uncle Joe, my overactive and very optimistic imagination was already putting the finishing touches on the plans for my big birthday party while I was still sitting on the holy ass whippin' chair. Talk about crazy.

So remember, Saturday, two days after Thanksgiving, November the 29th in the afternoon. I still gotta check with my mom on the exact time, but don't worry, so far mom's still pretty flexible. It's going to be the bestest birthday party of all time. I'll be blowing Jap planes to smithereens with my Mattel Bulldog Tank before you could say, Kevin, where's the book of matches that was in this drawer?

5

Grandma says birthdays are guaranteed to come once a year no matter what my mom says. It doesn't mean it's gonna be fun, but of course my Grandma was already talking me up as the first Catholic priest from the family, which probably didn't hurt my prospects. 'Evangeline, leave the lad be. Kevin's gonna be a fine priest sumdae.' Grandma said it often and always in her lilting Irish brogue that seemed to give her the credibility of a higher power, the patron saint of troublemakers.

So I actually pulled off the first officially recorded miracle of 1956. November the 29th is here, and so is, "Hey, Tony Boy, c'mon up, you're the first one." Fat Tony Boy's big easy smile broadened as he handed me a tiny box wrapped in shiny paper. "Thanks, Tony Boy."

"It's a yo-yo."

"Wow. I need a yo-yo." Fat Tony Boy was still lumbering up the stairs when the doorbell rang again. "I betcha a dollar it's Big Louie," guessed Fat Tony Boy. "I betcha it's Stevie... Hey Eric. What's up?"

"Kevin, who's at the door?" Mom was peering down from the top of the staircase with the bearing of a squinty eyed gunslinger, feet apart, hands on hips, at the ready with a friendly warning. Mom's got the patience of a nun for loud annoying kids, probably why we get along so well. Her jet black pixie hairdo highlighted bright probing eyes on top of a tiny frame gave many the impression of a fragile porcelain doll, but impressions are funny things. Mom's energy level ran a hundred miles an hour for the sixteen hours she was on her feet, and for the eight hours she did sleep her brain could've won the 100-yard dash every night. Mom was a marauding force of nature in a tiny house dress.

Eric was all excited as he raced up the stairs ahead of me, red muffler wrapped snuggly around his neck, black horned rimmed glasses crooked on his perfectly round face. "It's just me, Missus Carroll." As I hit the top step the telephone rang. Mom hurried to the kitchen wall. Her conversation was short.

"Don't worry, Lilly, I'll handle it." Stevie's mom had called with the usual warning, Steven's on the way. "Oh, hello, Eric. Why don't you and Anthony go into the living room, sweetheart, but first hang your

29

coats in the closet." Mom patted Eric gently on his woolen beanie that was still pulled over his ears.

"There's plenty of goodies in the living room." Ding! dong! "Kevin, ya better slow down before ya break ya neck."

"Hey, guys, c'mon in." Timmy, Big Louie and Little Louie stood on the stoop bundled against the cold, scarves, woolen beanies and big old play coats hid everything but happy eyes and frozen breath. I closed out the howling winter and raced up the stairs. Eric was still standing at the open closet door when the telephone rang again. Mom was in the kitchen doorway yapping away when Eric realized who was on the other end of the line. "Oh, no, definitely not... Oh yes, of course... No, Helga, don't worry, Eric's a good boy." It was Eric's very nervous and highly excitable mother, and my mom quickly talked her in off the ledge. There was only room for one on the ledge and my mom already had it covered. "Eric, you go inside and have a good time, sweetheart. Go." Mom hung the phone on the kitchen wall, hurried down the hall into the bedroom and closed the door.

The boys were already attacking the crunchy delights in bowls strategically placed around the room when I entered the party and jumped up onto the arm of dad's big green chair. This of course is against the law. Fortunately, the law was already busy in the bedroom doing secret birthday stuff. Straight up. Steady... Steady... with outstretched arms like a tightrope walker. I was still looking down as the boys anxiously awaited my next move. Steady... Steady... when I suddenly jumped up into the air and across to the couch. It was an absolute thing of beauty, and just when I was halfway through a world-class somersault, Ding! Dong! Ding! Dong! The doorbell startled the living crap out of me so I over-shot my soft touch-down on the couch and crash-landed on the corner of the wobbly end table. "OUCH!" Fat Tony Boy was standing next to the table trying to inhale a bowl full of M&M chocolate covered peanuts when the whole bowl popped into the air along with mom's favorite statue of a big nosed guy with long hair, and guess which one Fat Tony Boy caught? Well, we don't call him Fat Tony Boy because he can juggle ugly pottery statues. Fat Tony Boy stood there in shock with the half empty bowl in his hands while the rest of the M&M's were rolling around his U.S. Keds.

"Kevin! What was that!?" Mom's startling explosion frightened everybody right through the living room wall. The boys stood frozen. "Nuthin!" Now, some might call that a lie, and considering that mom was still in the bedroom, a pretty damn effective one if I say so myself, but better than that is the one that came next. "I tripped on the rug, Missus Carroll and the M&M's spilled on the floor." Shy, timid Eric was begging forgiveness like an old pro. "Eric, you be careful, sweetheart. I told your mother you would come home in one piece." Eric held a hand to his mouth. "Okay, Missus Carroll." Eric couldn't hide his excitement with a paper bag over his head.

I jumped up, carefully stepped around the M&M's and picked up mom's favorite statue that was face down at the edge of the table. The boys huddled around. "Holy shit," I whispered, "da nose broke off." This is potential for a full-blown disaster and a definite party pooper, but faster than you can say Humpty Dumpty I realized I could fix mom's ugly statue and save my party from certain doom. That's right, I could perform nose surgery, but first we had to recover that nose. "Tony Boy, stop eatin' 'em. Just put 'em in the bowl."

After placing mom's ugly statue upright and turning the mutilated face to the wall, I whispered my concern to the boys. "Find dat nose before my mom comes back."

Ding-dong! Ding-dong! Ding-dong! I flew down the stairs in a fright. "Kevin, I'm not gonna tell you again to stop running!" The fear of discovery left me panting. "Wha' took ya so long?" Stevie looked mad, so I quickly motioned him in. My best friend stepped up into the vestibule, but his shadow lingered on the stoop, only Stevie's shadow had his hair in his fist and was sucking his stupid thumb. With my outstretched arms blocking the door I quizzed Carmine like a pissed off cop. "Who told yudda come, stupid?"

"My mom's goin' shopping," interrupted Stevie. "She said Carmine has to come. Here. My mom says this is from both of us."

"Thanks." I took the little present and started up the stairs. "Hurry up. I think I might be in trouble."

"It's a yo-yo."

"Thanks. I need another yo-yo."

Timmy rushed over as soon as I stepped through the doorway into the living room. "Here it is, Kev." Timmy opened his hand, exposing the severed nose. I was still half in shock, but the other half of my brain instantly figured out a genius plan to make it go away. It's what professionals do in times of great crisis.

Mom was still futzing around the bedroom doing secret birthday stuff. I plucked the broken nose from his palm and slipped it in my pocket for safe keeping. Then I went to work. I picked out a rather nice looking red M&M chocolate covered peanut from the bowl, and with the delicate touch of a seasoned plastic surgeon I pushed and twisted the shiny red treasure into the hole where the nose goes. I did a hasty post-op examination and realized I was probably staring at maybe the greatest M&ectomy of the twentieth century. An absolute work of art and probably, maybe, hopefully un-de-tectable to the naked eye. Actually, it depends on how you're looking at it. My colleagues were already rolling around the living room floor, yelling and kicking themselves into hysterical fits of pandemonium.

Mom suddenly appeared in the doorway. Not actually part of the plan. "Kevin, ya better put that down before you break it." Well, it's a little late for that.

I placed mom's statue on the table with the surgically altered face turned to the wall. "It moved a little when Eric hit the table. I just wanted to straighten it out." Sometimes I amaze myself when the heat is on. "What exactly is so funny? What's going on in here?" Eric finally calmed to a giggle. "This is a really neat party, Missus Carroll."

"I'm glad you're enjoying yourself, Eric." Little honest Eric could've sold my mom flood insurance if she lived on an aircraft carrier in the middle of the Mojave Desert. Mom paused and stuck her head back through the doorway. "Don't go anywhere. I'll be right back." Ding-dong! "Kevin, stay there," she insisted, "I'll get it." But who could be at the front door? Is someone else trying to crash my birthday party? All my friends are here. Another deadbeat like Carmine and we could have a serious situation.

I ran to the banister and hugged the floor trying to listen. "Wha' took ya so long?" mom sighed, "I thought I was on my own. These kids are already getting me a little nuts."

"Is everything alright, Eve?" That voice: it's Big Bonnie Bigelow, Little Louie's mom. Mom called in reinforcements, and Big Bonnie's even tougher than Sister Mary Monster.

Mom ran up the stairs grinning with relief while her big buddy slowly lumbered behind. I jumped up and peered over the banister to make sure there were no other birthday surprises, and what did I see tiptoeing through the darkness of Big Bonnie's very wide shadow?

"Maaaaaa! No girls allowed!" None other than the biggest crybaby in the whole world, stupid Judy Bigelow. Mom calmly strolled past me into the kitchen and sat at the table. Big Bonnie was still huffin' n' puffin' and totally out of breath with one meaty hand on the baluster post and within seconds Little Louie's mom sucked all the happy birthday spirit right out of the air. "MAAAAAA. NO GIRLS ALLOOOWED. I'M NOT KIDDIIIIN." Big Bonnie covered her ears. "Eve, this child has to calm down. He's gonna give himself a heart attack." Did she say heart attack? I don't get heart attacks, I give freaking heart attacks. Dad's right, there's never a cop around when you need one.

Stupid Judy was still ducking and grabbing onto the back of her mom's big black coat in an attempt to hide from me, now the tiny terror of the staircase. Big ole Bonnie would've had an easier time smuggling in a freaking hippopotamus. Little Louie ran into the hall. "Ma you said JuJu wasn't comin'. Maaa, you said."

"Louis, if you don't go back inside and be quiet you'll be marching yourself right back home."

"Maaaa, I said no girls allowed!"

"Kevin, if ya don't calm ya self-down I'm gonna chuck this whole party thing right out that damn window. Bonnie couldn't get a baby sitter. Judy has to stay, do you understand me?" My plea for sanity was obviously falling on the ears of a crazy lady. "I don't understand nuthin'. She's a girl. No girls allowed." I almost started to, let's just say I was really, really pissed off. My party was officially pooped. A girl. I can't believe it.

The utter despair was all too much. I ran into mom's room to clear my eyes. I mean, head. I wasn't crying, it just looked like crying because there was something in my eye. Really. Why would I lie about something like that? Sonofabitch! So here I am, calming down, all by myself in the bedroom. In a few very long minutes though my composure was back, and it's a damn good thing, too, 'cause I was practically on the verge of kicking somebody's big fat ass. And a little one, too.

When I finally stepped into the hallway I glared at stupid Judy already seated at the kitchen table. I stuck out my tongue and stepped into the party. Steven popped to his feet. "Kev, you okay?" Stevie was smiling with the expectation of coaxing the same. "Yeah, whaddaya think?" I was still settling in when mom abruptly came through the living room door with a smile and a bribe disguised as the biggest chocolate birthday cake I ever saw. Mom was obviously desperate to devert my attention from stupid Judy and nothing turns my head like chocolate birthday cake, decorated with five little blue candles and one giant number six stuck right in the middle. The last time I felt that much heat so close to my face, I was burning down the lots. Mom started the celebration, "Haaaaappy biiirthdaaay tooo yuuuu… "

Everybody was singing along when my sister walked into the room with her arms wrapped around a big box and a smile wrapped around her head. "Kathleen, put it on the floor like a good girl," instructed mom. My little brother Tommy sat like an Indian as I tore away the paper. "What is it, Keb?" Whajaget?" I lifted it out. A calm, collective "Wow" circled the room. The Mattel Bulldog Tank. It seemed the perfect moment for a rousing rendition of Stars and Stripes Forever. "The batteries are right here," said mom, and with palpable reservation she took the four 'D' batteries from her dress pocket and placed them in my itchy hand. "Now play nice," she warned, "we'll be right out in the kitchen, listening."

The happy birthday commotion was all the diversion stupid Judy needed to weasel her way into the party. She was already looking way too relaxed at the far end of the couch, her big brown eyes popping out all over my new tank. Stupid Judy seemed to be getting some really stupid ideas as she inched closer to the action. I'd hate to accidently kill a stupid American female with my new weapon.

After freezing the intruder with a hard stare I placed the four 'D' batteries in the rear compartment. It was combat ready. "Hey, Kev, look at these." Big Louie pulled a little plastic bag from the bottom of the box and tossed it in my lap. "Wow, bullets."

"I can't wait 'til Christmas," boasted Timmy, "I'm gettin' one of these for sure."

"Me, too!" bellowed Eric. "Shit," whispered Stevie, "this thing is really neat." Everybody's eyes were wild as I quickly loaded a bullet into the breach. The troops got to their knees, ready for action. I hit the switch. Rrrrrrrrrr! Mighty rolling thunder, just like on the commercial. Rrrrrr! Of course it only went one way. Rrrrrr! Straight-ahead. It rumbled into mom's cherry wood RCA television cabinet, Rrrrrr! Then it banged into the leg of dad's big green chair. Rrrrrr! Then it thundered into the hall and crashed into the Rrrrrrrr! banister, Rrrrrrr where it got—Rrrrrrrrrrrrr—stuck. It was a good thing I was right there, because in seconds it could've tore through the wooden balusters on its way to obliterating the front door. God only knows what could've happened next. It might've thundered right down Taylor Avenue and blown my freaking school to smithereens. Like I said, good thing I was right there.

We crawled behind it for another minute and a half, and then it was time to start blowing stuff to kingdom come.

In times of war it's sometimes necessary to sacrifice a few small unsuspecting gatecrashers for the greater good of mankind, which means that either dumb Carmine or stupid Judy would have to die. But with two possible enemy targets within range we had to narrow it down to which one was the most dangerous. Which one posed the most substantial risk to the security of the living room if left alive. Since dumb Carmine was an idiot and not an actual threat, my choice was all too clear. Stupid Judy would have to bite the dust.

The stupid enemy infiltrator was still surveying the terrain from high atop her mountain perch, I mean couch, while the Bulldog Tank ever so mightily rumbled to a position far out of view of enemy mothers that were already preparing rations out in the mess hall. Or maybe mom and Big Bonnie were doing some hard drinking. Probably not, but you never know, these are dangerous times.

Unfortunately for stupid Judy, the battle lines had been drawn the second she was spotted sneaking up behind the enemy's giant Trojan hippopotamus. So just when stupid Judy was sloshing down some whiskey, err, soda, I opened fire. A direct hit under the optical observation portal in the uppermost portion of her little stupid face, but you couldn't tell it the way stupid Judy was screaming. You would have thought I plucked her eye out with a rusty bayonet. "Oww! I can't see! Maaaaa! Kevin Carroll hit me in the eye!"

The wounded enemy jumped off the couch in rage, one arm flailing, the other hand covering her stupid eye. Mom rushed through the doorway into the middle of ground zero. "Kevin, what the hell did you do this time?" Everyone scattered for cover. As usual I was first to make a move, diving head first under the couch to wait out the fireworks. Mom was about to explode all over the living room. Big Bonnie finally squeezed through the doorway.

Mom uses a well-documented enemy scare tactic: screaming and yelling. I always say yelling and screaming is good for scaring, but it never kicked anybody's ass. And besides, I believe I'm protected by the Geneva Convention. After all, this is war.

Stupid Judy was still hopping and howling and holding her stupid eye, trying to get me in trouble and doing a bang up job. "I can't see!" Mom's tentative hold on sanity was being pulled apart one nerve ending at a time. "Kevin, get your ass out from under there… now!" There was some mighty tuff-talking going on inside my head, but "no" just meekly rolled off the tongue. Mom grabbed hold of my exposed ankle. "Let go!" My hand was anchored to the rear leg of the couch, but she yanked my ankle and snapped my grip. I was pounding the floor with both fists and stupid Judy's big mouth was still pounding in my ears. "I can't see. Owwww!"

Stupid Judy finally stopped howling long enough for Big Bonnie to wipe the flood of tears with a napkin she snatched from under the popcorn bowl. Big Bonnie was tenderly wiping, blotting and staring when she suddenly spotted the tiny, tiniest red mark on stupid Judy's dumb cheekbone. "Oh my God, Eve will you take a look at this." She lifted stupid Judy's dumb chin with a finger. Mom was already glaring directly into my brain from over her shoulder. "Jesus, Kevin!" mom shrieked, "you could've taken an eye out! Now say you're sorry." Mom stood like a statue, arms folded, waiting, but the only thing I was sorry about was that stupid Judy wasn't taken out on a stretcher to a waiting ambulance. "If ya don't say it, mister, everybody's gonna go home. Then ya really gonna get it."

"I don't care." This is what's known in the biz as a judgment call. For as long as I could remember mom was real good at stomping her little foot and shaking her tiny finger and looking tough, and nobody's developed a better evil eye. Threatening physical harm? As loud as mom is when she says, Kevin don't make me run after you, I'd have to be a stoned deaf moron not to be scared, but with a room full of witnesses mom was just a foot stomping, finger shaking, scary eyed, screaming marshmallow, and the best thing about it was that I knew it, probably better than she did. I'll stand here looking mad until my feet grow into the floor before I'll say, I'm sorry.

Stupid Judy had a teeny tiny spot on her cheek bone hardly detectable without a freaking magnifying glass and not even close to the eye. If I really wanted to hit her in the eye we'd be calling her stupid Judy, the cyclops from across the street. "So what exactly happened in here, mister?" Mom was still in my face and Big Bonnie was now blocking the doorway, and make no mistake, when Big Bonnie blocks a door, it's blocked. Everything in stays in, everything out stays out. Not even the smell of Bosco could escape. "I'm not sure, it just went off." Mom rattled her head, which rattled her eyes, and just as I was coming up with my second best option, the old Stevie made my hand slip defense, my eyes flashed to my brother as he placed his pudgy little hands at the base of mom's ugly statue and turned it around to its normal position, naked to the world. The six of us held our breath. Mom's eagle eye caught the first glimpse. It was beauty alright. There was that big old shiny M&M chocolate covered peanut shoved into the hole where the nose goes. It was so life-like I wasn't sure if she noticed. I pretended not to see.

"Tommy, what did you do? Lemme see that statue." Of course my little brother probably thought that mom meant, bring her the statue, but that's not really what she meant at all, because Tommy's not allowed to touch anything around the house that's not made of reinforced concrete or steel, which basically means Tommy can't even take a whiz unless mom holds it for him. Tommy grabbed the base of the statue. Mom's eyes flashed with panic. "DON'T!" But mom was already way too late, little Tommy was already half way through his first quick stride when I happened to be stretching out my leg. Not on purpose, that wouldn't be nice. No, actually I was getting a little cramped. No, really. So just as I was… stretching, Tommy kicked me right in the foot. Yeah, can you believe it? The little guy kicked me right in the freaking foot. Tommy went flying across the room and mommy went flying to catch Tommy, but nobody was flying like they were about to leap a tall building in a single bound with the same determination as mom's ugly statue. That baby flew across the room faster than Superman, and not even The Man of Steel could crash a wall like mom's ugly statue. That little guy splattered into a zillion pieces. In fact, the biggest piece now was the little porcelain nose at the bottom of my pocket.

Tommy started crying all over the place. The way he was carrying on, you would've thought he was going to be arrested for murdering the nose. Mom squeezed between Fat Tony Boy and Stevie on the couch, stretched her arms to heaven and prayed aloud. **Please, Lord, let this be over.**

I learned a powerful lesson on my sixth birthday. Whenever you're in over your head like mom, forget about second string saints that nobody ever heard of before except Grandma. Go right to the source, because not a second had passed before mom got a true revelation. She jumped off the couch, threw her hands up once again and begged, "Kevin. Please. Everybody's gotta go."

Swift thinking in times of great crisis happens to be one of the many attributes I employ daily like a suit of armor, but my brain was still locked into survival mode, so there was a bit of confusion. Everybody's gotta go? Could she possibly mean leave? Did mom forget we're in the middle of my damn birthday party?

When Tommy destroyed the evidence, mom could only wonder, was that really an M&M chocolate covered peanut I saw stuck in the nose of my lovely statue? Or maybe I was just upset, because I thought my wonderful son just blinded my best friend's little girl. Mom looked pretty much confused as she lifted little Tommy into her arms. "Excuse me, Missus Carroll." Mom grinned at Fat Tony Boy as my second best-est friend slipped off the couch and picked something from the floor as if collecting a rare jewel. Fat Tony Boy fell back onto the couch while a very wide grin expanded across a big moon face.

After a quick ride on mom's hip, Tommy dried his nose with his hand and instantly returned to his usual happy self. Mom put him down and patted him on the head. "No running, Thomas. You already gave me enough to clean up. And don't touch anything in this house 'til you wash those hands." Tommy looked up and smiled. Mom, looking ready for a nap, finally turned to leave.

Fat Tony Boy's eyes grew wide and his grin even wider as he slowly opened his clutched fist. Giggles and smiles circulated the room faster than cheesecake at a fat farm. Fat Tony Boy popped the nose in his mouth. No, not the real porcelain nose, that was still in protective custody. It was the M&M chocolate covered peanut that was inserted during emergency nose surgery. "What's so funny, Tony Boy?" wondered dumb Carmine. Fat Tony Boy practically busted a gut laughing. He spit the peanut nose clear across the room and almost hit mom in the back of the head as she headed for the door. Pandemonium had once again erupted all over the living room.

My little brother had no idea what was so funny, and neither did dumb Carmine, stupid Judy or Kathleen, but the laughter was contagious and they all caught it. Even mom and Big Bonnie were beginning to grin.

"Okay," mom pleaded, "that's enough now. You're going to hurt yourselves. Let's go, ice-cream and cake in the kitchen." Big Bonnie backed away from the doorway, allowing the smell of chocolate birthday cake to permeate the living room. One by one the boys followed me aaaaall the way around big Bonnie towards the aroma.

We laughed about the untimely demise of mom's ugly statue as she sliced the cake. Before we knew it, everything was gone: all the cake, all the ice cream, all the M&M's, all the everything, inhaled through a vacuum of smiling wonder. Mom finally settled into her regular mom stuff, clearing the table and washing stuff in the sink. Big Bonnie standing guard by the refrigerator suddenly abandoned her post and went down the hall towards the bedroom. Seconds later she emerged from the room and wiggled into her big black coat. "Alright, Eve, I'll be going."

"Okay, Bonn. I couldn't have done this without you."

"You're welcome, Honey. C'mon, JuJu, get ya coat, we gotta go, ya father will be home soon." As stupid Judy readied to leave, the boys got up from the table. I was still walking away from the kitchen, but something was seriously wrong. How do I know? It's my damn job to know when stuff is wrong. Mom was making that "tch, tch, tch" sound with her tongue. It sounded like she was trying to suck a tree between her teeth. I glanced over my shoulder. Mom snatched the dish towel from the refrigerator handle. "Kevin, where is everybody going?" It didn't sound like a good question. Actually, it didn't sound like a question. It sounded like mom wanted us to pack up and take it on the road.

"Living room," I said with a wonder. Mom was wondering, too. She was wondering what the hell we were all still doing in the house at four o'clock on a Saturday afternoon. "Oh no, you're not," she begged. "C'mon now, please. It's been a very long day." Mom was hardly subtle, so the boys definitely got the hint. Besides there wasn't enough birthday food left in the house to fill a cavity. "Let's go to the fort!" yelled Stevie. Everybody jumped for joy as we all joined the chorus. "Yeah, let's go!"

The boys were still attacking the hall closet to rummage for their coats as I looked towards mom, who was already wide eyed with delight. Her smile said it all. And don't let the door hit ya in the ass on the way out. She didn't actually say it, but that look was unmistakable.

The boys flew down the stairs, buttoning and zippering as they thanked mom on the run. "Thanks, Missus Carroll," Eric sang. They all cheered, "Yeah, thanks, Missus Carroll!"

I hurried towards the big grin at the kitchen sink. "Thanks, mom." Then I planted the usual right on the old kisser, and as usual mom prayed as I flew down the stairs. "Kevin, now stay outta trouble and be a good boy, please!" As I pulled the door shut behind me I wondered again: When the hell did my mom learn to speak Chinese?

6

To say that Stevie and I repeated the first grade because we weren't ready for school would be a gross understatement. We also weren't ready for a Russian attack or nuclear fallout. After two full years together with Sister Mary Monster we still weren't a whole lot smarter, but we were getting tougher every day. It would've been redundant and probably illegal to make us repeat what we couldn't learn the first two times, so Sister finally smacked us along to the second stage of the cross. Our ability to suffer through Sister Mary for two full years in a row should've put us in the running for a purple heart. Although I'm tougher for the experience, I still break into a cold sweat when I see penguins.

School years were still dragging along like the passing of ice ages, so by the time I started third grade I felt like an old beat-up prize fighter and I was still only eight and a half years old. Being older and a little punch drunk, I began to range even further from the sound of my mom's voice. "Stay within' earshot, mister." That was literally anywhere in the northern hemisphere. Stay on the block, mister or else is what she actually meant.

The giant lot just the other side of Taylor Avenue had overgrown with trees and various tall flora. Swampy areas dotted the entire expanse as far as the eye could see. All I had to do to get to my favorite unauthorized play area was to sneak around the corner. Mom's got excellent vision, but she still can't see through a solid line of two story brick houses. I'm pretty sure.

It was the beginning of summer. Steven and I were strolling through the lots on our way towards the biggest swamp by the biggest rock. Just two best friends contemplating important kid stuff, like how to catch the giant alligator lurking at the bottom of the muck. The big kids explained the need for patience.

"Ya 'member that girl two weeks ago?" Stevie wondered. Though pretty much dumbfounded I still managed to be indignant. "No, stupid, what girl?"

"You know, my cousin? With the long red hair? At the movies?"

"I don't 'member no freaking red headed girl." I didn't actually say freaking. Me and ole Stevie already knew most of the good bad words by third grade. "Yes ya do. Member? Godzilla. She was on line talkin' to me n' Wally, 'member? I think maybe she likes you."

"Why ya say that?"

"'Cause she told me."

After Stevie explained the whole deal we decided to do a little undercover investigating so we could see first-hand what we were getting into. Nothing confused me more than my next encounter. Not even arithmetic.

The sound was as regular as a smack in the head without the pain. The eerie drone of an organ followed by the deep scary voice of the announcer. "The Edge of Night. Brought to you by... " Once the music stopped and the show began, Godzilla could step on Taylor Avenue, but as long as he didn't pull the plug on the TVs we could set the whole block on fire and burn it to the ground because every mom in the neighborhood was transfixed to the biggest soap opera on television. Steven, didn't I tell you to be quiet? And that's exactly what we were when Stevie snuck me into his parents' bedroom that next afternoon. Quiet. We were so damn quiet we could've been confused with the dead.

From the moment Missus Guardino propped her feet up on the coffee table she was engrossed in her daily ritual. Stevie and I slipped into the darkened bedroom just down the hall. The second biggest troublemaker on Taylor Avenue cautiously slid the heavy mahogany night stand across the rug to the closet while my eyes kept a nervous vigil on the partially opened door. Stevie stepped up and stretched on tippy toes while his little hand searched under a small cardboard box at the edge of the shelf. My best friend slowly pulled out a flattened brown grocery bag and quickly passed it down to me with a grin and the ever-present, "shh" across his lips. The split second his foot hit the rug I instinctively handed it back. If anybody is going to get caught at this point I definitely didn't want it to be me, Stevie's mom can get a little crazy.

We crept past the bureau to the far side of the room by the windows. We still needed a lot more cover. I'm thinking Australia. Stevie whispered, "under." We knelt down and slipped under the giant bed until the only thing left exposed to danger was the top of our heads.

We were shoulder to shoulder when Stevie opened the paper bag and pulled out the shiny magazine. "Wait 'til you see this." I was already smiling like we were about to split a bag of money. He flipped right to the good stuff. "Wow, look at 'em," slipped out of my mouth. "Shh—quiet. Wally says those are for sex." My eyes grew to alien sized proportions. "Whadddya mean?" "I'm not sure. Wally says they don't do nuthin'. They're jusfalookin'." He turned the next page. "What the heck is zat?"

"No stupid," Stevie whispered, "ya gotta look at it like this." He turned the magazine upside down. It didn't look a whole lot different. "What the heck is it?" My imagination was still puzzled way beyond normal capacity. "Wally says that's for sex, too."

"What does it do?" Stevie just shrugged and kept turning pages. I figured he didn't know, either. "Does your mom look like that?"

"I don't think so," I assured with utter confidence. Mom's real pretty, but I don't think she looks like this with no clothes on. "Does yours?" Stevie held up a hand to cover laughing teeth, "I don't think so." He quickly flipped through the final pages. "This ya mom's?"

"No, stupid. My dad bought it the other day in the candy store when he was with Wally. Wally says he thinks this is sex."

"How come?" Stevie had already studied this material and he was still failing this question and answer session like it was a high school biology exam. "Wally says he heard Mister Bongivani and my dad talking. Then Steven explained the encounter at the candy store in detail…

"Hey, Walt, whaddaya got there?" Mister Bongivani wondered, "gonna' have a little fun when you get home?" My dad covered Wally's ears with his hands and hushed Mister Bongivani. "Shh quiet, Mike, the kid." My big brother still heard my dad whisper to Mr. Bongivani, "This is the only sex I'm gonna get today. My wife's friend is coming over."

"Who's ya Mom's friend?"

"Shhhh… I'm not sure." Wally said nobody came over except Carmine, but whoever she is, she don't like my dad. Wally said dad got real mad just talkin' about mom's friend. He said if Mom's friend don't leave real soon he's gonna go broke buying magazines. I looked at Stevie. "What does that mean?" Stevie looked at me, but not a peep passed between us as we studied every last picture until our eyes caught fire.

The droning organ alerted us to the end of his mom's soap opera, so I never got the answer, but it nevertheless signaled the beginning of our latest adventure. "So ya wanna' come?" offered Stevie. It sounded like a great opportunity, but I still had serious reservations. "Yeah, I guess?"

"Ya hafta tell me now. She wants to come tomorrow."

"Are ya sure she's gonna come?" The blood to my brain was getting thinner as I contemplated all the possibilities. "She said she would as long as you come, too."

"How old is she?" Stevie shook his head. "I told ya a hunit times, nine." After flirting in the face of death for nearly thirty minutes my main concern was getting out of Stevie's house in one piece. "Okay, I'm comin'."

♣

We always searched around the fort to make sure nobody was lurking in the high weeds, no big kids, no little kids, no old people and no nuns. The coast was clear, so we crawled inside. "I think I have to take a leak," Stevie alerted. "Hurry up, dummy." Stevie pushed the secret door and scurried back out. We didn't actually have a secret door, we just called it that because everything in and around our fort was a secret. Stevie suddenly pulled the door open and frantically crawled back inside. "I think I heard somethin'... in the bushes."

"Whaddaya mean ya think?"

"I think she's comin'." The two of clubs was nailed over the secret peephole. I bent it up and squinted through the tiny crack, but I could already hear the sound of crackling twigs, then a sudden movement. "Holy shit, ya right, she's comin'." Her bright orange hair was like a walking neon sign. Knock, knock. Was that a knock on the roof? Didn't anybody tell this stupid girl you don't knock on the damn roof? That's why we built a secret door. "C'mon in," invited Stevie. I looked at my best friend. What the hell do we do now? Me and ole Stevie are about to get educated right here in the lots, and considering it took us both two years to escape from the first grade, I for one figured a little education couldn't hurt.

Long, straight, shiny, orange hair covered her face and swept the floor as she crawled in, boldly dragging the door behind. Our little visitor parted the tresses in the middle and pulled it all behind her ears, exposing a little button nose and red cheeks dotted with tiny freckles. I really don't like freckles, but I guess they look okay. The little girl finally adjusted to the darkness, her emerald green investigators penetrating the glare of a rabid Leprechaun, and when she spoke her tongue slashed

44

out like an angry shillelagh. "What are you doing here, Steven?" Stevie shrugged, but her demeanor quickly softened when she spotted me in the other corner, kneeling up and ready to run. "You're Kevin, right?" This time she sounded like a tiny cartoon mouse as she refocused two big Irish marbles. "Yeah. What's yours?" Her smile finally brightened the darkness. "Jolene."

We were still both grinning, but Jolene bright eyes seemed lost in thought. I had a quick thought myself: where the hell is she hiding all the giant sex parts? "I'm not taking my clothes off until he goes outside." The pushy little girl seemed to be changing the game plan. After all, this whole thing was Stevie's idea. Jolene was glaring at my best friend. I was looking around for an escape hatch when I realized I didn't build one. "I'm gettin' outta here," Stevie decided. And don't let the secret door hit ya in the ass on the way out. Jolene punched me in the arm, hard when I grabbed Stevie's collar to stop him, but my best friend angrily pushed the door that hung by one rusty hinge and crawled away. "I'm tellin' ya mother, Jo."

"Ya better not, Steven. I'll tell ya mother you steal candy." Jolene pulled the door back with a bang and a sigh. "He wasn't supposed to be here," Jolene clarified, "jus you." Fear of the unknown was worse than any horror perpetrated by Sister Mary Monster. In that case I always knew what to expect. In this case I didn't. "So, ya want me to take my clothes off, now?" I figured Stevie would be the spokesman, so I never imagined any talking. Looking and listening, that was the plan. "I guess... If you want." Jolene smiled as she slowly pulled her tee shirt from the waist of her dungarees. I was still anxious, but gaining confidence until the moment she snapped her shirt over her head, pulled it back through a mass of flaming hair, and like the shock from a smack in the ear I was staring, eyes wide, stupefied at the two little red dots on her very pink chest.

Now, if we hadn't studied that magazine we wouldn't have known what to expect, but we did. For one thing, I was expecting bigger dots. Much bigger. In fact I was expecting them to take up a whole freaking page, and at the very least they should've been bigger than mine. "Do you want me to take my pants off, now?" Jolene was already untying her sneakers. "But when I take 'em off, you have to take off yours," insisted Jolene. "That's the deal." Deal? She made it sound like this was actually going to happen. "Are you crazy?" Jolene had a better chance of watching Popeye eating a can of freaking string beans. "You know what I'm talking about," she blurted. "He said you would do anything." Stevie told Jolene that I would take my pants off if she did it first. "I don't care what he said, I'm not takin' my pants off." I was still gazing in stupefied wonder when the enormous power plant inside my head abruptly short-circuited. "C'mon," she interrupted, "I jus wanna see it."

This was like traveling to another planet. You have to figure it's going to be really different, but when you actually land your space ship it's not quite what you were expecting. Where the hell are the monsters? After traveling all this way to another planet I wanna see some big freaking monsters. One second I was transfixed on Jolene's little red dots, the next my mind is buried up to my eyeballs in giant things. You know? Things. "If ya wanna' take ya pants off, why don't ya jus do it," I suggested.

"But I jus wanna' see it," she begged. "Why can't I see it?"

My eyes were still glued to Jolene's little red dots as if I expected something to happen, but they didn't grow. Not even a bump. If they did I would've been out that secret door faster than my best friend. "'Cause ya can't," I blurted. "That's why."

"How come?" Both faces nose to nose. "'Cause you're a girl." Now that we finally straightened out the sides and Jolene was returning to planet Earth, the planet where boys don't take their underpants off in front of crazy little girls, I pushed back against the wall and kept staring at those two little red dots. "Ya not gonna run out, are ya?"

"Hell no." Sounded pretty damn confident, too, but I was treading in virgin waters so to speak, though you couldn't tell it the way Jolene was undressing. "If you run… "

"I'm not gonna run."

"Ya better not." Jolene turned and peeked through a crack by the door. "Ya have to kiss me first." For a pretty little girl with the voice of a cartoon mouse her determination was like a punch in the face. "No." My head jutted forward to intensify the point. "Why not?" Because I'm scared shitless, that's why. "Because it's dumb," I blurted. "You have ta. My big sister said if a boy doesn't kiss… "

"Ya big sister's crazy." Jolene sat back on her heels with a pout. "Don't ya like me?" My brain is now spinning out of control. "Yeah, I guess." Big mistake. That slip of the tongue left the freaking door wide open. Not the secret door, Jolene had vacuum sealed that like a coffin five minutes ago, but she obviously sensed my overwhelming trepidation. "Don't worry, I won't tell anybody." Now if I don't kiss her she'll say I'm a chicken. If I do I'll be a girl lover. Time stood as a monument to my dilemma. Birthdays seemed to pass faster. "Whaddaya waitin' for?" Jolene closed her eyes and puckered, so I closed mine and put one, right on the old nose. "You have to do it on the mouth." This can't possibly be happening. She's actually giving me a do over. **Please, make it fast.** I gulped down enough anxiety to explode and finally made contact, right on the old kissie thing. The overwhelming fear of girl germs destroyed what should've been a beautiful moment so I unpuckered fast enough to pop.

Jolene turned and peeked again through the crack. "Are ya ready?" Of course I'm not ready. How could I possibly be ready? Her wide eyes expelling the notion that this was a good time to run. "Okay, yeah, sure." Jolene inhaled, and with two tiny fingers she unbuttoned her dungarees. "I have to kneel," she protested, "I can't even move. This place is too small." If she was trying to tease me she should've said I have a veal cutlet parmigian hero right in my underwear because stress always makes me hungry.

Jolene leaned forward, put her hands on the cardboard floor and knelt up. She swept her hair back and once again tucked it all behind her ears. Then she ran down all the people I had to swear not to tell. "And especially my stupid cousin."

"But he's right outside."

"I don't care. Swear anyway."

"Okay. Swear to God."

"And hope to die?" I was praying it wouldn't come down to this.

"Yeah."

"Say it." **Okay, God I got my fingers crossed.** "Okay, hope to die." The "O" was barely out of my mouth when Jolene unzipped her dungarees. Then I did what I always do when I get anxious. A big nervous smirk creased my lips. The little girl I met less than five minutes ago is about to take off all her clothes. This had to get funny sooner or later, and just like that my smirk turned into a smile that quickly made its way to my ears. My legs were still folded in front of me as I attempted to cover my teeth with my hands, but I had a better chance of stopping the sunrise on a school day by throwing a blanket over my head. "Ya better stop laughin' or I'm gonna' go."

"No. Go ahead. I'll stop." Jolene looked away, sort of disappointed, maybe mad. "Don't ya wanna see it?" I wasn't sure what it was, but "yeah I guess," rolled right out into the dark. Yeah I guess were prob-

47

ably the magic words. Jolene's eyes grew wide and her smile wider as she slowly wiggled and jiggled her dungarees and bloomers right down to her knees.

Jolene was smiling, I was smiling, but the biggest smile was the one on Jolene's little friend. Actually, I think it was smiling and winking at the same time. It looked sort of funny, like a little piggy bank. Yeah, I guess it looked just like a little piggy bank, but Jolene wasn't here just to add to her savings account. She was here for the exact same reason as me, trouble, plain and simple.

From the moment our eyes met, Jolene seemed anxious to get down to her birthday suit, and by the time she got there Kevin the Troublemaker was anxious to say happy birthday. Happy birthday to me! My eyes were still in shock.

"Jo!" A distant voice boomed from just beyond the edge of my universe. "Joleeeeen!" And it didn't sound like the voice was trying to inform Jolene that her minestrone soup was getting cold. This guy is loud, angry and in a hurry, and all of a sudden, so is Jolene. "Shhh," she whispered, "it's my father." Jolene redressed in a blur of arms and legs and electrified orange hair with the speed of my favorite super hero, and I was praying just as fast that she was about to fly out the secret window.

Jolene's dad seemed to be on automatic seek and destroy because he was getting a whole lot louder in a real big hurry. "Jo!... JOLEEEEN!"

The fort was well hidden from nearby intruders by a gigantic rock on one side and surrounded everywhere else by those tall skinny bamboo things with the fuzzy feathers on top. By the sound of crunching twigs and weeds we could tell he was headed directly for us, about twenty yards and closing fast. Time is of the essence. "Let's get outta here," I pleaded.

The natural progression of life as I knew it seemed to be right on time. That's how it is with professional troublemakers. Sometimes we don't even realize that we're on the job when all of a sudden, it's time to get paid. "No, no, you go." She didn't have to tell me twice.

My crawl into the sunlight was so fast and furious that I almost tunneled my way into a hole as I scrambled to my feet. From just inside the secret door she whispered, "Hurry." I ran away with the kind of fear I held for giant nuns, but not before his ponderous footsteps were pounding in my ears just beyond my actual field of vision, although the virtual field of vision in my brain was already showing the coming attractions of this afternoon's feature presentation, 'Kevin the

Troublemaker gets his ass busted by a very large stranger.'

"Oh, shit!" There he is, but instead of going towards the fort, he started running, towards me. Not exactly what I had in mind.

The very large pursuer was dressed like a construction worker, with big black boots, dirty overalls and unfortunately, no shirt. A shirt would've covered those massive bulges popping out in places I didn't even know you could grow muscles. A big droopy orange mustache hung on his face from cheek to cheek and he was still wearing his hard hat. The silver hammer dangling at his hip was ominous, and though my imagination was pretty wild, it wasn't wild enough to imagine Jolene's dad happening by to start construction on the new Fat Tony Boy memorial wing. The man was here to kick somebody's ass, and it was up to me to make damn certain it wasn't mine. His puffy face and bulbous red nose made him appear old. I naturally assumed he was slow. His second problem was that he was running on my turf. Nobody knew this environment better than me. Some old guy can't come into my lots and chase me around without getting a few lumps. Every rock, rat hole and tree stump were obstacles to reckon with, and I reckoned with them every day of the week.

I was practically flying through tall bamboo weeds with the fuzzy feathers on top and attempted to lose him before hitting the street. The well-broken path is a long winding traverse through stuff six feet over my head and barely wide enough for Fat Tony Boy. The sound of crunching twigs beneath my feet could hardly be heard because I was still but a small muffled noise in the vast overgrowth of swamp stuff. Besides that, my feet were hardly touching the ground.

Surprisingly, he was pretty damn fast for an old guy. He was cutting into my lead right up until, SPLAT! "SHIT!" He fell over a tree root onto his big dumb face. It was probably my imagination, but I swore I heard rosary beads jingling behind me. **Okay, God, it's time to choose sides. Remember, I didn't do nuthin' this time.** "Get over here you little sonofabitch!" Uh oh, he knows my name. Mister coordination scrambled to his feet and started screaming all kinds of bad stuff. "Where's Jolene you little bastard?" He started moving at the speed of, "I'm gonna get ya, you little shit." Let's just say he got a second wind. I took a leap. Still can't fly, so I turned on the afterburners and finally hit the edge of the lots, but somehow the massive monster was keeping up with me step for step. Seven thirty-three Taylor Avenue seemed a million miles away, way beyond the range of my mom's earshot.

When I finally stepped onto a running surface built for speed I realized that some dads no matter how old can still keep up a pretty good pace. If he tripped on the way out of the lots he would've banged his head on my heels. The wind is now running in second place.

A helicopter suddenly appeared above the roof tops. A Tarzan rope is dangling from the cabin and just long enough to save my life. Okay, my imagination was always in play, but this was merely a prayer and I didn't have a prayer. **Try to pay attention!**

My arms and legs were pumping like an Olympic high hurdler in a last-ditch effort to increase my lead, but somehow the mustache monster was still gaining ground. I frantically grabbed the stop sign pole on the corner and whipped around the front of old Mister Mulligan's car. It was a thing of beauty and probably my greatest mid-course correction ever, but when I glanced back Jolene's dad was already reaching for the pole. BANG! "Sonofabitch!" Terror filled the air when the big red klutz slipped and tripped to his knees and banged his silver hardhat into that old brown jalopy. "Now ya dead ya little bastard!" He scrambled to his feet and now he's calling me names my ears never heard before. Of all the language hurled from the time the race started the word, castrate was suddenly hitting me in the back of the head like a ball peen hammer. I didn't know castrate, but I naturally assumed it was gonna hurt. "I'll castrate ya, ya little bastard!" Ouch! Castrate. I was hoping castrate was just a fancy word for kicking little kids in the ass.

My tiny lungs were so out of air I was practically praying for a holy ass-whippin' chair to catch my breath on. Jolene's dad was still closing the gap like a champion racehorse.

Formulating plans on the run was essential for keeping my tiny movable parts in good working order and something I was already quite good at. For the most part. Usually The idea also needed to be ingenious, and I knew I had both the moment I glanced towards my home away from home at the very end of the block.

Fat Tony Boy spent most of his Summer days at the Shore Haven Beach Club. When Fat Tony Boy jumped on the bus with him mom and little sister Angie for another day of sunshine and recreation, his ancient Italian grandma always stayed home, usually cooking something, always something Italian.

I raced up to Fat Tony Boy's house but tripped on the top step and banged my Ouch! knee, but still managed the door knob, crashed through the front entrance and splattered into the tiny foyer. My attempt at breaking the land speed-mark for eight and a half-year-olds came to a very unceremonious conclusion. I was sucking air like an old fat mailman on Christmas Eve.

I was still on all fours when I opened the inner door. I was about to crawl behind it when the giant red monster stumbled through the doorway behind me, his silver hard hat flying past my head through the living room and into the kitchen. He got to his knees, chest heaving, veins bulging, totally out of breath. It looked like the old guy was having a heart attack right here at my feet. **Okay, God. Just make it look like an accident.** Jolene's dad slowly stood on thick wobbly legs and put a hand the size of a catcher's mitt at the scruff of my neck. "Where's... Jolene... you little... sonofa... bitch?" It was time to give the Big Guy one last shot. **Dear God. Please kill this horrible man right now. If you do, I'll start being good tomorrow. Promise.**

The power of prayer appears to be reserved for those that wouldn't know a calamitous situation if it smacked them in the head, people like dad and grandma, but there are kids down here in jeopardy of serious consequences if only a simple prayer be answered. What do I have to do? What's the secret word?

As usual, getting into trouble was easy. Getting out of trouble with a full complement of body parts is a feat reserved for the truly great. Escaping this latest bout with a very large, very pissed off old person could someday be used as a course study for the next generation of professionals, titled, How to make an idiot out of a jackass.

Fat Tony Boy's ancient Italian grandma was so wrinkled she looked like she could've written the original manuscript for the history of mankind before it actually became history. We called her Grandma Macaroni, and she was no taller than your average eight-and-a-half-year-old. Grandma's long silver tresses were always pulled tight to a braid that cascaded to a very slight waist, and that stately mane was always covered on top with a black babushka that she tied snuggly under her pointed chin. Even on the very hottest of days, grandma worked her little garden along the side the house dressed in her favorite color, dark black. Long-sleeved black dresses flowed over the tops of black grandma shoes, and the entire ensemble gave grandma the look of a wicked old witch, but Grandma Macaroni wasn't actually wicked and never looked very old chasing a mouse or squirrel through the tight rows of corn or around the tomatoes and through the squash. Taylor Avenue was full of healthy young adults, and none had enough stamina to keep up with grandma

51

when she was in hot pursuit of aggressive, vegetable loving rodents.

Whenever I came into Fat Tony Boy's house there was always a gesture hello and a friendly word or two in Italian. That's right, Italian. Every audible whisper that escaped her toothless mouth was in Italian. "Uppa stair." It means Tony Boy is upstairs and it was practically her entire English vocabulary. I'm pretty sure.

When the inner door opened with a crash, Grandma was straightahead in the kitchen standing by the stove, her dark eyes ablaze upon witnessing me and some crazy shirtless monster in a struggle for life and death. The big idiot was stretching the collar of my sweaty blue and white striped tee shirt as I was explaining in no uncertain terms what would happen if he didn't let go. "Ya better lemme go before I tell my Grandma to calls the cops." Grandma rolled up on this guy with a wooden spoon the size of a shovel. She raised it high over her head and started whacking him from every angle. If I hadn't smelled the tomato sauce I would've thought Jolene's dad was bleeding to death. He was blocking her attack with one hand as my body twisted in the other. Grandma was already explaining the deal in the fastest Italian I ever heard. She said, "Ifa you no letta hima go, umma gonna sticka thisa blacka shoe so far uppa you ass, ummagonna needahelpa to pulla my leg outta you butt." I think, either that or Mister Musclehead was as fluent in Italian as Christopher Columbus. Or maybe the beating he was getting was taking its toll. Grandma's tone was unmistakable. Jolene's dad walked into an Italian buzz saw with an attitude and her name is Grandma Mac. I mean Carroll.

Grandma circled at a dizzying pace, and in her excitement she actually gave me a few whacks by accident, one shot almost taking my arm off at the shoulder. "Alright, alright," Mister Muscle-head protested. "I just wanna know what your grandson was doing with my little girl?" That's right, Grandma Macaroni turned into my own blue-eyed Irish grandma faster than you could say Saint Patrick, patron saint of meatballs and spaghetti.

When the massive intruder finally relinquished hold of my little shirt, grandma grabbed my hand and pulled me to her side. Grandma was still catching her breath while she introduced Jolene's dad to the Sicilian death ray. Upon witnessing that stare I would've bolted for the exit door faster than Superman, and not even Superman's x-ray vision could burn a hole through somebody's concrete head with the laser intensity of grandma's evil eye.

I was still excited, though considerably calmer and a little tougher after realizing that things were actually working out according to the script, so I stepped forward and displayed one of my best terrifying sneers. He was lucky grandma was holding me back. Damn lucky, because I was getting pretty damn close to kicking his big stupid ass. "I don't even know your daughter." Jolene's dad growled. Quickly, I retreated. "Yes you do. My son said she was playing with my nephew Steven and another kid named Kevin in the lots behind Walt Guardino's house. What's ya name?" Big freaking deal, so he knows my name. "None of your business," I blurted. He took a step forward. I took one back. Grandma sneered and the big red monster snorted like an angry dog. "When do your parents get home, sonny boy? I know you did something."

I never cracked a smile, but the one in my brain could've starred in a toothpaste commercial. "I know you did something!" he yelled and thrust a big dirty hand across the threshold. WHACK! "Ouch!" The Italian ninja cracked the offending digits with her giant spoon as she blurted another barrage of Italian so fast and furious the big guy looked like he got smacked in the mush with a plate of lasagna. She shook her bony finger up in his face. "NO CROSSA DA LINE!" Grandma didn't actually say it, but the meaning was all too obvious. Like the startling clank of a prison gate, Mister Musclehead was shocked back to reality. WHACK! "Ouch!" See what I mean? No crossada line! Grandma's giant spoon managed to be one hell of an interpreter.

Mister Musclehead was dazed and confused when he splattered through the front door, and my plan was to make damn certain he left in the same condition. "You wait. Ya not gettin' away with this. If I find out you touched my little girl I'll be back to talk to your father." I won't hold my breath, you old fart. The words never actually reached the air, but they were right on the tip of my tongue. He was damn lucky Grandma was still holding me back. That's right, damn lucky.

Grandma and I watched from the relative safety of the foyer while the big man rushed off the curb, stopped and hurried back to the foot of the stoop. "Can I please have my hardhat?" Grandma shrugged and squinted sideways. "Che Cosa?" In English it's probably "eh." I ran across the room and picked up his silver hardhat lying against the leg of a kitchen chair, and when I walked back I hit him with another hard glare. He glared back, snatched his hardhat and strode across the street, where he finally disappeared among the tall bamboo things with the fuzzy feathers on top. He's an awfully large man, alright. Too bad he has a brain the size of a walnut. Nevertheless, he was gone, so my work here is done.

With a thankful smile and a cheerful, "gotta go, grandma," I stepped towards the open door, but Grandma Macaroni had other ideas. Grandma put a vise like grip on the handle on the side of my head and dragged me like a jailer to the nearest kitchen chair. "Ow! Ow! Ow! Ow! Ow!" She pointed. "Seat!" She meant, sit. Usually, right after seat comes mangia. I think it means meatball or cookie, but unfortunately I wasn't expecting my usual treat. Grandma finally placed her giant spoon on the counter. After witnessing how she handled that thing when she wasn't stirring tomato sauce, it was a comfort to see it on the counter.

Grandma was pacing along the sink and stove while wringing her fragile hands so tightly I thought she'd snap off a finger. She didn't seem mad, just sort of, different. Grandma paused at the back of my chair. I thought maybe grandma was trying to tell me something, but how could that be? Grandma Macaroni only speaks Italian. I can't even hear good in Italian. The only words she spoke that I understood with certainty were uppa stair and mangia, but Fat Tony Boy was still at the beach club and there wasn't a meatball or cookie in sight. Maybe I'm just nervous. Maybe all this sex stuff has me wound a little too tight. Or maybe I got this thing all mixed up. Maybe grandma's not mad at all. She doesn't look mad. So why is she still standing behind my chair?

Grandma patted me on the head and slowly walked to the opposite end of the table and sat, staring. She whispered, "I no tinka you bada boy. I tinka you gooda boy." You could've knocked me over with a soggy lasagna noodle. Here she is, maybe the first little dark eyed girl to stroll off the Santa Maria and say ciao to the Indians, a refugee straight off a spaghetti farm from the hills of Sicily. Grandma Macaroni, Fat Tony Boy's ancient Italian Grandma who only uttered uppa stair or mangia that I could decipher suddenly sounded like an Oxford English professor. "So, you likea da little a girl, eh?" My jaw flopped open as I scrambled for a plausible response. Grandma cautioned, "aspetta." I'm pretty sure it means, "closea you moutha, unlessa you wanna finda little tiny Grandma shoe parked uppa your little tiny rear enda." She had my undivided attention. "Shhh, stata'zitta. No you worry. I no tella you momma. You gooda boy." The ancient Taylor Avenue watchdog obviously knew who to keep in the dark. Grandma fixed a twinkle in her eye as a thankful smile grew with wonder and wrapped its magic all the way around my tiny innocent face.

Grandma patted the table and stood, paused and stepped towards the big cookie jar shaped like a pig on the counter. Then she lifted the pig's head, reached inside the belly and took out my favorite, a big fat homemade chocolate chip. For a second she held it for me to gaze at. My eyes were as big as the cookie with anticipation. Once again, very, very slowly, finger to lips she whispered, "stata'zitta." The meaning was all too clear: big secret. Jolene who? Grandma didn't have to tell me twice.

7

The next few months brought nothing but new troubles. Big troubles. First of all, school always seemed to be lurking around the corner, but that was hardly a problem compared with my latest dilemma. Mom and dad had been talking about moving away to a bigger apartment, and of course they expected me to go with them. I was actually thinking about running away, but where to? We had no cooking or toilet facilities in the fort.

As it turns out dad didn't travel very far to find us a bigger place to live. Actually, dad didn't travel at all. The Castle Hill Housing development was being constructed way over on the other side of my unauthorized play area. The boys and I watched from the edges of Taylor Avenue as the fourteen massive buildings slowly rose into the sky. Long before their completion my anxious dad with me in tow stood in line outside the temporary trailer on Randall Avenue where he picked up an application for one of the many sought-after after apartments.

It was an unusually dark cloudy morning towards the end of summer. Fat Tony Boy's house was always pretty quiet, but it was especially dreary this morning: no Grandma shuffling about or standing at the stove carefully tending her pot. When I passed through the living room her rocker wasn't rocking and the Victrola wasn't rolling with her favorite Italian opera stars. Wonder was spinning around my brain, so with a mouthful of cookie I wondered aloud, "Where's Grandma, Missus Nardello?" I kept looking over my shoulder. She had to be here, somewhere. Missus Nardello's eyes grew wide as she put a hand to her face and looked up towards the high kitchen cabinets. Fat Tony Boy's mom seemed visibly unnerved by my query. When she turned back a tear had pooled and streamed down her cheek. Her voice began to quiver. "Oh, Kevin... I thought your mom... would tell you." She looked so terribly sad. I almost cried myself, but I didn't. I'm not a cry baby. "What, Missus Nardello?" I braced for really bad news.

Fat Tony Boy's mom calmly sat in the same kitchen chair where Grandma Macaroni only a few weeks before put her finger to her lips. "Grandma went away." Her voice broke again. "To heaven."

The vagueness of everlasting eternity as taught by the crazy old nuns was as baffling a concept as Chinese arithmetic. Grandma is the only person I knew who actually left here to go there. I had no idea what to think. So I sat there dumbfounded, puzzled and even mystified by the saddest news in the world. I stole a quick glance over my shoulder. Grandma still wasn't there.

So, unless Jolene's dad happens by with more wild accusations I'm thinking my secret is safe and locked away for a really long time and probably forever and ever in the soul of my new Italian guardian Angel, good old Grandma Macaroni.

♣

My last few days at Holy Cross Detention Center were every bit as miserable as the previous four years, with nerve-wracking, stress inducing, painfully long terms of confinement.

My nervous, highly explosive mom was practically dragging me up the block towards the school by the wrist. She was explaining for the thousandth time what I should do when we got there. "Remember, keep ya smart mouth closed. I'll do all the talking."

"What if she asks me a question?" She almost yanked my arm out of the shoulder socket. "This is why you're always in trouble. You have a smart mouth. Try to keep it closed."

During the final conference before my release to a new valley of death, the principal told my mother exactly what she should expect in the future: big trouble, and my permanent record was discussed in front of me in detail in order to bear out her assessment. Mom was now in the uncomfortable position of being my lawyer, which is usually dad's job, but as usual dad was at work.

The principal reminded mom that leaving me back in first grade would have an enduring effect and go a long way in keeping me out of prison. "This boy has to grow up." She said I needed to mature in a big hurry. I didn't know mature so I figured mature had something to do with not pissing in my pants. Principal Godzilla seemed especially intent on getting to the bottom of that fire alarm thing. "Did you or Mister Carroll ever ask him why he did it?" Mom turned and looked

58

me right in the eye before she confronted the big principal. "He was angry!" Mom blurted it out with a new authority, like if Mother wasn't wearing a habit she might've clawed her eyeballs out.

Mom told the principal exactly what she told her almost four years ago, that I wasn't normally a pants pisser. That I actually pleaded with Sister Mary whenever the need arose. That little push from my pushy mom almost four years ago wasn't quite good enough then, and Mother Godzilla still didn't get it. Forcing little Christians to whiz in their pants comes with consequences, for the abuser. Mom said that my dad gave me an especially long-winded talking to. The principal didn't seem impressed.

Mother said that PS 69 is full of daydreamers and hooligans. She said I should fit right in. Mom was forced to send in the A-Team. Dad went to the convent behind the church and he didn't take on the mission alone. My Aunt Jeanie happens to be my godmother, but everybody else calls her Sister Regina Teresa, and apparently my aunt Jeanie was more firepower than Mother Godzilla could handle.

After a good holy arm twisting, Mother grudgingly let me stay in the school. Mother also promised my Aunt Jeanie that she would omit the little thing about the fire alarm from my permanent record. Aunt Jeanie told the principal that a blemish like that might damage any prospects for employment with the civil service and may even keep me out of the armed forces. Mother Godzilla wasn't exactly thrilled about the promise she gave my godmother almost four years ago.

After a long day of work and a very long conversation with Mother Godzilla, dad finally came home and sat at the kitchen table. Dad said that Mother never mentioned anything at all about Sister Mary forcing me to whiz in my pants, which happens to be the reason for this entire misunderstanding. Mother Beatrice Godzilla also didn't mention the fact that she was the spiritual head of a dark hooded gang of unmerciful bullies who were too stupid to recognize the difference between ignorant rebellion and lazy immaturity, but Mother did write enough bad stuff in my permanent record about my lackadaisical efforts and smart aleck mouth to make the necessary impression on my new holy instructors. So before you could say "where's your homework, Mister Carroll?" I found myself in the place of honor, in yet another valley of death and displacing John Federico in the third row, first seat, cell block-A.

♣

Dad always wore a smile, and moving day seemed to bring out a particularly cheery side of his personality. With thoughts of despair spinning around my brain, dad was doing his best to keep me in a good mood. What better way to advance the generous side of my dad's disposition then when he was trying to make me feel special. By the time the Bungalow Bar ice cream truck rolled into Taylor Avenue I was playing up the ole Kevin the starving orphan routine like an old Bowery bum.

The big red moving truck was parked at the curb. Stevie, little Louie, big Louie, Fat Tony Boy, Eric and I were all parked next door on Stevie's stoop when the bells began to jingle, Ding-a ling, ding-a ling. Ding-a-ling, ding-a-ling, as the white truck with its brown shingled roof slowly pulled to a stop.

Everyone raced to the far corners of Taylor Avenue except for me and Stevie. "Maaaaaa! Can I get ice cream?" The simultaneous pleas could be heard in New Jersey, all eyes darting back and forth between the ice cream truck and their respective kitchen windows as if disaster were moments from reality. After all, the ice cream man only comes by twice a day, and nobody wanted to blow the first opportunity.

Nobody was home at Stevie's house except for dumb Carmine's mom. Missus Pucharelli was a screaming beating awaiting a good excuse, so Stevie's only prayer for having ice cream today was me. My only prayer was still loading the moving truck. But extracting a whole quarter from my dad to buy ice cream for me and my best friend was like trying to rob a bank with a water pistol while the bank teller trained a bazooka on my nose. The two of us ran to the back of the moving truck. "Dad, can I have a quarter, please?" Grandma calls it the face of an angel and I put it on display every time I was begging my dad for ice-cream money.

The boys were already charging the ice cream truck with dimes clutched tightly in their fists and smiles as wide as the Lincoln Tunnel. I stood there fighting the urge to scream while my dad slowly reached in his pocket. "A quarter?" inquired dad. Here we go again. As the ice cream man was handing down push-ups and chocolate pops, Stevie and I were about to get a college education on what you could do with a whole quarter back in the day, when quarters weighed five hundred pounds and spending one took imagination and at least one best friend. "What are ya gonna' do with a whole quarter, Luke?" Dad's arm was practically down to his shoulder inside his pocket. "I want to buy ice cream for me and Stevie." Dad was smiling as he jingled the change. "Do you have any idea what I could do with a whole quarter when I was your age during The Depression?" First of all, I didn't believe for a second that my dad was ever eight and a half years old and he never actually explained The Depression, although what he did say always sounded like the greatest time in history for kids with a whole quarter.

I was still staring up at the babbling mouth. Dad's hand was so far down his pants pocket I thought he was trying to pull up his socks. "Luke, did you know that I could go to the Lowes Paradise Theater on the Grand Concourse, see a double feature, newsreels and three cartoons, take me and all my friends in a limousine around to Jahn's Ice Cream Parlor on Kingsbridge Road and buy banana splits for everyone and still have enough change to buy candy for the entire week? Luke one time I even bought a new bicycle with a quarter and a scooter and, and, and…" And by the time my dad finished explaining what he could do with a whole quarter I thought he was dragging a manhole cover up from the bottom of his pants pocket. I finally caught him in the middle of breath. "Well, can I have that quarter now, please?" The ice cream man was already back in the driver's seat, impatiently awaiting the end of my dad's enlightenment. "Sure you can, Luke." Just sign on the dotted line.

As late morning was rushing towards almost time to leave, Stevie and I were eventually left alone on Stevie's stoop. Dad hopped onto the back of the big moving truck for the very last time and I found myself staring down in total disbelief at my P.F. Flyers. This is actually happening. We're moving away, and never coming back.

My Uncle Jack Reagan walked out the front door, hopped down the four steps and paused at the red English racer inside the stone gate. "Gerry, we takin' this bicycle?" His big easy smile and joyous tone didn't even make a dent in my miserable attitude. "Luke, we takin' the bicycle?" My dad and my Uncle Jack were desperately trying to make a joke, but it was about as far away from being funny as my new address. I looked at Stevie as my uncle sat on the seat of my red racer and peddled it to the edge of the curb by the rear of the truck. "Jump in the car now, Kevin," urged Uncle Jack. "It's time to go."

I was still staring at Stevie and he was still staring at me as I sunk into the front seat of my Uncle Jack's big yellow Cadillac convertible. Fear is now my closest friend. I quickly wiped my eye. I wasn't crying. It just looked like crying. Stevie wasn't crying either. Sonofabitch. I said nobody was freaking crying.

By 1960 those crazy Russians had already taken a lead in the space race. They launched a satellite called sputnik, and it seemed every time their tiny communist orb was passing over the free world every school kid in the home of the brave was ducking under his desk while klaxons blasted along along Soundview Avenue announcing another civil defense air raid drill. But I wasn't scared of the Russians. John F. Kennedy was now the President. I remember listening to my parents talking in glowing terms of the first Irish Catholic to run the country.

As a young kid John Kennedy was molded by crazy nuns, so he was actually pretty tough by the time he graduated from grammar school. After his service in the Pacific during World War II the man was ready to chew glass and kick ass. Those Ruskies didn't stand a chance. They were probably ducking under their own desks every time they heard his name.

☘

The Castle Hill Housing development opened for occupancy on the 12th of November, 1959 and we moved in the very next day. Fourteen buildings with two thousand apartments and dad said we were the sixth family to inhabit the entire complex.

Uncle Jack dropped me off on Randall Avenue at the side entrance. "Remember, Kevin, the eleventh floor. Eleven C." I quickly dashed past the temporary orange wood fencing and the mounds of dirt and entered the building, where I found an iron stair case. I sprinted around and around the iron stairs a half flight at a time at a dizzying pace until I finally reached eleven. I followed the sound of my mom's voice and rushed through the open door. "Did you run up the stairs?" mom wondered. "Yeah... why?" I practically sucked every molecule of oxygen out of the kitchen area. "Next time try the elevator."

"Wow... .we have... an elevator?"

Our new place was huge. Tommy and I had a whole bedroom to ourselves. We could look out our eleventh floor window and practically see Canada. Kathleen also had a giant room, and mom and dad had enough space in theirs to play hide and seek. The five of us were actually pretty comfortable in the one bedroom apartment on Taylor Avenue. Now we had a mansion in the sky with enough room to play sports, and it even came with an elevator.

The next morning dad walked the three of us across what was left of the lots to the ten o'clock mass at Holy Cross. After forty minutes I'd been blessed enough to keep me in the good graces of the Lord for at least another hour and a half. After breakfast I couldn't wait to investigate my new territory.

Mom gave me the first official warning when she caught me slipping out the door. "Stay out of the mud, mister and don't get into any trouble." Mom should've come to church, she might've had a prayer.

It was a beautiful sunny day, but even sunshine couldn't compare to the bright smile on the pretty young girl with the tiny freckles and long blond hair. She was standing under the front entrance by the perambulator room, just ignoring me, gazing out towards the lots on the other side of Olmstead Avenue. Even without wings, her brilliant white dress and shiny white saddle shoes gave her the look of a heavenly body. So far this place is showing great potential.

I was still daydreaming when I spotted a kid throwing rocks. Like the pretty girl, the kid was about nine years old, but this kid probably lingered at the breakfast table and maybe the lunch table too, because unlike me with the sun behind him, the kid actually cast a shadow.

The kid obviously had some previous training in the arts. He was standing atop a large pile of dirt in front of the adjacent and still unoccupied twenty story building and breaking windows in the third and fourth floor apartments. Every time the kid shattered another pane of glass he threw up his arms like a triumphant fighter. It looked like something I might enjoy. By the end of the day I was running around the empty projects with my new best friend Sean O'Connor. Sean pointed out his older sister Kate. She was still standing by the front entrance and still smiling. I love this new place. I think I'll stay.

I was pretty much finding trouble on a regular basis and the stress it was causing mom should've, under mom's rule of thumb come with a good beating. I was grateful that dad maintained a higher tolerance for stupidity.

Dad uses love as a persuader. It should've been enough to induce the truth, but I'd stick to my stories out of stubbornness, borne out of fear inflicted by outside sources. My less than honest accountings usually tested dad's religious tolerance on a regular basis. Some days I got hit and some days I didn't, but the days I didn't, I wished that I did.

Those were the days dad searched my eyes in hopes of a flicker of recognition for my newest disaster. The moment I failed his latest test he'd merely look up to his friends in the sky and in silent resolution he'd give me up to their divine wisdom and heavenly grace. My dad never prayed aloud, except during mass and right before dinner, and just before bed he'd lead us again, but I'm absolutely positive that the Holy Ghost was right over his shoulder when dad needed him most, probably about once a week. Okay, maybe twice. Actually, I don't remember.

Mom believed I had serious problems. "Are you crazy?" I wasn't exactly sure myself, but I was being embarrassed, slapped, poked and preached the word of God by crazy women disguised as holy people. If I had to put my finger on it, I'd probably break my little finger. Those crazy nuns were really darkening my cheerful smiling outlook. If education comes with constant beatings, I'd rather be an idiot. Why do I have to know who discovered America or the nine times table or the Ten Commandments? Can they send me to jail if I give the wrong answer? Will the cops stop me on my way home from school and ask me, who was the first President of the United States? I didn't understand the need for learning so I rarely tried. Opening a book meant looking like I was reading it.

♣

Dad was talking to mom in a low tone in the dining area. Mom doesn't have a low tone, so I could easily hear her from my bedroom with the door open. They were sort of agreeing that my new school might possibly be a great opportunity to change my attitude, but mom didn't sound nearly as certain as dad.

Holy Family Grammar School appeared as your average, run of the mill, old fashioned three-story school building, but that outer facade was merely camouflage designed by ancient architects inspired by holy people to obscure their ultimate plan to recreate a medieval torture chamber for those troublemakers dumb enough to walk into their trap.

The old fashioned desks were probably unearthed from the last ice age, and they were constructed of wrought iron and dark petrified wood that unfortunately went well with the petrified rear ends that sat in many a front row seat. Attila the Nun was crudely carved into mine. We stored our ugly winter coats in a long walk-through closet. In the event of a breakdown of Christian decorum the cloakroom was also used as a temporary jail cell. A long wooden pole with a brass hook was used to unlatch the high windows in order to vent the stagnant smell of fear that hung way up by the ceiling, and it was said that Thomas

Edison himself had designed the very first electric lights that hung precariously overhead as an apparent reminder that electrocution was not beyond the possibility for the noncompliant or thick headed. For any student inclined with a troublesome spirit, the holy people in this dark foreboding dungeon had the original diagrams showing how to smack insolence through one ear out the other and back to a time when people walked the earth in long white robes and leather sandals.

The nuns of Holy Family Grammar School tortured my sluggish brain with history and geography, preached religion with the insight of medieval monks and pounded arithmetic with the enthusiasm to inflict the pain of crucifixion, but the only portion of the curriculum administered with any passion was the ancient Christian art of inflecting pain without leaving marks. Corporal punishment was administered regularly by no less than generals, and even the lowest ranking nuns had four star attitudes.

The future Saint John Vianney's Grammar school was still a grand idea envisioned by our new parish elders, and by the time they turned their dumb notion into a valley of death, many of us project kids were forced to trek a half mile to that giant hell hole on the other side of Bruckner Boulevard, The Holy Family Grammar School for wayward Christian soldiers. **And the Lord have mercy on our souls.**

One by one new families filled the fourteen massive buildings. One hundred and forty-four apartments in the eleven twelve story buildings and one hundred and sixty families in each of the three twenty story buildings. Hundreds of kids and one valley of death for all of us.

Project kids quickly overwhelmed Holy Family Grammar School like a swarm of locusts. It appeared that the older people in that well-established community didn't like it. It wasn't just the many unfamiliar faces that stuffed their school to the point of ridiculous absurdity that caused their concern, but rather that our flourishing neighborhood existed in the first place. The city of New York built the expansive Castle Hill housing development just eight blocks south of their peaceful little enclave, and that was probably all it took to piss off existing property owners. I for one could've used a football helmet.

♣

For me and my friends, the deep swampy areas were the main attractions. The massive lot surrounding them had been greatly reduced in

65

size with the building of the expansive Castle Hill Houses, but the lot was still a half mile long and a quarter mile across. The water that oozed from below was once Pugsley Creek, but the creek had been damned off years ago at Lacombe Avenue. Before city planners destroyed it with landfill, the water flowed all the way to Watson Avenue on the other side of the Bruckner Boulevard. It was also the exact same tract of land I ran through with my friends from Taylor Avenue, but now I merely entered from the opposite side, and I didn't have to sneak, all our windows faced the other way. Mom's good, but she still can't see around the corner. I'm pretty sure. "Kevin, stay out of those lots."

"Okay!" I'll be in the library.

The marshes attracted every critter that could scamper or slither across Lacombe Avenue: snakes, skunks, raccoons, pheasants, rabbits, rats, cats, wild dogs and wilder kids merely looking for a playground or a place to run and hide. The entire area was Disneyland for project kids, and the entrance was right across the street in front of my new building.

My new best friend Sean O'Connor was younger than me by a year. My second best buddy and third year apprentice Charlie Dineane was two years junior but tall enough to look two years older. Troublemaking was second nature to both of them, and altogether we were three very annoying peas in a pod.

The three of us were struggling with an old wooden door and some partially burnt two by fours that we picked off a pile of junk that some local knucklehead dumped on Lacombe Avenue. As we trudged through the weeds, my eagle eye suddenly spotted an intruder climbing down from our tree fort, about fifty yards as the crow flies. "Look." The kid was still hanging from the lowest branch. We dropped everything and sprinted to defend the territory.

The black horned-rim glasses and studious freckled face gave Jonathan Patrick the appearance of a bookworm, or possibly a very intelligent tree fort burglar. Jonathan lived in our building on the third floor. If he could drop to the ground and run a hundred-yard dash and up three flights of stairs faster than me he might've saved us all a whole lot of grief.

Jonathan spotted us racing in his direction and the second his feet hit the dirt he took off like a thief, but we were on top of our prey like a pack of hungry wolves. Sean and I were still pushing him back along the path trampled in the high grass when Charlie climbed up the tree to the fort with the ease of a chimpanzee. "What were ya doin' up there?" I grilled. "I didn't do nothin', I was just lookin'," pleaded the intruder. Seconds later Charlie tossed the old Tarzan rope to the ground. Not a word passed between us, but we seemed to be thinking along the same crazy lines.

I was holding Jonathan's arms behind his back while Sean tied his ankles together. With the same rope I then bound his wrists and threw the other end over the lowest branch. The squirming prowler was relatively calm because Jonathan still hadn't realized the gravity of his infraction until Sean and I were actually hoisting him off the ground, and even then our ill-mannered neighbor was still threatening us with the fires of hell, but Jonathan was actually a whole lot closer to getting burnt.

A frenzied moment became two harried moments. Before we knew it we had a pile of dry kindling a foot high and mere inches from the black high top sneakers of our very first swamp prisoner. It was like playing cowboys and Indians with Jonathan running right smack into a raiding party of angry Iroquois.

He wiggled and jiggled as he dangled from the rope, but once I struck the match that lit paper that started the fire, Jonathan started yelling for his mother, my mother, God's Mother and every other mother within earshot and beyond. Jonathan didn't actually get wild until the flames were licking the cuffs of his dungarees. "He's on fire!" alerted Charlie. The bottoms of his pants were smoking. I'm not sure what we were expecting, but I for one wasn't expecting smoke. "Put it out! Please put it out! Ow!" Jonathan was screaming at the top of his lungs. "Hurry up! Ow! Put it out! Ow! Ow! Ow! Ow!"

We frantically kicked away the twigs and branches. The little fire quickly scattered and died. I quickly untied the rope and slowly lowered Jonathan to the ground, where Sean untied his ankles. One medium rare book worm anxiously patted his smoking pants and streaked away like a cat spooked by a fire cracker. Jonathan was already through the lobby door before we climbed up and into the fort.

Three scared peas in pod were sweating, and not just because it was humid. The realization struck like a lightning bolt thrown by the good right hand of God. This was big time professional trouble, and it wasn't sixty seconds before it was time to get paid, again. "Charrrleeeeee!" Jonathan's mother had quickly located the apartment of the closest hangman slash pyromaniac. Diana Dineane charged out the lobby door screaming like a crazy woman. "CHARRRLEEEEEE!"

"I think I'm in trouble," said Charlie. I shook my head and swallowed hard. This time the heat was definitely coming our way. My second best buddy crawled backwards out the door and slowly shimmied down the tree, which left Sean and I to wondering, who's next?

On a clear day I could probably hear my mom's voice from outer space, but from a mere hundred and yards it sounded like she was screaming inside of my brain. "Kevinnnnnnnn! I know you can hear meeeeee!" So could my dad, and he was working in Yonkers. "You better get outta here, Sean before—"

"Shauuuuuuuuun! Get your stupid ass upstairs, this second! Shauuuuuuuuuun!"

"Damn." My best friend closed his eyes and hung his head. "She's gonna kick my ass."

"You? What about me? My mother's crazy."

Three terrified Musketeers slowly slinked from behind the trees into the line of fire. Three angry mothers were already pointing fingers like saber swords by the front entrance. "Kevin! Move it! Move your goddamn ass over here. NOW!"

The furious action that erupted was like an episode of Batman and we were the bad guys. It didn't matter which way we turned because there was no way of covering every vulnerable portion of the body simultaneously with only two hands. Smack! "Ouch!" Bang! "Ouch!" Crack! "Ouch!" Boom! "Ouch!" Mom's last hop in the ass sent me flying through the lobby door and sprawling on the floor, where she quickly grabbed the handle and hustled me into the elevator.

Seconds later, three battered and bruised buddies were standing at attention in Jonathan's living room. "Come out here, Jonathan." The burnt dungarees spread in obvious display over the back of the couch. Missus Patrick was still grinding her teeth when her son entered the room wearing short pants. "Turn around, Jon." Three petrified parents still out of breath were suddenly aghast when Jonathan turned to display the bubbly flesh on his ankles and calves. Jonathan's mom was still visibly upset, but calmed enough with quick breaths, in out, in out in order to describe the telephone conversation with Mister Patrick. She looked each one of us in the eye.

"My husband said to use my discretion... as to whether or not we should have you all... " She pursed her lips tight enough to suck the liquid that encased her brain as she glared directly into the soul of the young sicko that barbecued her little boy. "Prosecuted!" she announced with fury. The situation was headed down hill, but Mary Patrick was making the ride to Armageddon a whole lot faster. A sneer turned up the corner of Jonathan's mouth as he sat on the end of the couch.

Three angry mothers were now terrified at that possibility of arrest. It was mine that started the chorus of begging. "I can't tell you how sorry I am, Mary. Kevin...... Kevin!" I was still pondering the consequences of incarceration or worse when mom suddenly delivered a vicious slap CRACK! to the back of my head. "Sorry, Missus Patrick."

"And... " Mom folded her arms in a tight knot. I was definitely really sorry so it wasn't a big deal to give a convincing effort. "Sorry, Jonathan. We were jus tryin' ta scare ya." Mom then assured Missus Patrick and me that our apartment would be the next closest thing to a concentration camp for the foreseeable future. Missus O'Connor assured her that Sean would see God before he'd visit the lots again, and Missus Dineane was already slapping Charlie around the living room.

When Dad arrived home from work he wasn't quite through the door before mom tossed him the daily hand grenade. "Your son set a neighbor's boy on fire this morning." No "how was your day?" No kiss on the cheek. The sudden alarm in mom's voice was hardly unusual. Dad remained calm as he gave the little lady a weary glance before bending over to untie his work shoes. "Eve, I never heard anything so stupid in my entire life." Dad was shaking his head as he placed his shoes on the floor of his closet. Mom's head was still smoldering since this morning and appeared moments from spontaneous combustion.

"Did you hear what I said, Gerry!" There isn't one person within a forty-mile radius that didn't hear, except dad. Dad has ninety percent hearing loss in one ear and the other one wasn't too good either. His disability from the war was usually thought of as a gift from God when dealing with mom's vocal explosions, but not today. "Even at Earth's closest orbit the sun is too far away to set anyone on fire." Mom sounded like she was ready to launch into orbit. "Gerry! I said your son set a neighbor on fire!" Well, now that's a whole other kettle of fish.

Mom usually blows things out of proportion, so the toughest part of my day was explaining the situation from an entirely different angle. One with a little wiggle room. Dad's aware of my tendency to get a little crazy, but he's also aware of mom's affinity to exaggerate. One of my greatest assets is my ability to feign stupidity under great pressure, but that wasn't even necessary. For this particular situation I merely needed to clarify a few details. "What is your mother talking about, Kevin?"

"This kid was in our fort. We were just playin' around." Dad looked a bit puzzled as he glanced towards mom. Mom looked like she was ready to toss me out the eleventh floor window. "There is something seriously wrong with this kid, Gerry."

"What exactly do you mean, playing around, Kevin?"

"Gerry, they hung the boy in a tree and set the poor kid on fire." Mom interrupted my train of thought just as I was gaining traction. Dad was shaking his head. The image was obviously mind boggling. "Mary Patrick called Jon at work and thank God they decided not to have them all arrested." Mom was tapping one little shoe hard enough to crash through the tenth floor ceiling. "Let me guess, Sean and Charlie. So what exactly was your part in this whole thing, Kevin?" Mom interrupted again, intent on turning up the heat. "The boy said your son lit the fire."

"Jesus, Mary and Saint Joseph, Eve will you please let me get to the bottom of this." Mom folded her arms in a tight knot, steam blasting from her ears. "We weren't trying to burn him. We just wanted to scare him." Dad made a quickie sign of the cross, then looked up to the Big Guy for added composure, but still shaking his head. "You could've seriously hurt that boy, Kevin. I just don't know what to do with you, anymore."

"I KNOW WHAT TO DO WITH HIM!" shrieked mom. "He needs his goddamn head examined, Gerry!" Mom could usually be counted on for going way over the top, but I guess it can't hurt to get a psychiatric evaluation. This way if I do anything in the future she deems crazy I can say I've already been assessed and cleared by a professional.

8

I was slaving around the apartment, cleaning things for the hundredth time that were clean before I started, when the phone rang. Mom catapulted off the couch and snatched the phone off the kitchen wall before the second tone. "Oh thank God. I was praying it was you, Helen." A very close friend was calling mom to lend a concerned ear, but apparently Helen Jardine was also calling to give mom the telephone number of an old high school classmate who just happened to have a degree in aggressive childhood stupidity. "I'll call you right back, Helen."

Mom hung up the phone and quickly dialed the office, and for the next ten minutes she described my colorful behavior with way too much color and way too much emotion to an obviously very patient doctor before she paused for a second breath, then she scribbled the date and time for my appointment. "We'll be a little early in case you need to talk with me first, Doctor... are you sure?" Apparently, the doctor had enough information already to clear me through the security desk at FBI headquarters.

Mom and I were riding the number thirteen bus all the way to Pelham Parkway, where we transferred to the twelve to take us to the Grand Concourse. The forty-minute trip seemed more like a twenty-year prison sentence. Every two minutes she reminded me of our purpose and the consequences of screwing it up. "When we get there you tell this man the truth. If you lie to the doctor, he'll know it. For god's sake, you're eleven years old. Your father and I need to know what's going on with you. Please, for your father's sake, Kevin be absolutely honest."

After their brief and very animated exchange in the reception area I slowly followed the short trim doctor with the shiny bald head to his inner office. He closed the door and quickly put my anxious jitters at ease. The doctor was pensively stroking his thick brown beard and made a quick professional assessment about mom's hyper-vivacious personality. "Boy... she's a real fire cracker." I grinned with relief because I thought he was about to say, boy... she's a real nut job.

The smiling PhD with the piercing gray eyes never took his gaze from mine while he strolled around his desk and gestured to a hard, straight back chair on the other side of his antique coffee table. "Please, take a seat, Kevin." The doctor was still smiling and still stroking his beard as he sat in his big plush chair and crossed his legs. "So why do you think you're here, Kevin?" Well, I thought I'd be catching a little shut eye on a nice comfy couch, but I see you don't even have one, you old goat. So twenty minutes after my ass fell asleep I was still spinning a world class story, and twenty minutes after that he wasn't any closer to finding out what was in my head any more than I was of finding the cure for schizophrenia. Psychiatry is the greatest scheme for seducing money from depressed crybabies since the invention of the strait-jacket. The idea is to let somebody talk long enough that eventually a glimmer of reality should rise up from the depths of the tortured soul. That's the idea, but I figured out a better one before I stepped off the bus. My plan was to simply convince Doctor Edelman that mom was crazier than me. How hard could that be? After her initial meltdown over the phone I figured he already made a preliminary evaluation. I thought he'd lock her in a closet as soon as she stepped off the elevator.

I eventually told the doctor that Jonathan didn't really get burned, a little redness maybe, but hardly scarred for life. I told him that mom exaggerates. I assured the doctor that dad only went along with her psychiatric evaluation thing to keep her calm. I explained that I like to scare big bullies with fire because it's more intimidating than a punch in the face. Jonathan wasn't a bully and he wasn't any bigger than me, but Doctor Wizard didn't know that. In fact, he only knew what I told him and I told him I was scared of my mother. I told him she was crazy and I also told him not to be surprised if she was already dusting the reception area.

Mom and I had finally switched rooms. I can actually hear better than my mom who can hear better than a NASA satellite dish, and with my anxious ear to the door I took in the doctor's unbiased assessment. The doctor actually tried to convince my mother to go a little easier with me. Can you imagine? He's lucky he didn't get smacked. He cautiously suggested that loving parents would be the key to my sanity, and he also hoped that she wouldn't worry, that many kids have this same fascination with fire. I've been telling my mom the same thing for years and never charged her a dime for the self-analysis. The man was a freaking jackass. I schmoozed my way around this PhD like a Harvard professor and I wasn't even trying hard. If I would've concentrated I probably could've had my mom arrested. The doctor seemed very accommodating. Maybe it was my Boy Scout face and sparkling personality that brought him around to my way of thinking, but on general principle I'm sticking with dumb freaking jackass.

The ride home was a breeze. "So, what did he say?" I was in my own little world, daydreaming, counting Volkswagens. Oooh, a red one. "What?" I hate it when she breaks my concentration.

"I said what did he say?"

"He didn't say anything." Mom pondered a moment, not wanting to damage my fragile psyche. "Whatddya mean?"

"I mean I did all the talking." Mom probed ahead. "Well, did you talk about what you did to Jonathan?" I pondered a moment, not wanting to destroy forty minutes of world class bull shit. "Yeah." Keep it simple.

"And... ?" I hadn't time to think this one all the way through, so I went with the first thing that popped into my head. "He said I shouldn't talk about our meeting... with anybody, especially you."

"We'll see what your father has to say about that, mister."

♣

It was Friday, payday, and dad was a little later than usual, but not actually late. I was seated at the dining room table doing a great impression of somebody studying history until dad finally came through the door at five thirty. "How'd it go today, Luke?" I wasn't exactly sure what to expect, but I still should've anticipated the calmness of Jesus because dad is always the calmest person in the room. He was already smiling as he held out dinner, two small pizza pies. I smiled right back "It went pretty good." I hurried to the door and greeted dad with a kiss. Then I carried our regular Friday night treat to the table with a little bounce in my step while dad slipped out of his work shoes.

"So, where's ya mother, Luke?" Mom was always home at dinner time, always cooking dinner. Kathleen and Tommy came from their rooms one behind the other and greeted dad the same way. "She's downstairs with Deni O'Connor," alerted Kathleen. Sean's mom and my mom are as close as Sean and I. Deni O'Connor was always home and always ready to entertain mom's early evening craziness with her own special prescription for calming frazzled nerves: scotch.

Kathleen, Tommy and I were sitting around the dining room table annoying each other with the usual annoying stuff. Dad washed his hands in the bathroom before he came out, opened the top box and looked at me with a prayerful twinkle in his eyes. "So, how'd ya mother do today, Luke?" Psychiatric evaluations weren't exactly my forte, but I stumbled along like a third year graduate and gave it the old college try. "She didn't scream." Dad smiled just a bit broader. "This might turn out to be a good night after all." Always the optimist. "Let's say grace. Bless us oh Lord and blah blah blah… blah blah blah. Let's eat. And save a slice for your mother. We don't want her getting crazy when there's nothing left."

We wouldn't want that.

♣

With age came the ability to run like the wind, and my greater speed was an absolute necessity because my mouth was also getting a whole lot quicker with maturity.

Calculating the exact moment to bail out of dangerous situations is a skill that I had fashioned from early on. Screening factors such as proximity to a threat and the size of opponent were just two of many dynamics I considered when determining how tough I should actually get before the only thing left to beat out of me was a very thin shadow.

My fourth grade teacher Miss Dingaloone wasn't a nun, so she wasn't nearly as adept at beating the crap out of a medium sized troublemaker, but what she lacked in a quick right hand she more than made up for with screaming and yelling, and Miss Dingaloone did some of her best work when I was doing mine. So it wasn't very long before my new name became Mister Carroll go stand in the cloakroom.

The long walk through the closet was really dark and quiet. That means you can't learn a thing in the cloakroom. So banishment to the cloakroom wasn't that bad as long as the ranting old fart stayed on the other side of the door.

Her dull orange hair was short and bristly and looked like a nest for small birds, and her two beady eyes were set deep and always on the lookout for shifty Christians. She might've been a mind reader because Miss Dingaloone could usually picture the funny idea in my head just seconds before I was turning it into a smart-ass answer, but most of the time she wasn't nearly as sharp. Those were the days that Miss Dingaloone ordered me to stand quietly in the cloakroom, an occurrence as regular as sunrise on school days.

The main point of contention between us was how she conducted herself when the need arose to manicure the inside of her nose. Miss Dingaloone's a nose picker. I'm talking professional. I pick my nose too from time to time, but I refuse do it in front of a captive audience. Whenever the urge struck, no matter what we were doing, she would order, "Heads down children." With lightning quickness she had a finger in her schnoz up to her elbow, and catching her in the act was one of my jobs. "I said put your head down, Mister Carroll." There she was as usual with a booger the size of a freaking bowling ball on the end of her fingernail. If I didn't already know how to pick my nose, I could've gotten a Ph.D. at it in fourth grade. In the blink of an eye she could do a complete excavation, and absolutely nobody could flick a booger with more skill than old Ding-dong. "Okay children, heads up."

My eyes were still trained on her two fingers as she nimbly readied to fire, but once she started strolling around the room it was impossible to calculate trajectory. It was every man for himself. Keep in mind that boogers cause skin cancer, blindness and even leprosy, and not even self-administered penicillin could wash away the stigma of getting hit with a booger. Every little kid knows that, especially Robert Bowden. Robert almost died in a booger attack. One day old Dingaloone got Robert right smack in the middle of his forehead, and Robert sits directly behind me. I could've been killed. Robert screamed like a girl. I quickly turned around, "Oh, wow! A direct hit! You better get to the nurse's office, Robert." After embarrassing the teacher to the point of infuriation, she once again ordered my incarceration in my favorite spot in the entire school. She pointed that dirty old finger like a used butter knife. "Mister Carroll!" she blasted, "Go stand in that cloakroom and don't come out for the rest of the year!"

"But I didn't do nuthin'."

"Now ya can do nuthin' in the cloakroom, Mister Carroll. Get."

♣

Another obsession mastered in fourth grade is the fine art of writing small. Really small. Imagine printing the fifty states and capitals so tiny it could practically fit onto a postage stamp. Instead of studying at home I spent my time writing a single word, then sharpening the pencil. Over and over, sharpen then write. I became so proficient I could almost write a book on a piece of paper an inch wide. Then I'd stick the little piece of paper up the hole in the bottom of my tie. I spent so much time preparing my cheating notes that I actually learned stuff without even trying. Imagine that, I was cheating, but I was still getting educated.

My mother was summoned to school by a note delivered by my sister Kathleen after I was handed the usual substandard report card from a very irritated teacher.

I was squirming at the end of mom's iron grip as she pushed me through the classroom door just minutes before the start of my regularly scheduled internment. Miss Ding-dong was seated at her desk and began slowly and cautiously, but gathered momentum quickly as she told my very anxious and highly volatile mother a whole lot of bad stuff about my big mouth and complete lack of effort. My teacher ended her five-minute monologue with a brilliant insight. "Kevin might possibly be the smartest child in my class, but Kevin never actually attends my class. Your son spends his days in the clouds." And why shouldn't I? That's where the freaking space ships are, ya crazy old witch. "If your son doesn't apply himself very soon, I'll be forced to leave him back."

Fourth grade taught me a whole array of fine arts. Thanks to my uniquely attuned skill as a booger detector I got through the year with no unusual diseases. And thanks to my expertise with a sharpened pencil, my promotion to fifth grade was right on schedule. One year. Poor old Dingaloone couldn't get me out of her classroom fast enough. Class dismissed.

9

Sister Joseph Marie proved as equal to the task of slapping the snot out of a medium size troublemaker as any of my previous captors. Sister would ask a question, usually towards the very end of my last maneuver, and before I could manage another harrowing touchdown on the aircraft carrier she was WHACK! smacking me from the cockpit and right over the side of the ship and into freaking Atlantic Ocean. "Go get your sister, Mister Carroll... And don't dawdle out in that corridor again or you'll be a very sorry young man."

The emergency bells were still ringing in my head as I followed my sister back through my classroom door. My class mates were now referring to my big sister as the substitute teacher. "Do you know why your brother doesn't have his homework, again? And why can't he ever pay attention?" Sister knocked her boney knuckles on my thick skull. "Does he even have a brain inside this empty head?"

Kathleen had a few years' experience in dealing with my daily interruptions. My big sister merely absorbed it all as part of her regular morning. "I don't know, Sister." That's right, keep it simple, Kat. "Your brother will be a rag picker if he doesn't straighten himself out."

Sister Joseph Marie had as much patience for my attitude as I had for arithmetic, and we collided like nine-times-seven every single day of the week. So after another exhausting year of guessing my way through math tests, pop religion quizzes and every other examination known throughout the black robed world of Christian prosecutors I was handed a final report card written with so much red ink that I thought the paper was on fire. At the bottom and printed in bold red letters, KEVIN WILL REPEAT THE GRADE.

Sonofabitch!

With the ever-present fear of an untimely death I attempted to slip through our apartment door like a ghost, but mom was in the kitchen and immediately scared up all the standard threats with an impassioned tone that still rings in my ears. "Wait till ya father gets home!" Dad was the least of my problems. Doing the fifth grade over was a thought that resonated like a smack in the ear from the left hand of God.

Missus Periwinkle's tolerance for aggressive troublemakers was the same as mine for annoying old ladies: none. If I had to listen to her daily babblings one more time about her four genius children my brain would be mush before the first report period. Fortunately for both of us my stay in her classroom wasn't that long.

My repeat performance of fifth grade was actually going better than expected because I quickly realized that my latest annoyance was a loud barker with no bite. Missus Periwinkle never raised a hand in anger, and her gentle demeanor was more like permission to be twice as annoying. I never gave her the correct answer because the smart answer was always the funny one. That was the only reason I was coming to school in the first place, to have a little fun. After a few very long weeks, Missus Periwinkle was probably rethinking her career path. Every time I opened my mouth she would shake her head and look out beyond the window. It seemed we both wanted the same thing, the ability to fly away.

I was in the cloakroom at the end of the day and merely putting on my coat while it was still on the hook, the top hook. Barbara Conway probably thought I was hanging myself after another torturous day of listening to Missus Periwinkle, but Barbara Conway didn't stay long enough in the cloakroom to ask me if I was a little depressed. She ran out yelling, "Missus Periwinkle. Kevin Carroll's hanging himself in the cloak room." Good ole Barbara Conway.

The crazy old goat wrote a two-page letter to my parents imparting information that if seen by the wrong people could've had me confined to a mental institution, and considering that mom and my dumb teacher were pretty much on the same page concerning my penchant for aggressive self-destructive behavior, I figured my next ill-advised adventure could land me in a tiny strait jacket.

Early the next morning mom was breathing down my neck while the principal administered the mandatory tongue lashing. When Sister Madeline finally lost the ability to breathe and talk at the same time I was transferred across the hall to a different cell with a new jailer, and not a moment too soon.

☘

It was said that old Sister Augustine was born in Italy during the reign of Julius Caesar. Sister was only four and a half feet tall wearing one-

and-a-half-inch grandma shoes, and so wrinkled her face resembled the fractured windshield of a Model T Ford. Sister was deaf and practically blind, but with the help of God the old battle axe could yank any size troublemaker out of his desk and shove him against the blackboard with the brutality of a six-hundred-pound sumo wrestler. Sister Augustine regularly nodded off in the middle of lessons, and the fun didn't stop there because Sister would make mistakes on the blackboard almost as often as she stood at the board with a piece of chalk, and George Dolan, a tall, golden-haired wise-ass never missed an opportunity to point out her blunders. That was usually my job, but George was a better than average troublemaker with a razor sharp wit, so I merely laughed along with everybody else and awaited my turn. "U-keepa you mawda closa, Meesa Doola. U-Puta you handowna, Meesa Carro."

It was early in the afternoon. My ability to concentrate on anything after lunch was the same as before lunch, except with a bad stomach-ache. The starving kids in China had no idea how lucky they were. The smell in the dungeon-like cafeteria on Thursdays was nauseating: a soggy gray hot dog wrapped in wax paper, watery tomato soup and half an orange. The other half probably goes to China along with all our missing hot dog rolls. Every Thursday I took my twenty-seven cents lunch money to Babe's candy store on the corner and feasted on two Milky Ways, two Snickers and a Chunky. What A chunk-a-chocolate. With two cents left over for a pretzel rod.

I was vectoring north over the West Side Highway and gave the locals a show with a screaming barrel roll under the George Washington Bridge at nearly Mach one. The mission was highly classified as usual and new coordinates were still coming in from NORAD. I was getting static through my ear piece that I thought sounded like an SOS, but it wasn't… Sister Augustine suddenly crashed into my desk. I really hate it when she does that. By the time I was fully conscious my good friend Wally Ferguson was leaning against the blackboard holding his arms up like a boxer covering his face in the corner, but it was like taking a beating from the wind with a pillow.

"Nexatimea," the old nun suggested. Smack! Smack! "U holda you smada mawda, Mesta Wise-a-guy." Smack! "You unastanda?" Smack! Wally was still smiling and still peeking through his hands above Sister's head. "Yes, Sister." The entire class exploded into giggles. Sister stomped her little black shoe and scanned the room with cloudy eyes no longer capable of detecting the offenders. Old Sister Augustine was the greatest nun to float across a classroom floor, and runner up for second place was probably still in heaven getting last minute instructions from The Holy Ghost.

♣

I bounded like a purse snatcher, three steps at a time down the rear stairwell of Holy Family Grammar School. Boom! Boom! Boom! Boom! Boom! The overwhelming hostility for us project kids and our new upstart parish will surely prove disastrous if I get caught. My frantic footsteps echoing throughout the empty stairwell sounded like rolling thunder. Boom! boom! boom! boom! boom! The blizzard of paper announcing the fourth annual Saint John Vianney Lady's Guild card party (mom's the recording secretary) that I snatched off my dining room table this morning and flung out the third floor window seconds ago will cause a firestorm of resentment if anyone of consequence puts them and me in the same place at the same time.

The two hundred raffle tickets the size of post cards appeared like a biblical rain of fire as I flew past the second floor window. Faster, faster. I catapulted around the banister onto the last landing, where to my utter shock and despair stood big Angela DiUbaldo the toughest hall monitor in twelve states glaring at me wide eyed from the ground floor. What the hell is big Angela still doing in the building after detention? The only person around this time of day is usually mopping up the lavatories or changing dead light bulbs.

The giant eight-grader was twice my size, so her menacing glare was hardly necessary, but I was still expecting a clumsy effort as I charged the exit door like an escaped felon.

The big monitor stood her ground, the shiny badge pinned to a grown up chest puffed out like a marine protecting the front door at the White House. Big Angela snatched the little silver whistle hanging from a string and started blowing like a big stupid cop. With only five steps remaining, my final bound towards freedom was so fast and furious that I actually sensed a little lift as my skinny ass continued flight on wings of a prayer. Big Angela can't stop me now. I'm pretty sure. I pray to God.

My timing was probably incapacitated due to the earsplitting noise whistling through my ears, so my last bound towards freedom was hardly the Olympic style effort necessary for escape. The fastest kid in the fifth grade is about to collide head on with the slowest girl in the Bronx. Big Angela snatched me right out of the air, and we were still wrestling to the floor when the door at the far end of the corridor exploded open as if hit by a speeding truck.

The Big Angela obviously had enough lung capacity to alert every nun in the valley, but only one responded to the racket still bouncing off the ancient marble walls like a locomotive whistle screaming through a long dark tunnel. Hitting the ground broke her grip and I was still squirming away from the frenzied attempts of the giant lunging hall monitor when a sharp talon reached up from the depths of hell and snatched my ankle and hauled me away as I frantically clawed towards my salvation.

Freedom was just the other side of the large red oak door, but the sudden reality of a holy ass whippin' of biblical proportions was as frightening a thought as getting hit by a freight train full of nuns. **Dear God. Give me a sign. A debilitating stroke would do it for me.**

"I didn't do nothin'!" Big Angela didn't actually see me throw anything out the window, but my frantic scramble for a plausible explanation was still coming up scrambled. **Please, God, please, God.** Mom still says it best, fat chance. This is about to get crazy ugly.

The principal dragged me screaming and squirming through the corridor. "I didn't do nothin'!"

"I'm not sure what you didn't do this time, Mister Carroll, but that's why we have hall monitors."

The search for a convincing denial was still being worked out in my brain, but the extreme gravity of the situation was causing a breakdown in reaction time. My plea for reasonable doubt was still echoing through the valley when we reached the principal's office. "Go into the office, Angela!"

Sister followed Big Angela into the main office and dragged me over the threshold. She flung my leg, which spun me three hundred and sixty degrees, and I would still be spinning except that I banged my head on a box of catechisms. Sister Madeline grabbed her big holy face. "What exactly didn't you do this time, Mister Carroll?" I didn't do nuthin. I didn't see nuthin' and I'm sticking to it. Sister closed the door and snapped the lock. She folded her hands into her sleeves and tapped an anxious foot. Her obvious lack of religious tolerance was already causing her blood to boil, which caused her eyes to bulge. "Get up and sit in that chair, Mister Carroll! What exactly is going on here, Angela?"

I barely settled onto the dark mahogany holy ass whippin' chair when someone's attempt to enter the principal's office startled the living crap out of me. Click! click!... Click! click! click! The knob flicked back and forth with such a vengeance it appeared the massive figure on the other side of the frosted glass was trying to yank it off. "Unlock the door, Angela." The giant hall monitor was also startled because she could also see the foreboding silhouette of the one and only prince of darkness. Not the devil. At this point the devil would be as welcome as a birthday clown. Father DeGenco's piercing black eyes were practically melting a hole through frosted glass as big Angela hurried to unlock the only thing separating me from an untimely death.

Sister snapped to attention, eyes focused as Father abruptly entered the room clutching a fist full of Saint John Vianney raffle tickets for a basket of cheer, and for some godforsaken reason The Holy Family hitman was already shaking the Saint John Vianney raffle tickets under my nose. "Where did these come from, Mister Carroll?" How the hell does he know my freaking name? "You can leave now, Angela," ordered Sister. That's right. We wouldn't want any children to see this. Not even a big one. "Please, leave us alone, Sister." Big Angela held the door wide. Sister smirked in my face and slowly floated from the room. **Okay, Lord. It's time we get on the same page, here. You know he's nuts, so if he trips and bangs his head on the corner of the desk nobody will think any less of You.**

"God has no time for delinquents, Mister Carroll." Father DeGenco's black eyes were like two exclamation points to every word regurgitated in anger. Father placed the picture of the Holy Family face down on Sister Madeline's desk. There will be no witnesses, on Earth or anywhere else. I clenched my teeth to protect my jaw. Keep your mouth shut. He can't break your jaw. That's what Sean O'Brien says. The holy lunatic couldn't pry my teeth apart with a crow bar.

Father grabbed my tie at the neck, lifted me up to my feet and rattled my head. Then he shook the raffle tickets in his other fist. Once he had me all lined up the holy hit man punch-poked a quick short jab to the tip of my nose. It wasn't exactly a Sonny Liston left jab in the mush, so it was only upon looking down at my brilliant white shirt spotted with my own red misery that I finally got scared. "I hope you're not going to cry, Mister Carroll?" Not on your miserable freaking life I thought. Upon witnessing my dripping nose he bit his lower lip. "I guess we'll finish this in confession." It didn't actually sound like an invitation.

FRIDAY MORNING

As the line slowly dwindled to one final sinner before my own entry into one of three confessional boxes, my focus narrowed with laser intensity as I calculated the odds of getting a friendly ear to receive my weekly breakdown of Christian values. Mary Gallagher exited the furthest soul cleansing station. Walter Stevenson ambled in. I still had a 50/50 chance of walking out of here under my own power until the maroon curtain parted to Father DeGenco's house of horrors in the wake of Kathy Dailey's long-winded accounting. Dark clouds gathered in my brain. Lightning flashed. Thunder cracked. What to do? Stand pat. Don't breathe. Run. "What's the problem? Move it along, Mister Carroll." Sister Edward Jean showed me the way with a friendly but determined smack in the head.

Now I'm kneeling in the darkness, a veiled screen the only thing separating me from the same unholy lunatic that punched me in the face on Wednesday. I lowered my voice and mumbled. "Blame Fa, for I haa sin." I already had serious misgivings about this ritual, especially with the likes of the heavy weight champ of Holy Family dishing out the forgiveness. "Go ahead, Mister Carroll." The dark avenger deciphered my new voice right through the damn partition. I shoulda ran. I bit my lower lip and gave him the regular. "I said five curse words. I disobeyed my mother three times and… aaaa, I also made fun of old Mister Morris who lives in the lots… one time." The sun shines green on Mister Morris's baldy bean. I only mentioned it as a last ditch effort to add substance in the absence of a real confession. What could it be, an extra ten Our Fathers?

The holy screwball smacked Jimmy Merlino in the mush two weeks ago for the very same infraction, leaving out the big sin. "Is that it, Mister Carroll?" The silence in my mouth was probably nothing compared to the dead silence screaming between his ears. I whispered, "Yes… Father." The words were hardly through my quivering lips when a large hand burst through the curtain and yanked me out by the handle so fast that my last dark thought was still floating around the confessional box. CRACK! The cavernous cathedral resounded from a smack in the mush administered with the kind of hatred you'd see in apartheid police stations.

Lines of dead-silent, very stunned medium sized sinners circled the perimeter of Holy Family Church all awaiting their turns to confess all the usual stuff. The bad kids all, rethinking their options.

I glared a loathing disgust through blue eyes ablaze with red rage into his thick skull, my own equivalent of a smack in the face. I couldn't have made a stronger point if my tacit message was connected to the right hand of Rocky Marciano. Father DeGenco grabbed the handle and hurried me down the aisle towards the main altar, where he pushed me onto the kneeler and simultaneously whispered in my ear. "There are no prayers for you, Mister Carroll. You will surely burn in hell if you don't change your attitude." If that's true, I thought, me and this poor excuse for a holy man will be burning in the exact same place.

My early years of professional experience had finally paid off, because I was never more prepared for a smack in my mush as I was today. So I calmly knelt there with my head down trying to remember who was pitching for the Yankees today... Ralph Terry, I think? Go Yanks!

♣

When my mother wasn't railing on and on to Grandma about my latest miscalculation in judgment she would sometimes sprinkle in a few rays of sunshine just to brighten an altogether cloudy week. "Even at twelve years old," she'd rejoice, "Kevin could already iron Kathleen's white school blouses better than a Chinese laundry." Need a quart of milk or a loaf of bread from the delicatessen? "When Kevin does anything, he does it with a smile." Doing good deeds or my chores around the apartment weren't unusual occurrences, but unfortunately the absurdity of my everyday life was a lot more regular.

My ability to run from zero to a white flash around and around the kitchen and living room partition with mom hot on my heels was a talent borne out of sheer necessity. The effort to keep myself at a safe distance from mom's little right hand had become a full time job. Mom wasn't a quitter, but sooner or later she would run out of breath because I never ran out of fear, and I was faster than fear, most of the time, usually.

Dad didn't require quick feet or greater lung capacity for dealing with my constant stupidity. Dad's a talker, but when he did finally get mad enough to bang the kitchen table I suddenly became a much better listener. In fact, I was much better at listening than talking.

All dad wanted was the truth. I can't handle the truth. As I struggled and stammered and plotted along with almost heroic type stamina to explain away my latest fiasco, Dad would simply sit there shaking his head.

I'm pretty sure dad would have accepted my alternative scenarios without givng me the two-hour lectures if I was given a decent opportunity to explain away the scary scenes being played out in my head, but I never got that chance. Dad had no patience for hastily manufactured fairy tales or psychodrama.

♣

The new E.J. Korvettes shopping center was a welcome addition to the Castle Hill community, and the big grand opening celebration was eagerly anticipated. The boys and I came to witness the commotion, but if an opportunity presented we'd probably, maybe do a little "shopping," and we actually had a foolproof plan just in case. Our plan was to split up and "shop" separately in order to keep the undercover square badges busy with three different targets. If the plan went as planned we planned to reunite outside in the parking lot. That was the plan.

The doors opened at nine-thirty on the nose. The massive crowd milling about the parking area quickly streamed into the store. Sean, Charlie and I were pushed through the entrance with the early morning rush. Smiling employees handed each new patron a wooden yard stick as they entered the building. I refused mine because I planned on keeping both hands pretty busy, "shopping."

I paused at the largest counter nearest the escalator. A half dozen bright eyed salesladies within the chrome and glass jewelry display were already hustling to help anxious customers. My attention was drawn to the opposite side of the counter. A thin, middle-aged woman with bright yellow hair and big bazoongas wearing thick Mister Magoo eyeglasses was gazing down through the glass display. With those thick magnifiers hanging on the end of her pointed nose she'd be able to spot a flaw in a diamond from Pluto. By the time I wrestled my way through the crowd and around to the other side, her nose was practically sucking gemstones up through the counter top. The woman's obvious need to cash in on the colossal opening day discounts seemed a great distraction. I snuggled close enough to the woman to appear related. As long as I don't break her concentration the practically blind consumer would probably see me as a coat rack, without a coat. I stretched my arm around her slim shoulder and nimbly plucked a little red address book from the straw basket while my super-blue investigators scanned the immediate area for undercover dick-heads. The coast is clear. I'm pretty sure.

I quickly slipped the tiny red address book into my front right pocket. On the same counter a chrome carousel held a hundred different

85

keychains, and on it dangled the very one I needed, the one with two dice—front left pocket. The bustling crowd was getting thicker. I carefully nudged my way towards the adjacent counter. Next to the Timex watch display I discovered the latest advancement for the written word, a blue Papermate ball point pen. I needed one of these for sure—back pocket. What a great new shopping experience, and I still had an empty pocket in case I happen by a small necessity on my way out the door.

Making my way towards the exit was going rather nicely until I was suddenly yanked up from behind by my collar. Not part of the plan. I wiggled and jiggled and struggled to break free, but the big guy in the cheap suit merely dragged me along like a rag-doll towards the rear of the store. Unfortunately for the Korvettes super sleuth, the jostling crowd enabled me more than enough cover to drop everything I glommed onto the floor, where the mornings take quickly disappeared among a thousand shuffling feet and long before we reached the security office. I'm good to go.

The big man shoved me into the room and slammed the door. "Turn out ya pockets." I was as cool as a cucumber, even belligerent. I folded my skinny arms in a tight knot. "Wha for?" His penetrating stare enhanced by a deep gravelly voice. "I'll give ya what for, ya little snot nose. Turn em' out." I dug my hands deep and pulled. "Where's the pen?" Damn, he only caught the pen? Steam was blasting from his ears because I was smiling like a little ballerina holding out my empty pockets. He quickly patted my back pockets. "I want to call my father now. He's a lawyer." And if dad really was a lawyer, not a printer, this guy would be standing in shit up to his freaking eyeballs. "I don't care if ya fucking old man is F. Lee Bailey." He pushed me over to the back wall. "I'll hang ya by ya thumbs, you slick little bastard. Don't move. Don't even breathe." He opened the bottom desk drawer and pulled out one of those newfangled Polaroid cameras. "Don't smile either." Two minutes later Dick Tracy was tacking my beautiful color image onto an empty cork board. I guess I'm the very first one. And look at that. I should've combed my damn hair.

My shopping technique obviously needed a major overhaul, and I planned on working out the bugs with lots of practical experience in the new Korvettes shopping center, as soon as I could grow a freaking mustache.

I'll be back.

10

For my ordinary or somewhat minor indiscretions, Grandma always begged the assistance of all the usual second stringers, but on this particular occasion she pleaded my case to the very top. By listening to mom's rantings almost twenty-four hours after the fact, you would have thought that I committed capital murder. Mom was losing control as she recalled my latest adventure. As she would retell it, it was a bloody mess. I recall it was just another day in the life of Kevin the Troublemaker.

The start of the school year is also the official beginning of crack top season, and the first rule of crack top is simple: no girls allowed.

The idea of the game is to hit the target top with the sharp metal point imbedded in your own wooden missile. "Yeah, I got some blood." Red paint from a target top is reason for a big celebration, but a direct hit on any color top is a triumph bragged about for the rest of the afternoon.

It was Friday, lunch recess, and all the big competitors were forced to be in school, so everybody was there, John Federico, Robert Bauman, Wally Stevens, Donnie Polacsio, big Donald Latimer and the king of Holy Family fifth grade crack top, me, Kevin the digger Carroll.

None of my closest friends and all of my biggest enemies in school were project kids, all of their homes within a few blocks of Holy Family grammar school.

We quickly wound our tops with the official top string, formed a wide circle and readied for the initial spinoff. The first top to stop spinning is the first target of the day. I counted down. "One, two, three, go!" Six tops were thrown to the concrete with a furious energy, but Donnie's attempt at a super duper spinoff was a disaster from the moment his top flew from his fingertips. His bright blue top merely wobbled around the sidewalk, sputtered and died. The first target of the day lay motionless as the vultures circled Donnie's little blue carcass.

Janie Holiday, Mary Sullivan and Kathy Killgalen were skipping double dutch at a feverish pace just a few feet away. Well, little Mary was skipping. Kathy and Janie were turning the rope. The usual game of ring-a-levio was well under way on Blackrock Avenue. In the school yard the first and second graders tortured each other in the daily rituals of red rover and dodge ball. The entire flock of nuns floated through the valley of death while maintaining eagle-eyed surveillance on all the usual contributors of havoc. The principal seemed especially concerned as she passed our little competition. Crack-top is being played all around the building on just another beautiful fall day, until Wally shouted, "One, two, three, go!"

I reared back like a major league pitcher about to deliver a ninety mile an hour fastball and threw my top towards the sidewalk with enough torque to pulverize Donnie's shiny dead target into a zillion blue splinters, but my steel-tipped rocket completely missed the mark. It ricocheted off the concrete and shot straight up into the brilliant sunshine. All I had to do now is wait for gravity to pull it back to Earth and start this thing all over again. Maybe in Kevin the Altar Boy's story. In my story there are no do-overs. My yellow missile suddenly whistled back through the tree tops and crash landed four feet short of the planet on top of Mary O'Sullivan's curly blonde noggin. If there was an actual pay scale for troublemaking I could've renegotiated my contract for a bonus clause.

Her soul searing scream could be heard to the heavens, but Mary didn't have to yell that loud to get a reaction from God because His agents were already patrolling the area like Japanese ninjas. Nuns floated towards the open wound like a school of piranha. My eyes were in shock, my brain frozen like a block of dry ice.

Mary was still shaking from head to toe when Susan stepped towards the emergency like a trauma surgeon and placed a calming hand on her friend's shoulder. "Stop moving, Mary." Susan was still unplugging my top from Mary's melon when Sister Madeline floated into the middle of my latest disaster, so I didn't actually see the little spurt of crimson that shot from Mary's head, but you can probably guess where God put it next. "MISTER CARROLL!" The principal exploded as she made a quickie sign of the cross. "Mister Carroll! Look at what you've done!" Sister Madeline's big white bib was suddenly spotted with the same color as Mary's bloody face. Thanks to good ole Doc Holiday the situation was totally out of control and about to get a whole lot worse.

Multiple signs of the cross appeared so fast and furious that I thought I was witnessing a new form of holy karate. I wish I had a prayer.

I was about to apologize for putting that unsightly hole in Mary's head when Sister Madeline hauled off and smacked me so hard in the mush she probably took three years off my life expectancy, which suddenly didn't seem that far into the future. The principal flicked a tissue from inside her sleeve. "It's just a little scratch," consoled Sister. Mary wasn't buying it for a second. "What's happening?" Sister Edward Joan floated up from behind me and yanked the left handle. "What did you do this time, Mister Carroll?" The pain in my ear was searing behind my eyes as she pulled it back and forth, up and down. Missus Periwinkle was barking orders as she rushed up and grabbed the other handle. "Stand at attention, Mister Carroll." I couldn't have been straighter if I was nailed into place.

Mary was still pressing the tissue to the hole. "I'm sorry, Mary." The freckle faced tom boy with the normally beautiful wide smile and sparkly green eyes was already considerably calmer than our raging principal. "It's alright, Kevin. I think I'm okay."

"You're going to get a whole lot sorrier real soon, Mister Carroll." Even somebody that got left back a few times could figure this one out. "Ring the bell, Sister. Lunch period is over thanks to our Mister Carroll." Sister Edward Joan floated through the front entrance and re-appeared seconds later, brass bell in hand and waving it frantically like a town crier announcing the end of the world. Ding! dong! Ding! dong! Ding! dong! Old Missus Ingerdoodle guided Mary towards the front door as the entire student body lined up, unfortunately, fifteen minutes ahead of schedule.

Missus Periwinkle and Sister JoanMarie each grabbed a handle and appeared to be walking in opposite directions as they hurried me through the middle of two columns of extremely dead silence. I figured I'd be able to fly from a running start by the time I finished my second stint in fifth grade.

Sister JoanMarie floated into the principal's office and pushed the holy hot seat to the edge of the threshold by the open doorway. "Sit!" I slowly settled onto the very warm chair. Old Sister Augustine placed an empty cardboard box outside the door, and for some unchristian-like reason she placed the contraband collection box within kicking distance.

One by one eight hundred angry Christians marched by the open door in solemn procession. "Drop em ina da boxa!" demanded the old nun. "You canalla tanka Messa Carro fadesa." Sister's steady glare at a bulging pant pocket or cupped hand was a warning, but only until the reluctant student surrendered the goods. "Ten cents down the drain," moaned Philip McSweeny, his big chubby face a mass of anger. "You keepa you mawda closa, Messa MacaSwewe." Friends winked or smiled as they passed me by, but the bigger kids were hardly in a forgiving mood. Michael Randle practically stopped in the doorway. "You're dead," he mouthed as he flashed the middle finger under his arm. A development to be considered, but hardly my primary concern. Michael should probably count on being at the end of the line for the ass kicking portion of the afternoon.

From the forbidden underworld of darkness where Draconian nightmares go to die, Monsignor Klinkenhimer appeared abruptly like a giant shadowy apparition.

All adults seem old to kids, but monsignor would probably seem old to Methuselah. His skin was scaly and so white he was practically transparent, as if the old coot had been drinking Clorox three times a day to strengthen his already bad attitude. The chief parish holy man was tall and skeletal. Long years of unholy aggression had creased his face with gorges deep enough to plant corn and his long floppy ears sprouted fuzzy gray hair that looked like squirrels nesting on each side of his thick skull. His thin lips and yellow teeth were constantly twisted in a simian like snarl. Monsignor floated through the valley in his long black cassock like a leviathan in search of his next conquest, and his every undertaking was sanctioned, of course by God. I didn't have a prayer so I didn't even try.

With my spirit now daunted way beyond normal capacity I was actually praying for Sister Madeline to administer the holy ass whippin'. Unfortunately, the principal was now outranked by a higher calling and would have to wait her turn, just like Michael Randle and Philip McFatso.

Monsignor was already pacing the office like a caged tiger awaiting his first meal at the zoo. "Cloze za door and vait outzide," he ordered Sister. The disgust in his booming voice a mere prelude to the onslaught. Sister calmly floated from the room, pulled the door, secured it with a click and stood sentry with her back to the frosted glass. With Monsignor now in charge of the valley my latest disaster had all the ingredients of a final holy ass whippin'.

His breathing labored as the old man summoned the strength of his robust days, but even a tired old dinosaur was stronger than me. Monsignor started mumbling in Latin with a German accent, and I was still praying in very clearly English when the crazy old lunatic started driving his middle knuckle into the top of my skull, over and over and over. "You haff a sof head, Mizda Carroll." And it was getting softer with every jab. "What is going on inzides here, Mizda Carroll." Jab, jab, jab! My eyes filled with rage as the anger in my head overflowed onto my lap. Monsignor read my face like a sage old Indian reads a fresh dirt trail and didn't like what he saw. If I had the nerve to add sound, I'd be dead, but I'm Kevin the Troublemaker, not freaking Godzilla.

The man of God grew in size as the insanity in his head took control of a balled fist. "You vill conform, Mister Satan. You vill not thrive here." I wasn't sure if the old fart was seeing things or confusing me with another annoying kid named Mister Satan. His knobby old fist suddenly expanded to the size of a frying pan and smacked me in the eye. I hit the floor. The religion of my dad and my Grandma was taking one serious hit to the stomach. I'll never look back. If I did I would've seen him kick me in the ass. Ouch! Can you believe this? The wrinkled old fart kicked me right in the freaking ass.

The holy screwball snatched me up by my belt and flung me into a box of geography books. Taking a holy ass whippin' by a large man is certainly different from all previous holy ass whippins'. The nuns can smack you around pretty good, but none of them had the strength for this kind of action. Even Father DeGenco could stand a few lessons in the administration of corporal emasculation from this old geezer.

"Gettoff your kneez, Mizda Carroll." I was still half in a daze when he bent over and stuck his wrinkled old mush into my little pink face. If given the choice between the smell of old people and another kick in the ass I'd probably take the kick in the ass. He pointed a gnarled and excessively long finger towards the holy ass whippin' chair. "Tell me somesing, Mizda Carroll." The tone hissing from the gray ashen face of a vampire pierced my ears like a razor.

I focused my anger on the crucifix behind his head. "Look at me ven I speak, Mizda Carroll." This kind of anger erupts like a volcano and sets my teeth firm, lips tight, jaw locked. It's like telling the truth without opening my mouth. I glared up. He stared down. "Crack!" That was one hell of an impressive look if I say so myself, so I didn't get anything I didn't expect. His open-handed smack in the ear rang bells in every dark corner of my brain, and they continued to chime as he back-handed the other side of my face and knocked me again to the floor.

Monsignor grabbed the handle and jerked me up to my feet. "I don't ever vont to hear your name again, Mizda Carroll. Do you understanz me?" The rage in my head oozed like acid from every pore in my body. "You vill speak, Mizda Carroll or you vil sit in zis chair until you are an olt, man." His angry ultimatum suggested little in the way of options. Sit in the holy ass whippin' chair for the remainder of the day with this ancient German goose stepper staring me in the face and beating me to a pulp or capitulate. I'm not that smart, but I had this one figured out ten minutes ago. Unfortunately my brain had been reduced to mass of red rage infected by an all-consuming hatred. Smack! "I said, do you understandz me, Mizda Carroll?"

"Yes" escaped with a hiss. I probably should've used a little more sincerity, but I managed every ounce of what I thought he was asking for. All the other words on the tip of my tongue had four letters. He wasn't ready to hear them, I wasn't ready to die, but my eyes had already sealed my fate because my eyes never lie. My mouth could tell parables that would make an apostle green with envy, but when anger takes control of my brain the fire it ignites in my eyes is totally incapable of twisting the facts. Grandma calls it the face of an angel, but when rage strikes my next expression would make your eyes bleed. "Zis attitude vill get you srone in za gutter vunday." The old geezer shoved me aside and slowly lowered his bony rear end onto the chair. "Za next time I hear your voice, Mizda Carroll it vill be in confession."

God knows I'm sorry and so does little Mary. Ten more Our Fathers aren't going to change a thing. "Try to learn somzing bezides causing chaos vile you're here, Mizda Carroll." He straightened a leg to forage for his nasty old handkerchief and proceeded to blow a nor'easter from hell as I realized that I had finally weathered the storm. "You're on sin ice. Get out of my zight." The old fart went from rage to mere disgust. I rose from the depths from where hatred festers, thankful to be alive. Get out of my zight means get out fast. The old Bavarian windbag didn't have to tell me twice.

My exit though swift was not to be confused with rapid. Rapid may be construed as joyous. Joy may be perceived as my being impervious to insult. Although I was as happy as a four-year-old on Christmas morning, I couldn't even manage a grin because my face hurt. Upon exiting Sister Madeline's chamber of horrors she abruptly reminded me of the first rule of Catholic School. "Do not run in this corridor, Mister Carroll." It was only the fortunate byproduct of three glasses of milk a day to strengthen my scrawny bones that I was even able to walk. Besides, I really wasn't in a big hurry.

After trudging up three flights of stairs as if climbing a gallows I entered my classroom to the moans and groans of a disgruntled mob. I felt like a Christian walking into the ancient colosseum in Rome with a pork chop hanging out of my back pocket. This was not an environment conducive to learning. This wasn't even a good place to daydream. Not with big Michael Randle and Philip McFatso whispering the method of my demise for everyone to hear, except for the ancient and terminally stone deaf Sister Augustine. My plan for leaving the building was rapidly unfolding as a scheme for survival.

As the biggest troublemaker in every classroom I was ever forced into, I was always accorded that special seat, the one within a pointer's swat. This year no different, second isle, first desk. On the other hand, Michael Randle and Philip McFatso were situated in the two rear seats on the opposite side of the room by the windows, their large sizes being the unfortunate determining factor in this placement, first seat by the front door, first to exit, last seat by the window, last to leave. This arrangement could possibly keep me alive for weeks if managed with finesse.

At the sound of the final bell we jumped up as one. Two days of no holy people. Friday afternoon is still my favorite time of the week.

Having been blessed with a razor sharp tongue and the guts to slash it with the precision of a Japanese butcher was a gift that was gaining potency with every passing birthday. By the fifth grade I could split the attitude of most big idiots like a Samurai sword through a ripe watermelon, but the much bigger kids weren't as easily scared off. That's when it paid to have a quick pair of hands or really fast feet. Fortunately, I had both, so on the days I wasn't kicking somebody's big dumb ass some big dummy was kicking mine or chasing me back to the projects with bad intentions.

Philip McFatso was determined to choke my scrawny little neck like a chicken. He kept coloring that picture for me all afternoon. "If you don't have any money I'm gonna' choke ya scrawny little neck like a chicken, Carroll." See what I mean? Old Sister Augustine was oblivious to the verbal assault. "I'm gonna beat the shit outta ya, Carroll." The ancient one never batted a blind eye or turned a deaf ear from the mistakes she was scribbling on the blackboard.

Philip the idiot was still attempting to scare ten cents out of me, Kevin the pauper, in order to replace his confiscated top, but even if I did have an extra ten cents I'd still rather take a beating. I'm not Kevin the masochist, just thick-headed. This was shaping up to be a world class sprint back to the projects.

The slow steady march down the three flights of stairs was going as well as could be expected under the circumstances. "When I get you outside, Carroll, I'm gonna choke ya scrawny little neck like a chicken." The aggression echoing throughout the stairwell sounded like a threat from the boogieman.

No one is allowed to pass the principal's office until the teacher reaches the front of the line. I was waiting impatiently on the last landing as seven kids paused in front of me, one on each step. John Federico, the second biggest troublemaker in the class was shuffling in place, staring at the ceiling on the safe side of Sister Madeline's office doorway. John was probably picturing the bright blue sky beyond the gloom. I was picturing a comfortable head start.

Old Sister Augustine was still floating down through the middle of two columns of anxious Christian soldiers. Just as she passed me I leaned over and looked up the staircase to show Philip my favorite finger. Sister didn't see it. Unfortunately, God did, so my silent message got lost in the chaotic maelstrom of screaming and yelling because God, for some unchristian-like reason placed my foot in the middle of nowhere. My books flew up in the air. When my wobbly foot landed one step closer to the outside world, somebody was already on it, Carol Rizzo. When I banged into Carol she crashed into Michael Manion; he knocked over JoAnn Baily who tumbled onto Timmy O'Sullivan and so on down to John Federico who was now spread eagle in the middle of the open doorway to the principal's office.

The dominos fell one on top of the other, and the only dumb Christian laughing was Philip. "Ha, ha, ha! Now Sister's gonna' choke ya scrawny little neck like a chicken, Carroll." Old Sister Augustine, oblivious to the quiet chaos in her wake, floated towards the exit, but no sound traveling through air ever slipped past the supernatural gift God bestowed on the principal, who suddenly rushed into the hall, startling everyone, especially me. "If the person that just spoke doesn't come down this instant the whole class will do an about-face." Smoke was spitting from her nose as a raging inferno burned in her eyes.

Although nobody got hurt in the melee of tumbling bodies it was still early in the event. Seven kids down. Somebody's gonna pay.

The first kid down was the first one up. Carol was reaching back to hand me my history book when Sister Madeline suddenly noticed my place, suspiciously at the top of the first landing: every kid behind me was standing. Every kid in front was not. Somebody started this mess and the principal was hardly surprised to discover the culprit. "Mister Carroll. What did you say?" Sister Edward Mary floated down through the middle of two lines of extreme Christian anxiety and hovered at my back just as my denial hit the air. "That wasn't me, Sister." SMACK! Right in the back of the head. My shock quickly turned to anxious apprehension. Without turning or even rubbing my head I maintained focus on the greater fear as Sister Madeline hastily ascended the stairs. "Tell me what you said, Mister Carroll." The principal was already sucking the majority of oxygen from the surrounding area, so it was difficult to breathe, let alone speak. "I didn't say nothin'. SMACK! Right in the mush. She didn't buy it for a second. Now they got me surrounded.

The last kid on line stood out like a giant among Lilliputians. "Do an about-face, Mister Latimer!" Sister Madeline's anger generated electrical impulses as the storm brewing around her head repelled both lines of nervous Christian sacrifices to hug the wall in fear, but their fear and mine could hardly be equated with the same logic. I was gonna' die. They were gonna' watch.

Sister Madeline appeared to be forming her own dark ominous cloud as she slowly circled the perimeter of the classroom. Around and around she floated while scanning the room for fear. Nuns can smell fear. The principal paused at the rear of the room, the heat from her eyes burning through the back of my head. Sister suddenly floated up my aisle, but mere inches from the back of my seat she stopped, whipped around and caught dumb Philip and big Donald in a stink-eye staring contest. "Mister McSweeney! Stand!"

My big friend Donald had just jabbed his long finger into my tormentor's fat neck. The principal quickly floated back down the aisle, and that was all the distraction I needed. I turned around and smiled a thank-you at big Donald. Alerted, probably by God, the principal spun back and caught my smile while it was still uncovering my teeth. "Mister Carroll! Stand up! What exactly is so funny?" Sister Augustine finally entered the classroom and jumped into the action. Actually, she didn't jump, she sort of floated very slowly. The ancient one grabbed the right handle and yanked me up out of my seat. With one nun holding a handle and the other one closing in fast I prayed for a miracle.

Please God. I need a diversion. Maybe a fire? Praying for miracles under extreme pressure will often do that to a person, even a professional, but, no fire, not even a diversionary puff of smoke.

The raging principal raced down the aisle and grabbed Philip by the long greasy hair above his ear. She quickly dragged his dumb fat ass up the isle to the front of the room and threw him against the blackboard. "Everybody stand," she ordered, "Mister McSweeney and Mister Carroll will be staying for a while. The rest of the class is dismissed." Old Sister Augustine was still out of breath and in obvious need of a nap. "I'm sorry, Sister. Please take the class down again."

Philip and I stood, arm's length apart with our crisp white shirts getting damper as they pressed against the blackboard. Steam blasted from the principal's head as she hovered in the doorway. The second the last kid made his escape she slammed the door and whipped into a raging black and white tornado. "Mister Carroll. What did you say in the stairwell?" I glanced at Philip. He gazed at the ceiling. "I am not going to ask you again, Mister Carroll." Oh yes she will. I got a world of crazy shit in my head and I'm still processing the crazy shit part. "Mister Carroll! Mister Carroll!" Sister turned into a raving holy woman. "Mister Carroll! This is exactly why you're failing all your studies." No it's not, you holy bag of wind. I'm failing all my studies because I haven't studied a book in six years.

Embarrassment is my least favorite emotion, so my reaction was hardly appropriate. This would've been a good time to show fear, but I wasn't that smart yet. Angry indignation illuminated my wild eyes, and the second the light flashed in my brain she ran around her desk and snarled with enough teeth to scare an alligator. "Mister Carroll. What did you say and who were you talking to in the stairwell?" Her right hand was cocked before the denial hit the air. "I wasn't—" Smack! Right in the mush. "Who spoke in the stairwell, Mister McSweeney?"

"That wasn't me—" Smack! "I didn't ask you who didn't, mister. I asked you who did." Her anger was still peaking. "Mister Carroll, I'm only going to ask you one more time. Who spoke in the stairwell?"

"That wasn't—" Smack! The back of her hand caught a smiling McFatso flush in the kisser. "Do you think this is funny, Mister McSweeney?" Philip ran one hand through his greasy pompadour, the other pressed his fat throbbing lips. "He did it," mumbled Judas McFatso. "Carroll said he was gonna get me outside and then he pushed everybody down the stairs." Sonofabitch. If I was a little bit bigger I'd still be kicking his big cissy ass down Castle Hill Avenue. "I want to hear from your mother, Mister McSweeney, as soon as you get home. Do you understand me?" She actually bought that? The big idiot is twice my size. Philip the rat nodded like a jackass. "Be on your way, Mister McSweeney."

Although the principal was now fully armed with all the ammunition necessary for an official holy ass whippin', she decided to bring my parents up to speed on this latest development.

Sister hurried me down the stairs and pushed my lazy arrogance into the office. The fuming nun barely under control as she plopped behind her desk. "What is your telephone number, Mister Carroll?" My brain quickly scrolled through all the potential responses to that one very simple question. Sister was tap, tap, tapping an anxious staccato with her hands on the green blotter as she impatiently awaited my reply.

Now, if I say I don't have a telephone she'll probably explode. If I say I don't remember the number she'll think I'm an idiot. I can live with that, but she'll probably pummel me into submission anyway. It's broke, it's turned off because my mom forgot to pay the bill, there's an F.B.I. wiretap because my dad's in the mafia. "T... A... 9... " When I hesitated she slammed the desk, smoke spitting, steam blasting, lightning bolts probing the deepest parts of my brain. "You do know your own telephone number. Don't you?" I stared back in wonderment, eyes as blank as an empty chalk board. She didn't like being ignored. Sister Madeline scooted around the desk and glared directly into my soul. "You will either tell me that number or I will drag you down to that project by your hair!" The emphasis on "that project" was Sister's way saying she'd prefer to see the place leveled by a Russian bomb. "2-2-9-4". She bit her lower lip and floated back to her seat. "Again."

"T-A-9-2-2-9-4."

Sister jammed her big holy finger into the shiny black telephone and spun each number. "I should know it by heart," she mumbled. Another bit of information she obviously forgot is that mom was working in the Castle Hill Day Care Center until four o'clock. "Where is your mother, Mister Carroll? She's not answering." Sister slammed the receiver into the cradle, snatched her fancy gold pen and grabbed the yellow legal pad from the top drawer. Furiously writing, writing, writing. She seemed to be imparting an awful lot of information when she suddenly tore off the page, stuffed it into an envelope, licked and sealed it. "Your mother or father will get this note as soon as they walk in the door, Mister. Carroll." Only if my name is Kevin the freaking retard.

Sister leaned waaaay across the desk, her big holy face right in my kisser. "Do you understand me, Mister Carroll?" Sister obviously had the soggy hot dogs for lunch. "Yes, Sister." The only plan on the drawing board was to get my freaking ass off this damn chair. "I'll be expecting them directly after the dinner hour, Mister Carroll. Is that understood?" Sister glared down her nose and folded her hands into her puffy black sleeves. Don't hold your breath you old fart. I'm not exactly sure how the words managed to stay in my mouth, because they were screaming like a complete lunatic inside my head. "Be on your way, Mister Carroll." She didn't have to tell me twice.

The system in my brain that controls the course of action during high pressure situations was forced into overdrive. Play stupid. What note? Act stupid. I didn't do nothin'. Within seconds I was moping down Castle Hill Avenue in a fog of rage and desperation as if headed to a guillotine inside a gas chamber.

11

It was just about this time in my troublemaking career that dad had fully refined an uncanny sense of detecting the truth, as opposed to something close to the truth. Dad certainly knew the truth when he heard it, but hearing it from me was still a rarity. Over the years he's developed an almost supernatural ability to weed out the bullshit while it was still being formed in my brain. Even before I'd open my mouth dad would hop out of his chair. "Kevin," he'd plead, "don't." Fortunately, dad's right hand was nothing compared to old Monsignor Klinkenhimer's. In fact, dad wouldn't even swat me as hard as old Sister Augustine. He could, but dad hates lying more then he dislikes hitting me in the head, and some lessons needed to be felt. This could be that defining moment.

After a few hours of running around the lots with my friends, that note was the last thing on my mind. When I pushed the elevator button for the return trip home, that note was the only thing on my mind.

As I passed the Chatterton Bakery I tossed the note down the sewer. By the time I was riding up in the elevator that note was well on its way to the Atlantic Ocean.

I held the doorknob like a ripe tomato and barely squeezed, but it opened anyway. Mmm boy, smells like meatloaf. When I peeked around the door mom was bent over, staring into the stove. Sensing atmospheric tension happens to be a daily requirement. "Hi, ma, daddy home yet?" She turned from the stove, big fork in hand, an acid sting in her voice. "What happened at school today, mister?" It didn't actually sound like a question. It sounded like I needed to duck. I managed a tight smile and one incredibly brave answer. "Nothing." Keep it simple.

Kathleen was setting the table and rolled her eyes when she passed me on the way back to the kitchen. "Nothing? Then do you have any idea why Sister Madeline would want to talk to your father and me tonight?" The fear factor is now registering solidly in the, you're about to get your ass kicked, portion of the scale. "Do ya?" The front door opened behind me. "Hi, doll," cheered dad, "smells like meatloaf." Dad kicked off his shoes and placed them together at the bottom of his closet. Then he strolled up to mom and planted the usual greeting, right on the old kisser. Dad was still beaming as he rubbed my head. "How'd ya do today, Luke?" What's with all the questions? Is there a gun hanging out of my back pocket? Dad was simply praying my day went without incident, but mom seemed to have information that could blow up any possibility of eating dinner before breakfast.

Mom's silence quickly degenerated to that annoying sucking sound she makes when her head is about to explode. "Tch, tch."

"Everything all right, Doll?" Dad knew the answer to that one even before he asked the question. "Maybe we should eat first… and talk it about this later." That is one hell of a timely suggestion if I ever heard one. Although the winds of an early evening disaster were already blowing a gale through the apartment, dad still surrendered with a smile. "Then let's eat. I'm starved."

Except for the fact that my name is Kevin the Troublemaker and not Jesus of Nazareth, we still had the genuine makings of a last supper. We're all going to eat. Somebody's going to rat me out. Then I'm going to die. "Kathleen, take some peas and carrots and pass them to your brother," suggested mom. "Kevin, take it easy with those potatoes. Leave enough for everybody else," she ordered. One by one we passed our plates to dad at the head of the table, where he laid upon each a big old steaming slab of meatloaf. I plopped a big lump of soft butter into the middle of my mashed potatoes as dad began the ritual. He folded his hands and reverently bowed his head. Just before he started he peeked towards me. "Kevin, put your knife down, please." Then he led us in prayer. "Give us oh Lord our daily bread and blah, blah, blah. Blah, blah blah."

The absurdity of my entire crazy day had been flashing through my brain since I rode up in the elevator. When I finally arrived back at the dining room table it appeared that I escaped for the entire meal. I was suddenly staring down at a plate so completely clean that I thought I dropped my meatloaf and mashed potatoes on the floor. "I guess you were hungry, Luke?" Fear makes me hungry. Fear of dying is a whole different story. "I think your son has something to tell you," mom blurted. I glanced at Tommy. Mom glared at me. Dad squinted at the guiltiest looking son seated at the table and he never hesitated a nanosecond in my little brother's direction. "Is everything alright, Kevin?" The man certainly has an unnatural gift of optimism.

100

My brain was now in a frantic search for an adequate answer. Could I find one in time to stave off the winds of war? Am I doomed to repeat history? Of course I am. This is largely a yarn about my dad's perennial search for the truth. What are the chances he hears any before sunrise?

As I frantically reviewed the day's events there wasn't one single portion of the entire freaking disaster that would ever be confused with 'alright.' So in order to keep the peace, and I'm still a firm believer in peace, I decided to totally evade the question. With the face of a young George Washington plastered firmly over the one I was born with I played stupid and begged confusion. "What do you mean?" Dad exhaled a long day's anxiety, "Eve… .can this wait?" Mom shuddered as she looked at Dad. Dad cringed as he realized mom's normally short fuse was tethered to a very large cache of explosives.

My dazed reflection was still staring up from an empty plate as I prayed for divine intervention. **Dear, baby Jesus. We don't have a lot of time here. I need something big, like maybe an earthquake under the convent. It's not a real nice place, so nobody will miss it. Thanks. See You Sunday.** As I finished praying Dad had already finished everything on his plate. The praying portion of evening was officially at an end. "I got a call today," announced mom. **Holy Mary, Mother of God.**

✣

As I stared out the back window of dad's big old brown Desoto on the way to the convent I was trying to imagine a best case scenario. *A smiling young nun opens the front door. "Oh, good evening, Mister and Missus Carroll. How can I help you?"*

"Hello, Sister," sings dad. "We have an appointment to see Sister Madeline and Sister Augustine about Kevin."

"Oh I'm so sorry you made the trip, Mister and Missus Carroll, because unfortunately Sister Madeline and Sister Augustine are no longer permitted to speak, as per papal decree. Can you believe it, Mister and Missus Carroll?" Not a chance in hell. Not even a fat chance.

Dad pushed the bell on the convent wall for the second time when all hope faded to black like the opening scene of a recurring nightmare. Sister Madeline opened the door in a huff. "Good evening, Mister Carroll," she moaned. "Hello, Missus Carroll," she muttered. The dark salutation sounded like an invitation to a fist fight.

The principal held the door wide as mom and dad stepped over the

101

threshold exposing me to the light. "Oh, I see we have a little visitor." Her slit stare and acid tone a welcome greeting compared to the one I got earlier in the day. Sister crinkled her nose. I thought I stepped in something. "Come along, Mister Carroll."

The convent was everything I was expecting, really, really dark and as quiet as a funeral parlor at closing time. The piercing brown eyes of Saint Joseph standing in the bosom of his Holy Family was already glaring a hole through my brain. Sister Augustine appeared from shadows. "Let'sa go ina ear." invited Sister. The principal had already disappeared down the hall, so we followed along in the tiny shadow of the ancient one as she floated like a ghost through the long candlelit corridor and humbly hovered under a white porcelain crucifix above the doorway at the end of the hall. Sister crossed herself and entered. Dad crossed himself and followed. Mom pushed me along. So this is the actual valley of death they talk about in the bible.

Not a sliver of sunlight dares breach the heavy forest-green draperies that hung ceiling to floor. A thick, oval, blue rug with gold embroidered trim muffles the sound of the heart beating out of my chest, and dark green walls danced with shadows from the small bank of votive candles at the base of a life-sized crucifix while Jesus hung in silence begging The Father's forgiveness for those souls entering His valley without a prayer. Dark mahogany chairs with leather padded seats and matching armrests circled a solitary chair in the center of the room. With mom and dad in close proximity I'm figuring there's no officially sanctioned holy ass whippin' on this evening's agenda, so the ordinary chair in the middle of the room is probably just an ordinary chair in the middle of the room. "Why don't you take the chair in the middle, Kevin?" suggested Sister Madeline. Why don't you kiss my fat ass, you old goat. The words never left my mouth, but they were right on the tip of my brain. Except for the wretched nuns who float around here in their scary black habits among the flickering candles, no one should be subjected to this type of torture.

After passing the normal pleasantries of the day, Sister Madeline turned the evening into exactly what she intended. The trial of Kevin the Troublemaker.

Dad sat erect in his chair while mom squirmed nervously, and both listened attentively while Sister Madeline and old Sister Augustine took turns portraying me as an up and coming mass murderer from the Castle Hill projects. Unfortunately, I wasn't here to listen. My presence was necessary to answer questions. How well I do on the answers will be determined by my reactions under extreme duress. So it's fortunate I majored in 'extreme duress' way back in first grade. By the fifth I could have written a thesis and been well on my way to a doctorate.

I failed to get clearance from the tower for an emergence take-off. Time is the enemy. I was already screaming down the runway at nearly a thousand miles an hour. The two massive engines, a blaze of orange fury as they rocketed me up into the clouds, the valley of certain death a distant memory.

"Kevin. Kevin." And I damn near made it, too. "Kevin, answer Sister's question," demanded Dad…

"What question?"

Now that I had everybody's attention except for old Sister Augustine, who seemed half asleep herself, the principal cocked her head to drive home her intense state of mind. "I asked you, Kevin to explain exactly what happened in the stairwell at the end of the day. You do remember what happened, don't you?" Of course I remember. I didn't do nuthin'. I was just standing around minding my own business when I heard Philip the big mouth mention that he was going to choke my scrawny little neck like a chicken. "You mean… when I slipped… and fell… on the stairs?"

Dad glanced at mom while she clawed ten extremely sharp red nails into the armrest. Sister Madeline was apparently on the verge of administering one, god awful holy ass whippin' while old Sister Augustine lingered at the edge of a nirvana. So I played like Kevin the mute until dad finally interceded.

"Kevin," he pleaded, "please tell ya mother and me what happened today." A rock and a hard place could hardly describe my situation. Being dragged by a big rock to the bottom of the ocean does.

I knew dad would never strike in anger in front of an audience. If fact, dad never strikes in anger at all. Corporal punishment is doled out only when absolutely necessary, and whether or not that happens, happens to be totally up to me. Though his nervous system was going through one hell of a workout, I knew his patience could be counted on for biblical type stamina. Sister Madeline didn't, so she had no idea what was keeping my dad's arms folded on his lap and his back side planted solidly on his chair.

Dad was still willing to explore all avenues before drawing any conclusions. On the other hand mom was hyperventilating, obviously ready to fly into the middle of the circle at the sound of my next denial. Shock is pretty much the expression around the room. "Kevin," begged dad, "Please tell me what happened today?" My latest adventure through unholy hell had taken a serious toll on my sunny disposition, so my brain simply closed up shop. Dad actually had a better chance of engaging a conversation with the life size Jesus, but unfortunately The Lord wasn't looking too talkative either.

Stress brought about by overzealous holy people is the stimulus that caused confusion, which agitated my overactive imagination. Confusion plus stress equals fear. I'm not that smart, but an idiot could figure that one out. Irrational fear is probably the reason I lumped my dad and everyone else who actually did do me harm into the same mental hopper, and it was because of that unholy fear that I knew a peaceful resolution was never a possibility. I always prayed for a way to explain what actually happened to my very patient dad, but I couldn't. If I knew why I could be curing psychological conundrums that would put the major pharmaceutical companies out of business, but I can't, because I'm a freaking troublemaker, not a goddamn genius.

Mom was on the edge of her seat and leaned into the circle, eyes bulging, steam blasting from the top of her tiny head. "Tell your father what happened today, mister." That didn't work either. My anger would not allow me to speak. I managed a great deal of explaining, but only in my head.

When the holy dinosaur finally awoke she once again stumbled through fractured English, but managed with the help of God to clarify all the many reasons my parents were summoned, and long before she described the seminal events of the day even I thought I should've been arrested. But dad was hardly unnerved until Sister Augustine blurted, "Mesta ana Missa Carro," the kindly old nun suggested, "you son," she turned and glared directly into my two blank eyes, "ezzada bigges a lie I ava wheatness ena fifey ear ateecha. **These nuns are killing me here, Lord.**

Now, if the kindly old nun had merely suggested that I was the biggest liar in fifth grade that wouldn't have been too bad. Dad might already figure me to be the biggest liar in the whole school anyway. Could I possibly be the biggest liar of the last half century? Sister Augustine must've heard some real whoppers back in the day, so I thought if I tried to shore up my defense at this late juncture I'd wind up looking like the biggest liar of all time. I certainly wasn't looking to break any world records.

Could the ancient one be stretching the truth? This is a nun. Nuns don't lie. There was absolutely no conflict for my dad. I was lying and there wasn't a tale I could manufacture that would ever be long enough to change that simple fact. Dad took a deep breath, closed his eyes and appeared to pray. To say he was finding it difficult to fathom what was still ringing in his one decent ear would grossly understate the obvious. She cut my dad to the core of his religious tolerance and she didn't exactly light my freaking celebratory cigar.

To get this disturbing testimony, particularly from a holy woman was a lot to endure, but dad's deep religious upbringing prepared him with the intestinal fortitude to battle through such an assault. As I peeked up every few seconds I could see the pain. Dad probably felt more like a failure than I did. Fire shot out of mom's eyes, smoke from her ears and steam blasted from the top of her head. Mom obviously felt the same as Philip McFatso because she seemed awfully eager to choke my scrawny little neck like a chicken.

"I'm not a psychiatrist," noted Dad, "but as you may already know, Kevin has a very active imagination. He probably thinks we came here to gang up on him." The two nuns chuckled as they raised their eyes to the Lord, as if dad's suggestion was the most preposterous scenario imaginable, but Dad was so on the money it was hardly a laughing matter.

Dad finally explained my need to confuse the facts as some un-natural fear of a possible reprisal. Possible? He still had no idea. If my parents weren't three feet away these crazy nuns would've been slapping the snot out of me for the past twenty minutes.

Although I was totally unaware of my Fifth Amendment right against self-incrimination, I was actually quite thrilled by my acciden-tal development of the silent defense. Dad is comfortable around reli-gious people, mostly because he is a truly pious man. His conviction and religious fervor are second to none. That impression was evident from the moment he opened his mouth.

The investigation was slowly grinding to a standstill, so dad finally decided to interrogate at his leisure. Two minutes later mom and dad were leading me back through the flickering candles and away from the piercing glass eyeballs and back to the light of day. **See ya Sunday**.

♣

Dad was prayerfully silent as he sat in his chair at the head of the table in what appeared a swirl of emotions: disappointment, worry, apprehension, but for the moment no apparent anger. As long as he stays calm this could be over by as early as eight o'clock, give or take an hour. On the other hand my emotions were totally out of control. Imagine a paranoid cat slinking through a dark alley behind a Chinese restaurant. In Beijing. Year of the dog.

Dad's trusting eyes should've been enough to extract the truth from the devil himself. "Kevin, I wanna' know what you said and why you pushed the class down the stairs today and we're not gonna sit here all night." With that codicil at the end of the question dad was practically begging for a menu and a cup of coffee. Of course we're gonna be here all night. We could possibly be here for the entire weekend.

Mom was already circling the kitchen and living room partition like a fuming cartoon bull, steam whistling through flared nostrils. She charged across the living room rug into the bathroom, where she angrily flushed a toilet bowl full of clear blue water as if she expected it to wind up in the Pacific Ocean. Dad suddenly slapped the table. "Look at me when I'm talking." His face was tight as a drum, his eyes searching the heavens through slits of pain. "Kevin, I'm not gonna hit ya. Just tell me what happened. Please."

"I'm losing my patience, mister. If you don't tell us what happened today you won't be going out for the rest of the year. LOOK AT YA FATHER!"

"Eve, just let me handle this, please." Dad took a deep breath. "Come closer," he demanded as he pointed to that spot on the floor. Having been on that spot for half of my career I hesitated with good cause. "Gerry, if this kid doesn't start talking I'm gonna chuck him right out that damn window." I flinched, anticipating a lightning quick smack in the head, but she only shoved me onto that spot. "Eve, please. You're not making this easier." Talk about an understatement.

With dad's lie detector on the verge of a circuit overload, mom's constant interference seemed to be adding additional amps to the power source. "There's something seriously wrong with this kid, Gerry."

"Alright, Kevin, tell me what happened today and don't tell me nothing." One simple question. Unfortunately the one truthful answer was stuck waaaay in the back of my head. Insecurity was stirring my fear, and my fear was stuck in a muddy pit. "I didn't—"

"Kevin." Dad paused, closed his eyes and looked towards the heavens. "If you lie to me one more time I'm going to do something we'll both regret." Mom was still fanning the flames. "Gerry, this kid is driving me crazy." Mom was driving dad crazy. Bang! Dad slammed the table. "Kevin, you look at me when I'm talking." The strain was beginning to show. His voice fraught with exasperation. "If you say that one more time you'll leave me no choice." So I sniffled and managed a single tear that rolled right down my sad little face, but that didn't work either.

Dad suddenly stood from his chair, which slammed into the wall. "That's it!" He stomped over to his closet by the front door, reached down and picked up his weapon of choice, the shot-gun, I mean the slipper. Dad's slippers weren't used for walking around the apartment because the hard rubber heels scuffed mom's white linoleum floors. The slipper was a threat, but fortunately dad wielded that old brown slipper like a soggy lasagna noodle. But he always made it sound like he was swinging a thirty-eight ounce Louisville Slugger. "Kevin. That's it. I'm losing my patience." Dad slowly walked back and sat at the head of the table, weapon held low like the old western gun slingers. "Please tell me what happened today in the stair case."

"I didn't—" Whack! Dad suddenly smacked the top of my head with the much softer end of the slipper. "No! Stop!" My two hands frantically attempting to cover the vulnerable portions of my skull, but dad was way too quick. Smack! Another shot, this one to my forehead. "No, no, stop, please. I'm not lying!" The beating he was giving was hardly enough to get my attention, so it wasn't easy convincing dad that I was about to die, but I was giving it one hell of an effort. "Stop yelling," dad ordered. "I hardly hit ya!"

"No. Stop!" I cried. "I'm sorry!"

Dad dropped the slipper to the floor and held his anguished face in his hands, and he stayed in that exact same position for so long that I thought he was falling asleep. Dad slowly shook his head and raised his hands as if giving praise and queried, very softly, "What are you sorry for, Kevin? Well, for one thing, it always works. This isn't my first rodeo.

Dad was praying for anything to break the deadlock. Anything, but another all-out fabrication would usually do the trick. Mom casually pulled the pin and lobbed a hand grenade under the table. "Don't stand there with that stupid face! ANSWER YOUR FATHER!"

"Jesus, Mary and Saint Joseph, Eve. Will you please leave this to me. Please." There was never any doubt as to who was in charge in our home. Mom was in charge of screaming and yelling. Dad was in charge of everything else.

Mom sat in a huff on the end of the couch, arms folded at her waist as dad pondered my fate in eerie silence, but once he dropped that slipper my brain escaped earth's gravitational pull. "Kevin... Kevin!" My mouth was hanging open, glazed eyes vacant to the possibility of a pulsing brain and mom and dad caught my stupid face at the same time, which means we might actually have to start this thing all over again. "Kevin... " But dad had seemingly passed on the idea of obtaining a full confession. If I'm sorry is good enough for the Lord, it's certainly good enough for dad. Besides, he doesn't have the stomach for this stuff. You couldn't tell it by me, but dad couldn't squash a bubble the way he was swinging that old brown slipper.

By accomplishing the more reasonable of two possible scenarios, which is getting hit and not bleeding as compared with getting killed and not dying I was able to avail myself of the kindness my dad spreads like brown gravy on two slices of Wonder Bread, and dad really loves his gravy and bread.

Half way through The Mitch Miller Show and not one second before a commercial break dad turned away from his favorite old fart television sing-along program. I was still standing next to the dining room table, holding the same position on the exact same spot. Mom seemed content to stare out the window towards the Whitestone Bridge, while the eyes in the back of her head kept me frozen to the linoleum. "Okay, Luke." The serenity of tone and use of my favorite name was an obvious gesture of peace. I finally drop my guard. "Why don't ya go to ya room and open a book."

Dad still wasn't smiling because the lesson wasn't over, but fortunately the last lesson of the day is always my favorite, and the only one that didn't require cheating notes because dad had been teaching me the same lesson for years.

I was sitting up on the edge of my bed, feet dangling, cloudy mind cleared of all the day's trials and tribulations and waited with a serene confidence that dad would think of something new to say that might actually work for the next time, and there was no good reason to believe that there wouldn't be another next time.

So, why was it so difficult to tell my dad the truth? If I knew the answer to that one my story could be titled Kevin the Boy Scout or possibly Kevin the Astronaut, but the paralyzing fear brought about by the few holy people charged with reinforcing the important lessons of life was such that any mistake, misjudgment or even apprehension was roundly ridiculed as stupidity. My first reaction was anger, the second, fear. "Kevin... ." The love for my dad is boundless. I looked up with bright anticipation. Dad sat close and hugged my shoulder. "If you had killed somebody today, Kevin, I would still be your friend. I would help you, but I can't do that if you don't trust me. All you had to do was tell me the truth." He squeezed my shoulder and kissed me on the head. "Goodnight, son." Dad smiled as he rose to his feet. His kindness couldn't be contained within the eight-foot ceiling as he paused in the doorway. "Now, say good night to your mother."

Another long day, another close call, another dad might have tossed me out the eleventh floor window. Just another reason to thank the Lord. **See you Sunday.**

12

Troublemaking is pretty much a full-time occupation, but getting into trouble is not the same as being bad. It's like being adventurous which leads to unexpected circumstances which leads to explaining things that have no reasonable answers. That's what I couldn't get the hang of, admitting how stuff actually happened.

Attitude is not something you plan. It's a process of adjustments. From the first grade on I was told I was an idiot, a moron, a hooligan, a snot nose, a malcontent, a knucklehead, Lucifer's helper and Satan himself, and I simply didn't adjust well to the embarrassment. And for those doing the labeling I had no problem showcasing my newly adjusted personality.

Minor distractions were hardly a reason to end a flowering career, and my stupidity was still rumbling down the track like a runaway freight train. So the next lesson was surely around the corner. And I mean the next corner. This corner... right here...

By the time I was twelve years old and staggered away from fifth grade after two very long years I was able to spin a compelling yarn under hostile conditions with the cool smooth swagger of young Samuel Clemens. I just needed a second or two to think of one. As long as I stuck to the new facts, everything would be okay. It rarely was and that was also a fact, but changing what I thought to be a dynamite story half way through an inquisition never seemed a viable option. Why go through an eternity of telling some really first class bullshit just to eventually admit to my latest adventure. "Kevin, don't lie to me. I won't hit you if you just tell me the truth." Nervous? Damn right. I stood firm with the conviction of a Benedictine monk and always reluctant, but usually willing to take a good smack in the head with a soggy lasagna slipper if things didn't go quite as expected.

Only a true great artist with years of practical experience could stand at the kitchen table, understate the obvious to the point of ridiculous absurdity and expect dad to believe every single word. Dad would say nothing. He'd look, mad. Silence. What? He didn't believe that? Was it the face? Did I tip him off with a stupid face? I've garnered way too many years of professional experience to get caught off guard with a stupid face again. I can't believe it. Did I forget something? Did I leave something out? "Kevin, I'm not going to ask you again." Sure he will. Dad would ask the same question until his brain explodes. "What were you doing today?" Sure, admit to one thing and sooner or later dad finds out about everything else. Usually one good story covered up the whole day's adventure. Keep it simple. Admit nothing.

With the inner peace of the Dalai Lama I looked my dad right in the eye. Of course I really wasn't the Dalai Lama, but the mild-mannered tone I adapted to ensure a peaceful resolution was scary, even for me. "I was in the lots… all day." Talk about guts.

♣

The constant itch for adventure was never far from a good scratch, and though my arms are a little short I have really strong fingers. It was a beautiful Friday morning in September, the last weekend before going back to school. It wasn't just beautiful because there was no school, but the sun was bright and there wasn't a cloud in sky. Oh, and did I mention there was no school, yet?

His thick, platinum hair and ice blue eyes gave Davy Swenson the face of a young model, but he wasn't. Davy was just a real good-looking troublemaker. When Sean, Charlie and I found Davy setting fire to the old junked car at the edge of the lots by the old man's shack he was immediately embraced as the fourth annoying pea in our ever-expanding pod. His pretty face was hardly a requirement to join the gang. Just the book of matches.

The four Musketeers were skirting around the biggest and deepest swamp in the lots on the way to our two-story granite hangout when another brilliant idea exploded in my head like a Fourth of July fireworks display. "Who wants to go to the zoo and shoot paper clips at the buffalo?" Sean was walking up ahead and yelled back over his shoulder. "I never been to the zoo!" Charlie and Davy were bringing up the rear. "Let's go." It was unanimous. We're going on a safari. All we needed was ammunition.

McCrory's Five & Ten cents store in the middle of the projects on Castle Hill Avenue had all the ammunition we needed, four little boxes of paper clips and a bag of heavy duty rubber bands and we'll be loaded for bear, I mean buffalo.

Stealing stuff from McCrory's was so easy we didn't even call it stealing. We called it shopping. While one of us did the shopping the rest of the boys distracted the old sales ladies by running around the other side of the store being annoying, and being annoying happened to be one of the many talents we considered a professional endeavor. The boys gathered in the furthest corner away from the school supplies by the underwear and socks. The old ladies circled around. The boys grew louder. The ladies moved in. "Come on now, who's buying?"

"He is," insisted Charlie, pointing towards Davy. "I thought you were," claimed Davy. "Okay, that's it. Everybody outside!" Like a well-oiled machine this same scheme worked every single time. By the time the old ladies were escorting the boys to the front door our little shopping spree was already over.

Mister Johnson, the young manager and chief law enforcement officer smiled as I strolled past him with the take of the day stuffed snugly into the waistband of my underpants. "Whaddaya need there son?" None of your freaking business, I thought. "A blue pencil case," I said politely. "Does it have to be blue?" Of course it had to be blue. He had red, yellow, green, brown, orange. He had every freaking color of the rainbow except my favorite. "Then I guess you don't want a red one or a green one?"

"No thank you," I mumbled as I pushed the front door. "Stay outta' trouble now, son." Thanks to Mister Johnson and McCrory's crack staff of roving police ladies, shopping was getting easier to do every time we strolled through the front door.

We practiced our aim on the way to the zoo, so getting there was actually half the fun. Okay, maybe a little more than half. Every big ass was a target and every target we hit made a serious effort to make sure we didn't do it again, with one big exception. And there they are now. I'm talking big. A thousand pounds. Maybe two.

Both big ladies wore tight pants, one blue, one white, and both garments obviously made from the latest space age material that was stretched as taut as a Hollywood facelift across the back of a freaking hippopotamus. We snuck up really close and fired at the same time. "SHIT!" Screamed one. "Don't let me catch ya, ya little bastards!" yelled the other. Well, there wasn't much chance of that. Not even a fat chance.

We ran around the parked cars, taunting and laughing when I pointed to the big woman in white. "Hey, lady, you got a license for that trailer?"

We disappeared through the traffic and quickly sized up our next victim.

The roly-poly square badge cop on patrol in the massive Parkchester housing development seemed an opportunity awaiting a bugle call. We very quietly tracked our prey from a safe distance as he waddled along the tree-lined avenue whistling a happy tune. We tiptoed really quick and readied the ammunition, and when close enough, but not too close I screamed the call to arms. "Fire!"

"Yeeoooow!" His wild yelp could be heard all the way back to the bakery. I mean station house. The frantic patrolman with the triple-x uniform didn't rear up and charge. He merely rubbed his fat ass with one hand while the other prayed for a trigger on the button of his trusty flashlight. The huge patrolman was suddenly face to face with four very annoying troublemakers loaded with nothing but paper clips and smiles. "I know all ya fathers ya little pecker heads." Yeah, we've heard that one a few times.

We circled the parked cars to keep him at a safe distance, but the madder he got the faster we circled and the louder we laughed. He tried to give us a good chase, but Officer McCheesecake's best days were behind him. So were his best weeks, months and years. The big man was wearing a whole career's worth of jelly donuts in the back of his pants, but he still managed one hell of an effort.

He took a few quick steps and yelled into his walkie-talkie, "Ten-five! Ten-six! Ten-twenty-seven! I got four little pecker heads running around Metropolitan Oval shooting people in the ass with paper clips. Send a black and white, I got 'em surrounded." His phony attempt was pathetic. The only thing he was going to surround today was a corned beef sandwich.

"Ya know what we do to little pecker heads in jail?" The four of us back-peddled as we laughed at every word. "No," cried Charlie, "but I guess ya gonna' tell us, fatso!" The big man caught his breath and charged, but the threat was hardly worth the effort. We could've had lunch before his second foot hit the ground. "We handcuff ya to the radiator and watch ya parents beat the shit out ya!" I laughed, "I don't think so, ya fat bastard!"

Officer McCheesecake threatened everything from incarceration to emasculation, but his angry frustration fell on ears deaf with cartoon-like hysteria. The big man had a better chance of catching a herd of wild stampeding buffalo. Buffalo? We were having such a good time we almost forgot our prime objective, two thousand pounds of big ugly buffalo heinie. If Officer McCheesecake thought he was having a bad day wait 'til we get to the Bronx Zoo. Those buffalo are gonna wish they were hanging in the butcher shop window on Castle Hill Avenue as two thousand pounds of prime rib.

We vanished up Unionport Road faster than a bag of jelly donuts at the 43rd Precinct eight AM roll call. An hour later we casually strolled up to the front entrance. BRONX ZOO – KIDS UNDER 12 YEARS ACCOMPANIED BY ADULT – 25 CENTS.

The lack of hard currency was rarely an obstacle. Getting beyond an enclosure of any height with the cunning of an Army assault team is something we considered an art form. It's called a "fence pass."

Every troublemaker born in the New York area gets one. It's right there in your head.

Just beyond the turnstile a young city cop was talking to a young park ranger. Both appeared to be in excellent physical condition, so we decided to look for another way in, one without armed guards.

We carefully investigated the deserted fence line along the Bronx River Parkway. An overhanging tree limb could help us over the barbed wire, and we were also pushing at the bottom of the fence to find a spot where the pole and fence were unattached. Five minutes of optimism is all it took. A recent visitor had dug a hole under the fence. On the other side, nothing but trees and high weeds. As far as we were concerned this was the front gate and the sign read, FENCE PASS ENTRANCE. FRIDAYS FREE.

Once inside we became the wildest attractions there, four twelve-year-old troublemakers loaded with nothing but rubber bands and paper clips and not a parent among the group. "Let's go to the gorillas!" yelled Davy as he ran up ahead. "I jus seen ya mother!" I shouted. "Let's go to the tigers!" When we finally stopped running we found ourselves by the elephants. The four of us leaned on the railing, still out of breath and already smiling at natures wonder. "Wow," sighed Sean, "those f@#%*!$ things are big!"

"Hey, Kev," chimed Davy, "I thought your mother went shopping."

"Davy, ya mother's so fat she has to wash the ring around the Atlantic Ocean every time she takes a bath.

"Oh, yeah."

We looked around. Hardly any people. No trainers, no tour guides, no cops, not even a stray vacationing nun. The coast is clear. One unsuspecting elephant turned away as we prepared the initial assault.

Arms stretched over the railing, heavy duty rubber bands pulled to the limit, the four of us grinning like professional idiots. Would the two massive giants rear up and charge? Maybe a stampede? A bead of sweat drips from my nose to the floor of the pen below. "Ready." My whisper reaches all the way down to Davy. "Aim... Oww! Shit. My damn rubber band broke."

"What's the matter, asshole," shouted Sean, "whaddaya doin'? He's moving away!"

"Shut up dick-head, I almost knocked myself out." I actually punched myself on the nose when my rubber band snapped.

I quickly refocused my watery eyes, and when I glanced at Charlie his eyes were already bugging out of his head. "Gimme that thing!" Some elephant lover had a lethal grip on the back of my neck, and he was already choking it like a chicken. I frantically jumped on the ground. "You stay away from those elephants, sonny boy." The man straddled over me, pushed the side of my face into the pathway and snatched the broken rubber band out of my grip.

"Get offa' him!" yelled Sean. "You asshole!"

"Yeah," demanded Charlie pumping his fist. "Get offa him!" Davy circled around his back. "We'll kick your ass, you little #$%&*#@ midget!" I flailed, twisted, kicked and cursed. Mother @#!$%&! Stupid +%#!@&*#$@# as I frantically crawled away and jumped to my feet. The little guy was the funniest thing we'd seen all day, a head shorter than me and the boys and as old as my grandpa.

The tiny tour guide was dressed in a red engineer's suit with big shiny gold buttons and his matching engineer's hat was pulled snuggly about his ears. "Oh yeah, who's first?" He put up his dukes like the old time fighters. The old coot sounded like Blutto, but he looked like Popeye's grand pappy. We were crying hysterically, screaming with laughter.

The red and tan trolley, half loaded with stunned passengers was idling in the pathway a few feet away. "Where are your parents?" he demanded. I pointed, "Right there." He turned... and it was the last time we ever saw the little engineer. We ran away faster than a herd of laughing hyenas and we didn't stop giggling until we reached the other side of the zoo.

When we finally slowed to catch our breath I noticed a little something extra special in the air. I smacked Sean in the back of the head. "Hey Sean," I laughed, "I wish it was Saturday. You need a freaking bath."

"Oh, yeah… Your mother smells like my ass."

"Oh, yeah… Your mother smells like monkey shit."

"Oh, yeah."

The fence looked like an old western horse corral. With our chins on the top rail we gazed in wonder as the giant herd thundered about. There had to be three hundred, maybe four hundred thousand strong. Okay, maybe about a hundred and fifty. Okay, five. I mean two. There were just two buffalo, but they were really big, and I'm talking really big. And I guess they weren't exactly thundering. They were just standing around drooling and snorting and looking ugly and smelling bad. They were covered in big ugly patches of brown matted curls with big ugly heads and great pointy horns.

From a distance I could see the sign. AMERICAN BISON. I walked closer. DO NOT FEED. But not one word about shooting paperclips and no sign yet of the little engineer. Another thing that sign didn't say was, do not enter. It might've been obvious to most, but we weren't most. This enclosure was an open invitation for professionals with special skills.

Four happy smiles were still leaning on the top rail as the smaller and seemingly more curious of the two very large animals ambled within range. The beast slowly plodded up to the fence and laid her gigantic head on a vertical post. Amazed by the creature's enormous girth, we stared. Mouths open. Eyes wide. She seemed to be checking us out, too, her profile as big as a garbage truck. One ebony eye circled around. It stopped. We froze. The huge, prehistoric creature was ten feet away, but we could feel her gargantuan mass with every exhale. Was the beast trying to scare us? I don't think so. She looked kind of old, with tufts of gray hair all over her giant body. The giant slowly raised her enormous head, "Ka Choo!" and sneezed. The four of us stretched up on tippy toes and stared in awe at the massive sniffling buffalo. "God bless you!" I hollered. The boys laughed. The beast shook its great curly head and clomped one mighty hoof into the dirt. "Maybe she's catching a cold?" thought Davy.

"Yeah," I chuckled, "maybe she caught it from your mother." The gentle behemoth took another step away from the fence and focused a big curious eye on Charlie. "Hey, Charlie," Sean laughed, "I think she likes you." Charlie crossed his eyes and put the middle finger on his nose. "Duh, I think she likes ya mother, Sean."

We yelled and laughed and waved our hands and frantically banged

117

on the top rail. "Yah! Yah!" We wanted to make it run like they do in the cartoons, rear up on her hind legs, front wheels spinning a thousand miles an hour and taking off like a locomotive, but she merely wiggled her tail and slowly plodded away.

The giant wooly monster continued her leisurely retreat from any possible encounter with the wild inhabitants from the other side of the fence. The farther she walked the tougher we got. "Let's get 'it!" I shouted. "Hey, Davy," shrieked Charlie, "I hope your mom's leaving to take a bath!"

"Oh yeah, doofus. That thing smells like your mother's meatloaf!"

"Get ready," I alerted, "she's gettin' away."

We quickly bent and broke the paper clips in half and plucked the rubber bands from pants pockets. We carefully readied the initial assault. The four of us stretched eight gangly arms over the railing and steadily pulled the rubber bands taut. "Readd-i-i-i-i-i... Aaaaaaaim... Fire!"

"I got it!!"

"Me too!" It was unanimous. All four of us claiming a direct hit, but how come she didn't charge? How come she's not breathing smoke from her nose? We had more fun tormenting those two hippos waddling through Parkchester. At least they made an effort.

I looked around for the little engineer. No choo, choo chugging down the pathway. The coast is clear. "C'mon you faggots, she's gettin' away." I stepped between the railings. Three anxious hunters quickly followed me onto the expansive field. Sean was already peering down the barrel of an imaginary Kentucky long rifle. "POW! I'm Buffalo Bob."

"You mean Buffalo Bill, asshole. Buffalo Bob's on the Howdy Doody Show!" When I yelled it over my shoulder I slipped in a pile of buffalo crap, stumbled and barely managed my balance. "Hey, Kev!" shouted Davy, "You can be Howdy Doody. Doody, get it?"

"Hey, Davy, your mother smells like Howdy Doody!"

We were running and screaming like rampaging Indians, but there was buffalo shit everywhere we stepped and as far as the eye could see. Nevertheless we were whooping it up, trying to make it move, arms spinning as we hooted and hollered, but still, nothing happened. "Watch out!" David's frantic alert wasn't nearly frantic enough because the gigantic prehistoric hairball from way across the pasture was already chug, chug, chugging like a massive cartoon steam engine, head down, horns fixed ready to send four little troublemakers back in time to meet the Flintstones.

118

I sprinted in a blur of arms and legs and bellied flipped over the top rail. Within seconds Davy and Sean followed me onto the relative safety of the pathway. "Hurry up, Charlie, he's comin' fast!" Charlie was running for his life, chin up, eyes bulging, sweat pouring, arms and legs pumping like long skinny pistons, but the angry beast was tracking the target on his skinny ass like a laser guided missile. "C'mon, Charlie, move it!"

"Faster, faster!" urged Davy.

The old grey beast merely wandered off, totally disinterested. On the other hoof, her perturbed, much larger companion was charging Charlie like Buffalo Bill Cody dipped in barbecue sauce. The hairy monster was rapidly closing the gap, the charging mass of rage appearing to have no thoughts of stopping at the fence. We scattered for cover, our fear of death greater than any need to help er… .what's his name? That kid better get moving.

"Arrghhh!" Charlie's cry could be heard all the way back at the projects. "Arrghhhh!" He was still yelling and still racing for the fence when he suddenly tripped and slipped into a world class, head first slide through a gigantic mountain of fresh warm buffalo shit. His fingertips were begging for the pathway. Charlie looked like Superman as he slid under the bottom rail while two thousand pounds of wild snorting beast came to a sudden halt at his heels. Charlie shot up to his feet, a rush of blood shot into his face, tears barely held in check, teeth gritted beyond despair. Charlie had buffalo shit from his chin to his knees. We were rolling around the ground, kicking and screaming as tears of laughter rolled down freckled faces of fractured hysteria.

Once again the sneezing, wheezing behemoth plodded up to the fence, drooped her massive head onto her favorite post and stared off into the trees. But Charlie's full attention was still focused on the curly locomotive. The massive beast walked off and whipped its tail from side to side in a final act of defiance.

We were still laughing and rolling around the ground when the sickly old beast let out another sneeze. "Ka Choo!" loud and again, "Ka Choo!" Charlie rushed up to the tired old buffalo. "You big ugly shit." Charlie was gagging as he gestured towards the fresh brown paste with cautious fingertips. "Look what you did!" Seemingly unfazed by the intrusion, the old beast merely gazed up towards the bright blue sky. "I'll kick your fat ass, you big dumb shit." The old buffalo didn't even blink.

Charlie carefully managed his smelly shirt over his head. Then he

119

wiped his shitty face with his shitty shirt, and upon doing his best, which wasn't real good, he pinched the filthy shirt with two tentative fingers and tossed it up where it landed on the tip of a giant horn and draped over one big black eye.

The weary old buffalo backed away from the fence and passively bowed her enormous head. "KA-CHOO!" The smelly shirt slipped off the horn, fell to the ground where the giant clomped it into the dirt with her mighty hoof. "Hey, Charlie," I cried, "I think she wants to play!"

"You should kick her ass," chimed Sean, "because ya mom's gonna kick yours when you walk in the door without a shirt."

The humor of his dilemma finally diminished his sense of loss. Charlie was still stretching his sneaky smile up towards a big inquisitive eye. The old buffalo didn't seem to be laughing, but rather recalling some crazy caveman shenanigans from back in the day when she suddenly and very violently jerked her massive head towards the freckled irritation on the other side of the fence. "Sneeezeooie!" The force of the blast could've blown out a raging forest fire, but this time what came out of the beast wasn't just noise. "Oww! The monster sneezed out what looked like a raw dinosaur egg that exploded in Charlie's face and I'd swear she did it on purpose. "Oww! I can't see!"

The massive snot covered Charlie's freckled puss like a grotesque Halloween mask and dripped onto his bare chest. Charlie suddenly yakked up a foul river of lumpy, brown oatmeal. Davy saw the disgusting mess and hocked up a torrent of ugly green farina. After witnessing both, Sean couldn't stop gagging. Breakfast was all over the pathway and from the nasty looking evidence nobody had Cheerios except me.

Charlie ran in a panic, wiping his face and flicking the oozing mess to the pathway. The three of us quickly followed along when Charlie stumbled down the grass embankment to the meandering Bronx River. Buffalo Charles Dineane was still shaking, still choking and practically in tears up to his knees in the river, bent at the waist, hands vigorously patting water up to his face. Davy, Sean and I actually were in tears. "Shut up assholes. I'm gonna' kill that bastard! You watch!" Charlie was going to do stuff to that beast that would've turned even Buffalo Bill Cody's stomach. "You wait, you'll see. I'm gonna kick her fat stupid animals' ass."

13

For the better part of an hour we laid on our backs staring up through a giant sycamore tree and mercilessly goofed on Charlie's dilemma. It took him at least that long to finally calm down. "Boy, Charlie," snickered Davy, "you still smell like shit."

"Davy… ya mother smells like shit."

"Whaddya gonna' tell ya mom about the shirt?" I wondered. We all knew the truth wasn't an option. We were five miles from home and four and a half miles from out of bounds. "Hey mister," yelled Davy, "what time is it!?" An old guy passing with two little blonde girls in tow paused on the pathway. "Four o'clock," he informed. "Thanks, mister!" yelled Davy. "Shit. We better get goin'," alerted Sean. "I gotta be home by five."

"Me too."

"Me too."

By the time we got to our building Charlie was actually in a pretty good mood, until we came through the side door into the lobby. While we were walking through the fresh air nobody seemed to notice that the odor actually followed us home. When we got into the tiny elevator it was hard to miss. The god-awful smell was smothering. Everybody held their breath. Sean quickly pushed the door when we arrived on three and I reminded him what we agreed as he hurried away. "Member, in the lots, all day."

"Got it," said Sean as he frantically waved at the awful stink.

When the elevator stopped on Charlie's floor his smelly half naked reality seemed to hit him like a sudden smack on the nose with a rolled up newspaper. Charlie merely pushed the outer door and held it ajar with his sneaker. He was obviously begging the heavens for ideas and fresh air, so he poked his head out the door, took a life-sustaining breath and turned back with a tortured smile. "I got a great idea."

"Ya better make it fast. I gotta vacuum my room before my dad comes home or my mother will kill me."

"I thought you said you vacuumed this morning,"

"I did, but my mother's crazy."

"Gimme' ya shirt." Charlie finally realized that walking into his apartment without a shirt was a risk and the consequences of getting caught disastrous for everybody. Davy and I hurried off the elevator and followed Charlie into the iron staircase.

The iron staircase goes around and around a half flight at a time. You can actually look from the top floor right down to the first, and you can also hear people coming up or going down from a mile away. Every move echoes up and down the thirteen flights in the iron staircase.

"How come we didn't think of this before?" Davy wondered. When Charlie kissed his mom good-bye in the morning he was wearing a red white and blue striped tee shirt. Mine was red and white. What's one freaking color? His mom will never notice.

I hastily snatched the shirt over my head and threw it in his face. "Ya better hurry up', I begged, "ya gonna' make me late." Charlie pulled it on and patted down the front of his hair. "How zit look?" Davy gave him the good news. "Looks like your shirt without the buffalo shit, asshole."

"It's a little damp under the arms."

"It's better than buffalo shit, dick head. Now hurry up," I pleaded, "I'll wait right here." Charlie hurried past the elevator and down the hall to show his mom his nice clean shirt while Davy ran down the stairs to wait in the grass under his bedroom window. All Charlie had to do was get past his mom in the kitchen, run to the bedroom in the rear of the apartment and throw my shirt out the window. How simple is that?

So here I am... waiting, minding my own business. Must be five minutes already. Just standing around the iron staircase all by myself with no shirt. It's a damn good thing Charlie didn't throw his pants away. Boy, it sure is getting hot... so... .I'm still, waiting... and getting nervous. How long can it take a tee-shirt to fall five freaking stories? A door crashed on the ground floor and somebody was coming up the stairs, fast. **Thank-you, Jesus.**

My eyes were riveted on the hand on the railing as it went around and around. As the pounding on the iron stairs grew louder my nerves grew to a frazzle. Somebody was flying up the steps three at a time and I finally heard Davy grasping for air. Fifteen minutes? It should've taken no more than two, but when Davy turned up the last half flight a cold chill went straight up my skinny naked spine. "Where's my fucking shirt?" Davy's eyes were bulging and he was sucking in air like an old lady. He pointed down, "Ya father's... home." I whispered under my breath, "Where the hell is my damn shirt?"

"He got caught."

"Whaddaya mean caught?" Davy shrugged, his wild blue eyes screaming S.O.S. I was already picturing those two fat ladies, Officer McCheesecake and the little engineer all sitting atop that big, fat, sneezing, wheezing, behemoth as my whole day came crashing through my apartment door. Are you Kevin's mother? Do you know what your son did today? "Hurry up. Call for Charlie, see what's goin' on."

"Ya gonna get me in trouble. I gotta get home." Another door crashed, this time from above. Mom started screaming my name with all the subtlety of a broken bottle jammed in my ear. "Kevinn!" And I mean loud. "Kevinnnnnnnnnn!" Something was wrong alright. The voice echoing throughout the iron stair case was resounding with the high pitch wail of an air raid siren, only this siren had short black hair and a very short fuse. Every kid in the projects named Kevin was probably jumping under his bed, and somehow I knew she knew that I could hear. "Your ass is grass." The shock was still on its way to my brain when Davy disappeared out the door leaving me all alone with no freaking tee shirt.

I knew my mother wasn't about to run down the stairs on the outside chance that I might be hiding out on one of the lower floors. Playing hide and seek with my crazy mother was a regular thing. I'll just stand really close to the wall and say a little prayer 'til she goes away. 𝕻𝖑𝖊𝖆𝖘𝖊, 𝕲𝖔𝖉. 𝕳𝖔𝖜 𝖍𝖆𝖗𝖉 𝖈𝖆𝖓 𝖎𝖙 𝖇𝖊 𝖙𝖔 𝖒𝖆𝖐𝖊 𝖒𝖊 𝖆 𝖓𝖊𝖜 𝖙𝖊𝖊 𝖘𝖍𝖎𝖗𝖙? But, no shirt. Not even a white one.

Conjuring a quick explanation for a typical day's disaster was still a work in progress. Plausible storytelling is conveyed with equal amounts of conviction and sincerity, and both those qualities happen to be my specialties, so it only took me another minute to get it all straight in my head so it wouldn't sound stupid when it all came out of my mouth.

During the earlier part of my career mom had been slapping her little hands on the back of my melon so often she probably developed calluses. When I got a little bit bigger she naturally adapted a more aggressive assault. Mom's itty bitty shoes were usually the first line of attack, but she quickly advanced to whacking away with handy plastic toys, giant spoons, flying wooden hangers plus any number of household implements she could fling in my direction before I made my

123

escape out the door. My development into world-class get-a-way expert was now unparalleled among the professional ranks. There wasn't a kid in the entire Castle Hill Houses that could run around and around the kitchen and living room partition faster than me. Mom and I would circle that wall at a dizzying pace until she finally paused for a… breath… gone, out the door. Mom never had a prayer. Not even a quick hop in the ass. Her screams would echo throughout the building as I flew down the hall. "Now ya really gonna get it, mister!" I'll take my chances with dad.

Ideas always sounded really good while they were still ideas, but as soon as they jumped out of my mouth they seemed to lose that little something special. That little, I don't know, something. If I knew exactly what it was I'd be eating dinner already.

I gently turned the knob and barely pushed the door and peeked through a scarcely visible crack of light. **𝕻𝖑𝖊𝖆𝖘𝖊, 𝕲𝖔𝖉. 𝕮𝖆𝖓 𝖞𝖔𝖚 𝖒𝖆𝖐𝖊 𝖒𝖞 𝖒𝖔𝖒 𝖉𝖎𝖘𝖆𝖕𝖕𝖊𝖆𝖗?** Kathleen and Tommy were already seated at the dining room table. They noted my customary hesitation and simultaneously rolled their eyes, leading me to believe, I should've prayed a whole lot harder. It seemed unusually quiet until the freaking door Squeaked! Mom's voice exploded like five cherry bombs. "WHERE! HAVE! YOU! BEEN! MISTER?" Her startling outburst scared the snot out of me, but I quickly gathered my composure. After all, I am, a professional. "Whaddaya mean? I was in the lots." That should do it. "Oh, is that right?" Mom poked her head around the exercise wall. "Where's ya damn shirt?" Mom doesn't miss a trick. "What shirt?" Mom rattled her head and squeezed her eyes. "Gerry! He says he was in the lots and he's standing here without a goddamn damn shirt on!"

Uh oh. Storytelling takes on a whole new meaning when dad's in the house. Dad calls it lying. I call it the truth the whole truth and nothing but. I swear to God. Unless of course you've heard something? Flexibility happens to be my other middle name.

Dad casually strolled from bathroom into the courtroom, I mean dining area, and sat at the bench, er' chair at the head of the table. The People versus Kevin the Troublemaker was officially gaveled to order. The judge didn't look particularly angry, just hungry. The prosecutor was already stomping around my usual comfort zone, which is usually ten feet in all directions under these types of conditions. I'm sensing major hostility here. I was actually ready for an intensive cross-examination, but praying really hard there were no surprises. I hate surprises.

As long as my story is solid they'll have to believe me. I'm pretty sure. The tension in the room was so thick you could cut it with a paper clip. I mean knife. Concentrate. Just stick to the facts. I mean story. Dad slowly shook his head while mom circled the half-naked evidence, her breathing, intense. I didn't shift my weight or even blink. "What's that smell? Gerry, you smell that? I'm getting sick. What the hell did you step in, mister?" Mom pointed her tiny finger like a scalpel towards the door. "Get out in that goddamn hall and take off those goddamn sneakers and pants."

"I don't smell a blessed thing, Eve." Dad pointed to my spot. I shuffled over to my spot next to dad at the head of the table. "Don't move." I didn't move. "Eve... can't we do this later?" Dad was exhausted and hungry from a long day at work and obviously in no mood for mom's delaying tactics. "I'm starved." 𝔜𝔬𝔲'𝔯𝔢 𝔡𝔬𝔦𝔫𝔤 𝔰𝔬𝔪𝔢 𝔯𝔢𝔞𝔩𝔩𝔶 𝔣𝔦𝔫𝔢 𝔴𝔬𝔯𝔨 𝔥𝔢𝔯𝔢, 𝔏𝔬𝔯𝔡. "Yeah," begged Tommy, "let's eat." Sounds like we're all on the same page. Mom marched over and stood next to dad's chair and folded her arms in a tight knot while glaring a laser of crazy into my brain. Her face red, ears red, eyes red. "Gerry, we have to get to the bottom of this." Dad appeared bored with her attempt so he calmly patted the table as mom began direct examination. "Okay, mister, so ya wanna tell us what happened to the damn shirt?" I didn't twitch a muscle. "Where's the goddamn shirt?"

Composure under this type of pressure is a job requirement. Troublemakers without it don't last a week. "Kevin, please just tell ya mother where ya shirt is so we can all eat." Mom squeezed her eyes and rattled her head. "No, first I wanna know where he was all day. Now, where were ya, mister?" Dad was also shaking his head in disbelief. "Jesus, Mary and Saint Joseph, Eve. Can't this wait?" Mom tightened the grip on her upper arms. "Don't ya wanna know what he was up to all day?"

"Eve, please. I just wanna eat."

Dad is the ultimate seeker of truth, but he's also the smartest person in the room. Dad realized even before Kathleen and Tommy that he wouldn't be hearing a whole lot of truth before breakfast, and dad looks like he could eat a buffalo. I mean pork chop. "I've been a nervous wreck all day!" mom yelled. "So where's the damn shirt?"

"Eve, whaddya wanna know?" Mom stomped her little foot. "I wanna' know everything. I paid good money for that damn shirt." My half naked body was still frozen to the linoleum. Mom's little face was right in my mush and still barking like a rabid Chihuahua. "Gerry! Ask him where his goddamn shirt is!" All dad wanted was a measly pork-chop, but instead he's being forced into the middle of mom's latest investigation. Dad slowly exhaled, "Kevin… where's ya shirt?" Think fast… remain calm… don't panic. "I didn't wear a shirt today." Simplicity. There is absolutely nothing like it. So, I very patiently waited for an invitation to the dinner table.

Kathleen slowly shook her head and stared up at the ceiling while Tommy placed his fork on the table and slumped in his chair. You didn't have to be Dick Tracy to see I that I didn't even convince my little brother and big sister and they're not even that smart. "Gerry, is this child crazy?" I actually thought it sounded pretty good. "You two." Dad pointed down the hall. "Go to ya rooms till I get to the bottom of this."

"Now, where were you all day?" Dad was getting jumpy in his chair because mom was still crazy in the eye. My next prayer mumbled through a tight crack in my mouth. "I was… in the… "

"Gerry!"

"Eve, please, go in the kitchen. I'll take care of this." Reality finally set in. We're gonna be here for a while. "Okay now, one more time. Where were you today and who were you with?" A two-parter? Holy crap. Dad's probably using a two-parter to confuse me. Well, there's no confusion in my head. I'll be Kevin the tattle-tale before the milkman hits the building if I tell on all my best buddies. "I was in the lots… all day… with my friends… really." Boy, talk about guts.

Mom flew into kitchen. The sudden explosion of cabinet doors slamming and pots and pans banging was ear splitting. Dad sat there shaking his head, listening, probably trying to imagine the action at full volume. Her aggression was still peaking as she reentered the living room where a blur of tiny fingers flashed about the wall dusting picture frames and statuettes plus everything else she dusted five minutes ago. Dad continued to gaze in stunned silence. "Gerry, WHAT are we gonna' do with this child?" Control is a relative term, especially when dealing with this type of pressure, but my brain was leading me to believe that I still had it. After all, dad's a talker and very much in charge. He wouldn't beat me up if I told him I went all the way to the Bronx Zoo and murdered the last surviving American Bison on the planet. "Kevin, we're not gonna sit here all night. I wanna know what you did today, who you were with and what happened to ya shirt?"

There it is! The freaking trifecta from hell. The constant pressure was finally wearing me down, and my ability to lie with a straight face was somewhat compromised, so I tried again with a slightly crooked one. "Really... I was... " The Rock of Gibraltar still remained calm. "Kevin." Dad shook his head and looked up for help. "Don't tell me that again." Mom's voice suddenly exploded like a run-a-way freight-train crashing into an out of control tractor trailer. "GERRY IF THIS KID!!!... "

"Eve, please, calm down."

It was pretty obvious that mom was trying to scare the truth out of me. I figured the next time I'd see a pork chop it would be walking around the Bronx Zoo disguised as a pig. A vacant gaze fixed in my eyes. "Pay attention to your father." Dad was obviously at the end of his rope with Kevin the storyteller so he started making up his own story.

"You were with Sean, Charlie and David today. Weren't you?" Is this an accusation? Is dad actually calling me a liar? I was perfectly willing to go to the electric chair rather than admit to any misrepresentation of the facts. I'll even go to bed with no dinner. Hold on, maybe no cartoons for a week. Troublemaking is a full time occupation and I can't possibly do it on an empty stomach. Kevin the Gambler stood at the crap table of life with no dice and shit out of luck. I didn't even have a shirt to lose. Not even a dirty one. "Sean, Charlie and David went to the Bronx Zoo today." And he sure as hell sounded like he knew what he was talking about.

When dad's good friend Stan Dineane, with a little prodding from the misses questioned his son's whereabouts from early morning till dinner time, Charlie fell apart like a three dollar suit, and a few minutes after Charlie spilled his guts my dad stopped by the fifth floor to ask Mister Dineane about the time for this Saturdays' softball game. Dad was actually loaded for buffalo before he got back on the elevator.

The worst thing about storytelling was watching the anguish in dad's eyes. Dad appeared to pray in that quiet unassuming way he does everything. No sign of the crosses, no begging the Lord out loud. Just silence for long pauses of reflection. By watching my Dad during these times of high stress I learned that professional troublemaking takes enormous stupidity. All I had to do was look in his eyes to see the disappointment.

Dad put his elbows on the table and hid his anguish in his ink-stained printer's hands. When he finally spoke it was barely above a whisper. "We go through this over and over every time, Kevin. What do you think I'm gonna do to you?" Just tell me the truth. I'm not gonna hit ya." When he slowly looked up I quickly looked down, at my sneakers. Damn, is that buffalo shit? I thought I got it all off. No wonder mom's turning blue. Phew!

The panic in my brain was paralyzing. I couldn't think, wouldn't speak and dad took my silence as an indication of guilt. The man certainly has a talent. "That's it." Dad suddenly stood and pushed the back of my head and forced me down the hall towards the bedrooms. "Now take it easy, Gerry." That is one hell of a timely suggestion. My whole life was passing before my eyes. Wow, I forgot about that. And that. And... Dad opened Kathleen's bedroom door with a crash. The noise startled my big sister off the pillow. "Kathleen." He pointed the way out. Then he flicked that big, hairy finger like a meat cleaver towards the window. "Get over there." Dad grabbed me by the wrist, held it over my head and dragged me along. "What are we gonna do with you, Kevin?" Dad's never shown this kind of anger before, and I've told him stories that could've been published. "Kevin, I'm only gonna ask you one more time." Dad was shaking from head to toe as he pushed the window up with such a force I thought he was trying to shove it up to the twelfth floor. "So if you don't tell me the truth I'm gonna throw you right out this window."

Dad was gambling that my new option of learning how to fly before I reached the grass would frighten the truth out of me. Yep, my dad's pretty damn smart for an old guy. He scared the living crap out of me. "This is your last chance, Kevin."

It was a long exhausting day and I was losing my ability to concentrate. Chris Carpenter and Mark Madden were playing fast pitching stickball in the park across the street. Was that a home run? That Chris Carpenter can really smack the shit out of a Spaulding. Dad gave me a quick shot in the head to get my attention. I've gotten early morning greetings from good old Sister Mary Monster delivered with more purpose, but my eyes suddenly sprung a leak anyway. I wasn't crying. Well, at least no noise was coming out, at least not yet. The wet stuff wasn't even fear because even when dad was really mad he really wasn't that scary, but when I suddenly saw the utter despair and anguish in my dad's trusting eyes overflow his own watery pain down his beautiful face I fell apart like a professional cissy. So I essentially told him the gospel truth, except the stuff about McCrory's, the fat ladies, the big slow cop, the little engineer and the buffalo shit. Keep it simple. Essentially. A little truth would normally settle things down a notch or two. Normally. Usually.

So after another grueling search for reality dad knelt to one knee and embraced me in a big old bear hug. Then he apologized for that brutal smack in the head. As I sniffled and blubbered through watery eyes over his shoulder dad reinforced the only thing I already knew for certain without the constant reminders. "I love you so much, Kevin. I don't know why you think you have to lie to me and mommy all the time." Dad said the exact same thing every time I told a good story, danced around the facts, exaggerated, understated, stretched the truth, got caught cold in a red-faced lie. Yeah, dad really hates that.

Even after all these many years of telling my dad great stories he still failed to realize that lying was just part of my job. The part I wasn't too good at, yet.

Boy, I guess I'm really gonna hate doing this again tomorrow.

14

It was late Friday afternoon. I was snickering my way through Sister Nicolas's dumb art class. Sister was drawing a chicken on the blackboard that was supposed to look like a turkey when the principal, Mother Anastasia, interrupted class with an urgent announcement over the intercom.

"Attention, please. Attention all children and teachers. I have very disturbing news. I have just been informed that President Kennedy has been shot and mortally wounded in Dallas Texas." There was a long pause for reflection and sniffling. "We will now pray for the eternal soul of our beloved president and we will also beg the Lord that his family and this great nation be given the strength to pull us all through this great tragedy." She then led us in a few Hail Mary's and couple of Our Father's and a glory be. "When you leave the building at the end of the day please be respectfully quiet and return to your homes immediately. God bless you all and God bless this great country."

The assassination of President Kennedy was a time of great sorrow and the beginning of great turmoil for the country. It was exactly one week before my thirteenth birthday.

The American political involvement in Viet Nam had been under way since the United States entered the Second World War. I couldn't comprehend the magnitude of war as a young teen, but our nineteen inch black and white television was giving me plenty of second-hand instruction.

By early 1964 every six PM newscast began the same way every evening, except for the body count. Today in Viet Nam nineteen American troops were killed in combat. And the commentators always made it sound like we were winning. And thirty seven North Viet Cong guerillas dead. For a short while I actually thought that our army was in a foreign jungle fighting real guerillas, but we weren't. This wasn't monkey business. They were killing our young soldiers and we were killing theirs and the body count was rapidly mounting on both sides.

♣

I was supposed to be asleep, but I wasn't even tired. The sound emanating from my tiny transistor radio was barely audible with an anxious ear pressed to my pillow, the rest of my head carefully hidden under a nice warm blanket. I was completely mesmerized as I listened in the dark to the live broadcast being announced by the former undefeated heavyweight champion, the great Rocky Marciano.

According to Sonny Liston, Cassius Clay should've been knocked out by the second round. According to the boxing experts, Clay should've stayed at home in Kentucky under his bed. Sonny Liston was considered by all to be the most devastating puncher in the history of the sport. Liston's gruff demeanor and menacing glare scared a few heavyweights to re-think their career paths, some into retirement. Sonny the bear Liston was supposed to thrash the young whipper-snapper with the big mouth, but Liston hardly seemed equipped for the young man with fast feet and lightning quick hands. Liston was swinging wildly at the air while Clay was peppering the heavyweight champion's mush with a constant pneumatic left jab and punishing over-hand rights that were about equal to what I received daily from Sister Mary Monster for two straight years. The fight ended with Liston on his stool, bleeding profusely under one eye, but it was the severe shoulder injury that rendered The Bear incapable of answering the bell for the seventh round. Sonny Liston would've never made it in Catholic school.

☘

The Boy Scouts were the closest I've come to joining a military organization. My enlistment was actually well thought out. Going to scout meetings was my only opportunity for hanging out with my friends on Friday nights. My dad had been a Boy Scout, so he knew first-hand the benefits of the national organization. Dad also knew the leader of troop seventy-five. Dad figured Mister Hart, the ex-marine war veteran might possibly, hopefully be the perfect influence necessary to change my aggressive behavior, but after my very first overnight camping trip to Senida Hills, New Jersey, dad was already having second thoughts.

Big Bruno Benedetto was big enough to fill a four-man tent by himself. Big Bruno was a junior troop leader with years of experience and his father was second in charge to Mister Hart. Charlie, Sean, Davy and I were shivering to death in our canvas freezer when Sean noticed a warm glow coming from our closest neighbor. I crawled into the frigid New Jersey wilderness and poked my head into Big Bruno's tent. Four warm and toasty boy scouts were sitting Indian style, huddled around a little blue flame in the ground in the middle of the tent. "How'd ya do that, Bruno?" Big Bruno looked up at the tenderfoot like I was a girl scout. "Ya dig a hole in the dirt, put a little tuna fish can in the hole and squirt in a tiny bit of lighter fluid, dummy."

"Thanks, Bruno." Asshole.

I quickly hurried back and told the boys the heartwarming news. We hastily rummaged through our knapsacks and gathered up all the cans of lighter fluid. Charlie crawled outside and retrieved an empty can of corn. With my handy Boy Scout spoon I dug a six-inch hole in the dirt. After I pushed the can into the neat hole the four of us squirted in enough lighter fluid to melt steel. Davy closed the tent flap and tied it tight while the rest of us searched for a lighter. "Who's got a match?" said Charlie. "My shit and your mother's meatloaf," I offered. "C'mon, find something to light it." Rubbing two sticks together really isn't a Boy Scout thing. It's a caveman thing. The acrid smell of fluid was already thick in the air while we searched through jacket pockets, pants and knapsacks for the means to start a fire. "If somebody farts we're all gonna die," blurted Davy. "So don't fart, dick head," warned Sean.

After a few minutes I finally found my lighter buried deep in my super-secret, water tight pouch inside my knapsack. I flicked it. The flame didn't even make it to the fluid when a flash of blue light exploded the tent up into the trees. "What the fuck!" yelled Sean. "Holy shit!" cried Davy.

Four stunned boy scouts were lying on our backs, staring up at the stars. "Whose genius idea was that?" I slowly sat upright and shook my head to clear my blurry vision. "You're an asshole, Kevin," said Sean. Everybody looked a little creepy. It took a second to figure out why. "Hey, you guys have no eyebrows."

"Neither do you, asshole."

"Whaddya we gonna do now?"

We were sitting under the stars, freezing in the New Jersey wilderness with very little facial hair and what was left was singed by the instantaneous explosion of gas. "You're an asshole, Kevin," suggested Charlie. "How do we know Davy didn't fart?" Charlie pointed his flashlight, "Hey, is that a bear?"

"No," I warned, "I think it's ya fat ugly mother, you dick."

We were still talking over our Boy Scout survival procedures when Davy came up with his own brilliant idea to keep us alive. "Kevin, why don't ya go and see if Mister Hart will let us sleep in his cabin before we freeze to death out here." The big ex-Marine snuggled up with rattlesnakes in mud trenches in the war with the Japs. Our plight was a mere discomfort and not life and death. I figured we had a better chance of sleeping in the White House. "Why me?"

"Because you're the dick that blew up the tent," noted Charlie.

After ten very short minutes I finally found enough courage and body heat to walk over and knock on the door of the big log cabin. "Come in," invited Mister Benedetto. "What can we do for you, Kevin? And what happened to your eyebrows?"

"I had a little situation, Mister Benedetto. It's sort of a long story. And… I… we was.. wonderin' if we maybe could we sleep in here tonight?" It was about forty degrees outside, but I was sweating like a ten-point buck on the first day of hunting season. "What's wrong with your tent, son?"

"We had a little mishap, Mister Benedetto." Mister Hart was sitting back in his big comfy chair with his legs propped up on an old wooden seltzer box. His square jaw a red glow three feet from a roaring fireplace. When he heard my incredible tale of misfortune he quickly stood up and marched to the door. He looked down and growled. I looked up and prayed. "Rectify it, Mister Carroll." The big Marine sounded like he wanted me to charge up Mt. Iwo Jima to rectify a machine gun nest. Rectify? I didn't know rectify, but it didn't sound like an invitation to pull a seltzer crate up to his blazing fire.

"What did he say?"

"Whaddya think?"

I managed a year and a half in troop seventy-five and I actually earned nine merit badges, one short of attaining the rank of Life Scout. I'm not sure if I had the right stuff for the Boy Scouts, but it did get me out of the apartment and away from my crazy mother on Friday nights. Mission accomplished.

♣

If Mark Madden wasn't the smartest kid in sixth grade he was certainly at the very top of the class, and because I wasn't nearly as bright I was able to engage a new classmate who also became a great friend. We were both born on the 29th of November. That coincidence of birth added that little extra something to an already thriving partnership.

Mark's gentle spirit and mild-mannered disposition were just two of his many good traits that kept him a safe distance from expressing any aggression. In this regard we were polar opposites. I had a schedule. Friday afternoon: who wants to fight? Mark couldn't punch his way through a soap bubble, but my attitude was big enough for both of us. If I couldn't scare away some asshole from pursuing a fight with my new best friend, my second best option was a tactic to clarify any lingering doubt that a miscalculation in judgment might possibly endanger your good health. For the much larger opponents a sudden knee in the nuts followed by a quick right cross would usually do the trick. Others were simply introduced to the anger in my head that rushed adrenalin through a brain that exploded on anyone thinking that strength has anything to do with muscles. But my sharp tongue was and still is my finest asset. I could stare straight into the eyes of a much bigger opponent and promise an ass kicking he'd remember for the rest of his life. "I'll punch ya so hard, I'll sprain ya fucking neck."

As an aggressive young teen with the verbal acuity of a crazy old poet I built up quite an extensive repertoire, but if my verbal punch in the manhood didn't attain the desired effect, well let's just say I learned to take a beating from the nuns for having a big mouth, and by the time I started the sixth grade my mouth was still my best means for getting educated. I've threatened some very large people with little or no capacity to do what I said, but as soon as that special look in my eyes registered in their feeble brains the battle was over, usually, but not always. Not everybody can be intimidated. Many can. I won a lot of fights with my big mouth and raging blue eyes and got my ass handed to me by some very large adversaries. It's good practice.

Wow, I never realized how big my ass is.

☘

The arrival of The Beatles on this side of the Atlantic was the cause of enormous social upheaval. The new British rock sensation triggered an explosion of musical interest in young Americans that spread like wildfire, and being close to flame, even a rock n roll flame was like oxygen for my brain.

Practicing my new bass guitar along with Mark and his supernatural ability for rock n roll strumming kept us both out of trouble for many an afternoon. Starting a band and the dreams that come with adolescence was the greatest cure for troublemaking since the invention of the electric chair.

Long hair was now mandatory for anyone considering music as a hobby, and Mark was a natural to be a star. Except for my size I was natural to be a nightclub bouncer, but Mark needed me to be a bass player so I practiced my new hobby with real determination in hopes of a career that wouldn't require any actual work. Or bulk.

Growing my hair longer than dad's was a feat yet to be conquered. Both my parents were hardly sympathetic to the plight of an up and coming rock star. Dad's hairstyle was the same as he wore in the Army. Mom and dad considered The Beatles to be four screaming mops of hair. "Why do they need all that hair? They look like freaks."

Monthly haircuts were now as traumatic as holy ass whippin's. "Felix. Please, just take a little off the back and nothing off the front." Felix the barber obviously had his orders long before I walked in the front door of Joe's Barber Shop on Castle Hill Avenue. Old cockeyed Felix appeared to be staring at a head in the other chair while his scary buzz clipper was shearing my noggin like a Marine drill sergeant. Growing my hair long was a major project that took a few years to develop, a great deal of cunning and a large consumption of green goop that congealed like lava and turned to rock. I could now walk through the eye of a hurricane without a single hair being out of place. So when I walked in the door I could show my mom that a buck fifty still buys one hell of a haircut.

The Beatles gave new meaning to places like Joe's Barber Shop. Long hair was in. Felix and Joe were men to fear.

Chris Carpenter wasn't just a good athlete, he was also a better than average troublemaker. The slight space in his teeth gave his handsome Irish smile character, and his tight, curly blonde hair was always finessed with an educated comb that kept my friend a safe distance from the barber's chair, which for the rest of us was more like a monthly bloodletting.

Chris and I were housed on the same cell block where we spent a year laughing at the expense of old Sister Augustine in the Holy Family reformatory for wayward Christian soldiers. I actually noticed Chris's talents from way across the classroom, so when we came together that next September in Saint John Vianney we hit it off like twin trouble-makers separated at birth.

It didn't happen often, but if trouble was staring me in the face and I happen to be standing around with my empty head in the clouds my other best friend could usually pull me back to earth with nothing but a mischievous grin. So when Chris and I walked into the office of the Texaco gas station for a soda the signs of a Saturday afternoon calamity were as plain as the pearly white character in Chris's sneaky smile.

Our regular Saturday morning basketball games at Saint John's schoolyard were almost always followed by a monster thirst. After getting thoroughly thrashed around the court for two hours Chris and I finally strolled across Castle Hill Avenue and into the office of the Texaco gas station to get a soda from the vending machine. But the scheming portion of my brain which happens to be the larger portion quickly noticed something amiss: nobody pumping gas, nobody sitting around the office, just a lone mechanic doing mechanic stuff in the garage area.

When I peeked through the door that connects the office to the garage area the regular grease monkey with the slicked back hair was standing under the hydraulic car lift. The bulky young mechanic was banging away with a ballpeen hammer at some old jalopy, oblivious to the two sweaty basketball stars standing at the soda machine on the other side of the door. "This place is practically deserted," I noted. Two smiles and four wide eyes quickly found the ancient cash register. "I betcha we can rob this place." Chris glanced through the door at the only person keeping us from a small fortune. "I bet ya right."

The 1964 World's Fair was about to open for business out in Queens, and slipping under the fence according to news reports would not be an option. The boys and I were desperate to see the future, but present day security was said to be extremely tight. Our collective brain power had been conjuring up different ways of getting us through the front gate, and I personally never gave a thought to paying. Until now.

By the time a few more of the boys walked into the schoolyard, Chris and I had already figured out a positively foolproof plan to get us into the World's Fair. We figured we needed three more fools.

Timothy Quinn and Mark Madden lived in the same building across the street from the school yard. When they walked onto the court together only one of them was actually ready to play ball. Mark was about as athletic as your average fat girl in stretch pants, but the pretty girls still came to the playground to watch him comb his black wavy hair between dribbles. Timmy, a quick thinking, fast talking string bean with long lanky legs and wispy brown hair was no better than me at basketball, though both of us could beat Mark with one foot encased in concrete.

Chris threw the ball and hit Mark hard in the chest as I was throwing out the most outrageous question of the year. "How much ya think they have in that register at the end of the day?" I was smiling towards the gas station on the other side of Castle Hill Avenue. Mark was never one to turn down a challenging opportunity, but not without a few point-ed questions of his own. "What the hell you idiots scheming about this time?"

"We're thinking about robbing the Texaco," I said. We robbed every-thing but the paint on the walls in McCrory's, but glomming stuff was hardly a challenge compared with robbing actual money.

"Every time you think too hard, Kevin, I get into trouble," noted Mark. Timothy was still grumbling. We expected resistance. "It'll be a snap," said Chris. "There's only one guy working in the garage." Timothy strolled in a wide circle, slowly spinning the idea around his brain. "Ya think we could actually get away with it?" One down, two to go.

Sean finally sauntered through the gate while Mark slowly dribbled past Chris and proceeded to blow an easy layup. "How do we rob the place without a gun?" wondered Mark. "We don't need a gun," I noted, we just need to be fast." Sean heard enough to be intrigued, but seemed to need further assurance. "Then how do we get the money?"

"I'm figuring three look-outs and two guys in the office. As long as the mechanic stays in the garage we'll be on our way in seconds." Mark was still shaking his head. "What time you geniuses figure we'll be out of jail? My mom's making lasagna today and I don't want to be late for dinner."

THE BIG GAS STATION HEIST

The look-outs casually strolled up to their pre-designated positions by the gas pumps. Mark and Sean were probably a bit nervous but played it cool, as if merely discussing the ridiculously high price of gasoline which had recently sky rocketed to thirty cents per gallon. Freaking A-rabs. Mark is so nearsighted that a patrol car could roll into the station, gas up and have us all in handcuffs before he realized a black and white was parked under his nose. Wearing eye glasses in public was not an option for Mark. God didn't make his beautiful face to have it screwed up by something that might actually help him see past the length of his nose.

Chris took up his post outside the entrance to the office. Timothy and I casually continued on through the door like two thirsty teenagers in dire need of an ice cold can of Pepsi.

When I glanced through the inner door the lone mechanic was scurrying around the garage area. The young mechanic didn't seem concerned or possibly never even noticed the regular neighborhood kids who visit his soda machine every other day. His likely thought process was also built into the plan. We figured the big guy would never suspect anything underhanded, especially from the same kids he sees every other day. The part of the plan that wasn't part of the plan was that he probably knew our names and where we went to school, which was right across the street, but it wasn't discussed during the planning so we didn't worry about it because we weren't planning on getting caught. Like I said, the plan was foolproof.

Last one out is a rotten egg! Chris will yell the alert when he sees us turn from the cash register towards the getaway portion of the heist. I slowly pushed the button down on the ancient cash register and held the drawer with the other hand so the bell wouldn't ring and carefully eased it open. Timothy plucked half the bills while I was grabbing the other half. Three seconds later we turned to go. "Last one out's a rotten egg!" Good ole Chris. Right on the money. We figured the young mechanic would never think it unusual if he saw us running from the station with twenty dollar bills flying out of our pockets if he just thought we were playing a game.

Ten bright eyes and five brilliant smiles exploded from the scene like a starburst. We streaked across Castle Hill Avenue in a blur of elbows and knee-caps past the church and around the corner and continued along the sidewalk past the weary glare of the Saint John Vianney statue on guard in front of our school. We picked up speed down the best hill in the area for sledding and roller skate scooters, dashed to the end of Seward Avenue and vanished into the lots. We didn't go far, but as far as we were concerned it was the safest place on the planet. No cops, parents, nuns or even eagle-eyed mechanics see us through the thick curtain of overgrown swamp stuff.

The take was a big one alright, one hundred and ninety-six large.

139

After Mark did the math and split the cash the skinniest kid in the gang announced a desperate need for nutrition. After all, we did run a whole block and a half. "I gotta' eat something before I faint," begged Timothy. "You gotta be kidding," I scolded. "I didn't eat all day."

"'Cause you're a fucking idiot."

The German delicatessen on the other side of the lots was actually very convenient. The store is just two blocks west of my old house on Taylor Avenue by the Beach Theatre. It was also the same store where dad worked behind the counter on Saturdays before we moved, but that little fact sort of escaped my devious mind.

We all rushed into the tiny store. Timothy quickly snatched a nickel bag of Wise potato chips from the display shelf and placed on the counter with a smile like he was purchasing a new Cadillac. Timothy dug in his pocket and pulled up a fist full of crumpled bills, quickly plucked a twenty and placed it on the counter. The ancient store clerk picked up the note and squinted through Coke bottle glasses while Timothy was stuffing the rest of the cash back in his pocket. "Don't you have anything smaller there, son?" I frantically scrambled for a dollar bill, but in haste dropped my whole fortune to the floor. The old man wiggled the bill. "Where'd you kids get all this money?" None of your freaking business, I thought. "Our parents are rich," blurted Mark. "Is that right? The old man fixed a quizzical glare. "And you, son, is your mansion down by the Castle Hill Projects? Aren't you Kevin? Gerry Carroll's boy." Before the nosey old goat could gather his next thought the five of us charged the door while Timothy's Jackson was still wiggling in the man's fingers. "Hey, get back here! Where are you kids running, to?" We were half way up the block before Timothy realized, "My change!"

"Go back and get it!" I yelled, "We'll wait for ya in the lots." Timothy kept pace as we headed for the hills and he was actually a tiny bit faster because he was suddenly twenty dollars lighter.

My plan for getting us back home without getting arrested had been well thought out, but this time my idea was overruled by an over confident democratic process, so instead of walking back through the lots, we headed south. Not Mexico, but any other direction would've been smarter.

We were still laughing about the big gas station heist as we strolled along Soundview Avenue. We finally calmed down to giggles by the time we reached Lacombe, the bumpy clay dirt road bordering the southern edge of the lots. Just as we were passing Pugsley Creek our attention was seized by the ominous cloud of brown dust billowing up behind the wheels of a speeding truck. The ancient red Texaco wrecker quickly came into focus. I frantically strained for a better idea and it came the second I spotted the steely eyes of the man with the greased back hair behind the steering wheel. Fear is a terrible thing and in times of great necessity, it usually makes me stupid, but it also makes me really, really fast.

Five frantic troublemakers raced towards the vehicle because the laws of physics would surely prohibit the speeding truck from stopping fast enough without the occupants going through the windshield. We passed each other going in different directions and the big angry predator screaming out the passenger window was expressing everything we needed to know to keep us all moving along as fast as humanly possible. I will choke all your scrawny little necks like chickens, mother#@$?&%'s. He didn't actually say it, but he didn't have to. His intentions were loud and clear, pain is on the way.

The truck was still fish-tailing all over the road and barely under control as it raised huge clouds of swirling clay dust. While the laws of physics and a very heavy foot were still dragging the truck to a stop, the passenger door flung open. Everyone but Chris had already darted into the lots. The second fastest troublemaker on Lacombe Avenue stopped on a dime and reversed direction back towards Soundview Avenue. Fear is now in a terrifying race with a front bumper, but not for long. The crazy young wrangler suddenly leapt from the passenger seat and tackled Chris like a calf in a rodeo. They looked like a human tumbleweed and Chris was wild in his effort to escape, but the big angry predator outweighed my friend by a thousand pounds and flattened Christopher into the high weeds along the edge of the lots.

By the time we re-grouped a few scary minutes later Chris was probably half way to the 43rd precinct, a development so far from the realm of possibility a few short hours ago that when reality finally sank in it was like the onset of malaria. I was sweating like a big kid being dragged by his mom through the brassiere section at Macy's. I planned on going to the World's Fair but nobody planned on getting caught. This evening had all the ear markings of a catastrophic holy ass whippin'… minus the holy. Dad is sure to explode. Mom will supply the atomic energy.

15

Only moments after the Texaco grease monkey had tackled Chris, Sean suggested an option that quickly gathered traction. By the look on his face I thought he discovered the cure for pimples. "Let's go see Father Wilson." The way too friendly parish do-gooder was always hanging around the school yard, so we were probably his biggest project. Or maybe his special penance. We needed somebody to soften the stupidity for our parents and Sean figured that Father happy-face would be the perfect Christian for the job.

Father Wilson was well acquainted with all of our parents, but he was especially friendly with mine because dad is one of the founding fathers of the Saint John's Holy Name society. Mom is recording secretary of the lady's guild and my Grandma is the cook for the rectory. Talk about miracles. I was living with the holy trinity of good luck. "I think it's a good idea, too" appealed Mark. "Maybe they'll let Chris go if we give back the money."

"Maybe if I click my heels three times I could ask the Wizard to come to New York so he could personally slap the snot out of you for being a dumb ass."

"I think it's a good idea, too" chimed Timothy. "Let's go see Father."

"Then we'll all be arrested," I groaned.

We were still standing in the middle of the lots, my favorite place in the universe on a beautiful spring evening, but the sky had suddenly turned black and my brain was churning like three pounds of mush. My only thoughts were stupid. I could've used a really special prayer. **Okay, God, What if I plead insanity?**

By the time we rang the bell on the rectory door we were really, really sorry for getting caught. I mean for the terrible breakdown of Christian values. All we needed now was for Father Wilson to express our deepest regrets and give back the money and that should be enough keep us out of prison. **Grab a glove, Lord. You're playing center field.**

I was the fastest talker and the genius behind this catastrophic disaster so I was elected to do the lying. I mean talking. After Father listened intently to all the shocking details he explained the need for prayer. Father told us that God already knows the truth, but hearing it in confession would go a long way in guiding us through the darkness. I for one could've used a flashlight.

We followed Father like nervous sheep through the front entrance of the precinct. As soon as we stepped through the door the big greasy mechanic and his large burly friend pointed us out to the sergeant seated up high behind the front desk. "Will ya look at this."

The good shepherd was quickly hustled away by a detective. The air was still escaping my brain when my jaw flopped open in preparation for the stupidity left dangling on the tip of my tongue. "Let's get out of here," I whispered. An Irish cop the size of the Empire State Building stepped over to block the way. I looked up. He looked down. "March over there!" When I flashed him the evil eye he glared and explained my option in no uncertain terms. "Move now before I give you a good swift kick in the ass, ya little shit." The copper had a foot the size of a freaking ironing board so I closed my eyes, and when I opened again Chris's mom was walking down the stairs from the detective's offices. "They came in on their own, ma'am," said the big Irish palooka. Chris's mom looked each one of us in the eye as we were being escorted up the staircase for the interrogation portion of the evening. "It's probably the first smart thing they did together all year." As I stared at each step that was spotted with various shapes of grey bubble gum I realized how wrong Chris's mom sounded. So far, this idea wasn't looking that smart.

I was seated at the desk facing the dumb fat detective when Dad rushed in the room. I couldn't look up. He put his hand gently on my shoulder. "I don't know where to start, Kevin. You stole money from a hardworking man and food off his table. Your actions have consequences, Kevin and telling it in confession will not make it go away." That's where dad started and he didn't stop talking for the rest of the weekend.

I never actually thought about where the money came from or what it was for. It was just money in a drawer and we needed every penny to go to the World's Fair, but dad made a very convincing and rather long winded argument against stealing from thy neighbor or even thy neighbor's gas station. Dad wasn't trying to make me feel guilty or even stupid. He was trying to impart the idea of ownership of one's actions. "If you break the law, Kevin you should expect consequences." Dad never actually explained, consequences. That was mom's job. "Do you think I should apologize?"

"That would be a good start, Kevin, but you'll have to wait until you're finished with court."

♣

Five scared criminals and five weary parents were dressed in our Sunday best as we waited in the corridor on the safe side of the court room door. The fear instilled by mom leading up to this moment was being recalled in vivid detail when a large round officer in glistening white shirt pushed open the door and leaned his head under the entrance to hell. "The judge will hear you now. Please follow me." His deep baritone voice sounded like it traveled from outer space.

We walked in dead silence towards the judge's bench and sat in the very first row of the empty court room. "Sit next to your own child," said the officer. Mom grabbed my wrist and dragged me along. Judge Goldfarb entered the courtroom. The little man with the Saint Anthony hair doo peered over black horned rimmed glasses towards the front row as he sat in his big leather chair. The judge whispered to the court officer, who stood erect and glared down. "Who represents defendant Kevin Carroll." Mom squirmed nervously and dug her nails into my leg. "I do."

"Please stand when you address the court, ma'am. For the record I need your name and your relationship if any to the defendant."

"I'm his mother. Missus Evangeline Carroll." She didn't sound real convinced about the association. "Please be seated, Missus Carroll." The officer proceeded down the row until all the other moms accounted. "Sergeant, please escort the defendants outside and make them aware of the consequences of leaving the waiting area." By the judge's tone a toasty corner in hell was not out of the question.

We scrunched together on the bench with the officer glaring down like an angry nun. "Now if I have to come out here for anything at all somebody will be introduced to the tip of my foot. Do we understand each other?" The man had the language skills of a mafia poet and a shoe the size of a freaking cinder-block. "Well?"

"Yes sir," we mumbled in unison.

The second the large round sergeant walked behind the door we very, very quietly debated all the possibilities being established for our certain demise. "Maybe he's gonna send us to the Six Hundred School," I said. Mark, chin in hands stared hopelessly at his shiny shoes. "I don't care. I just don't wanna get another haircut."

"Me either," prayed Timothy. We all grumbled unanimous agreement.

Twenty minutes later five squinty eyed, very tight lipped expressions emerged with the verdict. The apparent ringleader, mom announced the judge's decision. "You boys are very, very lucky," blurted mom. "The judge released you to us. He said whatever punishment we decided would be far greater than anything he could impose." This can't be good. "Push that hair out of your face, mister." I slowly combed my pride and joy with my fingers and patted it back in place on the top of my head. "First things first," mom declared, "We've already decided. You're all going for haircuts."

"I rather go to jail." mumbled Mark.

"This is not debatable, Mark. I don't need any more of this long hair nonsense from you. Do you understand me?" Missus Madden was irate. My best friend was inconsolable.

The length of my hair was the least of my problems. The penalty for committing mortal sin in the Carroll house has escalated to screaming, hellfire and brimstone, which in some states is considered mental cruelty.

Mom and Dad had decided, without my personal input that maybe, possibly, perhaps conceivably the most effective way to curb my aggressive behavior was to send me away to camp. Yeah, that should do it. Dad was thinking a week, mom suggested a year. My enterprising parents compromised on a month, but before dad drove me up state to spend half my summer with a bunch of fresh air sucking hillbillies my mother the clean freak had me scrubbing the apartment like a live-in servant. She'd enter the living room and squint in search of her mortal enemy. "You didn't get under that couch." She wasn't even in the room, but mom can hear dust collecting before it settles. "I did under the couch." She stomped her little foot. "Do it again! And don't answer me back. And get under that damn TV."

"I already did under the TV." Whack! The vicious smack to the back of my head stung her hand and messed my hair. I was still mumbling and mom was still shaking her little fingers. "Next time," she shrieked, "ya gonna' get a good hop in the ass! Now do it again!"

☙

I was staring through the windshield, bewildered, confused and downright angry. The front entrance of the camp seemed thirty feet high and topped with razor wire and there wasn't even a freaking fence. Just a sign on a poll next to a little yellow house. I think it read: WELCOME TO HELL, MISTER CARROLL.

Mom has her faults, but cooking a tasty meal on a budget wasn't one of them. On the other hand, the camp cafeteria was reigned over by a large muscular man with bulging red eyes and a shiny bald head who was constantly standing over massive iron pots with one dirty finger stuck in his nose and a smelly cigar the size of a freaking telephone pole stuck between his yellow teeth. I was a string bean when dad dropped me off and now I'm thinking I might have to drop a few pounds.

Somebody had spread a rumor that old Cookie had learned his trade as an inmate in the New York State penal system. After my very first breakfast I realized it probably wasn't a rumor. I should've insisted on having his parole revoked.

My third day of confinement began the same as the first two: angry cold and hungry, but this time my entire breakfast tray was taken away because I said a bad word when I got back to the table. Old Cookie seemed to be living up to his reputation. A freaking cockroach was doing the dead man's float in my oatmeal. "Holy shit. There's a fucking cockroach in my bowl!" My voice was barely loud enough to be heard by the big dumb kid sitting next to me, but the skinny pimple-faced female counselor behind me seemed to have the listening skills of a monster nun and my crazy mother put together.

After staring at a species that managed to stay alive through nuclear fallout, a bug that actually thrives on insecticides, I realized that old Cookie's next entree would probably send me to an early grave. I hate oatmeal anyway, but oatmeal flavored with cockroaches was enough to turn me into Kevin the explorer because Kevin the camper was about to hit the trail. I had no particular plan of escape, but I knew I wouldn't be staring into a bowl of death in the morning. That's the plan. Something will come to me. I think. I'm pretty sure.

♣

Day four, crack-a-dawn. I was leaning back at the edge of the jetty, watching the sun rise, feet dangling above clear blue water, eyes staring beyond my prison of green in the black mountains of Mordor. Breaking out of this hell-hole and getting back home to hang out with my friends was an obsession enabling my devious mind to think with decisive clarity. But there were a few minor complications. I don't know where I was. I was seventy-five miles from home and I still can't fly. When I finally envisioned a plan of escape it wasn't exactly a masterstroke of the human spirit, but absolutely doable. Just leave. That's the plan. **Might need a little help here, Lord.**

The early morning stillness before mandatory wake-up was the perfect time for the perfect crime. Nobody about but me and the early birds pecking the early worms. I casually strolled towards the front entrance when The Lord suddenly gave me a sign and a plan. An old girl's bicycle lying in the weeds by the little yellow house was whispering my name. I hear you. **Thank You, baby Jesus.**

With seventy-five cents in my pocket and the good sense the Lord gave me buried in the deepest hole of my subconscious I mounted that ratty old miracle and headed for home.

I quickly raced to an adjoining road, pedaling faster and faster as if the cops were hot on my heels, but nobody was there except the monster in my head, and this guy was a whole lot scarier than Sister Mary Monster. Second thoughts were infecting my brain like mathematical equations. Follow the sun? Which way is the wind blowing? Look for the North Star. What the hell is the Taconic State Parkway? Signs everywhere leading nowhere and massive trees as far as the eye could see.

The next road was even bigger, and cars were speeding past me in a blur. Lunch time had come and gone and hunger pangs were twisting my stomach, diminishing my enthusiasm and causing my clouded brain to rethink my options. Cookie's roach infested oatmeal was already floating around my head disguised as a plate of mom's lasagna.

Well, not really, but I was freaking starved and ready to chew off my damn foot. The bright yellow ball in the sky seemed like the jaundiced eye of a fire breathing monster. **Dear God. A few clouds would not dampen my spirits.** The sun continued to blister my skinny pink torso. That seventy-five cents was now burning a hole in my pocket as I raced towards a sign on the side of the road, WHITEY'S ICE CREAM PARLOR. A big bowl of ice cream would be like a seven course meal. The sign practically grabbed me by the handle and dragged me into the store like a five-star chef holding up a veal cutlet parmesan hero.

After five hours of furious pedaling the wooden bench in front of the store seemed the perfect place to rest my sweaty bones. I devoured the chocolate ice cream cone so fast, anyone watching would've thought I dropped it on the floor so I bought another, this one vanilla.

I love vanilla. Why didn't I get two freaking vanillas? I'm so confused.

Within minutes I re-mounted and searched up and down, north and south, east and west in order to gain a sense of direction and make certain the coast was still clear. The coast was still clear. No snakes, bears or raccoons, no pimply faced counselors, no giant nuns and no dumb cops.

I was back on the road for less than a mile, but my body was already drained of every ounce of enthusiasm. I was practically praying for the back seat of a highway patrol car to rest my skinny ass as the high noon sun continued its assault.

The sweltering heat was now pushing my exhaustion towards total collapse, plus the constant fear of being flattened by a speeding Plymouth. Destination signs were still passing and still giving no clues as to my whereabouts. I was lost in the wilderness with twenty-five cents in my pocket and a stolen bicycle under my dumb skinny ass.

My frantic pedaling was still pushing me faster and faster in my head, but my numb, weary legs were actually moving slower and slower. The sun was so freaking hot, but I was no longer sweating. I was so tired. It was so damn hot… I just wanted to fall… asleep…

"Kevin."

Was it an echo… of a whisper… "Kevin… "floating through one ear… "Kevin."… out the other? Is someone calling me inside my head? "Kevin… " The echo drifted away… and back. "Kevin… " The echo pulsed louder, the voice coming faster and going, "Kevin." Faster. Time… stopped… eyes. "Kevin," open…

The fluorescent lights above illuminated the first signs of peril, the second, mom's voice. "Kevin… you awake?" My eyes were open, but I still couldn't fathom my surroundings, and what the hell is mom's voice doing inside my brain? And why is that damn light so bright? I'll tell you why. You can't conduct a first class interrogation without bright lights. "Kevin. Can you hear me?"

"Lemme see, Eve. Luke. Can you hear me, son?" Dad's soothing tone was a welcome embrace compared to the panic spinning around my head, but I still couldn't clear the cobwebs. "Luke?" Dad's face was a blur. The blur quickly vanished and a darker blur appeared above me. From inside the dark blur a stream of a light shined directly into my

149

brain. "Let's get a look see… I believe this here child gonna be just fine, Mister and Missus Carroll." Just fine? Who the hell is this freaking old dark blur, anyway? Does she have any idea?

After being held against my will for three torturous days and nights I had finally stolen a ratty old bicycle and peddled it fifty-six miles like a fugitive from justice in ninety-five-degree heat and apparently in the wrong freaking direction until I fell unconscious on the side of the road from ingesting ice cold ice cream, which rapidly passed through my undernourished, overtaxed and probably contaminated digestive system. An ambulance then picked my red roasted carcass off the road, drove it six miles further from my friends to a hospital where I laid in coma for twenty-two hours. I'm not fine you freaking angel of stupidity. My mom will be blasting the whole ridiculous scenario into the side of my head until I get married. I'd rather stay in a peaceful freaking coma.

The interrogation after the investigation was still in the preliminary stages. I slumped in the back seat of the car and awaited the onslaught. "You're not going out for a whole year." And for the next two very exhausting hours mom blasted away with both barrels. "Your father and I paid good money to send you away to that damn camp for a month and you run away after three damn days? Are you crazy?" Dad appeared dazed as he stared out the windshield. He shook his head and prayed for silence. "That's enough, Eve. It's been a very long week." Her relentless bombardment was an impressive display of stamina. A smoker could never build up this kind of lung capacity. "If you think for a second that you're going home to play with your friends you have another thing coming, mister." Over and over for the entire ride home, but one question kept spinning around my exhausted brain like a pizza pie. What's for dinner? I could eat a chipmunk. I mean cheeseburger.

16

My seventh grade teacher wasn't a nun, but that doesn't mean he wasn't just as crazy. In fact, Mister Balboa served up old time Christian behavior modification with the brutality of a young Roman centurion. My latest educational irritant bared an uncanny resemblance to Wimpy from Popeye, and with the same cheeseburger diet he developed a short squat frame just south of his little pea brain.

The pimply faced gas station gangsters were all still together and yours truly still the primary target for all the usual slap-happy corporal humiliation.

Although I still had the quickest mouth in the class, I now managed it sparingly and usually with great caution. "Mister Hurley, what is the capital of Vermont?" The Howdy Doody look-a-like gazed towards the heavens without a prayer, so when nobody answered Alfred quickly turned his desperation in the other direction. But the devil was still busy with me so he used my big mouth to lend a helping hand. "Montpelier." I was trying to whisper from two aisles away, but long distance whispering was never my strong suit.

If old bubble butt Balboa wasn't absolutely certain as to the exact location of the meddlesome voice, it didn't much matter because my presence in the general vicinity was usually enough to turn my hands into raw hamburger. "Mister Carroll?" The little man was barely tall enough to spot me from his standing position in front of the classroom. He quickly opened his desk drawer, grabbed his handy attitude adjuster and strode with his usual arrogant determination towards the disturbance. Balboa was so fond of his little green rod that he actually gave it a name. "Herman" was an inch around and the length of a ruler and Herman was brought to bear at the first utterance of voluntary stupidity.

"Do you have an opinion on this subject, Mister Carroll?" Of course I have opinion on this subject. I have an opinion on everything, ya fat bastard. "Stand up, Mister Carroll and stick out your hand." My left hand was about to pay the price for being attached to a big mouth. A protective rigidity coursed my entire body as I nervously extended a solid ball of taught bone. "Open your hand, Mister Carroll. And remember, if you flinch we start over." Every nerve in my body pulsed as I awaited a series of blows that would split knuckles like a razor across a fat lady's ass. I slowly turned up my palm. He quickly went into action. Whack! Whack! My hand snapped back as a red welt obliterated the life line. Eyes ablaze kept a steady glare as my mouth twisted a grotesque line of anger, but not a peep escaped my teeth that were clenched like a steel trap. "Put it out, Mister Carroll." Whack! Whack! Whack! Whack!

The anger management portion of my nervous system alerted my brain which pulled a blistering piece of flesh from a stove, but the heat on my palm was nothing compared to the fire in my eyes. "I'll tell you when I'm done, Mister Carroll." No you won't, you fat bastard. You're done. The words were right on the tip of my big mouth, but the teacher was apparently on the verge of insanity and one peep could push him over the edge. I managed the middle digit with my eyes and if I had the size I'd still be kicking his fat stupid ass down Castle Hill Avenue. "Sit... and if I hear your smart aleck mouth once more you'll be sitting in Mother Anastasia's office for the rest of the year." I rather go to jail, ya fat tub-a-shit.

Baseball's my favorite sport, but it was impossible to get more than a few guys together on any given day, so like everybody else in the neighborhood, basketball became my primary source of exercise. Everybody I knew played round ball, so pickup games in the park or Saint John's school yard were as common as troublemaking. Almost. Saint John Vianney hadn't yet developed a sports program except for dumb gym class, and dumb gym classes don't count.

Benny Russo was the best athlete in the school and Chris Carpenter the best basketball player in sixth grade. The two of them got a bunch of us together in an effort to start a basketball team, and together they also persuaded Mister Balboa to be the coach. Balboa wasn't my first choice. I'd rather have a giant nun punching me in the face for forty minutes, but when he wasn't knocking somebody around the classroom old bubble butt was actually pretty good at the game.

In order to compete in the league we needed uniforms. Getting Mother Anastasia to open her Christian purse strings to buy uniforms for troublemakers was like asking her to eat kosher hot dogs on Fridays. We had a dumb fat coach, nine troublemakers and a whole lot of enthusiasm. We needed uniforms. Sounds like a job for Kevin the, aaaa, uniform getter...

Mister Balboa was babbling in front of the classroom. As usual I was staring mindlessly at a picture of planet earth in my geography book. The flashing red light above my head indicated a problem with the vacuum intake valve that feeds liquid hydrogen to the forward thrusters. I slowed Voyager back to Mach three and typed in new coordinates for an emergency landing, I'm thinking the middle of the lots or maybe the top of my building.

Denny Sullivan poked me in the shoulder and startled me awake. "Turn the page," he whispered. I turned the page that displayed the same globe split in half at the equator. The earth split in half reminded me of a basketball split in half. I'm not exactly sure how these things happened in my brain, but I was suddenly picturing the old basketball on the floor of my closet, and my old dead basketball was already enhancing a plan that was scary close to being an actual idea. The problem was a dead fuel cell. I landed on the roof and transported myself via osmosis thigg-a-magiggy back to geography class. "Mister Carroll." Mayday! Mayday! "Mister Carroll. I said take out ya history book." History book? Damn. I hope I didn't leave my freaking history book on the launch pad.

♣

I awoke just after dawn and instantly recalled my purpose. With barely enough patience checking my enthusiasm and hardly a body movement below a very still blanket, the squeaky hi-riser refused to yield under the weight of fear as I cautiously sat upright while guarding against anxious breath. Mom could sense changes in atmospheric pressure, and awake breathing is quite different from sleep mode. Mom was probably, maybe, hopefully still asleep, but you never know. A full frontal attack at six in the morning was always a possibility. I could throw a brick of firecrackers under their bed and dad wouldn't even stir. Dad's not the problem.

I crawled past their partially opened door like the shadow of a wary cat not daring to unfold until I reached the living room. From there I could sense my heart rate doubling as I entered the kitchen, better

153

known as the lock down zone. In terms of bravery under mom's restricted early morning movement policy this effort was way over the top, and considering mom's supernatural ability to hear a mouse fart in the lots, this maneuver was quite astonishing, but hardly a done deal. I had a long way to go and time like the sunrise my enemy with a slap happy right hand.

I very slowly pulled the silverware drawer without disturbance and carefully plucked the long pointy carving knife and pushed the drawer back without so much as a tinkle. I retraced my steps, slipped back under the covers and slooowly exhaled. I slipped the knife under my pillow without cutting my ear off and waited a few more minutes to make absolutely certain that mom wasn't playing possum, which happens to be her favorite exercise, catching me unaware with my back turned. Mom was obviously dead asleep because I'm still alive and breathing... normal.

I took the knife from under my pillow and quietly crawled into the back of my closet. I sat in the corner, held my old bald basketball between my knees and very carefully pierced it with the razor sharp blade like I was doing brain surgery. Kevin the surgeon continued dissecting right down the equator, one hundred and eighty degrees, but my dead orange dust-collector still resembled a live ball. A few hours later I had a new bounce in my step when I met Christopher across the street in the park.

Chris was sitting on the bench outside the park by the concrete chess tables. As I walked up he looked up. I tossed the dead basketball and when he caught it it was like the toss up that starts the action at a Knicks game. Chris stared up at the twinkle in my eye. "Where's your new ball, baby?"

From the moment I proudly strolled up to Christopher wearing my new black chinos, black suede Beatle boots and a long-sleeved black turtleneck shirt in the middle of August I was, "oh, baby."

Chris jumped up and added his mischievous grin to mine. Together we ambled past the Parker House. Chris was still examining the ball, spinning it between his hands as we walked onto the nearest court. He suddenly shot the dead ball flat footed straight through the rim where it plopped to the asphalt like a ten-pound pumpkin. "It's home, baby."

The first time Christopher strolled into Willie's luncheonette with the very same get-up I started calling him the very same thing. "What are you thinking?" The smile on my face was matched only by the

154

brilliant idea in my head. "I got a great idea, baby." But Chris had that figured out the second he squeezed my old dead basketball or else we'd already be playing basketball with my new Spalding.

As we strolled away from home court advantage I described my ingenious plan for removing sporting goods merchandise from a sporting store. Christopher thought it was the greatest idea for boosting stuff since the beginning of time when Adam bagged an apple that belonged in someone else's tree.

An hour later we casually sauntered through the front door of Modell's on Fordham Road. The dead basketball was cradled under my arm with no pressure to the outer skin so it appeared as your everyday ordinary basketball, but this old ball had as much bounce as a bag of flour.

We matched smiles with the bright-eyed salesmen on our way towards the staircase where we quickly hopped down to the team uniform section. Modell's had basketball jerseys in almost every color of the rainbow. They had red with white trim and white with red trim, blue with yellow trim and yellow with green trim, black with white trim plus ten other colorful combinations. We searched through every rack in the basement. We needed maroon and gold to start the very first ever basketball team from Saint John Vianney Cure of Ares, but they had no maroon with gold trim or gold with maroon trim so we went with the black and whites.

Chris ambled around one way, I strolled the other. Two minutes later we came together on opposite sides of the same rack. "Walk away 'til I line up the right sizes." So I slowly walked around the team uniform section like an old lady searching for bloomers in Sears and Roebuck. My partner held up a jersey and shook his head as if annoyed he couldn't find the right fit. Then he removed the hanger and then he did another and another until he gathered up all the correct sizes for all nine kids on the team. Chris held the take between the remaining stock on the rack and clapped a bunch of shirts together to secure them tight so they wouldn't fall to the floor. He was still shaking his head when he gave me the signal: he scratched his ear. My smiling partner then moseyed over to the football jerseys and proceeded to check them out like any other discerning customer in need of quality merchandise at a reasonable price which was now the second best way to get a really fantastic bargain.

I was still strolling towards the rack and casually turned the split in the basketball for easy access. "Check it out." Chris was holding up

155

an Oakland Raiders football jersey, but he was actually watching my back for store personnel. I was casually doing the same. The second he winked I tightly balled all nine jerseys together and stuffed them inside the ball with the finesse of a master magician. The next part of the plan wasn't even part of the plan. I tossed the heavy ball to Chris who tossed it right back and we kept flipping it back and forth as if it could float. With no obvious bulges under our shirts or down our pants we glided up the stairs, two at a time and strolled out the front door the same way we strolled in, smiling.

A basketball sliced half way around its equator is the greatest tool for stealing stuff since the invention of the hand gun.

We were still smiling like idiots as we hurried down Webster Avenue and continued up 188th Street, where we quickly pulled the shirts from the ball and stuffed them into a paper bag that I brought from home. Five minutes later we repeated the same process, only this time the ball was stuffed with nine pairs of silky black shorts. I love Modell's.

To say the nuns were less than enthusiastic about the new school colors would grossly understate the obvious, but they refused to buy us maroon and gold and we couldn't return the black and whites without a receipt. The Black Commandos of Saint John Vianney Cure of Ares were ready to play ball. Unfortunately, we still pretty much sucked, but we were now the scariest looking team in the league. We were already scary enough without uniforms and black seemed to highlight our felonious personalities.

The Souls were now the loudest thing around school since they dynamited to build the foundation. Paul O'Neil on drums, Vinny Maiello strumming a mean Stratocaster, Mark Madden wailing away on lead guitar, and keeping the base lines as simple as possible, yours truly.

The four of us got together every evening in Vinny's basement two block north of the projects on Homer Avenue. Hour upon hour we practiced The Beatles, Stones, The Animals, Bee Gees and The Rascals, and after all the tedious months of rehearsing we finally realized we could play these songs in our sleep. It was time to take the show on the road. Or anyplace with electricity other than Vinny's basement.

It was lunch time, normally the most productive part of my day. Mark and I were in the school playground talking band stuff as usual when we were approached by two friends from the eighth grade. Martin Cudlow and Anthony Nixon asked if we were almost ready to do an audition. We thought we were ready to play Madison Square Garden and we agreed to do a showcase.

The stage was set, the assembled committee ready, Father D'Antonio sat next to the rectory secretary Adrianna. Father Wilson sat directly behind them next to three nuns and six eighth graders. We played them our five best songs. Right after we rock n rolled all the Sinatra out of our school auditorium we were roundly applauded and invited to play our very first gig.

The anticipation leading up to The Souls' first appearance at the fifth annual Saint John's Bazaar was more exciting for me than watching the lots burn. The Souls rocked that Bazaar with classic rock n roll that wasn't even classic yet, and when it was all over we bathed in the glory of our new found fame and fortune. The Souls were now professional rock n rollers with a cool twenty-five smackers to prove it. We're gonna be freaking rich.

Vinny seemed unusually quiet and even distracted after the show. After we returned to his basement and unloaded the equipment our rhythm guitarist told us why. Vinny said that his good friend Johnnie had approached him after he stepped away from the stage and Johnnie asked him to join his band. Johnnie is the drummer and leader of The Ghost Raiders. Vinny said the idea of playing lead guitar with his closest buddy in an established band with a drummer as great as Johnnie was really exciting and there wasn't much to talk about it after that.

The only member of the band not pissed about the sudden departure of a key member of the group was Mark because Mark already had a great solution. Mark's older brother Mickey was equally if not more talented on rhythm guitar. According to Mark his brother was very interested in joining him in The Souls. Mark's brother was already in high school. Mickey was also pretty smart. Mickey Madden took control of all band business, which suddenly included finding us a new place to practice.

At six foot four Alex Berry was the perfect classmate to play center on Saint John's basketball team. Al loved music and trouble, so when Mickey asked him if we could use his empty basement for band practice Al assured Mickey that he'd ask his parents. Al said that his mom and dad gave him everything he wanted. Al came through. Alex said his mom and dad didn't care who he brought into the basement as long as he made sure that we didn't burn the house down. And why should that be a concern? Mister and Missus Berry don't even know me yet.

Homer Avenue was now the loudest block in the Castle Hill area because big Alex Berry and Vinny Maiello were next door neighbors. "Lemme get a little more volume."

"Excuse me!... ..what?"

Mickey soon recruited a friend of a friend from Saint Raymond's High school. Big Bobby Murphy is a drummer and Murph was also friends with everybody in The Souls. Murph told us that he had practiced a few times with this really exceptional organist who had been playing for ten years. Murphy explained that Bobby Perillo was sort of shy and somewhat introverted and not really interested in playing in a group, but Murphy finally convinced Perillo that The Souls might be a great way to break out of his parent's basement and into the exciting world of rock n roll. Murphy also assured Perillo that we wouldn't beat him up. Within a few weeks Murph talked Perillo in off the ledge so the organist finally came down to Al's basement for a highly anticipated audition escorted by big Bobby Murphy for protection.

He looked a little freaky with his shaggy black bangs, black horned rim glasses, and he seemed a little freaky because he hardly spoke, but Bobby Perillo didn't actually get freaky until he sat behind that organ. Bobby Perillo was a player and a music reading artist and fortunately for The Souls he liked everything he heard. So did we.

A few months after that we were ready to play again, this time with an organist with a shiny new outlook. The Souls treated Bobby 'Pupus' Perillo like a long lost brother and he treated us to rock n roll played on a monster Hammond organ that sounded like a ten-piece band.

We started our tour of the Bronx on Morris Park Avenue. The tiny Our Lady of Solace Grammar School auditorium could hardly contain the yelling and manic applause from the opening song 'til we walked off the stage at the end of the show.

Next on the New York tour was the Mount Saint Michael's Valentine's Day Mixer. The high school dance was widely publicized with posters in local stores and church bulletins, and with all the teenage chatter we mixed in over three thousand screaming rock n rollers like sardines into the massive gymnasium. The place went wild when we opened the show with one of my new personal favorites, In the Midnight Hour, by The Young Rascals. We ended our night by getting a raucous call back and sent the crowd home smiling with House of the

Rising Sun by the Animals. Electricity was still buzzing through the massive building when the curtain came down. We were still laughing when we drove away in the truck, but it wasn't until we played the big battle of the bands when The Souls became neighborhood favorites and the band with the wild dancing bass player. I didn't even know I could dance.

The big spring dance and band competition in nearby Saint Raymond's Girls High School Auditorium was drawing attention from all corners of the Bronx, and when it came time we filled that venue with enough project kids so when the master of ceremonies asked for applause to determine the best band, it wasn't even close. The Souls ran away with the two hundred smackers for first prize. I wasn't sure if we were the best band, but when we split the cash it didn't matter. We were playing in a rock n roll band and making money. I love freaking money.

♣

I was finally fifteen years old and on my way to Crazy George's Diner on Westchester Avenue and I wasn't even hungry. Okay, I'm always hungry. But Mark was quitting his job as the clean-up boy and our plan was for me to apply for the position. Some might consider my application tactics as more of the same old stupidity. It certainly is debatable. I'm personally thinking heroic.

Crazy George's Diner was located under the Zerega Avenue train station along Westchester Avenue. The wages for scrubbing the giant pots and pans and the smelly toilet bowl was a dollar an hour. Mark was using every penny earned to buy equipment for the band, but Crazy George was already driving Mark crazy, so my best friend decided to retire. I decided that mopping Crazy George's floors was probably better than my present summer job of walking ten bottles of milk up five flights of stairs for five dollars a night. Strolling to the milk factory on Hermany Ave in the middle of the night wasn't exactly a walk in the park. A doogan (young helper) will work like a dog for whatever it takes to empty the truck, sometimes seven or eight hours.

Mark's last day a Saturday was also pay day. When I walked into the empty restaurant just before closing time in the early evening Crazy George was getting crazy because Mark did a real crappy job of mopping the floor, on purpose.

159

As I sat at the empty u-shaped counter Crazy George was yelling from the kitchen when he suddenly jutted his big angry face around the doorway. "Mop it again," he snarled, "or you're not getting a fucking nickel." Mark slammed the bathroom door, walked around the counter and whispered as Crazy George continued his tirade inside the tiny kitchen. "He said he's not paying me unless I mop the floors again." I stared at Mark, he stared at me. We glared at the doorway as Crazy emerged from the kitchen slapping a meat cleaver the size of a freaking tennis racket on his palm. "I'm not gonna repeat myself. Mop it again or you will not get paid." Crazy pointed a big hairy finger towards me, seated and already smoldering on the other side of the counter. "You can wait outside, ya girlfriend still has a lotta work to do."

I was already mad because my best friend was pissed about Crazy's verbal assault so I didn't move a muscle, except the one that contorts my brain before it explodes. Crazy George was losing his patience while mine was being tested like a burglar in a bank vault. "Why don't ya just pay him so we can get outta here, ya fat bastard." Professional bank burglars probably have a lot more patience than annoying teenage troublemakers.

Crazy rushed around the counter as I sat shaking with fear, but too defiant to move. He quickly grabbed me up by the collar and tossed my skinny ass out the door like a rag doll. I lay sprawled on the concrete, momentarily stunned, but quickly re-armed my mouth. "Ya dumb fat bastard!" But crazy George was already back inside and couldn't hear so I decided to open up the front window. I rushed over and grabbed an empty metal milk crate from the stack next to the garbage cans. Then I marched back to the middle of the diner, spun like an Olympic discus athlete and flung that baby for gold right through the biggest window in front of the store. CRASH! Take that!

Mark ran out the door shaking his head, eyes begging a thousand questions, but managed only one. "Are you fucking crazy?" As usual his question was rhetorical in nature, but considering we were both staring wide-eyed at crazy George's newly air conditioned restaurant I guess I could admit to some disturbing feelings of anxiety, but this was no time for a good cry because my focus was suddenly staring wide-eyed at a much greater problem: a patrol car happening by on the way to the next bakery screeched to a stop at the curb. The passenger door flung open. A dark blue officer abruptly unfolded from the front seat like a giant stick figure. The officer sauntered behind the car while slapping his trusty night stick on the palm of his hand. He calmly studied the scene of the crime, big hole in a window, two nervous delinquents looking at the hole. No words, just the steady slap of intended possibilities.

His crime busting partner was still struggling from the vehicle like an awakening mastodon. The light blue blimp finally wiggled free from the hole crushed deep in the front seat, straightened up, took a life-sustaining breath and finally settled a meaty hand on the reason cops don't need to be in shape: a thirty eight special filled with very fast bullets. I had no intention of running for my life and leaving my best friend to answer for my stupidity. I'm actually quite experienced giving my own stupid explanations.

Crazy George rushed out the door, the milk crate hanging from one fist while the other was shaking a threat in the air. "Don't try to run you little shit head!" I had no intention of leaving yet. I wasn't quite finished being an idiot. Crazy was cursing and shouting. I was yelling and screaming and the craziness went on and on because a few minutes was all crazy George needed to obtain his objective. Mark's dad suddenly squealed to a stop on the corner and jumped from the family Chevy and glared at the guilty party, and if there was the slightest bit of hope in his eyes it went right over my head.

According to Mark his dad says I'm out of control. His deep baritone voice could scare the crap out of a mafia hit man. Mister Madden left no doubt as to who he came to rescue. "This is my son here," he growled as he yanked Mark to his side. "You can take that other one to jail." Mark's dad was now on the record. "That Carroll kid is nothing but trouble."

Mark's dad and Crazy were still yapping away as they walked towards the car. Mark was already sitting within swatting distance in the front seat. Crazy and Mark's dad continued talking through the front window when the Saint Johnny on the spot holy man to the rescue pulled to the curb in front of the restaurant. Father Wilson exited his car with a swirl and a flourish of his long flowing black cape and an anxious look on his face. Crazy marched away from the car and into the diner while Father quickly floated up to the driver's side window and never opened his mouth. When Mister Madden finished his brief and very animated tirade he sped away as fast as he came. Father was left at the curb holding the bag and his chin.

"What's going on, officers?" pondered the kindly parish problem

161

solver. The cops were still unscrambling their blue brains when Crazy George walked out the front door with a garbage can full of giant glass shards and slammed it on the sidewalk. "We had a little misunderstanding here, Padre," his anger somewhat subsided as he insinuated my involvement with a glare. "I'm sure we can work something out, here" implored Father. Crazy was now staring wide eyed at my holy advocate as if Father was crazier than me and Father was only throwing out options as opposed to metal milk crates. Father begged again, "His parents are really fine God fearing people. I'm hoping for their sakes we can work something out here." Crazy George seemed to be wearing down from the full court press. "If you can see it in your heart, maybe Kevin could work this off. He really is a good kid." Father better go to confession. Now he's just making shit up.

Crazy was now staring me in the eye. He needed a cleanup kid by Monday afternoon. A crazy clean-up kid might just be the right way to go. "I take all his wages until he pays for the window. If he's a worker, I'll keep him on. If not, he goes after he pays for his dumb mistake." Though stern in the eye, Crazy actually sounded encouraging.

Crazy George hurried over to the curb and shook hands with New York's hungriest. After a good laugh the smiling blue freak show drove away, probably to a real emergency, the box of mixed donuts screaming for help at the Chatterton Bakery. Father and Crazy then strolled around the corner. A minute later they strolled back and explained the whole deal. "Mister Blah, Blah is giving you a break, Kevin," said father, "So you have to blah, blah, blah and make sure you're not late and blah, blah, blah… .blah blah, blah." Crazy extended his hand to lock the deal while Father patted me on the head.

This could be the start of whole new career. I'm thinking demolition expert. Or maybe broken window fixer upper.

The lessons of the whole crazy day weren't actually that crazy after all. Okay, they were probably pretty crazy, but I learned a few things, too. I learned that first impressions are very misleading. I realized that hard work rarely goes unnoticed. But the most important lessons were learned by merely observing the boss. During that very first week Crazy George worked my fat ass for twenty hours and exercised it into a skinny ass. Saturday evening he smiled and handed me a whole twenty-dollar bill. "You're a good kid, Kevin, no matter what they say. Keep your head down and your nose clean and my restaurant spotless and you and me will get along famous."

"Wow." I was still examining the crisp twenty-dollar note when my happy grin expanded way beyond normal capacity. I'm gonna be rich. "Thanks."

Working at Crazy George's Diner taught me that elbow grease and not Brillo pads was necessary for cleaning the crusty lasagna pans. Growing the nail on the index finger extra-long was necessary for scratching the shit stains that stick under the rim of the toilet bowl. When Crazy saw me once again using Ajax and a scrub brush, he said, "Try the fingernail. I told ya, it works like a charm." I learned that truck drivers have a lot of sex with cheap whores, and I learned how to curse in Greek. My new job taught me that metal milk crates were necessary for carrying fresh milk and not for sports. Crazy George also taught me that tolerance of stupidity and understanding of human frailty are just two possible means towards building a friendship. Who needs an education? By the time I left Crazy George's Diner a year later I had a Ph.D. in how to succeed in the grown up world, and I learned it all from my new friend, Mister George Andropolos.

17

Why was it necessary so to further a good Catholic School education? I sat for hours mostly doodling cartoons while everyone else was taking the high school entrance examination. I refused to prolong the agony one more minute when the last nine and a half years were so annoying. So when the scores finally came in I wasn't surprised that I failed with flying colors, but dad was still optimistic. According to dad all was not lost. I thought I won. No more Catholic school.

Dad suggested that some of the public vocational schools were perfect for a kid like me. He didn't mean annoying troublemakers who preferred traveling to the outer solar system on regularly scheduled visits, but rather kids with other talents. I was pretty good in art, and just like my Uncle Joe I drew the nativity scene in colored chalk on the blackboard in Miss Moran's sixth grade class. Dad thought my artistic aptitude might possibly, hopefully, maybe open the door to the exciting world of mechanical drafting. I would've never thought of it myself. The man had waaay too much faith, and considering mathematics is prerequisite to enter that particular field, dad was probably a bigger daydreamer than me, but I gave it a shot anyway. A little one. One you couldn't even measure with a freaking micrometer.

Graduation from eighth grade came two years later than legally possible, but actually right on time. The accomplishment was exhausting for mom, satisfying for dad and after ten years of Christian behavior modification I thought the diploma to mark the achievement should've come with a purple heart, or at least a check for damages. Nevertheless, my escape did come with compensation from other sources.

Relatives and family friends thought my promotion was such a great triumph that they each gave me cash as a reward, and when I put it all together I had just enough to purchase my very first bass amplifier. The small Kustom amp I borrowed from a school friend needed to be returned, so my graduation money was gratefully accepted just in the nick of time.

Mark and I had been spending enough time in world famous Manny's Music Store on 48th Street in mid-town Manhattan to qualify for workmen's compensation. We would stare for hours at Gibson, Gretch, Rickenbacker, Guild and Martin guitars, plus Fender, Ampeg, Marshall and Vox amplifiers along with all the many accessories needed to be a rock star. We also knew the price of every piece of equipment in the very large showroom, but I didn't know shit about inflation.

When Mark and I last visited the store a week ago the Ampeg B-15 was one hundred and ninety-five dollars plus tax, but when I arrived alone with just enough cash to purchase one on the Monday morning after my graduation party the price had ballooned nineteen dollars. When I questioned Tommy the young salesman he told me that inflation was the reason for the higher price. "What the hell is inflation, Tommy?" Tommy wasn't exactly sure, but he was certain it would cost me another nineteen big ones at the cash register. I was devastated. I hate freaking inflation.

I stood there in shock for another ten minutes before I finally shuffled towards the exit. It was a beautiful summer morning, but not in my head. The disappointment was overwhelming until the moment I walked out the door. A little man suddenly stepped from the shadows of the recessed doorway adjacent to Manny's front entrance. He seemed like a tiny apparition in a cloud of cigarette smoke. "Hey, Kid. I'm Billy. I work in Manny's... Puff, puff. You know that. Right? Puff." I always thought the little guy was a little freaky looking with his jet black Elvis hair doo and lambchop sideburns, but up close the little guy was really freaky looking.

"Yeah... so?" He was a few inches shorter than me and was too close for comfort, but he wasn't looking at me. The weird little man was looking everywhere else. He smelled like chocolate covered tobacco. "Listen, kid. What's your name? Puff, puff." He was smoking the nub of a Camel cigarette down to his tiny yellow finger tips. "Kevin."

"Well, listen, Kevin, I saw you really wanted that B-15. Puff, puff. You don't have enough money, right? Puff."

"So... Cough!"

"So, listen. I have all kinds of amps and guitars in my apartment around the corner. If you want you can check 'em out. Puff , puff. It's all new stuff and if ya see one ya like I might even give it to ya." I was looking around for a fire extinguisher. "Can you stop, Cough! blowing that shit in my face?"

166

"Sorry."

"You mean, for free?"

Puff! "Yeah, free." This must be my lucky day. For a short walk around the block I could be stepping off the train with a new amplifier. Or lung cancer.

Freaky old Elvis and I hurried down 48th Street. We quickly turned the corner onto 7th Avenue and rushed up 47th to an old rundown tenement building in the middle of the block. He paused on the stoop and turned around to look me in the eye. "I only have fifteen minutes so we have to hurry." We hurried up five filthy flights of stairs where the little man quickly opened three different locks with three different keys and pushed the door. The first thing that hit me was the smell. Like old coffee, wet tobacco and shit. The weird little man was a freaking pig. I was still adjusting to the darkness and the odor when Elvis pulled up a badly torn shade covering his grimy kitchen window. The single stream of light was thick with dust and barely lit the room, but I could already see well enough to know that the dirty little freak wasn't bullshitting.

There was a tiny Vox, two Fender Twin Reverbs and a Marshall stack, three different Ampeg's and too many other amplifiers to count. He had a Martin acoustic, a shiny black Gibson Les Paul, a blond Rickenbacker twelve string, a blue Mosrite six string plus ten more top brand guitars all cradled on chrome stage stands. Old Elvis had a wide variety of Zildgian cymbals and blue sparkle Slingerland drums, two silver trumpets and one gold trombone hung on his dirty beige wall. The little freak had tambourines, harmonicas and hundreds of packets of guitar strings scattered about his filthy area rug. The dirty old stock guy had enough musical equipment in his tiny one room shit hole to open up Little Billy's Music Store. Without a second thought I knew exactly what I was looking at. Freaky old Elvis had been dancing Manny's musical inventory across the roof to his own private storage facility.

The place was magical except for the putrid smell. I was wide-eyed, and not because of the awful odor. The equipment covering the floor space was every young musicians dream. Freaky old Elvis locked the door, three times with different keys. "Make ya self comfortable, Kevin." There was only one possibility. I cautiously settled on a litter strewn love-seat next to a small cardboard box filled with music books. A filthy food-encrusted TV table held an ash tray the size of a freaking turkey platter and it was filled to a peak with his disgusting habit. "You look a little pale, Kevin. Can I get you a glass of water?" I was kind of thirsty, but I was imagining a gazillion roaches scurrying around his kitchen cabinets and freaky old Elvis shaking a few out of a filthy Flintstone's jelly jar. "No. I'm good. Thanks." And actually germ free until I sat on your smelly couch, ya little freak.

He was standing by an ancient Kelvinator refrigerator door when I noticed a thick textbook the size of the Manhattan Yellow Pages on the floor by my feet. Physician's Assistant/Nurse Practitioner. He called out from the tiny kitchen, "Ya know I'm studying to be a physician's assistant, Kevin." And by the time the old freak finishes this book he'll be in a nursing home and he'll probably need all this education to change his own diaper. "I give free exams and check-ups and get credit towards my degree." I didn't know what the hell he was talking about or why, but he wasn't talking music or free equipment, and the dark notion in my head quickly turned left towards a much darker reality. I wasn't' here to pick out a free amplifier. I really hate freaking surprises.

I've known fear for a long time. God demands it, Christians enforce it, but this was different. I could hear my fear. I could smell it. I could already taste the chemical bile working its way to my mouth. The visceral sensation was overwhelming, but I was not over-taxed. I wasn't ready, but I was definitely prepared.

Freaky old Elvis stepped from the kitchen wearing a sly grin on his dumb face and a stethoscope around his dirty neck. He carefully nudged between me and the box of books. My body tensed. I couldn't move. He put his sweaty little hand gently on my trembling knee and squeezed. "Kevin, why don't ya take ya shirt off so—" I shoved two hands into his chest so hard that his little legs flew over his greasy head and he collided into two very expensive guitars. He crashed to the floor with a tiny thud. In two frantic steps I was over his prone carcass and into the tiny kitchen, where I grabbed a ten inch carving knife from a sink crawling with roaches and filthy dishes.

Freaky old Elvis was already standing in the middle of ten thousand dollars worth of musical madness when I turned towards the exit. "Unlock that fucking door."

"You can't leave now, Kevin. You have to calm down."

"I will slice your mother fucking head off, you little fucking queer. UNLOCK THE FUCKING DOOR!"

This was suddenly my business. I knew it the moment his wide eyes flashed with panic while his new reality was still smacking him in the mouth. My flat facial affect showed only a resolve. I will hurt this little

168

man. He saw it the moment my crazy blue intimidators flashed red with hatred.

Freaky old Elvis very carefully backed up to the door and with three different keys opened three different locks. The little freak pulled the door wide and stepped away. "Guess where I'm going, mother fucker." I'm going to get a free amplifier. "Please, Kevin… " I threw the knife in the door and flew down the stairs. "Wait!"

A minute later I was sucking all the musical magic out of a million dollars worth of equipment when I confronted the owner of Manny's Music Store. "Your queer stockman… . just tried to… molest me." The elderly gentleman with the beautiful mane of shiny white hair stood at the cash register with his mouth open. "Who are you talking about, kid?" I was still hyperventilating. "You know who I'm talking about! Billy! I'm talking about little Billy! The stock guy!" The confusion on Manny's face was the real thing. He didn't know what the hell I was talking about. "Kid, Billy's upstairs working. Maybe you got the wrong guy."

"Billy's not upstairs because he just tried to attack me in his apartment on 47th Street." Manny turned to the intercom on the wall and pressed the button. "Billy! Come downstairs right now!" If Billy could fly he might walk down those stairs, and apparently he can. I was shocked. Manny was livid.

I frantically told Manny the entire crazy tale from the moment I walked into his store to the second his stock clerk put his hand on my knee. "Billy, what the hell is this kid talking about?" Billy managed calmness under fire like a fighter pilot. "Manny, I don't know what this kid's talking about. I was upstairs taking my coffee break." The pained expression in his eyes was disturbing, even for me. Manny finally came around the counter and put his hand on my shoulder.

I felt comfortable around Manny. I've watched him attending customers and he seemed like an old grandpa that knew his business better than most of his patrons could play their instruments. "Listen, kid. I don't know what you want, but I'll tell you what I know." Then he put the other hand on freaky old Elvis. "I've known Billy here for over thirty years and I know he would never do such a thing. So you take your story and get on out of here and don't ever come back."

I knew how it appeared. I wasn't offended, but I wasn't ready to surrender, either. I still needed a freaking amplifier and if I get off the train without one Mark will be pissed. "That's okay. I'm going around the corner to get his address. His apartment is 5B and the kitchen window faces 48th Street. Then I'm gonna get a cop."

I ran out the door and up and down the block in a frantic search for New York's finest. I was in the middle of the most heavily populated, highly protected tourist area on the planet and there wasn't a cop to be seen on the entire island of Manhattan that wasn't presently in a bakery shoving a donut in his face.

I finally raced around the entire block in an anxious quest for New York's hungriest when I passed Manny's Music Store for the tenth time. Freaky old Elvis suddenly stepped from the shadows of the doorway next to the music store. "Listen, Kevin. I'm sorry." His voice was trembling, so was his little hand as he warily pulled it from his pocket. "Please, take this."

All I wanted was an Ampeg B-15, but inflation screwed up my entire morning, though not my entire day. "It's fifty dollars. You can go across the street to Sam Ash and still have a few bucks left over." What a great guy. He squeezed my knee and it cost him fifty smackers. I should've let him squeeze both, I could've strolled off the train with an Ampeg B-15 and a shiny new Fender Jazz bass guitar.

Freaky old Elvis has left the sidewalk and in a damn freaking hurry, too, and with a little help from my little freaked-out benefactor I casually rolled my brand new graduation gift up 48th Street towards the subway. I really hate the smelly subway. Gotta love Uncle Elvis, though. So he's a little freaky. What's the big deal?

♣

Taking the bus and subway all the way downtown to Ninety-Sixth Street and Lexington Avenue just to attend Manhattan Vocational and Technical High School' home room class with Mr. Zeckowski was an abject waste of forty minutes and one seat on the overcrowded subway.

The third floor lavatory is the room where those inclined students were taught the fine art of rolling, smoking and ditching before detection the finest marijuana grown on the planet. But smoking pot was not my excuse for failing all five subjects in freshman year. Smoking pot didn't seem any smarter to me than smoking cigarettes, and I never tried that either. My excuse for total failure was being a smart ass and not attending classes because the few courses I did attend were as exciting as watching somebody pick their damn nose. I already knew how to pick my damn nose. I got a PhD in nose picking way back in fourth grade. The need for an education was still a foreign concept.

There should be a law against summer school so I instituted my own. I registered for all five subjects at James Monroe High School in the Bronx and failed to make another appearance.

♣

Birthdays were still passing as often as Halley's Comet. The eternal wait for the legal drinking age to arrive was like waiting to see pigs flying spaceships. But buying alcohol to fuel my new best distraction was as simple as finding Spanish Louie up at the stores, and finding Spanish Louie was as easy as finding the mailbox on the corner.

It was a typical Friday evening. The boys and I were sitting on the low wall along the edge of the parking lot in front of Willie's Luncheonette. We hadn't had time to get bored or even anxious before our favorite bilingual alcohol procurement specialist came a bopping across Castle Hill Avenue. Our eyes met. Spanish Louie was already smiling, stroking his wispy goatee. We came together and shook hands, already a carefully choreographed ballet, and without breaking stride my ninth floor neighbor casually peeled the bills palmed in my hand and bopped into fat Julie's Delicatessen.

The boys and I strolled around the corner to wait by Walter's Cabs. A few minutes later Spanish Louie bopped up to the cab stand with a large brown paper bag filled with four quart bottles of Colt 45. "Here jew go my frain." I smiled and handed Spanish Louie an extra dollar for underage tax. He placed the bag in my arms. "Kebing. Jew a gentleming ana scholar chip."

"Jew welcome my frain."

With an entire housing development filled with thirsty teenagers, Spanish Louie could always be found with his favorite pint bottle of Night Train whiskey sticking out of his back pocket and a big happy smile on his face. Me and the boys could be found in the parking lot right behind the stores, giggling shit faced, awaiting a better idea.

Eighteen is also the legal age for driving. I figured I'd probably see God before I ever got that old, but other options for cruising around the neighborhood were practically around the corner.

♣

Working as a doogan for the milk company had taught me lessons way beyond my years. It taught me that carrying bottles of milk up five flights of stairs was not something I'd be pursuing after high school. It taught me that my calf muscles were under-developed, and it also taught me the rudimentary skills for driving a standard shift transmission. But the best lesson learned about the milk delivery business was that you didn't need a key to start the trucks. You just push the button on the dashboard. No key? Now that's a business with an eye on the future.

Driving lessons at the milk company weren't actual lessons. I was simply observing the old milkmen. One hand was needed to pull and push the stick shifter. One foot was needed to depress the clutch pedal while keeping at least one hand on the steering wheel. Paying attention to anything on the other side of the windshield was way too much to consider. All I needed were the fundamentals.

FIRST NIGHT—OJT

Nobody was working the loading dock. Conveyor belt stopped. Trucks stocked and ready to go. A lone driver was backed into the ice house, shoveling shaved ice over the bottles of milk before heading out to the route. Most of the drivers were still inside the building tallying up the paperwork, and those that weren't, weren't paying attention to me and Chris. Christopher and I gazed at the button on the dashboard. We didn't know what we were doing, but it wasn't the first time we started an adventure without reading the manual. "I do the clutch pedal and you do the stick," I whispered. "Don't forget. We have to do it at the same time," warned Chris.

Milk trucks are equipped with one seat for the driver, but once the driver starts the route he usually folds it back in order to get in and out of the vehicle for quick house to house deliveries. We were both standing. "You ready?"

"Let's do it," urged Chris. I stretched my little leg and barely toed the clutch pedal while Chris wiggled the stick into neutral. When I pushed the button on the dashboard the ratty old truck rumbled to life like an old farm animal. Chris looked right. I glanced left. The coast was clear. We shifted that baby into first gear, KLINK! I mean reverse, and backed two feet into the fence. **Okay, Lord. I wasn't expecting You to drive, but a little help, here.** But no help. Not even a push in the right direction. "Towards me and up for first gear, baby," I instructed.

"Ya right," agreed Chris. "Do it again." We frantically readied a second attempt. This time the vehicle lurched forward and so did the entire load of milk. I turned the truck towards the gate and slowly drove out onto Hermany Avenue.

Just up the next block Castle Hill Avenue was completely deserted, the darkness bathed in a yellow haze from the old street lights. I turned right onto the avenue and was still driving past the Castle Hill Bake Shop when I noticed a dark blue van parked at the curb in front of the bakery, both rear doors wide open. "You hungry, baby?"

"Why?" said Chris. I pointed out a possible late night snack opportunity, made my very first U-turn and drove alongside the van and stopped. Chris jumped out. Three seconds later he jumped back with a smile and a large tray of fresh custard donuts. "Ya better be really hungry, baby?"

"I'm always really hungry." Christopher carefully wedged the tray high atop the cases of milk while I kept a steady gaze on the front of the store. The baker suddenly hurried out the door with another tray of fine baked goods and a weary stare at a milk truck idling next to his delivery van. "Let's get the hell outta here."

"Hey! Where you go!?"

I jumped on the clutch as Chris anxiously wiggled the shifter into first gear. We began our frantic escaped into the night. In my side view mirror the old baker was shaking his fist in the air as he hurried into the van. "Faster, baby." The transmission was straining for second gear as I pushed the gas pedal to the floor. "Second gear, baby! Second gear!"

Two hungry driver trainees were off on our very first high speed adventure. We raced towards the projects, rumbling down Castle Hill Avenue like an out of control stagecoach. The intersection at Lacombe Avenue at the southern end of the projects was deserted like everywhere else so I blew the stop sign and continued on past the long block of King David private homes on both sides of the avenue. We flew past the egg store, then the corner of Norton: the last cross street along the ever narrowing peninsula. Castle Hill Avenue was quickly turning into a trap. Within seconds we'll be staring at the concrete barrier and beyond that, the creek. We were running out of blacktop with the baker already close enough to smell his chocolate covered, yellow custard donuts.

As we passed the entrance to The Castle Hill Beach Club on the right Chris pulled the stick as I pushed the pedal for the super duper get away gear, but it didn't have one. "Sonofabitch!" A sharp, hairpin louie by the WMCA at the end of the avenue would've shifted the load and toppled the truck so we sped past our last best hope for a clean getaway. Fifty yards past no-man's land I jammed my anxious foot into the engine block. We screeched to a scary stop mere inches from the retaining wall and bailed out of the old truck like it was on fire.

Unfortunately, I still can't fly, but I was already running fast enough to leave sparks. Chris and I raced across the street and headed for the cover of the beach club. Seconds later the old baker skidded to a stop in the middle of the avenue.

Climbing over the ten foot, chain link fence by the usually deserted, heavily shaded picnic area in the back of the property early in the morning was usually a piece a cake, but once the old blue-haired grannies staked their claim with lawn chairs and a pack of cigarettes it was like trying to infiltrate an enemy encampment fortified with silver whistles and yelps. But the granny's were all still in bed like everybody else except bakers and troublemakers.

Chris and I climbed that obstacle like young Marine recruits. The old baker charged the fence and ranted, right after he caught his breath. "Summaday... umacatcher!" Yeah summer day, but not tonight.

We ran around the handball courts, arms and legs in a blur of fear, and continued onto the outfield grass of the softball field like Mickey Mantle chasing down a looooong fly ball and finally slowed down by the baby pool. We continued an easy trot towards the opposite end of the beach club where we scaled the fence and jumped to the ground and stuck a two point landing like a pair of gymnasts. "That was pretty... close," said Chris. "We're gonna need... a few more... driving lessons," I noted as I sucked every molecule of oxygen from the surrounding vegetation.

We caught our breath under the trees at the shore line of Pugsley Creek. A minute later we hurried up the block towards the avenue and peeked around the entrance to the beach club. The bakery van was gone. We walked to the middle of Castle Hill and watched the taillights as they were passing Lacombe Avenue on his way back to the store. "He's leaving," I noted "What if he calls the cops?" said Chris. "The cops are half asleep, but if it comes over the air as a donut heist this place will look like the parking lot of the 43rd precinct."

"Good point," agreed Chris. "Let's move."

We raced along the fence line in the shadows of the beach club.

174

When we reached the milk truck we quickly inspected the area. The coast was clear, no cops, nuns or milkmen and no little Italian bakers. Chris reached high over the stacked cases of milk and pulled the tray of freshly baked donuts that were still wedged between the metal cases. "He was so pissed he forgot his donuts," laughed Chris. "Maybe he just couldn't see that high?" I suggested. Chris stuck his finger into the center of the chocolate icing and shoved the whole thing into his mouth and chewed everything but the finger. My buddy smiled, the yellow custard filling his mouth, oozing onto his chin. "You're a dick." I stated. "Ya mudder," Chris mumbled.

"You wanna drive this time?" Chris jumped out the door and ran around the rear of the truck because the front of the truck was practically kissing the concrete barrier. I slipped around the stick shifter to the passenger side. Chris grabbed the steering wheel and peered through the windshield towards the blackness of the river, hand over hand turning the wheel in exaggerated circles. Chris then grabbed and giggled the stick shifter. His imagination roared to life as he throttled into high gear like an Indy race driver. "Rrrrrrrrrrrrrrrrr."

"So, asshole. Ya wanna drive?" Chris reached back for another donut. "I just did," he laughed. "Now let's get the fuck outta here before we get busted." We each grabbed a quart of milk in one hand and three donuts in the other and walked along the avenue like we owned it. "The cops will owe us big time when they find that tray."

"We should've parked it outside the 4-3 while they were still warm," noted Chris, "we could've been heroes."

"Maybe next time."

Probably not.

18

With a housing development full of young girls, finding one with an appetite for an up and coming rock star who has tendencies towards unconventional education was one of my top priorities. Ellen Flax emerged as a redheaded dream with the patience for such a task and, if you can believe it, a part time librarian. I love the library. I go there all the time. "Excuse me. Is Ellen here?" I mean do you have War and Peace? By, what's his name?

At five foot eight, Ellen is tall and her long red hair enhanced by a beautiful Irish smile and a lean well-proportioned frame that every project kid was gazing at from a distance.

The Mount Saint Ursula Girls High School dance was the latest gig for the band. The Souls were the entertainment and the only girl in the building worth entertaining was standing just to the right of the stage. Ellen and her best friend Lily were the tallest girls in the crowd, and Ellen was paying enough attention to me to qualify as my parole officer.

After we broke down the equipment Ellen came up onto the stage and planted a kiss on my cheek. "You were great," she applauded. Her smile didn't lie. I was in love with a big gorgeous redhead with a great kisser and a pair of legs that stopped just below her neck. Being a teenager was finally worth the pimples.

Boredom is a main contributor towards troublemaking, and at sixteen years old there was plenty of down time leading to some very disturbing choices. It was an unusually warm summer evening. Some of the local talent were hanging around the front of Willie's luncheonette in hopes of a brilliant suggestion and Derrick Warlord just happened to have one. Joe the Swede O'Leary and Charlie Deneane were all ears and I was pretty anxious myself as the three of us listened to Derrick's alternative to the malaise of late summer.

With a name like Warlord, crazy came with the moniker. Crazy Derrick, whose dad is Scottish and mom, Filipino looks Chinese, with slanted, half squinty eyes always on the prowl for the next rush of adrenaline. Joe O'Leary, who is all Irish, was the perfect complement for Derrick's crazy schemes. Why do they call Irish Joe the Swede? I thought it was because he was freaking nuts. Together or separate, Joe and Derrick made my exploits look like a handbook for the Boy Scouts. I was getting into trouble, they were finding new ways of inventing the word insanity. "You know," informed Derrick, "the workers in the library get paid in cash and they keep the money in the safe under the counter from the night before." The Swede nodded. "City workers get paid on Fridays."

"How the hell do you know when they get paid, Derrick?" I demanded. "You don't believe me?" I was shaking my head. "No. My girlfriend works in the library, Derrick, and I'm pretty sure she gets paid by check."

"Well my mother is friends with the head lady, and my mother said the workers get paid in cash because it's cheaper for the city." I glared at Derrick. Derrick smiled at Swede. "You're an idiot, Swede," I mocked. "No, he's right." At six foot two the Swede was taller than all of us by a lot, his brilliant green eyes wide with enthusiasm. "I seen it myself last week."

"You trying to tell me you were hanging around the library, Swede?" Joe quit school two years ago. It sounded like a stupid idea, but even a dumb attempt at something would be better than doing nothing in front of Willie's luncheonette.

The library was right around the corner in the basement of the Food Fair Supermarket in the middle of the projects.

Derrick had previously flipped the lock on the window inside the library and Swede had already unscrewed the heavy metal mesh that protects the outside of that same window from vandals. All we needed now was a vehicle big enough to haul away a small safe, and considering that I was the only one with recent driving experience, I elected myself as the official getaway driver. "I know where we can get a truck."

The big gate at Hermany Farms was wide open as usual and the area inside the chain link fence completely deserted. I casually strolled onto the property like a very young milkman anxious to start my route. I stepped into the first truck in line and within seconds I was pulling it onto Hermany Avenue. Two minutes later I parked the empty milk truck by the emergency exit in the rear of the library, stepped out and calmly walked around. Nothing to see here.

The four of us sauntered about the immediate area to make sure the coast was clear. No cops, no nuns or milk men and no librarians. We're good to go.

Charlie watched from Cincinnatus Avenue by the entrance to the parking lot while the three of us slithered under the security gate and then through the small window. With the get-a-way vehicle at our backs, no one in the area could see us before Charlie would spot them. Swede, the tallest stood on tippy toes and peered out the window. Derrick and I hurried around the counter and quickly rolled the small safe towards the emergency exit. A sign above the push handle on the door warned, ALARM WILL SOUND WHEN OPENED, but Derrick had previously investigated the area and saw the sign, so we planned on being fast. By the time the cops get the call over the air and dust the powdered sugar off their uniform shirts, the plan was to already be in the lots and dividing up the big library payroll. That's the plan.

Swede concentrated a steady green gaze out the window and patiently awaited the signal to go: Charlie passing without a cop attached to his wrist. "We're good," whispered Swede. "Remember, fast. I hit the door, start the truck and you guys get it in the back."

"Let's do it," said Derrick. I pushed the handle and the door opened without so much as a squeak. I hurried through the passenger side of the truck and jumped in behind the wheel. Derrick and Swede quickly rolled the small safe down the sidewalk towards the rear of the vehicle. When I looked over my shoulder through the body of the truck the boys were already grumbling. I started the engine with an educated finger. "One, two," and by three Derrick was already pissing and moaning. "Holy fuck!" They were still shouldering the safe against the lip of the bumper and finally managed it up and into the truck. "Get in," I ordered. Swede and Derrick were already on their backs behind me, huffing and puffing like under-developed weight lifters. Charlie hurried through the passenger door. I flipped the emergency brake and slowly drove through the parking lot behind the stores and carefully exited onto Randall Avenue.

Two minutes later we're in the middle of the lots, twenty feet from Big Jumbo: my favorite two-story granite hangout. The tiny Rock of Gibraltar is thirty feet high at one end and tapered at the other so you could step onto it without tripping.

Getting the safe out of the truck was a piece a cake. We slid it out the back door, crashed it on the bumper and it shook the earth when it fell to the ground. The four of us were now staring at what looked like a solid piece of hardened steel without a clue as to how to get it open. All smiling turned to serious reflection. "What the hell do we do now, Swede?" I wondered. "My father's got a big chisel and hammer," said Derrick. "That's good, dick-head. Maybe we can chisel it open before Christmas?"

"Look," said Swede, "there's a lot of fucking money in this damn thing and were gonna get it open if we have to throw it off the twenty story building. "I'll be right back," promised Derrick.

Five minutes later, Derrick was back with a smile, a solid looking chisel and promising sledge hammer. "Alright," cheered Swede. "Let's get started." Derrick placed the point of the chisel on the dial and banged away for five minutes before giving way to exhaustion. Swede, the biggest and strongest didn't do a whole lot better. Charlie took his turn, but the only difference after he pooped out was another hundred scratches in the gray paint. Whacking away with a furious attack, I focused every stroke like a diamond cutter with a pile driver. After five more minutes of frustration I slammed the chisel and hammer onto the safe. "What do we do now, asshole?"

Eight bright eyes concentrated the power of four criminal minds as we gazed at the conundrum like an idiot staring at a science test. Charlie was kicking through the weeds around the base of Big Jumbo and suddenly picked up a rock the size of a basketball. The three of us were suddenly smiling as if Charlie had figured out the combination. "What do ya think?" said Charlie. "I think it's Swede's turn," I informed the mob. Swede picked up the combination rock/safe cracker and held high over his head and suddenly slammed mighty stone onto the safe. His very first attempt was the first sign of hope. "You're a fucking genius, Charlie," congratulated Derrick. He completely crushed the silver dial. "Holy shit!" noted Swede. "It made a dent."

My entire body coursed with enthusiasm as I picked up the rock and struggled it up to my shoulder. The veins in my neck were probably blue from the lack of oxygen. I felt like a ninety seven pound weakling trying to clean and jerk five hundred pounds and finally managed it over my head and brought it down with a vicious thud that connected to the same dial that was keeping me from my freaking money. "We're gonna be rich!" cheered Charlie. I split the silver dial right in half, but my attempt also split the safe cracker in half. "We need bigger rocks," suggested Swede. Derrick and Charlie were already tramping through the weeds and quickly found two more hefty sized granite safe crackers and for the next three hours we pummeled that safe with enough explosive force to cause an earthquake.

With every new crash the safe was showing additional signs of stress. It was actually coming apart from the hinges. "We almost got it," I applauded. The heavily damaged door was hanging together by the slimmest of prayers. **Okay, Lord. A small electrical bolt from the sky would really brighten my prospects for the future. And if You could concentrate on the bottom hinge.** But, no lightning. Not even a little static surge.

Swede was now wandering along the edges of Big Jumbo, kicking through the weeds when he squatted and lifted a giant boulder, twice the size of anything attempted. The strain of a thousand pounds of granite was pouring down his face. The weight hung between macaroni legs as he staggered towards the encased fortune that was up until now, a dream. "If this don't do it," he grunted, "we can all go home."

The battered safe was looking more like a battleship used for target practice. The top hinge was pleading for mercy. Swede dropped the rock on the ground and jumped up and straddled the edges of the safe, standing above the criminal element like Superman. "Gimme that damn rock." Charlie and I took one side each and placed the massive boulder on the safe between his feet. A few deep breaths later, and Joe 'The Swede' O'Leary was ready to chew glass. He squatted over the boulder and in one fluid motion lifted up and held it high over his head. The three of us stared up at the awesome display. "Don't hit ya feet, asshole!" I warned. "Don't make him laugh, you stupid fuck!" cried Derrick. Joe suddenly split his legs to the sides of the safe and crashed the boulder onto the bottom hinge with the explosive force of nitroglycerin. The sound ricocheted off 2125 Randall Avenue and back again.

Fireflies flickered above the getaway milk truck that stood out like a silent billboard for whiter teeth and stronger bones. "Okay, assholes," I ordered. Let's pull it off and see what we got."

"He did it!" cheered Derrick. It took another hour, but we finally maneuvered the battered safe door just enough to squeeze my arm in down to the shoulder. I felt around the bottom. "Will you hurry the fuck up!" pleaded Swede. I pulled out two black and white composition note books. Swede was shaking his head. "Will you please get the fucking money."

"I don't wanna cut my damn arm off, asshole!" I grabbed onto a small metal box that was just large enough to contain the payroll and small enough to squeeze through the hole. My stomach was already churning with thoughts of despair. For a vessel containing thousands of dollars it seemed unusually light. "Grab the corner, Derrick," I pleaded. My elbow cleared the safe wall and my hand was still underneath the box when Derrick grabbed hold of the partially exposed fortune and pulled it out and held it up to the collective gasps of four exhausted safecrackers. Derrick rattled the box. It didn't sound promising. He pushed the little button on the side and flipped open the lid. "You're a fucking dick, Derrick!" I condemned. I snatched the box and shook the contents onto my cupped palm, two nickels, one dime and three fucking pennies. "You really are a big dick, Derrick."

CRIMINAL ACTIVITY 101: Inside information should actually be obtained from somebody actually on the inside.

Charlie and I were walking past the old man's shack on the our way to our building. "You're a dick, Derrick! You too, Swede!" Safecracking as a possible income enhancer was officially off the table, and with a serious lack of motivation towards education, other options weren't exactly on the horizon.

I went to sleep, still broke… **Dear God. Can You throw me a few dollars till next week?** Not even a dime. Not even a shekel. Sonofabitch!

Grandma says an idle mind is the devil's workshop. When I was sixteen years old the devil was probably building a skyscraper in my head, and I think he even took on a protégé in case he died on the job.

Me and the big redhead were getting closer every day and still doing everything, pretty much by the book. Her book. My book contained all the dirty stuff so I tried educating Ellen on the human necessity for the exploration of sexual experiences for the greater good of womankind. Ellen didn't buy it immediately. She was somewhat intrigued by a few of my well-developed theories.

Ellen and I were sitting on one of the many utility poles being stored at the edges of the lots. The long wooden poles would eventually be installed to bring electricity and street lighting to all the buildings and private homes yet to be built throughout the swamps. We presently occupied one directly across the street from Ellen's building on Olmstead Avenue.

We were talking teenage dreams. I managed to slip in a few personal goals. Ellen, as usual managed to cut me off at the knees. I was about to further my cause when a few boisterous colored guys happening by on their way to the PS 138 after-school program slowly, but steadily grabbed my attention. I knew them all by name. They all knew mine. They lived in the King David Houses, the small community of private homes the other side of Lacombe Avenue just south of the projects.

Physical altercations were almost a weekly occurrence. I had a few good ones with two of the colored guys that were walking towards me and my new girlfriend. The first was about four years ago during the summer. I walked out the lobby door early in the morning on my way to the fort and quickly noticed an intruder. Billy Blunt had one foot on the chain at the edge of the grass and turned suddenly when the door closed behind me. He looked at me crooked. I hate that. I stopped and looked at him sideways. "What the fuck you lookin' at white boy?" I'm not normally sensitive about being a white boy and rarely very talkative with people I hardly know, especially this early in the day. As if some colored kid from the King David Houses standing in front of my building wasn't enough to piss me off, but I still had a few options here. I could walk away and completely avoid a confrontation. Not possible. I could call him a fucking tar-baby and sound as prejudiced as he is. Better, but not great, but that would only lead to what came to mind in the first place. I cracked a short right cross into the side of his head, hurt my little hand and knocked him senseless over the chain into the hedges.

A few months after that Eugene Ellis and I bloodied each other for an hour in the lots the day after his dog Queenie chased me up a tree where the crazy little mutt showed me his snarling teeth until dinner time. His. I went to school and got along well with Tommy Simson, considering his ill-mannered associates, and then there was big Henry Moore. I knew big Henry well enough for friendly hellos and good-byes, and he seemed like a big slow teddy-bear, but big Henry had a reputation for sticking up for his annoying little friends, and with his size I imagined the big guy didn't get much lip or exercise.

Ellen was oblivious to my past with the approaching troupe of brothers. Ellen was still talking when I picked out Billy and held his gaze. They were still ten yards away, taking their time. One by one Big

Henry and his noisy entourage slowly sauntered by, but Billy seemed to have grown a bigger pair of balls since the last time I knocked him out, and he was bopping like a badass behind them when he decided to put them to work. "Lookin good, blondie!" Billy and I were suddenly locked in mental combat. His eyes were nervously back peddling away from a superior opponent. Mine doing flying drop kicks on his face, so I nudged my girlfriend off the telephone pole so she wouldn't get hurt when the real stuff started. "Get out of here," I insisted. Ellen hesitated and grabbed my hand.

Big Bobby Murphy and Patrick Welsh had been sitting on the benches way up the block when they probably noticed four colored guys too close to me to be having a casual conversation. My two friends started hurrying down the street. Ellen stood above me. I finally wriggled free from her white knuckled grasp. Now I have two hands balled in a fist. "Run!" Our eyes were locked. She saw rage. I saw panic. "Go." Ellen finally scooted away and ran up Seward Avenue towards Bobby and Patrick.

Billy paused, his arrogant smile more like the weary confidence of a weasel in the protective shadow of a friendly lion. I hate freaking lions and weasels. My blood boiled into my eyes. I slowly stood up in his face. We were nose to nose. "She's a redhead, ya dumb fucking nigger." That wiped the shine right off his teeth. Billy wound me up and they all laughed. The second I turned the table everybody stopped and nobody was smiling, but me.

This wasn't my first opportunity to get my ass busted by a crowd. Grandma says I look like an altar boy with the map of Ireland for a face, so it must be the Italian-German part of my brain that generates my hyper-aggressive personality, which pretty much assures it wouldn't be the last time I'll be facing death by an angry mob.

Big Henry quickly back-peddled and put a meaty hand between our noses. He looked Billy back. Billy stepped aside. I stepped forward. Big Henry growled. "Excuse me honky, but I believe you owe my friend here an apology." I guess everybody forgot my name. Big Henry didn't seem particularly angry. Just prejudiced. He merely folded his arms high on his chest, looked down and calmly waited for me to apologize. Or cry. "Fuck you too, asshole." I bet he didn't expect that, but then again neither did I. It was sort of a last second implosion due to a long standing resentment for those too big to punch in the face. This group of laughing clowns tried to punk me out in front of my scared

184

girlfriend and now their designated enforcer expects an apology? Not today.

I was looking straight up his nose into his brain and watched as it glowed fire red just before it exploded. He was obviously way faster and a bit more hostile than his reputation, because I'm certain I was ducking before big Henry introduced a very solid and rather large black bar of soap to the tip of my dirty mouth. I mean nose.

I'm not exactly sure how long I was out because I don't count real good when I'm unconscious. Actually, I don't even count real good when I'm awake. But when I came to they were all still laughing, and dumb Eugene was still stepping over my head, so I'm figuring three. I was up by the count of three.

They were hardly twenty yards along when my marbles fully realigned. Ellen was already standing at the top of Seward Avenue by the benches looking frantic. Big Bobby and Patrick were hurrying across the street when I waved them away. "Are ya sure?" urged Murphy. "I'm sure."

Big Henry and his rowdy troop of giggling bozos were still laughing and still within range when I picked up the only element on Earth harder than big Henry's thick skull and threw a golf ball-sized rock hard enough to shatter the back of his melon, but I missed and hit Billy in the back of his neck. "CRAZY WHITE CRACKER MOTHER FUCKER!"

I got their attention, but I was actually aiming for big Henry's bowling ball sized melon, but I'm kinda glad I missed because big Henry would eventually corner me in Willie's Luncheonette and mash my face into white crackers topped with strawberry delight. The fastest kid in the projects was gone before the rock hit the ground.

If there is anything funnier than watching four colored guys trying to catch a scared white cracker I haven't seen it yet. I was running so fast I was leaving a freaking vapor trail. They were so slow I thought they stopped to catch a bus. I flew down the very long block and crossed Randall Avenue, hopped the chain into the grass and raced along the edge of my building and crashed through the lobby door. I continued up eleven flights of stairs and ran down the hall and burst through my apartment door and snapped the lock without taking a deep breath. The apartment was empty so I merely stood behind my personal iron curtain and anxiously awaited the folly sure to be riding up in the elevator... .any time now.

185

Anyone that has ever lived in a city housing development knows how ridiculous it looks when a T.V cop kicks in a steel calamine door with one determined effort. It's like kicking open a bank vault with a wooden leg. Not going to happen. If the bad guys don't open the door it don't get open. You could kick it until your foot falls off. Four angry teenagers banged and kicked that heavy steel door for less than a minute, because unlike the TV cops they knew it wouldn't dent, buckle, bend or break, and they knew it without getting frustrated. Their appearance was mandatory. I dare say the only word they use regularly to greet each other, but when a skinny white adversary utters the same word it almost always comes with consequences. "You're dead. We're gonna get you outside, Carroll!"

"Fuck you, Henry! I'm gonna knock you out again, Billy. You dumb faggot!"

Big Henry Moore and his little troupe of angry slowpokes made their way back down the hall to the elevator. I quickly went into the bathroom to check on my throbbing nose. I was bleeding, but at least it was still there. Then I went back and thanked my door.

I always got along well with Tommy Simson and we remained friends after I apologized for my liberal disregard for his heritage, and I eventually apologized to big Henry Moore, too, so he wouldn't beat me to death.

Under normal circumstances Big Henry was always a big teddy bear. There were also abnormal circumstances and I was the latest. But we soon discussed our little altercation. Actually, I discussed it. Big Henry couldn't stop laughing about it. After a good giggle and handshakes we were right back where we started, friendly hellos, friendly goodbyes. He said as long as I didn't call him an asshole again he wouldn't have to rearrange my pretty face. I decided having Big Henry as a friend was probably better than having my regular face rearranged in the back of Willie's Luncheonette. Billy Blunt ignored me and dumb Eugene and Queenie growled whenever I happened by, but Eugene kept Queenie on a tighter leash and I kept my big mouth closed because I knew Queenie the mutt was crazier than Eugene. That little mutt chased me over more fences around the projects than angry cops trying to run me down to issue a two dollar fine for being on the grass. Like that could actually happen.

I was already getting tired of my new way of making friends with colored guys, but at least it was keeping me in shape. I needed to be in shape. I still gotta lotta colored friends to make.

19

My education finally came to an end because I no longer felt safe riding the subway. I mean the door was locked. I got a ear ache? Okay, I quit. I figured I wasn't exactly lighting up the scoreboard, so I bailed out of my repeat performance of ninth grade before wasting any more of my precious time on the smelly subway. I really hate the smelly subway.

With all this extra time on my hands Ellen was pretty much my entire focus. It took a while, but I finally convinced my girlfriend to think outside the Catholic Church. Be aggressive. Why should you be the only sixteen-year-old girl not having fun? We could both die from a brain aneurism. Tonight. Don't ya love me? Really? You will? Wait a second. Not in the elevator. Let's go up to the thirteenth floor.

After that initial breakthrough all we needed was a thought and a look and place to throw Ellen's clothes and we were doing a new dance in a different location before my girlfriend could manage a quick act of contrition.

It was just another Friday evening in late Spring. I was meeting Ellen in the usual place, the circle in front of her building. We called it a circle, but it was actually an oval. Two rows of wooden benches back to back extend the length of the circle. A concrete saddle at one end of the circle, monkey bars at the other. Ellen's friends, both girls and guys, were also regulars in the circle, and because of my new girlfriend I was already more regular than the ants and spiders.

Ellen was sitting on the bench with her best friend Lily when I approached. Two best friends deep in conversation. Neither noticed me until I interrupted Ellen with a kiss on the cheek. "You better sit down," Ellen insisted. Big Lily screwed a hairy eye ball into my brain, got up and quickly walked away. What the hell was that for?

I tried to look into my girlfriend's eyes, but her head was bowed, long red hair draped like a veil, so I pulled it away and saw a tear. Ellen's beautiful face was suddenly a quiver. "My friend... is late." My brain was suddenly in the middle of a mathematics test in the center of a circle on the outer limits of a conundrum. I turned and squinted towards Ellen's friend as Lily's fat ass hurried through the lobby door. I thought her timing was perfect. Keep moving. I got Ellen all to myself. What's the freaking problem, here?

Ellen's eyes widened as she pursed her lips and rattled her head as if attempting to turn her mouth inside out. "My period," she insisted as tears burst through watery eyes. "My period. It's late." It was beginning to sink in. Ellen's period must have to do with Big Lily. Or something? Ellen grabbed my cheeks tight and pulled. "I'm pregnant, Kevin."

"Why didn't ya say that?" I mumbled. **𝕳𝖔𝖑𝖞 𝕸𝖆𝖗𝖞, 𝕸𝖔𝖙𝖍𝖊𝖗 𝖔𝖋 𝕲𝖔𝖉.** I've gotten actual wake-up calls from Sister Mary Monster administered with less of a shock. We temporarily suspended all practice sessions. Temporarily. I think. I hope to God.

♣

Finding meaningful employment was now imperative and my resume was well stocked. Two solid years collecting with Mark after school on his Journal American newspaper route. Never sick a day. Four productive months working as a doogan for the milk company. Never dropped a single bottle, and one fruitful year of scratching the shit stains under the rim of the toilet bowl in Crazy Georges Diner. I'm thinking Wall Street, but I settled for the mail clerk position at Crown Publishers on Twenty Eighth Street and Park Avenue South.

♣

Dad explained the important stuff right after I admitted to practicing without a license. Dad sat in his chair and crossed one leg over the other. I stood just to his side looking nervously out the window towards the Whitestone Bridge. "You know, Kevin," explained dad, "you have to marry Ellen." With the calmness of Jesus he actually made it sound like a good idea. But even if it wasn't he didn't give me another option. I shrugged my shoulders that normally accompany my best dumbfounded expression. "Yeah, I guess?" His eyes widened to impress the seminal point. "Don't guess, Kevin. You and Ellen are going to have a baby." It was the first time anybody said it without the code words. So, I'm going to have a baby? And so is Ellen. **𝕯𝖊𝖆𝖗, 𝕷𝖔𝖗𝖉. 𝕬𝖗𝖊 𝖄𝖔𝖚 𝖘𝖚𝖗𝖊 𝖄𝖔𝖚 𝖜𝖆𝖓𝖙 𝖙𝖔 𝖌𝖔 𝖙𝖍𝖗𝖔𝖚𝖌𝖍 𝖜𝖎𝖙𝖍 𝖙𝖍𝖎𝖘. 𝕮𝖆𝖓 𝖜𝖊 𝖍𝖆𝖛𝖊 𝖆 𝖉𝖔 𝖔𝖛𝖊𝖗, 𝖕𝖑𝖊𝖆𝖘𝖊?** Maybe in Kevin the Magician's story. Apparently, in my story there are no do-overs.

We were too young to marry in New York State without permission from our parents and we didn't want any trouble with the cops, so Ellen's older sister Beatrice kept the big redhead hidden in her house in New Jersey until the big day. Practice was officially over. The next time we did it we were licensed by the great state of New Jersey. I love freaking New Jersey.

Except for the fact that Ellen looked like she was walking around with a stolen pumpkin under her shirt, everything else was pretty normal. Ellen and I moved in together in October, with little Marilyn due some time in December. Not a lot of time to get acquainted before the big day, but we made the best of a delicate situation. We had our own apartment, a big grown up bed and plenty of time to practice   .

TWO AND A HALF MONTHS LATER

Minding my own business was easy. Nobody was talking. Three nervous fathers to be were walking trenches in different directions. An angry outburst suddenly crashed through the double doors electrifying the air and bringing three solemn processions to an awkward standstill. I shrugged. They shrugged. The march of the anxious continued.

I was trying to pay no mind, but the boisterous lady was obviously having a very bad day. My wife only came to the hospital to deliver our baby, and besides, my wife doesn't curse, she doesn't even yell, but what kept my ear in the air was the name. "Kevinnn!" Was it an echo? "YOU SONOFABITCH!"

Something in the air was choking my ability to think. Was it simply fear, of having a baby? Or that familiar tone? I shuffled around the corner and tip-toed down the hall towards the delivery room. The voice grew in magnitude. I cracked the doors, though I did not step through. I am a troublemaker, not a damn idiot.

Somebody in the delivery room was mad at somebody. I'm thinking the guy that just left for the bottle of gin in his glove compartment. I thought he looked more like a Leroy. I drew closer and lingered a few seconds to better distinguish the voice, but it lowered to a growl so I moved even closer, an anxious ear straining for a foreign pitch that would lighten my fears. The vocalizations degenerated to a guttural gurgling, then lowered even further to a threatening hiss like a rattlesnake. My brain was churning my stomach because something in the voice was waaay too familiar. I was praying like a crucified sinner that it wasn't my little Ellen. I pushed the door. "You sonofabitch! If you ever touch me again I'll cut it off! You bastard! Kevinnnnn!" Yup… that's her, alright. So I slowly backed away in case the little lady could smell me and continued to walk a trench in the middle of the waiting area.

Three and a half hours and a whole lot of screaming later a nurse informed me that little baby Marilyn was actually a seven pound, six-ounce baby boy. So we named him Richard Gerard and he came into the world screaming even louder than his crazy mother on the 14th of December 1968 at three seventeen in the morning. A boy!

♣

It was a typical Saturday morning. Six hours of Sesame Street the only thing on the agenda for all three of us. I was heating up my Beefaroni on the stove when Brendan knocked at the door. Ellen's older brother and his wife had recently moved into our building at 373 East 188th Street in the Fordham Road section of the northeast Bronx. Brendan is the second oldest in a family of eight and senior to Ellen by five years. Ellen's brother and wife Jamie were expecting twins in late spring. Brendan asked if I'd help him paint his new nursery. It was like being handed the keys to the jail cell. Big Bird was already driving me nuts and the Count, all that damn counting.

Crocus Yellow from Martin's Paint Store was like blinding sunshine in a one gallon can. We only painted half the room and it was already bright enough to get a freaking tan. I was meticulously brushing the trim while Brendan was supposed to be rolling the walls, but every time I looked around his chin was on his chest and the roller stuck on the wall above his head. "Let's take a break," suggested Brendan. I thought he was on a freaking break. Brendan wiped the drool from his mouth and dropped the roller in the pan.

I shadowed Brendan down the hall into the living room and plopped on the couch. Brendan stood in front of his bookcase and fingered the four hundred record albums lining the middle shelf. My brother-in-law then pinched his fingers between two albums and extracted a tiny glassine envelope. On the top shelf he grabbed a cigar box, and from inside the box he plucked a tiny plastic straw that was cut to a point and sharp enough to draw blood. "I need a booster," informed Brendan. Ellen's big brother held the tiny bag up to the light and tapped it gently with a finger, then he carefully inserted the straw. When he pulled it out a barely visible white powder was evident on the tip. I wondered from my seat on the edge of the couch.

"This is some good shit, Kev."

Brendan held the straw to his nose and sucked the powder up like an anteater. He repeated the process two times each nostril, then placed the straw and glassine envelope on top of the cigar box and walked out to the kitchen. "Wow, Kev, you're legal now. Ya wanna beer?"

"Yeah, thanks." Brendan came back a minute later with a frosty bottle of Old Milwaukee.

"Wow, Kev. I hope you not thinking I'm cheap." I already knew he was cheap, he just handed me an Old Milwaukee Beer. Brendan motioned towards the little bag and pointy straw.

It was the first time I ever witnessed anybody sniffing white powder so I had no idea what it was or what he was up to. I didn't know if Ellen's brother was being cheap or stupid, but the look on his face should've been my first clue.

Brendan gathered the tiny straw and glassine bag from atop the cigar box. "Ya wanna get nice?" His big shit-ass eatin' grin suggested great things to come, but I would soon regard that query as the stupidest I would ever answer incorrectly in my entire life. "Why not."

I'll tell you why freaking not. When given a test in a small room full of paint fumes with a brilliant yellow sun in my eyes and clarity further veiled in a mysterious white substance that appeared to be twisting my brother-in-law's face into an oblique mass of mush I needed to ask at least one question. Will it kill me? I didn't, and paid for that omission for the next twenty-seven years. "Let's go in the bathroom," prodded Brendan. "Whaddya call this stuff?" My generous benefactor looked over his shoulder as he pushed open the bathroom door. "Skagg. It's called skagg." Brendan pulled the string for the light and handed me the gun, I mean tiny glassine bag and pointy straw. "Put a little on the tip. Don't exhale or you'll blow two dollars into the mirror."

Brendan's white powdery booster seemed to be sagging the corners of his mouth while his eyelids were practically drooping onto his lips. Twenty minutes later I looked pretty much the same way as I half stumbled, half crawled down a flight of stairs to my own apartment where I violently yakked up my Beeferoni into the toilet. Later that very evening while Ellen was lying down for a much needed nap, good ole Brendan knocked on the door to enlighten me further. "You know, Kev you can shoot that stuff." In my head I was still floating on a peaceful lake in Vermont behind the house my parents rented for summer vacations. Nevertheless, the subliminal seed was planted in the fertile mush that used to be my brain.

That Saturday afternoon in March was the first and very last time that I ever snorted skagg. When I explained my experience to a friend on the job I realized what I had inhaled on Saturday. My friend explained that skagg usually goes by another more popular name. My friend John called it heroin. That I heard of. Very popular.

The next Friday afternoon set a course that would see me crash and burn, day in and day out until the only thing left inside me to brighten was the very dark corner in the back of my head. The place where little Kevin was finally laid to rest.

❧

At two dollars a bag the cost of heroin was actually quite reasonable. Within a year I had become a weekend warrior, shooting heroin on Fridays and soon Fridays and Saturdays plus any other day of the week that I could scratch up two bucks.

My best friend Mark was given his wings (shown how to inject drugs) by another neighborhood knucklehead, so during that same period I was becoming a weekend warrior, so was Mark. Shooting heroin is not something you advertise, even to best friends, but within a few short weeks of getting 'nice' we both came clean as to our new found distraction.

During the late sixties the heroin epidemic was spawning a fertile culture around the Castle Hill Houses like bacteria in a Petri dish. The seeming necessity to infuse the darker spirits of my neighborhood with hard drugs had become no more of an effort than purchasing a loaf of Wonder Bread from fat Julies Delicatessen.

My stumble towards addiction began on that last weekend in March of 1969. I was eighteen, married with one child. Six months later I found myself in unbearable pain, lying across two dinette chairs in front of the open stove, gas turned high enough to melt the refrigerator door, the heat barely mitigating the stabbing ache in my legs. It was August in New York. It wasn't cold. "Knock, knock!" When I opened the door my best friend was clad as usual in a black tee shirt, black chinos and black suede Beatle boots. Mark wasn't even through the door when he posed the usual query because I was usually always broke. "Ya wanna' get high?" The natural chemicals in my brain instantly neutralized the pain in my legs. When I told Mark of my instantaneous relief he combed his fingers through shoulder length curls and calmly suggested the probable cause for my sickly dilemma. "Welcome to the club. You got a dope habit."

♣

Richard Nixon had been elected the thirty-seventh president of the United States back in '68. War protestors had taken to the streets in every major city in the United States and throughout the world and the major battles had yet to be fought. America was in the middle of a firestorm and the people in charge of putting out fires were still busy buying gasoline.

♣

The meager wages for my efforts at Crown Publishing didn't actually seem meager while I was still living at home with mom and dad. But with two additional mouths to feed and rent to pay, meager was putting a major strain on my new family budget.

I'd been working at Crown for a whole year and my climb to the top of the publishing industry was already taking way too long. With steadfast determination and a head full of doubt I walked up to the manager's desk in the corner of the tiny mail room. "Morning, Oscar." The little old German from the mountains of Bavaria rubbed the top of his bald head. "Vat is dis, Kevin?"

"I told ya that I have a baby now, Oscar, and I really need a five-dollar raise."

Old Oscar looked up as he slowly rubbed a three day stubble. "Not at diz dime, Kevin. Bezides, long hair drop outz a dime a dozen." Oscar said that he didn't want to hurt my feelings, but if he could hire a monkey it could probably do my job. If I had any self-respect I would've stiffened my leg to send my little foot up his tight German ass, but climbing the corporate ladder was still my main objective, and besides, violence was probably my least best option when applying for a raise.

I was riding home on the smelly subway while perusing the *Daily News* want ads and quickly found my next entry level position on my way up the corporate ladder, "Willoughby Peerless Camera. Repair de-

193

partment. No experience necessary. Seventy dollars a week." The only thing I knew about cameras before I started at Peerless was how to stand in front of one without moving. When I left I wasn't a whole lot smarter.

The job was taking in cameras for repair. Tag 'em, put 'em on the shelf and give a receipt. I was handling five thousand dollar Hasselblad cameras with ten thousand dollar Leica lenses that could take a photo of a fruit fly in mid-wing flap on the surface of a cantaloupe in California from New York on a cloudy day.

The typical customer rushes up the stairs in sweat. The reason for the panic? The one undeveloped negative stuck inside his camera. The same rich genius on safari in Africa standing next to the usually elusive purple spotted tigarillagis only moments after B'wana blew the magnificent species into extinction. "Film stuck."

I would stare at those black contraptions and imagine the inner workings of gears and springs and little tiny screws and magical shudders as if it had just landed on earth from a distant star system. I smiled. "No problem." Of course I was supposed to whip out the black bag from under the counter so the killer could actually witness the entire process. First I place his camera inside the black bag in order to remove the stuck film. Then I take a small metal canister in one hand and wiggle both arms into the specially fitted sleeves. Once my two hands are inside the bag I decipher the problem inside the camera without actually seeing the camera. Not a freaking chance in hell. If the cameras were all Kodak instamatics I could possibly be the CEO at Peerless by now, but they weren't. "Little problem. I'll have to use the big dark room in the back." Then I'm going to fly my new spaceship to the outer solar system where they made this contraption and have it fixed like new before you could squash a bug, you murdering piece of shit.

Unfortunately, there was no black room in the back room. So I went behind the door, unzipped the bag, opened the camera, removed the roller, exposing it to light and personally ruined more filmed vacations in one week than a whole year of hurricanes in the Caribbean. By Friday I was looking for a new career.

The way Dad explained it, a friend of a friend who knew a guy in construction needed a kid to work like an indentured servant with the strength of Hercules and the brain of a newly formed amoeba to haul construction crap up and down six flights of newly constructed apartment houses and he didn't want to pay me shit. I started Monday.

"You okay, kid? Ya look a little tired." Mike and Nick Santullo were never actually concerned for my well-being and they never held back on the sarcasm. They wanted to see my skinny ass in perpetual motion, so when I wasn't flying around the construction site carrying two-by-fours or banging eight penny nails my new name would fly around the building and pierce my ear like a freaking nail gun.

"Hey Kid!" Mike would yell, "bring that rope up to the roof! I ain't no damn kid, you fucking grease ball, I thought. I'm nineteen years old. I'm supporting my own kid, ya damn shithead. "Kid, I need it today. Kid, hand me your ruler. Move your ass, kid."

"Stop calling me kid, Nick!" I told them both a thousand times. "I'm not a fucking kid, Mike!" The fact that my hair was down past my shoulders and I looked like an ugly fifteen year old girl probably didn't help their perspective.

Nick paused midway up the ramp that extended from the ground and gradually rose up to the second floor terrace, stubby legs apart for balance, big ugly cigar hanging under a greasy little mustache. "Hey, Kid. Bring ya hammer up to the second floor." The boss continued trudging up the ramp when I decided to look for a new job. One that didn't require a hammer. I flipped the twenty-two ounce Plumb hammer from the metal belt holder and fired it like an angry Apache, right at Nick's fat head. He threw his hands up for cover, "SHIT!" and ducked. Missed by an inch. "You're fired, Kid!"

"Fuck you, Nick!"

It was still only nine thirty in the morning when I walked in the door. I passed Ellen reading at the kitchen table. She quickly followed me into the living room. I plopped down on the couch. "What happened?" I emitted enough angry frustration to keep the questions at a minimal. "I lost my hammer." That should cover it. My beautiful wife seemed to take it in stride. "What do you mean ya lost ya hammer?" Ellen sat in the chair across from the television, a slow burning intensity simmering behind normally sparkly eyes that suddenly lost any hope of sparkle or compassion.

I already felt stupid enough for walking away from a job that was paying the bills and Ellen wasn't helping with my insecurity. "What do you mean, what do I mean?" Ellen waited for something plausible, her dark gray orbs still probing the inside of my brain for a flicker of hope or light. "I threw my hammer at the boss." Richie was napping in the playpen and awoke with his usual smile and slowly stood up at the unusual tone in mommy's voice. Mommy never gets this crazy. Ellen stomped over and flicked the dial on the television, Sesame Street. She lifted Richie from the playpen and placed him on the floor in front of me. Richie is the only one in the room smiling. Cookie Monster caught my attention. I love Cookie Monster. "I'm going out for a walk," she blurted, the brilliant red face matching the shiny red hair. "See if you can manage to stay out of trouble 'til I get back."

"Where ya goin?" I mumbled. I didn't dare say it loud enough to be heard. I'm a troublemaker not a damn idiot.

I should've stuck with, I lost my freaking hammer.

If there was any difference between the arrival of Richie and little Joe it was the fact that little Joe was actually expected. We finally figured it out. Practice makes perfect. We also realized that Richie needed a little friend so we made him one. Piece a cake.

20

I'd been searching through the *Daily News* classifieds once again for all the jobs listed under the caption, no experience necessary, until a friend told me that the United States Government was looking for a few good men. I could be good if I had to. I think, maybe. Actually, I'm not sure, how good are we talking?

When I walked away from the written test at the General Post Office it was the first time in my life that I felt like a freaking genius in a classroom setting. I also remember thinking that the government didn't seem to be looking for a few good men. The Post Office was actually in the middle of a major hiring campaign. As I looked around the very expansive room full of misfits I wasn't the only one there with a big happy grin. Actually, there was way too much smiling going on. It looked like a line up for meds at a freaking insane asylum.

The Post Office was hiring alright and only those applicants with a least a third grade education and normal sinus rhythm need apply. I learned to read Dick and Jane in first grade out of fear, and before my departure from Catholic school hell I could probably comprehend a parole release transcript like a district attorney. Because I was spending so much time watching The Count on Sesame Street with Richie and Joe my math skills had progressed to a level the government might consider a threat to national security so if you can write your name and address and maintain normal sinus rhythm while reading this sentence you too can be a postal employee. Breeeeathe...

My blood pressure examinations always say I'm the healthiest troublemaker in the doctor's office. I passed the test because I wanted to. I needed a damn job.

As a new mail person I was emptying mail shoots in skyscrapers and hotels like the St. Regis and The Algonquin. I was also servicing corner mail boxes in the same area along Fifth and Madison Avenues in the fifties. As a sub-carrier I wasn't issued a uniform until the Post Office investigated my background and cleared me to work alongside all the other lowest level government employees in the United States of America.

My curly brown freak flag was flowing rather nicely, and with no uniform I looked like all the other hippie freaks walking around midtown. Only I'm not. I'm an undercover federal agent with a long brass chain and a big shiny key and not afraid to use it.

The blue mailbox at the corner of Madison Avenue and 56th Street was filled to overflowing. As I shoveled the contents into my big canvas bag I found myself staring at my own reflection in a pair of very shiny shoes. I straightened up. "Can I help you?" I stated abruptly. Gabe Pressman, the NBC newsman stood back, letter in hand. "How long has federal government been hiring hippies?" wondered the information gathering old fart. "I think I'm the very first one, but they have a long list of pissed off veterans and I hear they'll be carrying machine guns." I thought it was pretty damn funny. He didn't get it, and quickly walked away, letter in hand, to deposit I assumed in a safer place.

During the postal workers strike of 1971 the government in their infinite wisdom activated the National Guard to maintain the integrity of an essential government service. Unfortunately for the government the lowly postal employees refused to tell the soldiers the essential tool for sorting the mail. It's called a scheme, and we kept it secret, classified, need to know basis only. The strikers decided that the soldiers didn't need to know, so the soldiers sat on their fat asses out in their army trucks and collected a check for doing the same thing we were doing: nothing. At least we were walking a picket line. They watched. What a country.

F.D.R. station on 54th Street and 3rd Avenue was the most modern of all New York facilities. On weekends I usually worked the second floor unloading dock. It was just another boring Spring evening until I decided to read the mail. Not illegally of course. That wouldn't be smart, or legal.

Jim and I started the job on the very same day and we were once again partnered for the shift. His long shaggy beard and greasy shoulder length locks gave Jim the appearance of an Apostle, Saint James the unholy Pot Head.

The first task of the evening was unloading the five ton trucks. The trucks were all filled with large canvas bins on caster wheels that are used for moving packages between local post office facilities. Once the trucks are empty we push the bins onto a machine that lifts and tips the bins where the contents fall onto a conveyor belt. The packages then travel to the fifth floor where the mail handlers separate the parcels by zip code.

On this particular evening the entire unloading dock was covered with bins, but my attention was miraculously drawn to the five we pulled off the very last vehicle. The bins were filled with thousands of three-by-five cardboard advertisements from the Rucker Pharmaceutical Company that were going from F.D.R. Station to every single doctor on the planet, including the ones in New Jersey. I love freaking New Jersey.

One side of the card displayed a picture of a brain and words describing how Rucker's new drug will cure the entire universe of depression and slow brain function like a smack in the head from a baseball bat, plus the all-important address label. The opposite side of the card contained six round pills that were big enough to choke a freaking horse, the number 714 imprinted onto each tablet.

So here I am, reading the mail on another boring spring evening when I suddenly realized that this Rucker Pharmaceutical Company was making drugs for unsuspecting drug freaks. "Hey, Jim," I whispered, "I think these things are downs." I took control of the dumping machine while Jim plucked a packet from the bin and read the back. My partner smiled the big happy grin of a starving pot-head staring at a cheeseburger. "I think you might be right." Freaking genius.

An immediate investigation was imperative in order to avert a national crisis. The country needs to be warned. Rucker Pharmaceutical is attempting an all-out advertising blitz to send depressed lunatics into outer space for the good of psychiatrists everywhere. We needed a test monkey, or at least a young enterprising doper willing to take a dose for the good of the country. I stepped up to the plate. Jim looked one way. I glanced the other. The coast is clear. No government spooks, no federal spies and no agency whistleblowers anywhere in the general vicinity. I'm pretty sure.

An enclosed catwalk suspended forty feet off the floor contained two-way mirrors allowing inspectors to view the entire work area. Catching would-be mail poachers is a full time job for government police. I palmed one packet and slipped the six pills snugly into the waist band of my underwear as if merely tucking my shirt. I looked busy for another minute before I casually strolled around the corner towards the men's room and away from suspicious eyes possibly peering down from above.

I entered the toilet stall and locked the latch. Then I sat my fat ass on my favorite seat, carefully pushed one pill through the foil membrane and popped into my mouth. I quickly rushed out again and cupped my hand under the faucet and took a sip of water before I choked to death. I waited about a minute and stared into the mirror. Nothing. I combed my long curly hair and repeated the entire process for the benefit of all those chemically imbalanced, depressed bi-polar Americans in the country.

♣

My chin was flopping about my chest and my lips attempting a foreign language. "Leeeme lone. Pleee. Lemme leeeeep." I'm not sure how long I was out, but I was still in dreamyland when I found myself being dragged around the outer roadway by Jimmy the pothead and another post office buddy, handsome Johnny the gigolo. My arms were draped around their necks as they held my wrists and dragged me along while my feet were mopping the floor. "Pleee. lemme leeeep!" The term shit-faced was informally introduced by the makers of Quaalude in the spring of 1971.

"What's wrong with him!?" yelled a stern voice from above. "Oh shit, Kev," whispered Jimmy, "you're lucky it's Mundy." Supervisor Mundy is the father of George Mundy, and George is another doper and trusted friend on the job. For the most part the boss and I got along just fine. For the most part. Usually. "Get him up here, Ericson!" ordered Mister Mundy. "He's all doped up. What the hell did he do?"

"I don't know, boss," informed Jimmy. "I found him on the floor in the bathroom."

"Punch his timecard and get him out of the goddamn building before we all get arrested."

Later that evening I was startled awake when some asshole kicked me in the foot. I was slumped against the side of the post office building, a small brown paper bag of Quaalude's in my lap and the blinding sun in my eyes. Now I got a freaking sun burn on half my face and a bag full of downs. Good ole Jimmy.

I struggled up to my feet and headed for help with the brown bag hanging tightly from my fist. The euphoric malaise in my brain was tabulating my options like an idiot staring at calculus. When I finally figured out my purpose in life I stumbled towards the smelly subway and headed downtown.

Ellen's best friend and my old drummer from The Souls had been

200

recently engaged to be married. The big celebration planned for Paul O'Neil and big Lily Kowalski at Quinn's Bar on Westchester Avenue was all the talk for weeks. Mark was picking Ellen up at nine o'clock to drive her to the bar and my brother was set to babysit. My original plan was to take a two hour leave from work, jump on the smelly subway and hit the party in full stride. That plan was now dead. My new best plan was to walk and talk without tripping over my freaking lips.

Ellen's brother had been working at The Underground Record Shop in the east village on Saint Mark's Place. Good ole Brendan had dropped out of college where he was studying to be pharmacist in order to study drugs from a much closer perspective. Brendan was now a walking talking drug store with a pocket full of antidotes for any situation, up or down. I needed to be conscious. Up would be a freaking miracle.

With his slicked back hair on a six foot two frame, Brendan gives the impression of a gazelle at rest. He looks like a greaser, but Ellen's brother was more like a peaceful beatnik. My brother-in-law can walk everywhere and nowhere at the same time. He would depress the angels in heaven if given an ear, but I needed crystal methadrene (speed) and listening to Brendan's crazy philosophies usually comes with every purchase.

I was laid out in the subway car, semi-conscious, but managed to get off at the correct stop with the help of a rather intuitive transit police blob. The fat bastard scared the crap out of me when he hit the bottom of my foot with his night stick. "Wake up! This is your stop, hippie!" Astor Place. He was lucky I was in a drug induced stupor or I would've planted a wobbly foot in his fat ass. "Fucking pig,"

"Don't let me see you sleeping on my train again, freak!" I staggered out of the car just before the door closed on my pride, I mean ass.

THE UNDERGROUND RECORD SHOP

So here I am, drooling down the front of my black tee shirt in the back room of the record shop and Brendan is forcing crystal meth up my nose with aid of a Bic pen cap. We needed a shovel.

Brendan appeared to have enough methamphetamine to wake up half the population of Haight Asbury, California, but it still wasn't enough to rid the effects of two Quaaludes. "Wow, Kev," consoled Brendan, "you really are pretty fucked up. Wow, listen. Do you think I should call my sister?" My tongue was still rolled up behind my tonsils. I sat there staring at the floor, semi-oblivious.

Brendan took a piece of tinfoil from the shelf and flattened it on the desk. He then tapped enough meth onto the foil to startle a gorilla. He folded it neatly. With a ball point pen he then carefully printed on the foil, SPEED in the event I might forget. "Put this in your wallet for when you get uptown." I mumbled my appreciation as Brendan helped me towards the door. Once outside I blended in with all the other stoned out hippie freaks that meander along Saint Marks Place and stumbled back towards the smelly Lexington Avenue subway.

I was peacefully shuffling along the yellow line at the edge of the deserted subway platform, minding my own business, slipping in and out of subconscious oblivion, just stumbling about like any other drugged out hippie freak when I, slipped... .oops, over the edge and poured myself onto the tracks like a rubber noodle dressed in a black tee shirt, landing right smack in the middle of the two rails, my precious bag of Quaaludes clutched to my chest like a Bible in the hands of a Baptist minister. Now this is professional troublemaking that goes way beyond cursing at giant nuns. This is heroic shit we're talking here.

So here I am, staring at the filthy gray ceiling without a care in the world. I didn't bang my head, twist my knee or wrench my back. I didn't even get dirty. Somebody up there was finally paying attention and I never had time to say a little prayer, but I'll say one now because I'm suddenly feeling vibrations and hearing the low, low rumble of the number four express train off in the distance, I'm praying San Francisco. **Dear Baby Jesus. J hear You can raise the dead. Well J'm not dead yet, and it would be really nice for my little family of course, if You would keep it that way. Nevertheless, can You give me a boost?** But no boost. The Lord didn't even flip me on my belly.

The number four express was still screeching through the tunnel in the distance while the conglomeration of jellied muscles and bones splattered on the tracks was already getting comfortable. Maybe somebody up there on the platform could throw me down a little blankie.

God must've realized it wasn't my time for final departure, so He quickly grabbed my hand and pulled me up to my feet. It's a miracle. **Thank you, Jesus.** He got me to the edge of the platform. "Come on kid," he pleaded. "Hurry up. Grab the fucking platform." I didn't know He was allowed to curse. To my right, the tiny headlights of the express train had finally impressed the few active neurons in my brain. I quickly wrestled my arms over the edge of the platform, and from there God boosted me up and out of harm's way. **See ya in church.**

Okay, so maybe God didn't actually push my rear-end up and over the edge of the platform to save my ass from certain doom, but the courageous stranger who did could've started his own religion with me. Now I'm holding up the steel column on the platform, and with the same ambition I'm attempting to keep my eyes from going blind. It's not as easy as it sounds.

The brave stranger never says a word until the doors of the subway car slide open and standing on the other side, two of New York's finest assholes, Sergeant Greaseball and Officer Dickhead stroll off the train. "Excuse me officers?" says the good Samaritan. "I think this kid might be sick because he just fell onto the tracks." Sonofabitch! Way to go, bro. I would've taken my chances with the speeding locomotive. "Thanks," says Sergeant Greaseball, "we'll handle it from here."

With his big black bushy mustache, Sergeant Greaseball looked like Mister Bacciagalupe from the Abbott and Costello Show, and his younger tall steely-eyed partner a dead ringer for G.I. Joe with the kung foo grip. The daring do-gooder casually walked into the number four express while I was abruptly grabbed by either arm and bum rushed towards the token booth for further investigation.

My jaw was hanging slack and the five hundred pounds of dead meat on top of my neck was bobbing like a broken doll. "So, hippie, ya wanna show us some I.D.?" My latest pair of blue annoyances held their night sticks at either end, impatiently awaiting compliance. "Oh! Let's go, hippie. Today!" The Quaaludes actually destroyed the common sense portion of my brain and substituted an abundance of bad attitude, which was already pretty bad without drugs. I pushed my stoned kisser up at his blurry face and rattled my head. "No, asshole. Ya can't see my I.D." Sergeant Greaseball jabbed his nightstick into my chest with enough force to leave a mark on my back, but my new super powers rendered the blow harmless. "Fuck you, asshole."

"I said give me your identification, hippie!" I puffed my chest out like Superman, "I said go fuck ya mother, dick face." Officer Dickhead flipped me around like an aggressive dance partner and pushed my kisser between the wrought iron bars and extracted my wallet like a forty-second street pick-pocket. "What's in the bag, hippie?"

"My lunch, asshole." Officer Dickhead carefully plucked the tinfoil packet from inside my wallet and smiled. "Well, well. I wonder what this is, Tony?" He handed the foil to the boss. Speed. "Well, hippie," suggested Greaseball, "It's a good thing you wrote here, because we woulda never figured it out." Sergeant Greaseball carefully parted the layers of tinfoil and nodded knowingly. As if he could tell the difference between crystal meth and Ajax scouring powder without tasting it. "I guess you'll be staying in the Tombs for the weekend, hippie." Officer Dickhead snatched my bag of lunch and slapped on the welcome to my world bracelets.

By the time I ended my tour of the Tombs, New York City's deluxe temporary housing and ultimate deterrent for adult offenders, I was ready to join the priesthood. **Dear Baby Jesus. Would You happen to know a good Jewish lawyer?"**

My first mistake was eating the baloney sandwich. The second was trying to exorcise it. **Holy Mary, Mother of God**. No toilet paper in the bullpen? If I learned anything in the criminal justice system I learned that the thirty hardened criminals I was spending the weekend with were all smarter than me. Apparently, nobody was hungry except the stupid white hippie doubled over in the corner from life threatening stomach cramps. Holy shit. I gotta take a freaking crap.

My third miscalculation came after arraignment. After thirty hours of confinement I finally staggered from the courtroom, where I quickly spotted Officer Dickhead standing in the middle of the corridor. "Kevin?" summoned officer Dickhead. His expression was somber, but the tone somewhat comforting. "Walk over here." I was a bit hesitant, really tired and very hungry, but I quickly followed the clean cut officer down the hall to the long bank of Superman telephone booths.

I was sentenced to probation for a misdemeanor drug possession which would hopefully be vacated contemplating dismissal, but I needed to be a good citizen for a whole year.

The handsome, well-muscled officer leaned against the ugly green wall, his two hands behind his back as he looked me in the eye. "I'm here because I spoke to your wife on Saturday. You were still pretty unconscious so I made the call to ya wife. When I found the meth in your wallet I also found your pictures." He grinned. "My wife is a redhead, too." It was the first ray of sunshine since Saturday evening. "She was crying." Okay, maybe not so sunny. "I didn't want you to lose your job, Kevin. If I turned these in," he held out my bag of lunch, I mean stolen Quaaludes, "the Post Office would've had you arrested for stealing the mail when you showed up for work. I did this for ya family, Kevin."

Officer McSherry grabbed my wrist and placed the bag of stolen doctors' samplers in my hand and quickly walked away. As the door closed behind him in a cloud of dust and a hardy hi ho silver I was still wondering, was that actually The Lone Ranger disguised as a New York City dickhead? Or, am I still in a drug induced stupor.

I love this city. Officer McSherry wasn't bad either. Considering his blueness.

♣

Getting in and out of trouble was becoming a way of life, but the effort on the getting out part was wearing me thin. By the time I got home from the Tombs, Ellen's nervous system was fried. After her brief conversation with officer McSherry, Ellen wasn't sure if I'd be spending the next few years in prison, so I quickly assured my distraught bride that this little misunderstanding would be cleared up after one year and the blemish to my criminal record was hardly worth the energy it would take her to make me a freaking sandwich. "Take it easy." I suggested. "I can't take this anymore, Kevin." Ellen's face was the same burnt red that flowed from the top of her head. "Take what? I was the one that spent the weekend in jail!"

I took my failures out on my wife. Ellen never embarrassed me further and she was always comforting, but stupidity was always my first line of defense. "You know what I'm talking about, Kevin!" I definitely knew what she was talking about, but I was hardly ready to deal with growing up after spending a few nights in the Tombs. I evaded the topic and walked out the door. I dropped a dime in the nearest phone. Ding-a-ling, ding-a-ling. Ding-a-ling, ding-a ling. "Hey, Mark. I need to get straight. I'm sick as a dog. Can ya lend me ten till Thursday."

"Where you been? I called yesterday. Ellen was crying."

"I got busted in the subway. It's a long story. I'll tell ya when ya get here. And I got some good shit we can sell up at the stores."

"Whaddaya got?"

"Downs. Good ones."

Wait till America sees what's coming to market. Quaaludes. They're not just for test monkeys and junkie assholes, anymore.

21

Sometime during the early winter of 1973 the city announced its intention to structure a new tougher physical examination leading to the job of Sanitation Worker. It would be the first time in department history to allow women the opportunity for taking the exam. Schools and neighborhood organizations were setting up practice tests all over the city and I dragged my fat ass and skinny frame to as many as I could find in the Bronx.

The next summer when everybody else was drawn to Brooklyn for a test of strength and endurance, I drove to the Brooklyn Navy Yard to buy little pairs of sneakers and tiny tee shirts and little bitty underwears for Richie and Joe, and for my wife, piece of mind. My motivation was clear.

Eighty-nine thousand very eager New Yorkers were scheduled for an opportunity to show their stuff at the sanitation department physical exam, but the day I was there it appeared that most of the guys left their stuff at home in their other pants. Muscle bound freaks were puking their guts into garbage cans while others were flopping around the obstacle course like old ladies, and the women just embarrassed the entire gender.

I maneuvered my one hundred and seventy pounds through each portion of the test like a man with a higher purpose, and when it was all said and done I was damn near king of the freaking mountain. Not a single woman passed the physical exam. My score was good enough to land this highly sought-after job in the very near future. Like tomorrow.

"Ya brother will be graduating before you if you don't smarten up, mister." My mother predicted it for years and she finally got one right. Tommy completed his four years at Saint Raymond's Boys High School in the Bronx and was presently attending classes at Iona College in New Rochelle.

Tommy's carefree spirit and smiling upbeat personality were probably a few of the many reasons behind my brother's wide circle of friends, but even seemingly happy people with high school diplomas can be swayed by the dark side.

I thought my brother was too smart to get involved with hard drugs. When I was told by a good friend that Tommy had been dabbling with heroin, I didn't think that my brother got stupid since last we spoke. I already knew that Tommy and I had more in common than our last name. Tommy was a gambler so I was heartbroken to get the news, but hardly shocked. I knew the temptation was great. Every freak with a criminal aptitude was selling something to sniff, smoke or shoot right up in front of Willie's Luncheonette.

When Tommy and I finally came face to face I questioned his tiny pupils and slurred speech. My brother came clean with a mere shrug of the shoulders because I was displaying the same hollow twisted mask. I guess my brother figured I wasn't exactly standing on moral high ground. Somebody as smart as Tommy would already know that I was standing in a very deep hole and sinking slowly every waking minute of every freaking day. At least he didn't laugh.

The black cloud of heroin that engulfed our neighborhood was rapidly smothering the prospects of some very good people. My brother and I were running a race with the devil on the treadmill of addiction, and from what I've witnessed so far around the neighborhood the devil was proving to be one hell of a competitor. And besides that, he fucking cheats.

♣

Mark Madden's father had been working at the New York Times for many years, and Mister Madden was able to get Mark a job as a mailer. The job is preparing the newspapers for delivery. My best friend hated the mind numbing monotony, but the Mailer's Union is as strong as any in the city, so the pay was great and Mark needed every penny. Mark's drug habit wasn't only keeping him high, it was also keeping him thoroughly in debt.

I hadn't picked up a bass guitar since marrying Ellen, but Mark had been working tirelessly at his craft and was establishing himself as one the best all-around musicians in the area. Mozart's People would be his ticket to fortune and fame. The band wrote and produced their own material. His younger brother Martin on bass, older brother Mikey keyboards and Fernando, a freak of nature with a talent like no other human I had ever seen on drums. Fernando Rivera produced more beat with a foot pedal than most drummers can with four limbs, but like many drummers, Fernando was inclined towards craziness and it was Mark's job to keep him focused. It was like putting the sly fox in charge of the crazy fox.

Mark's brother Mickey, the brains of the operation, was the only musician in Mozart's People with money two days after pay-day because Mickey Madden was the only one in the group not addicted to drugs. Mickey's clear head kept Fernando focused, and for his brother Mark, Mickey often imparted his insight that Mark needed to keep his eyes on the prize, a recording contract. His youngest brother Martin was also a mailer for the New York Times. He was also addicted to heroin, and because of that daily drain on his pocket Martin's bass guitar spent more time in pawn shops than jewelry thieves, so Martin always had a pawn ticket and big brother Mickey always managed the money to bail it out before the next practice or gig.

♣

During the mid-seventies the national economy had taken a turn for the worse and the financial outlook for our state was even more dire than the rest of America. Abraham Beam, the pint-sized mayor of New York City had flown to the capital with his traveling band of bookkeeping wizards to show Washington that the economy here was on life support. The headlines in the next day's *Daily News* set the agenda for the next few years. PRESIDENT FORD TO CITY, DROP DEAD.

When President Ford pulled the plug on a federal bailout for New York City, our tiny mayor went to the major unions for contract concessions and didn't get them, but the man in charge of our big city had an alternative plan. The ex-city controller immediately pushed a program through the city council to sell municipal bonds, and because those bonds were backed by the great seal of New York, the mayor was able to raise enough cash to balance the city's budget for the coming year.

The dire fiscal crisis subsequently forced the mayor to institute an immediate hiring freeze on all city jobs, including the one I hustled my skinny frame and fat ass for around the Brooklyn Navy Yard. The one for sanitation worker. Little freaking piss-ass!

♣

During the time I was still evolving into a weekend warrior, long before the realization of addiction, the fear of becoming a strung out junkie was merely a foreign notion, not a tangible concern. I was always strong willed, which some considered pig headed and normally independent of thought, which some considered not normal and possibly crazy. I say calculating. No one led me anywhere I wasn't willing to go, and I never felt embarrassed walking away from an uncomfortable situation. When David, Sean and Charlie went into the lots to smoke their first cigarettes I went right along with them, to watch. And although the education 'professionals' would have me believe I was an idiot because of my grades, I was aware of my minimal efforts and knew different. But as clever as I thought I was, I thought I was smarter. I thought I could outsmart addiction.

Sydney Berger was a Castle Hill addict with a legendary dope habit. All my darkest thoughts of addiction can be attributed to my personal experiences with the young man carrying the largest gorilla. Syd was a few years older and his greasy black hair and pock-marked skin added three more, and the ever-present white scum at the corners of his mouth seemed to fit his felonious personality.

Sydney and I were sitting on the thirteenth floor of his building, inside the exit door leading to the roof. I had a duce a bag ($2 per) and Sydney had a bundle (10-bags). Every addict I knew used either a spoon or bottle cap to cook their drugs, but Sydney was cooking so much dope that he was using a Hellmann's Mayonnaise cap for the same process.

Because of his daily bill with the drug dealers, Sydney became a thief of some renown, which was necessitated by his lack of employment. Sydney would casually stroll into the Food Fair Supermarket or any other large food store in the area and walk out two minutes later with enough beef to supply half the restaurants on Castle Hill Avenue.

An addict's habit is whatever he could afford on a daily basis, so if you shoot two dollars of dope a day every day for more than two weeks you better have two dollars for day fifteen. If you could manage to scrape up a hundred bucks a day for the same period you better have a real good job or the extraordinary ability to walk a cow past the butcher with the same cunning as Sydney.

It is not possible to get physically addicted to anything, including heroin, after only one dose. The process of addiction takes time. The body must first absorb this new substance into its fat cells, skinny cells and all the other cells that appear to be enjoying this new treat. One dose will simply run its course with no ill effects. But take away that opiate after the body has acquired a need and the body will send the gorilla to the brain to get it back and the gorilla never comes back empty handed. The gorilla will actually sit you down and explain your new reality. Go get me heroin or I will beat you to death, you dumb fucker. That's right, the gorilla curses when he's really pissed off.

The cost of a dope habit directly correlates to the amount of heroin the body gets accustomed to. That means that you don't want to get too crazy when you're starting off on your new career. Sharing syringes was a common occurrence during the nineteen sixties and seventies. If the needle clogged with blood, and it usually did, we would break the nearest light bulb, straighten the filament and stick it through the end of the needle until it forced the clotted blood through the point. I'm next...

A bobo is hypodermic syringe minus the plunger. The plunger is removed and replaced with a baby pacifier that's fastened tight with a rubber band. It enabled the clumsy addict to draw blood without having to pull up a plunger, a difficult one-handed task for many. Watching the free flow of blood gushing into the syringe is the only way to know that you're actually well situated in the vein. Then you just squeeze the bobo, which shoots the blood back plus the all-important liquid relief.

Once the actual drug high has waned it's not long before your body is craving more. You become tired, and within twenty-four hours you will be sick. The body will sweat, as if with fever. The ache in the legs, particularly knees and calf muscles can be debilitating. Stomach eruptions are especially disturbing, but it is the overall lethargy that leaves the body crying in pain for more heroin. The body's physical reaction to the overwhelming distresses of dope sickness, (lack of heroin) in no way resembles the hysterical kicking and screaming portrayed in movies and television. The body has no energy for theatrics. The body simply curls up in a tight ball while the feeble brain prays for enough money to purchase the necessary daily requirement.

A friendly neighbor from my old building in Castle hill was well known throughout the junkie community as the last resort. If a desperate addict was in need of works (syringe), you could knock on George Beady's ground floor bedroom window at any hour, day or night, and George would rent you his for a dollar. It was without a doubt the

211

filthiest bobo and bottle cap imaginable, but what can you expect for a freaking dollar?

It didn't take very long to realize that heroin was something to fear. By the time I got scared enough to fear for my life I was already facing Sydney in my mirror, and every time I looked, freaking Sydney was sticking his damn tongue out. My problem wasn't the amount of drugs I was injecting or even how I'd obtained the money. It was the simple fact that I no longer had a choice. Addicts do not recognize choices. From the moment I opened my eyes in the morning the focus was getting high. Not getting high was like not breathing, the absence of either, even for a short while will have a sick addict praying for a quick death. During my addiction I prayed many times for a peaceful ending.

Sydney and George succumbed to the AIDS virus over thirty ago. I'm still here and relatively healthy so I obviously didn't contract that particular infection from sharing their needles. I could write the names of thirty friends and acquaintances who also didn't suffer the same devastating disease, but unfortunately they're all just as dead. They simply died a lot faster, and as crazy as it might sound to the unfamiliar, they passed on to the way beyond a lot happier. Heroin-induced death merely begins as blissful oblivion and slowly darkens to a peaceful unbroken sleep.... without dreams.

♣

I'm not sure if every neighborhood has a hero, but we did, and big Joe Costello was ours. His curly red hair topped him off at six foot three and his large athletic frame was like a free ticket to enter the wide world of sports. Big Joe had a mild manner and casual way, but the football coaches at James Monroe High School saw something different: a big red-headed gift. They quickly turned their friendly new freshman into exactly what they needed, a raging giant with the strength to inflict serious pain on everyone breathing on the other side of a line of scrimmage. Big Joe was a terror in his football uniform and a big fun-loving teenager when he took it off. Aggression is a learned experience. I know. Sister Mary Monster taught it to me in first grade, and after nine more years of Christian mind development applied regularly by defective Christians I'm lucky I haven't murdered anybody along the way.

Like many other young men in the Castle Hill housing development, big Joe would eventually be drafted into the Army. After his ser-

212

vice in Vietnam Nam the big handsome neighborhood good guy was called from a list of hopeful civil servants and soon became a sanitation worker for the greatest city on the planet.

Our neighborhood was fortunate to have many parents willing to give their time to the kids, but Mister Murphy stood out. His easy smile and friendly manor weren't any different from my dad's, but mom kept my dad pretty busy with three different jobs, so unlike Mister Murphy, my dad had very little time for socializing. Or breathing.

Mister Murphy started the Castle Hill Boxing Club in a large room behind the stores, and it was in that dank smelly gymnasium where many young men, including big Joe, first took their urge and crude street fighting ability for a major tune-up.

Day in and day out Coach Murphy trained the friendly giant in the sweet science while instilling the psychological toughness necessary for the battle of wills within the squared circle. After six long months of punching speed and heavy bags, as well as all energetic sparring partners, big Joe was a marauding force of nature chomping at the bit to begin the ultimate test of amateur boxers. When the final bell sounded the referee was holding up his big hand as the Madison Square Garden announcer proclaimed big Joe Costello the 1970 New York Golden Gloves Heavy Weight Champion.

The Castle Hill colossus was never one to start a street brawl, but he did end a few. Big Joe could hit like a mule so he was a menace in every rowdy bar with a tough guy because after a few beers every other neighborhood tough guy seemed to have a need to build on their reputation, and going up against big Joe was never a morale booster.

My 65 Impala was parked at the curb in front of the Castle Keep, a bar on East Tremont Avenue at the intersection with Bruckner Boulevard. I was leaning against the car and big Joe was facing traffic on the busy avenue. Just two neighborhood buddies in a different neighborhood discussing world peace on a beautiful warm summer night. Big Joe and I each had a cold bottle of beer in one hand and I was scratching my fat ass with the other when a car suddenly screeched to a stop at the light behind me.

When I looked over my shoulder the smiling young driver of the electric blue '67 Chevelle SS head turner was rolling down his window. The skinny kid with the sparkly blue shirt was staring out through beady bloodshot eyes in our direction, but he didn't actually open his yap until his mumbling buddy started egging him on. When he finally started stumbling over his lips, the two barely teenaged girls playing grownup in the back seat began laughing hysterically through a cloud of pot smoke that was already wafting across the avenue in our direction. I stopped scratching my fat ass and scratched my empty head. The tedious comedy routine was winding down when big Joe and I suddenly realized that the babbling bubblehead was asking directions to the Throggs Neck Bridge. I was amused by the antics, but after a few cold ones Big Joe was in no mood for the giggly carload so he gave directions "right down Tremont Avenue and keep driving, straight into the East River." I thought it was pretty amusing. The young driver with sparkly blue shirt didn't.

The humorless dumbass flipped the transmission into park. He ejected off the seat and slammed the door behind. The angry idiot then half hurried, half skipped across the avenue with one arm behind his back, but he half stumbled, and when his fist suddenly arched high over his head it was wrapped tightly around a tire iron that he slashed out, slicing a hole above my right eye that went deep enough to slip my pinky into down to the first knuckle. The kid obviously had a screw loose and he definitely loosened a few of mine that were already pretty loose.

The startling shock to my nervous system was still being calculated as I went to my knees. It was no mistake. Big Joe was simply too big. I was the logical outlet for his misplaced anger, but the young idiot should've hit big Joe, but I quickly called no backsies. Blood was streaming down my face onto my favorite red flowered shirt. Now he has to pay for the hole in my face and the shirt.

Big Joe knew me well enough to know where this was going the second he looked me in my good eye. The big sergeant at arms grabbed the squirming knucklehead by the neck and yanked his scrawny wrist up high behind his back. Every other limb below his sparkly blue collar gyrated wildly in a frantic attempt to break free, but the angry idiot was my size and no match for the Castle Hill heavyweight champ.

I calmly opened my car door and grabbed the hammer from under the front seat. You never know when you might run across a nail sticking up in the middle the highway. I casually strolled towards his shiny attention grabber as if I were merely headed to the bus stop. The first thing I addressed? The nail sticking out of his windshield. CRACK! When I banged it home the knucklehead's frightened partner jumped from the vehicle screaming like a girl. The hot rod king of East Tremont Avenue was suddenly threatening all kinds of police action. The idiot put a hole in my face. Now he wants the cops? The girls couldn't climb from the back seat fast enough. They jumped around screaming loud enough to alert the cops, but the 45th precinct was a whole block away. I blocked them out and went about my business like a CPA at tax time. And look at that, a shiny tack protruding from the headlight. Bang! I was actually admiring the glimmering blue muscle monster growling in neutral when I noticed a spike sticking up from the hood. Bang! Bang! Bang! Those spikes can be pretty stubborn.

Before I addressed the screaming bad ass personally I smashed every single pane of glass, every light fixture, and mangled every shiny blue piece of sheet metal as I calmly strolled around the entire hot rod that was now a battered wreck in the middle of East Tremont Avenue. I took one quick step towards the squirming cry baby, but big Joe just let him fly. Without the tire iron weighing him down the guy was actually pretty fast, but he wasn't faster than my freaking hammer. He was still running down Bruckner Boulevard when I flung it like a tomahawk and caught him right in the back of his melon and knocked him head over heels where he skidded to a halt on his face. Now we're even.

Charlie Dineane had been inside the Castle Keep and he came out in time to witness the ending of the show, along with half the bars patrons. "You better get outta here."

"I think ya right." Charlie drove my car and my bleeding face to Jacobi Hospital.

A young intern had just finished the last stitch in the emergency room when Charlie suddenly parted the curtain. The hot rod king of East Tremont Avenue and his angry entourage had no problem finding the hospital. They came by ambulance. Charlie whispered in my ear as the doctor was cleaning up. "The cops are here and they have your hammer. We gotta go now." I knew my way around the hospital better than the janitor. "Follow me."

It was already three in the morning and the bar closed, so I drove Charlie straight to his apartment. Then I drove myself home to show Ellen the great job by a seasoned New York intern. Ellen was asleep on the couch and awoke when I turned the key in the lock. She was still rubbing the sleep from her eyes when she noticed my face. "What happened?" Ellen is always the calmest person in the room. "I lost my hammer." Keep it simple.

"What?"

Without a prayer of an intelligent come-back it was always import-

215

ant to sound angry, or at least very annoyed. Keep the wife on the edge. If she senses vagueness in my normally convincing demeanor she might investigate a bit further, and I'm pretty certain my first answer didn't go over too well. Actually, I'm pretty positive. "Goda bed before ya wake the kids."

So, I guess I'm gonna need another hammer. For carpentry. And stuff.

22

Getting high on dope was almost as regular as eating. Actually, getting high was a lot more regular. From two dollars a bag in nineteen sixty-nine the cost of sucking my socks had sky rocketed in a few short years to ten dollars per. Every nickel earned that didn't pay a bill or family necessity was going into my arm. The monkey on my back that started off as a tiny chimpanzee had grown within five years into a silver-back gorilla. The gorilla was now picking my damn pocket and stealing my lunch. Sonofabitch. I hate freaking gorillas.

Most of my closest friends were like most other people. They considered being injected with a needle, even in a doctor's office as a nerve wracking experience. Chris Carpenter and Joey Jackson were in that category: beer drinking pot heads.

The blustery frigid gale whistling outside Charlie Brown's bar on Starling Avenue at three in the morning could freeze brain tissue before we could hurry up a single block. I'm pretty sure that's what happened, because our destination was a block and a half. By the time we stumbled up to the AB Cab stand on Westchester Avenue I couldn't feel my feet. My fingers were like frozen sticks of numb flesh. My face hurt. Alcohol is supposed to lubricate the system like antifreeze for blood, and I had enough alcohol to float a freaking aircraft carrier. It doesn't work.

My long grey, double-breasted, lamb skin coat with its wide lapels looked like a Confederate general's uniform. It was a beautiful looking coat, but as warm as tissue paper. The three of us staggered up to the cab service under the elevated Castle Hill Avenue train station next to Volare Pizza. I grabbed the phone attached to the building that was wired to the dispatcher on the second floor. The taxi parked at the curb was calling my name. It was running, probably heated, the driver, nowhere in sight. "Where to?" said the dispatcher. I mumbled three different addresses. "Five minutes," said the dispatcher.

"We could be dead in fymina," I slurred and slammed the phone. "What did he say, Baby?" wondered Chris. "He said take the one at the curb, just bring it back in the morning. Jump in. I'll drive."

Joey and Chris smiled wide through numb lips and chattering teeth. Chris then opened the rear door and gestured Joey in like an attentive chauffeur. One by one they poured themselves onto the back seat like we were going for a Sunday afternoon cruise. I actually found Joey's house on Virginia Avenue by magic. Three minutes later Chris's building on Randall Avenue was swaying a bit, but it was right where we left it in the middle of the projects. "See ya mornin'," garbled Chris. My buddy barely slid off the back seat when three hundred AB cabs came screaming down the other side of the Randall Avenue mall, one by one. Okay maybe it was only six or seven, but my eyes were really blurry and they actually looked like an armored tank division. It was definitely time for a little prayer. **Dear Lord, we have a little situation here. I specifically remember grandma telling me how You take care of drunks. Grab a glove, Lord it's time to get in the game.**

I jammed the gas pedal to the floor. I blew the light on Castle Hill Avenue and should've been doing a hundred and eighty miles an hour, but I was driving a ten-year-old six-cylinder piece of shit, and after a long block of going nowhere forever I finally rumbled through the stop sign at Olmstead Avenue. Half the cab company was in my rear view mirror. The other half were all over their radios looking for their missing car. I kept hearing my address over the radio. "1965 Lafayette. The last idiot is going to 1965 Lafayette."

"We're on 'em, Vinny. 1965 Lafayette."

"Check it."

"Check it."

My building was just up ahead, so all I had to do is get there faster than everybody else and get my key in the rear exit door and slam it shut. "Check it, Vinny. We're comin' in from the White Plains Road."

"Check it."

"Check it, Vin." Everybody checking except me. I should've pick up the radio under the dash board and given the dispatcher another address because the one I gave him over the intercom was drawing A-B cabs from all over the freaking Bronx. The old bald tires screamed into the turn. My mind and the car were barely under control as I frantically straightened out. Suddenly my nice warm bed and my very hot wife were just up the block on the left. Five or six cabs were racing straight at me, another thousand practically choking on my exhaust.

I squealed to a jarring stop and shouldered the door and stumbled from the cab. I was still squinting through bleary bloodshot eyes towards the rear entrance about oooh saaay maybeee three thousand miles away. Okay, actually about thirty feet, but in my drunken stupor that door appeared like a tiny red speck in freaking California. I really hate freaking California. I don't even like the freaking Beach Boys.

Fifteen car doors slammed shut in rapid succession behind me. My brain was begging my legs to run very, very fast, but my brain was no longer in charge. My legs merely wiggling my body around and around in a circle. I actually remember the first punch in the head because the big angry cabbie who threw it said it was gonna hurt. He was wrong. It put me to sleep. I slept like a baby. When I awoke in the middle of the next day I remember thinking, something isn't right. I remember my beautiful suede coat hanging over the bedroom door, ripped to shreds, and I remember it was in better shape than me. I remember Ellen telling me that a friendly neighbor had knocked on the door in the middle of the night to tell her that her stupefied husband was bleeding all over the sidewalk by the rear entrance. I don't remember hearing concern, but Ellen did mention that my wallet was missing. When the telephone rang I remember wondering, why the hell is Ellen handing me the damn telephone?

"Is this Kevin Carroll?"

"Who's this?" The massive headache pounding behind my eyes was about to blow two blue holes into the refrigerator. "Who's this? This is the freaking owner of AB Cabs. This is the man holding your freakin' wallet and two telephones. One has an asshole at the other end and the other has a freaking lieutenant from the 43rd precinct awaiting my request to pick up your dumb ass up and take you to freaking central booking. You ask me one more stupid question you stupid dumb fucker and I'll personally pull your eyeball out and stuff it in ya freaking mouth." He was a bit annoyed. Then I remembered why. He found my freaking wallet and wanted my stupid ass as a generous reward. "My office is at the end of Morris Park Avenue by Eastchester Road. Don't take a freaking cab and get here yesterday."

When I turned the key in my own car I remembered it still had a very dead battery. Then I remembered everything else, except for where I parked that freaking cab.

AB CAB SERVICE

My nerves were fried. Extremities numb. The screaming wind had been slapping my face like an angry nun for an hour. I shook it off, stiffened my spine and stepped through the only door of a dingy yellow brick, two story commercial building.

I cautiously introduced myself to the big scary goon seated behind the 'reception desk'. The large brooding 'receptionist' grumbled under his breath as he pointed the way. I walked down the hall and slowly ascended the stairs with a bad feeling in the pit of my stomach, like the sensation of rancid mozzarella floating in sweat. My brain was in a black fog of fear, but this had to be done. I need my wallet.

I barely knocked on the partially open door and hesitated before peeking in. "The man told me to come up. I'm Kevin Carroll."

It was said that the owner of AB Cabs was 'mob connected.' I wasn't sure if it was fact or unfounded neighborhood gossip, but I was still hoping for the best when I found myself staring at death. And why exactly do I need this wallet? It was already waaay too late to run.

My timing would've only been worse if he was cleaning his gun. The big man with the rather large Roman nose was about to subtract a good six inches from a nice looking meatball hero the size of my leg when he noted my unfortunate interruption with a sigh and a menacing glare.

Now I would never say that the man I was face to face with was Italian because I'm not an idiot, and besides, he might still be alive. So this well-tanned gentleman slowly placed the steaming hero back on the desk and gently patted two hairy hands on either side, his dark eyes still glaring through my brain and actually inflicting pain. I felt like a banana split standing behind a thick glass partition in the BIG HOUSE.

So, this gentleman of possibly say, maybe mid-Mediterranean ancestry, but definitely not Italian was dressed in the standard uniform for Morris Park area tough guys, short-sleeved black Banlon shirt stretched way beyond the capacity for standard cotton thread. The gold chain around his thick neck was probably heavy enough to anchor most small water craft and it was floating above a chest of fuzzy black curls that looked more like a mohair sweater on steroids. Dark wide set eyes were still glaring through my brain from a head the size of a pumpkin. "Don't sit, Kevin. This won't take long." It was an exhausting walk through frigid wind swept temperatures and my legs felt like soggy macaroni. No offense, I mean jelly. "My boys told me you dropped this last night." The big man pushed my wallet across the desk while wiping a curious smile with a napkin. He pushed his girth back with his feet and looked up with bemused delight.

"Ah, yeah. I guess I did. Thanks."

"You look like a fairly intelligent young man, Kevin, except you need a freakin' haircut. I wasn't too concerned about my car, but the radio in the trunk is worth forty-five large. I could install the radio on a freakin' scooter and use it as taxi so I was happy to get everything back in one freakin' piece. I was a wise ass when I was your age, Kevin so I won't ask why you stole my freakin' car. Do it again though and your beautiful wife there in your wallet will be planting your stupid ass in Saint Raymond's Cemetery. You understand what I'm saying to you, Kevin?" Oh yeah, and who exactly is going to pay for my freakin' shredded suede coat? And your goons kicked me in the freakin' head and look at my freakin' face and I can't take a freaking crap because they kicked me in the freakin' ass, but I didn't actually say a word. From what I remember he didn't look to freakin' receptive.

"Yes, I understand. Thank you." Anything resembling bad attitude stayed in my head where it was scrambled up with the alcohol and all the other dumb shit that felt like a massive freaking brain hemorrhage.

I remember walking all the way home again and I remember Ellen asking me, what happened? The stupidity turned embarrassment turned devastation of the last twenty-four hours was still sinking in, so I was hardly ready for the third degree in my own living room from my own wife. So I made something up and I hope it was freakin'good because Ellen really deserved some freakin' peace of mind.

Yeah, no freaking shit.

♣

Some of my friends were already calling my wife Saint Ellen while others were shaking their heads in disbelief. How can a very intelligent and beautiful woman be so deficient in the ability to see beyond despair? Love is the indefinable capacity to act irrational. The love for my wife is easy, her love for me the most special gift one idiot could ever hope for.

Addressing the physical needs of my addiction was usually, but not always a once a day occurrence, the cost rarely exceeded thirty or forty dollars because that's what I could afford without resorting to drastic measures, and I was certainly capable of the occasional drastic measure. Occasionally.

The anxiety portion of my day finally flipped in my head to a nervous comfort after conjuring up a believable tale to borrow money, who I'd approach who hadn't heard it before, and both my story and person of interest were as necessary for getting high as my dealer and my left arm.

Anticipation of the drug produced a sort of euphoria when the cash was finally in my pocket. The drama of hide and seek with the cops a mere inconvenience and the last part of the experience necessary for heightened awareness. The methodical preparation and finally shooting the drug was far more satisfying than the actual effect of the drug itself. Getting high was no longer guaranteed, but rather a once in a while occurrence. After ten years of feeding the gorilla it was impossible to get high without a major infusion of cash. What my regular dose did do was take away the sweats, the ache in my legs and the loose feeling in the pit of my stomach that I'd crap in my pants. Thoughts of not getting straight by sun down and lying in a dope sick pool of my own perspiration was always a constant fear. If and when that happened, anything resembling sanity blew out the window, and that's exactly what I was up against until I ran into my old buddy from Castle Hill. The fireworks of the fourth of July didn't actually light up the sky until I hooked up with my old buddy Sean O'Connor.

Fifteen years seemed to flash by like a single lunch period in Sister Mary Monster's class since I first partnered up with some kid to break windows in the still unoccupied twenty-story building in the brand new Castle Hill Houses. Although Sean and I were best of friends for a while we eventually walked our own paths. The trust we established during that early partnership never changed and never wavered, so when I realized that Sean was looking for trouble I couldn't imagine going home without seeing what he had in mind. It's only neighborly.

Our move to Spring Valley in upstate Orange County just six months earlier wasn't quite working out as we expected. The strain of the weak economy put me out of work and on unemployment. That, combined with the gas crisis on top of a dope habit had all together driven my imagination to come up with innovative ways of accomplishing the impossible on a daily basis.

Car insurance is required by state law, but not actually necessary for driving a car. What is necessary is that the car appear to be legal.

License plates are obtained from the state of New York with proof of insurance. This year's down payment for insurance was also the only payment made. When the bill came in the mail for a second installment I went to work. First, I procured two New York State license plates by... stealing yours. Thanks. I love this state. Then I returned my hardly used plates to the DMV before the state imposed the four dollar per day fine. All I had to do now was drive like an eighty year-old woman and obey every single law instituted by God and the state of New York in order to avoid a possible confrontation that would require me to produce my registration. Of course I had a registration card, but the new stolen plates no longer resembled the numbers on the card which would surely get me thrown in jail. Can't have that.

With the price of gas soaring and my daily trip upstate choking my wallet, it was essential to reduce the high cost of traveling. The answer to my latest dilemma? Free gas. It's sort of a no-brainer. If it wasn't, I would've been running out of gas all the time.

I merely pulled into a friendly station. Sometimes I check the oil. After that charade I get back behind the wheel and calmly pull a dollar bill from my pocket and stick it out the window and make it appear, larger. Eyes in my rear view mirror watch as the gas guy closes the cap behind the rear plate. While he was still reaching the nozzle to the pump I slowly drive away. The frantic attendant screams, "Wait!! You forgot to pay!" Then he scribbles the stolen plate numbers on the palm of his hand as my taillights vanish into light traffic.

It was such a great act that I kept it on the road, sometimes at the same stations at different times of the day with varying degrees of subtlety for the next three years, but it wasn't free gas that inspired my stupidity on this particular evening. It was the gorilla. Gorillas get gas too, but first they gotta eat.

It was early evening. Hot. Muggy. Fourth of July. I'd been driving around the old neighborhood in my latest set of wheels, a comfortably air-conditioned silver '68 Olds Cutlass. The frantic search for drug money was driving my devious mind to think way outside the box. The black toy gun stashed in the glove compartment happened to be just inside the box. Another no brainer. I took it out of the box and slipped it under my fat ass. The measly twenty-two caliber snub nose was never used for an illegal endeavor, but this was shaping up to be as good a time as any to see if I could make it look a whole lot scarier than it actually is. On the other hand, the car was a mechanical monster and worked rather nicely, but when it stalled at a most inopportune moment I prayed to God as usual and as usual He was right where I left Him, still busy talking with dad and grandma.

I finally parked in front of Willie's Luncheonette to gather my thoughts and nerve when Sean suddenly walked out of the luncheonette. I hadn't seen my old buddy in years. "Hey, big dog. What's up?" Sean was startled at the sound of my voice, and when he turned his big Irish smile was even bigger than mine. "Oh, what's up, madman?" Everything after hello was a disaster. Two dope sick brains in the same place gets ugly in a hurry. We decided to rob a cab driver. What a great way to rekindle an old friendship.

We jumped into my car and I drove to the end of Castle Hill, made a left in front of Saint Raymond's Church, and continued past the massive Parkchester housing development and finally parked by the wide intersection of Tremont and Rosedale Avenues. We were looking for a gypsy cab, but hailed the first car that happened by, a yellow medallion. Not a regular sight around this part of the south Bronx and the cabbie was about to find out why yellow cabs avoid the outer boroughs by any means possible. The young oriental driver stopped and opened the window. "I go downtown. Where you go?"

"Columbus Circle."

"Downtown?" Fucking idiot. "Yeah, yeah, downtown."

Sean opened the door behind the driver and slid over to the other side. Before my partner got comfortable I got in, leaned over, stuck my arm around the opened plexiglass partition and put the stub nose threat in the side of the cabbie's brain. "Gimme ya money."

CLICK! The little Chinaman locked the doors, electronically. Who ever heard of this? "Oh, fuck!" And hit the gas. The kamikaze cabbie was suddenly speeding so fast in a tight circle that centrifugal force was sucking the air from our lungs and knocked us back against the seat. I frantically leaned over as far as I could while drawing my left leg tight into my chest and suddenly uncoiled like a cobra, the heel of my boot shattering the glass. Crawling out of the fast moving hole was a bit more challenging. "Hep! Prease. Hep!" The little Chinaman was screaming out the window at the top of his lungs. "Hep, prease!" But the nearest bakery was a good ten blocks away. "Hep! Prease!" The cabbie was still flying around and around in a tiny circle. One by one we struggled head first out the window and tumbled onto the middle of East Tremont Avenue. The yellow bolt of lightning exploded from the scene and raced away with our freaking drug money still in his shirt pocket. Sonofabitch! Crazy freaking Chinaman!

I had just failed at my first attempt ever at armed robbery and I didn't want the bad experience to linger over night. We hurried back to my car where I quickly dreamed up another brilliant plan, and the best part of plan B was that it killed two birds with one stone. We both needed money for drugs and my car needed gas.

The Esso gas station a quarter mile north of the Highway One motorcycle precinct in the middle of the Bronx River Parkway was perfect. Except for the police station thing. And considering Sean's father is a retired motorcycle cop on disability from a serious motorcycle accident, we had all the ingredients of a major fireworks display and it wasn't even dark yet.

We entered the parkway at East 177th street and made a u-turn in the station in order to be headed south. The Fordham Road exit is less than two hundred yards away, handy for a quick escape into the shadows.

I pulled to a stop and shut the engine. A young Puerto Rican attendant strolled from the small building in the middle of the station. "Filler up. High test." I rarely ever skimp on free gas. Sean was gazing out the windshield on the lookout for flying saucers or passing motorcycle cops. I got out and popped the hood. "Ya got a rag?" The unsuspecting attendant grabbed the greasy rag from his back pocket and placed it on the battery as I carefully inspected the dip stick. "Looks good," I noted. "Looks a little dirty," he suggested. Yeah, I gotta change it this week before I go on vacation. When I get back from Europe I'll be breaking ground for a new hospital wing that will be erected in my name for mentally impaired gas station attendants.

I got back in behind the wheel. The short skinny gas jockey with the long greasy hair hung the nozzle to the pump, walked up to my door and held out a hand, the other hopefully clutching a fist full of twenties in his pocket. "Eleven dollars." I lifted the threat into the open window. "The money or you're fucking brains all over that building." I put a little extra crazy in my eye because I was pointing a little plastic toy that wasn't even loaded with little plastic bullets. The startled attendant stepped back, tripped and fell with one hand stuck in his pocket, the other breaking his fall. I turned the key. A light blue Volkswagen Bug pulled up to the gas pumps on the north bound side of the station. I turned the key. A tall clean cut citizen emerged from behind the building and notices something amiss. A crazed hippie gangster is pointing a twenty-two caliber pistol at a young, hardworking, Puerto Rican gas station attendant. This definitely looks like a situation. I turn the key. The situation quickly degenerates when the Lone Ranger disguised as a New York City dick head draws a freaking cannon the size of a howitzer from a shoulder holster and points it at my head, specifically, between my eyes. "Drop the gun, mother fucker. I'm a cop." Of course he's a cop. I wouldn't have expected anything less.

My little toy pistol was still trained on the fallen prey as my eyes were searing a hole through the hero as he watched his own casket being paraded past a sea of blue in the front of Saint Patrick's Cathedral to the eerie sound of Amazing Grace being squeezed through the lungs of a sick cat by a large man in a kilt. He blinked. I caught it. "I'll blow his fucking brains all over ya car, dickhead." I prayed and turned the key for maybe the last time. The engine roared to life. "Get up!" The startled gas kid sprang up like a Mexican jumping bean. He threw the money in the window and staggered back against the pump. I floored the gas pedal on my '68 Oldsmobile heart attack on wheels and never gave a second thought to the off duty altar boy pretending to be a cowboy motorcycle cop. After all, I was driving a big bloc Cutlass. He was driving a light blue lawn mower. "Ninety-seven dollars," calculated Sean. "You did a great job, Big Dog." My buddy smiled. "Let's go get straight."

"You're haven't changed. You're still a dick."

"Ya mother." Twenty minutes later I was oblivious to life on planet Earth and still as broke as I was twenty minutes ago. Can't wait 'til tomorrow.

23

It wasn't very long before Ellen and I were having regular discussions about moving back to the Bronx. The fresh air and wide open spaces were originally the big draw to upstate Spring Valley. The relative safety compared with the rapidly deteriorating Bronx was also a big consideration, but when we actually settled in, the air didn't seem any cleaner, the spaces no wider and crime was probably down because Snooze Valley was too boring for the muggers. But the biggest frustration was that both our families and all our friends were so far away. After two whole years in what seemed like purgatory we finally packed up the kids and headed home to watch the Bronx burn up close and personal.

The war in Viet Nam was finally over. The economy was getting worse and I was still out of work, but the family was making due with whatever half assed jobs I could manage.

The Café El Toro was right next to Willie's Luncheonette. My friends and I were regulars in the local establishment since we were old enough to drink, legally.

It was a hot Saturday afternoon. I drove down to the Bronx to have a few cold ones with the boys. Baby and I were sitting at the bar listening to the owner rambling on and on about the new dance club he was constructing in the basement. Reuben was telling Chris and me that he needed help finishing the club before the advertised date announcing his big grand opening celebration and he asked me if I was interested in a little work. I was interested in a lot of work. Reuben promised that if we completed the nightclub on time he would keep me on as the part time clean-up guy. We did and Reuben kept his word, but I thought I could do better than being a part time janitor. A few weeks later I found another job through the *Daily News* classifieds. This one was installing four-way locking devices on apartment doors in the poorer crime riddled neighborhoods around the borough. The locks were fastened inside the center of the door, and when you turned the key it sent three aluminum rods into the frame and one into the floor saddle. The locks were cheaply made in China and the old rotted pre-war doors and frames I was installing them onto were probably made in South

Korea because they weren't sturdy enough to keep out hyper-aggressive three year old's. The salesmen were fraudsters who prayed on the old and weak. They should've been slapped. When I walked away from the first installation I felt like I robbed the old woman of her social security money.

I quit at the end of the day, but I did have a plan and as usual it was freaking genius. Join the Army. Ellen thought I finally lost my last marble. So did Chris Carpenter. Baby spent four years in the service, so he tried to give me the benefit of that experience. "Some twenty-year-old corporal from Georgia is gonna tell ya ta get down and gimme fifty, yankee, and you'll be writing Ellen all about it from the brig." But my mind was set. I needed steady work and nothing is steadier than the U.S. Army. I knew I could do it. I'm pretty sure.

Baby drove me to the recruiting station on Fordham Road in the middle of the Grand Concourse. Sergeant Strafford said that if I had a high school diploma he could get me into the Rangers. He said the Rangers would be my best opportunity for quick advancement and a higher pay grade, and that was the only reason I was joining, a steady pay check, benefits for Ellen and the kids. I was thinking I'd probably like to be a Lieutenant General.

A few weeks later I took the test for the GED at Roosevelt High School. Of course I didn't study, but apparently the standards for public high school graduation are the same as Catholic grammar school graduation, and because the nuns beat education into me with such efficiency it was still there when I needed it most.

A few weeks after the test I got the results in the mail. I'm gonna be an Army Ranger. Ellen was absolutely thrilled. Only kidding. Definitely not thrilled. Actually, I'm not sure, but pissed off comes to mind.

My plan was to kick the dope habit in boot camp. Soldiers gotta be tough. I can be tough. I think? That was the plan. It wasn't great and I talked myself into thinking that I could actually kick heroin cold turkey without too much of a problem. I think I can. Maybe, hopefully... I'll have to see...

A few days later I went back to the recruiter with my poor excuse for an education. After I filled out all the essential government paperwork that would bind me to the army for two full years I was given a date to be sworn in. Sergeant Strafford gave me exactly three weeks to get my family and personal obligations ready for my absence, but as my luck was still holding up, a friend called with a job opportunity only eighteen hours before I was supposed be getting my head shaved by a government barber. Close call. Scary thought.

Tony Boombatz said that his bosses at National Frozen Foods in Long Island City were hiring hi-lo operators and food pickers and the job was union. That meant benefits, and that alone sounded better than jumping out of airplanes over Georgia and way better than crawling through mud trenches in Kentucky. I didn't show up the next morning to swear the oath and the Army couldn't make me. "Na, na, na, na, na, naa."

♣

I was walking along Castle Hill Avenue when I ran into a friend that I knew since Holy Family grammar school. We talked about the old days and caught up on the new ones and before Jimmy Grande thundered off on his '77 Harley Shovelhead my future seemed that much brighter.

My old buddy hooked me up with a job working in his father's construction company. Jimmy said that the old man needed a few rough carpenters to work in the twenty-one story apartment building that was rising up alongside the Major Deegan Expressway, a mile south of Fordham Road. The job was also union and sounded way better than working in a freezer, so after freezing my fat ass off for six long months I gave notice and started the following Monday.

The kids were already enrolled in the Castle Hill Day Care Center before we moved back to the Bronx with help from my mother, who was still the payroll clerk and front desk receptionist. Ellen applied for a part-time sales clerk position in Korvette's. I told the wife not to mention my name on the application in case my beautiful color image was still tacked to the cork board in the security office. Ellen's easy smile and talkative personality gets her friends waiting for a bus, so she easily talked herself into the job. Ellen and I were back home and everything was smooth sailing. Well, at least for me. Ellen was still navigating uncharted waters.

♣

I was home early from work. The material to be installed, aluminum studs and track weren't delivered to the job site in the morning and the foreman said that he couldn't keep us on the clock, standing around pulling our puds. So we were sent home early, to pull our puds on our own time.

I should've waited around to pick up the boys from daycare before Ellen would hike the six long blocks after her shift, but my priorities hadn't quite developed to full grown-up status, quite yet. I always felt guilty for not doing enough, but never verbally expressed it to my beautiful and very patient wife. Ellen carried her weight and mine and never cried about the extra load.

After a quick shower I drove straight to the Cozy Corner Bar and Grill, the heroin supermarket of my universe. I pulled into Commonwealth Avenue and parked under the shade of massive oak trees that line both sides of the street. The little black kid with the toothy smile already knew my car and hurried down the block to intercept me before his competition.

Little Beamo was one of the friendlier runners and also the most credible. Beamo was also the youngest, about the same age most kids are in third grade. After a few encounters the little street hustler asked me my name. "Kevin." Beamo beamed. "Yo, that be ma name, too." Within a few weeks of calling me by name every runner and dealer on the block caught on. Within a month I felt like a celebrity at the Cozy Corner drug spot.

I slipped Beamo a dollar bill. He casually directed me to Star Wars (street name), who was presently selling the best bag of dope on the block. I got home before Ellen and the kids, shot it up in the bathroom, paused for result and went back out to do nothing in particular, which I do particularly well.

I drove to the park to meet up with my brother at his regular hangout, the playground at PS 125 on Watson Avenue. When I pulled up, Tommy was looking under the hood of his new wheels, an old but very clean '67 Ford Taurus. For me, looking at a car engine is like staring at the inner workings of a spaceship. Mystifying. Tommy knew that so he closed the hood and walked me around to introduce me to his new girlfriend parked in the shotgun seat. "Kev, this is Bernadette." She wasn't ugly and didn't look annoying, with flaming red hair like 'burn ta death' from first grade so we shook hands. "Nice to meet you, Bernadette. I guess you like the Yankees." She turned to Tommy already in the driver's seat. "You didn't tell me your brother was smart." I smiled, "I'm not that smart, Bernadette, but I do try hard and I know my brother. If Tommy didn't meet you in a bar while watching the

230

Yankees, you probably wouldn't be here."

"Oh, a smart ass." Yeah, we hit it right off. "Jump in. We're going to the Power Test for more beer." But Tommy wasn't actually going to the gas station for more beer. He was about to drive five blocks to the convenience store so Bernadette could take a whiz, and Tommy didn't want to blurt it out and embarrass his new squeeze.

I opened the back door and slid onto the seat. "Here, finish this." Tommy plucked a Miller nip beer bottle from a tiny brown paper bag and handed me the half empty bottle over his shoulder. My brother crumpled the small bag in his other fist. A minute later he pulled up to the busy convenience store in back of the crowded gas station. Bernadette shouldered the car door, entered the tiny store, dashed past the cash register and into the restroom, but in her haste Bernadette probably didn't notice the red and white sign I was staring at in the front window, RESTROOM FOR PATRONS ONLY.

Tommy and I are about the same size, medium, but Tommy is thicker. If Tommy hit you in the face your knees wobbled. When I hit you in the face I usually hurt my hand and went looking for a big stick. And nobody ever said I was thick, except for my teachers, but they were referring to the consistency of brain matter.

From my partially obscured view in the rear seat I noticed a big guy wearing a red Power Test tee shirt sitting on a little bench outside the store. As we pulled up the guy seemed to be enjoying the relative calm of a beautiful spring evening until Bernadette dashed past him on her way into the restroom. His big Fred Flintstone face was barely above my line of sight and his thick wavy hair still probably blowing from the passing emergency whizzer. The guy started cursing loud enough under his breath to sound like an idiot that I assumed had everything to do with the fact that Bernadette was probably already resting on the seat reserved for paying customers.

Tommy still had the tiny paper bag balled in his fist when he suddenly hooked it out the window over the roof of the car towards the garbage can by the front door and missed. The big man whose head was already turning red abruptly blew a gasket. The guy poked his big ugly mush inside the rear window behind Bernadette's seat. "You some kinda pig?" Tommy held his tongue and turned completely around. Eyes wide. Cheshire grin. "I'm talking to you, mother fucker." My brother readjusted his line of sight and focused a hard glare long enough for the idiot to rethink his options. "That's right, ya dumb mother fucker."

231

Tommy was now straining to keep his long fuse from burning up his good will, but this asshole really needed a lesson in civility and my brother was certainly capable of teaching it. Tommy turned back again and slowly shook his head. I knew where this was going while Fred was still grumbling under his garlic breath. This is about to get stone-age stupid.

The Power Test windbag obviously needed further motivation to get off his big dumb ass. I happen to be an excellent motivational instigator. I calmly looked him in the eye. "How 'bout I rip out ya tongue and shove it up your fat ass so you could talk out your rear end on a regular basis, dick head." I'm pretty sure I couldn't actually do it, but that wasn't the point. The point was to get this party started. Fred leaned his big ugly mush even further inside the window and growled. "How 'bout I kick both your asses up and down Bruckner Boulevard, you fucking hippie faggots." He was big, but he certainly wasn't that big, but I was still more amused than anything. "In twenty-four-years I never got beat up by a big mouth, asshole. I hope you got more than a big mouth?"

The thoroughly offended and extremely pissed off gas station jockey rushed into the office adjacent to the store. Seconds later he emerged swinging a baseball bat and immediately started blasting home runs all over the front hood of Tommy's new car. "How's this, mother fuckers!" Bang! Bang! Bang! Bang! Tommy frantically exited the front door. I was already out the back. "That's right, I got a big mouth, mother fuckers. Whattaya gonna do about it?"

After four home runs in a row it was time for the opposing pitcher to put a fast ball in the side of his head. We charged at the same time. The big man tossed the bat to the ground, drew a gun from the back of his waistband and pointed it like a cop at the firing range. I got left back a few times in school, but I learned enough along the way to know the difference between a baseball bat and a handgun. I can dodge a baseball bat. I grabbed Tommy by his collar and pulled. "Another time."

"Yeah! Next time bring a few friends, you fucking hippie faggots!"

The Korvette shopping center at Bruckner Boulevard and White Plains Road was usually the cause of traffic nightmares under normal circumstances, but this Friday evening before Mother's Day was especially hectic. Bernadette finally opened the car door as total insanity was dragging us down to the next level. Tommy floored the gas pedal. "What's the hurry? What's going on?"

"We had a little misunderstanding with that guy." Tommy pointed towards the big smiling idiot standing in front of the office aiming his pistol towards the moving windshield. "I'll explain later." The wheels spun out as Tommy turned towards the boulevard, but he suddenly braked hard at the sight of traffic blocking the way. The Miller nip beer bottle was still in my pitching hand. I shouldered the door, stood, reared back and threw a purpose pitch that buzzed his ear at ninety-seven miles an hour and quickly jumped back in behind my brother.

The Power Test tuff guy was now tracking the car while screaming threats of annihilation as he held the thirty-eight caliber pistol high over his head like a sheriff clearing the town of rowdy drunken hooligans. Tommy made a sharp left around the gas pumps and suddenly stomped on the brake again to avoid a vehicle entering the station. He couldn't reverse and the fire hydrant on the right side of the car was practically in Bernadette's lap. We were almost out of options.

From under her seat Bernadette quickly grabbed an option, I mean a piece of heavy duty Con Edison cable, half the length of a cop's nightstick and thick enough to teach a hard lesson. I was already leaping from the car, when Bernadette handed it off. Tommy, not nearly as stupid but extremely loyal, followed his older brother with only his anger as a weapon.

Rubberneckers in cars and stupefied oglers walking by the station came to a complete standstill. The big tuff guy was still screaming bloody intentions in the hopes of scaring us away. He obviously misunderstood my level of stupidity.

When I rushed forward I discerned his fear for the first time. The big idiot quickly backed away, eyes bugging out of his head and screaming like a lunatic with the pistol pointed at my face. The highly agitated candy-ass suddenly squeezed a shot towards the ground that felt like somebody banged my big toe with a fist. I yelled above the crowd noise to alert my brother. "This asshole's got rubber bullets!" The man's eyes were now possessed of a manic horror but his anger was still managing the conflict. "Keep comin', mother fucker. I'll blow ya fucking brains out!" But it actually was a bullet, and it ricocheted off the ground and sliced into my work boot, but I didn't know that. I charged, this time with absolutely no apprehension and cracked the cable across his nose that split and bled like a running faucet. The Power Test windbag tripped backwards where Tommy met him with a haymaker off the side of his jaw. The frantic loud-mouth was still stumbling around when he fired another shot that whistled over Tommy's head. I cracked the cable with a vicious blow across his left eye. He fired another shot towards my head and a forth shot went straight in the air. The fifth CLICK! jammed and the sixth CLICK! Now he's in deeper shit.

The next left hook from my brother was delivered to the right side of his thick skull with enough rage to punish his unborn children. Big Fred was still reeling every which way so I carefully lined him up and swung the cable with a savage anger and cracked another opening under the same eye. This time he kept stumbling and crashed to the ground like a sack of shit where he pissed his bloomers and cowered in fetal position like a crying sissy.

The cumulative fury amassed for bullying authority figures from first grade on was still raging through my right arm like a pneumatic piston. I continued swinging that length of cable like a crazy man until I actually sprained my wrist. His every extremity paid the price. The man was a pulsing mass of lumps and bruises and open gashes left writhing on the ground in the bleeding heap of pathetic arrogance. I walked away, slowly, satisfied.

Tommy grabbed his gun off the ground, smacked it good in his bloody mush and flung it over the roof of the convenience store. The entire crowd applauded as we slowly exited the gas station via Virginia Avenue.

As far as we were concerned we did nothing wrong. A lunatic pulled a gun and shot it from point blank range in our direction. If he had the balls we'd be dead, but he didn't. We did what troublemakers dream about the world over: got the best of a punk with a gun. We're on our way to get beer, this time for real and I definitely needed a drink. I worked up quite a thirst.

Tommy dropped me off at the park by my car. He and Bernadette continued driving along Watson Avenue on their way to the bodega at the corner of Gleason and Pugsley Avenues. Ten seconds hadn't passed when a blur of blue and white screamed past the school yard. Shots fired will often bring out the Dirty Harry in police departments.

I left my car parked at the curb and sprinted in the opposite direction. By the time I turned the corner onto Pugsley Avenue Tommy and Bernadette were already in handcuffs. Blue and whites, flashing lights and undercover sedans blanketed the area. The regular Friday night crowd gathered around. I was already rushing across the street while Bernadette was being placed in the back of the patrol car, but hesitated when Tommy nodded me away but continued on towards the man attached to his wrist. "Excuse me, officer," I said to the back of the man in blue. He quickly turned. The young officer with the hard glare and twisted mouth placed something on the roof of the patrol car, I'm thinking half-eaten jelly donut. "Get back before you go with them." I was hoping for a friendlier reception. "Listen, I saw the whole thing. That guy shot at them. He got what he deserved." A short stocky detective with a big foomanchew mustache overheard. "You saw the whole thing?"

"Yeah, I did." A tall, uniformed lieutenant with a head of shocking white hair stepped between us. "Would you like to be a witness for these two? They're gonna need one." Think fast. Don't be intimidated. "Absolutely."

The three of us were now seated in the back of the same squad car. The little blue officer riding shotgun turned around to look me in the eye. "So, what did you see?" pondered Sherlock the blue dickhead Holmes. I stared back and quickly ran down the entire scenario with a little too much emotion and detail, so the driver, officer clairvoyant wizard thought, "He might be the other guy were looking for." I didn't deny the obvious for obvious reasons. My brother was in trouble and needed a lawyer and I was perfectly willing do the talking until one showed up. "I am the other guy," I confessed.

By the time we arrived at the 43rd precinct a quick two minutes later Tommy and I had already convinced the two blue geniuses that our actions were necessary and motivated by an unglued moron for no less an infraction than Bernadette taking an unauthorized rest and Tommy missing a hook shot. "I heard he's done this before," noted Sherlock. "I guess he pulled a gun on the wrong brothers."

"I guess you're right," I bragged.

From the moment I became aware of his presence the big idiot seemed intent on confrontation, and according to the cops it wasn't the first time he's pulled a gun. Officer Lewis told us that the enraged loudmouth was the owner of the gas station. Officer Turner said that he's pulled the same stunt a few times before except for the shooting part and those incidents were probably covered up faster than the Kennedy assassination. Discharging a weapon in a crowded gas station on this Friday evening before Mother's day will not be laughed about over beers in his back office.

Tommy and I were escorted into stationhouse and quickly hustled into a glass-enclosed interrogation room on the ground floor. Bernadette was finally uncuffed and showed to a chair across the room.

We were made comfortable with the hopes of release, but that notion blew out of my head faster than the answer to 7x9 when the angry investigators finally arrived back from the hospital. "Where are they?" A uniformed officer pointed the way. The two dickheads burst into the interrogation room, one behind the other, aggression overflowing through raging eyes and balled fists. The first one through the door looked like he swallowed a freaking Volkswagen. The second like he owned a donut factory. The sloppy disheveled leader of the pack paused and stuffed something in his back pocket. I'm thinking cream donut. "You!" He pointed at me. "Up!" His big ugly mush right in my kisser. "You better hope he makes it, because if he don't, you and ya partner will be spending a lot of time with Bubba up in Sing Sing."

I shook my head and stared at my partner. My partner stared back. We both glared at this stupid ass detective like he needed a new perspective, so I gave him mine. "I hope he's already dead, you dumb mother fucker!" The room was crawling with cops. He shoved me against the wall. "Cuff 'em both, robbery and attempted murder."

Well, that didn't exactly go down as expected. We expected to be released. The two arresting fabricators in blue had already suggested that Stanley Madoff, the angry owner of the gas station, who was also the dumbass shooter was probably presently cuffed to gurney at Jacobi hospital for aggravated stupidity. Instead, the upstanding bruised and bloodied big mouth told the fat-ass detectives we attempted to rob his gas station. Liar, liar, pants on fire.

If you discharge a firearm anywhere anytime for anything in New York State you better have a damn good reason, and our lying accuser probably sounded very convincing when his fairytale spewed from the battered face of a man unrecognizable to his own wife.

The following Tuesday Stanley Madoff's claim of a robbery and subsequent ass whipping was the head line story in the Bronx Press Review. PARKCHESTER BROTHERS ROB AND BEAT GAS STATION OWNER.

Mom and dad had moved to the massive Parkchester housing development a few years back and my brother was still living at home. The press was simply making a statement. Parkchester was no longer the crown jewel of the Bronx. Crime was rampant in the area, with Parkchester following the Castle Hill Houses down the sewer.

24

After quick handshakes and hurried introductions, the trim young attorney at Grey & Associates gestured to his imitation leather chairs. "So tell me, Mister Carroll, what brings you and your brother to me on this beautiful spring morning?" The baby-faced attorney leaned back and laced his fingers behind a very short head of ginger red hair, and since his probing gray eyes were focused on me I stated my case with the calm resolve of an innocent man and ran down each moment of the evening of Friday the thirteenth of May.

Except for a few minor interruptions by Tommy I did all the talking. No colorful descriptions, no youthful bluster, no bravado and no offer of rhyme or reason for the actions of another. I gave the man the facts. Just the facts. Plain and simple.

Mister Grey nodded aggressively and interrupted occasionally. When I finally concluded he calmly suggested, "I could win this thing outright, but I'm gonna need two thousand dollars. A thousand up front." He definitely started off on the wrong foot. I looked at Tommy. We both squinted sideways at the aggressive young lawyer. "We didn't know if we were gonna like you," I offered, "so we didn't bring any money." It was the first lie I told him and apparently he believed every word, from how I met Bernadette to the moment Tommy and I were charged with two class-A felonies. We didn't bring any money because we didn't have any money. "That's all right. If ya decide to hire me before you leave the office we'll make an arrangement. Maybe installments if ya need time."

I forgot to inform Mister Grey that I was feeding an eight-hundred-pound gorilla every day and that the gorilla eats before me, so his chances of getting paid any time soon will be when Tommy throws him a few bananas, but it wasn't explored further so I sort of put it in the deepest hole in the back of head and left it there. Five minutes hadn't passed before he tried again to close the deal. "So, whaddaya think? We have an agreement?" He seemed a bit pushy and we needed an aggressive hungry lawyer. I nodded at Tommy. He nodded back. "It's a deal."

Our new attorney quickly delved into every moment of the evening in question. After we expanded on everything he needed to know he grabbed a yellow legal pad and put pen in hand. "Okay, let's start over again from the beginning." I assured Mister Grey that he didn't need a pen. I told him he didn't even need a good memory because I have one and I can recall every moment of this incident the same way it happened then and now and Tuesday and next month and next year. I was emphatic. "He has to lie and when he does I'll whisper in your ear and you will make him look like the lying piece of shit that he is." Our new mouthpiece looked us both in the eye and smiled. "Okay, okay. I like it. You convinced me."

"I'm glad to hear it." He placed the pen on the pad and slowly shook his head and gave me his first legal counsel. "Try not to be too sarcastic on the stand." I didn't think I was sarcastic at all. But I nodded a half-hearted apology. "I'm gonna put you two in front of the grand jury." Mister Grey assured us that our entire testimony would then be public record and potentially used against us at trial. Mister Grey expected us to be indicted, but he expected our Grand Jury testimony to work in our favor.

THE GRAND JURY ROOM

Tommy and I told the same story to the grand jury that we imparted to the two blue wizards in the patrol car the evening we were arrested. Stanley Madoff, owner of the Power Test gas station was the only prosecution witness. We were indicted, attempted murder and robbery in the first degree.

THE TRIAL

Tommy is likable and wasn't really challenged by the prosecutor. According to my lawyer I was considered the instigator and the more serious aggressor. The young prosecutor had no idea. "Mister Carroll, you testified before the grand jury that when you first saw the man in the red tee-shirt, the man you now know as Mister Madoff, he immediately got up from his seat outside the store and ran to the office and—"

"I didn't say that."

"Your, Honor?"

"Mister Carroll, you will wait for the entire question." The judged glared at my lawyer. "Mister Grey, if you can't control your client, I will. Continue, Mister James." The smug little man was pissing me off already and we were just getting started. "Mister Carroll." The genius paused for dramatic affect. "In your previous testimony before the grand jury you said that after the man in the red tee shirt saw you, he ran into a nearby office and when he came out again he was pointing a pistol at your face. Is that correct?"

"No."

"Then do you care to elaborate on what you did testify?"

"If you would've actually read my testimony." The little prosecutor stomped his tiny wing tip shoe. "Your Honor?"

"Mister Carroll, just answer the question." I glared at the angry little prosecutor. "I said he stuck his big head through the back window and asked my brother if he was some kinda pig."

"And what did he do, or what did you do next, Mister Carroll?"

"I suggested that I'd rip his tongue out and shove it up his fat ass. I didn't say anything yet about running or a gun."

"Your, Honor. I object."

"Don't editorialize, Mister Carroll."

The little sissy Mary assistant was already coming unglued. Well, he huffed and he puffed. "And what did you do next, Mister Carroll?"

"I didn't do anything."

"Mister Carroll, what did the plaintiff say or do next if anything?"

"He said how 'bout I kick both your asses up and down Bruckner Boulevard you fucking hippie fags. Then he walked through a door and when he came back out he was screaming and swinging a baseball bat."

The agitated little prosecutor started flipping pages, looking through my grand jury testimony so he could shove it in my face, but he should've actually read my words before he walked into court. My very accommodating advocate leaned across the aisle and pointed to the relevant information. The little prosecutor read it, probably twice. When he sat back he looked like he was squashing a big dump in his little diaper.

I repeated that same scenario another ten times with varying degrees of contempt, so when the angry little prosecutor finally took a breath to catch a clue he seemed to be standing right where I spent half my career, in very deep shit.

After a lengthy day and a half and closing arguments the six jurors were charged before lunch break. The three of us walked confidently from the room and stood just beyond the double doors. We were discussing what we thought was a solid case of mitigating factors for dismissal of both chargers. Then we discussed the important stuff. "They take lunch, too, said Mr. Grey, "so the jurors won't be back till at least two o'clock and probably later. Get something to eat and come right back. There's a waiting area right here." He pointed to a door and pushed the elevator button. The court room door flung open. The officer was practically out of breath. "Mister Grey. Don't leave. We have a decision." Our lawyer glanced at his watch. "Already? Six minutes?" I looked at Tommy. Tommy looked at me. "Does that mean we can't eat?" Mister Grey glared at me like I was a cheeseburger deluxe. "I'm hungry too, but I think we can all wait a few more minutes."

Stanley Madoff was still huddled with the little prosecutor when the battling Carroll brothers and our young stud attorney re-entered the room. His shoulders slumped, head shaking and with good cause, Mister Grey had essentially beat the snot out of his big dumb ass all morning long, but the lying weasel suddenly puffed himself up like Popeye after a quick gulp of spinach when the door behind us secured with a click.

If looks could kill I was suddenly staring down the barrel of a sawed-off shotgun. Missus Power Test turned towards the isle and glared her two beady lasers when I walked back to my still warm seat. Missus Tuff Guy looked like a raging pair of shiny red lips on a stick. Most skinny people wouldn't look as emaciated after three or four years of decomposition. She was overdressed and way beyond agitated as she squirmed nervously and babbled incoherently from just behind the prosecutors table. I insisted that my Ellen stay home. I didn't need support, our show was the truth with a little attitude. "All rise." We stood as one and watched as the Judge entered the room. He sat. We sat. The jury filed into the box. The court officer looked towards our table. "The defendants will please remain standing."

"Madam Foreperson," announced the judge. An older woman in her sixties with a thick head of shiny white hair wearing a fuzzy white sweater stood at the right end of the box. "Have you rendered a verdict?"

"We have, Your Honor."

"Is it unanimous?"

"It is, Your Honor." I was staring directly at the woman, but hardly noticed her face. I could barely hear my brother whisper. "This is it, bro." I turned imperceptibly towards the man who testified being two hundred and thirty-five pounds at six foot three. I would be that with sixty pounds of rocks in my pockets standing on a step stool. He tightened a crooked mouth in a jackal snarl when he noted my attention. Our eyes locked. He was here to watch me suffer. He should've shot me in the face with the third bullet. "What say you madam foreperson?"

"Your Honor. We find defendant Thomas Carroll innocent on the charge of robbery in the first degree." The grumbling behind the prosecutor's table was already growing like a flame fueled by the hot gases of judicial frustration. "And how do you find for Thomas Carroll on the charge of attempted murder?"

"Your honor, we also find Thomas Carroll innocent of the charge of attempted murder."

Mister Grey tapped my leg and distracted my brain, which interrupted my whimsy as I was putting the finishing touches on the second ass whippin' I had given this asshole within three months. "We're not quite out of the woods."

I gazed towards the jury, but my anger was still in charge of my brain. I gave no response, but tight control. "Madam Foreperson, how do you find Kevin Carroll on the first count in the indictment of robbery in the first degree?" Mister Grey had already informed us that this charge should've been dismissed at pre-arraignment because the gun was retrieved at the scene. I was as confident as Elmer Fudd pointing a double barrel shotgun down a rabbit hole. "Your honor we find defendant Kevin Carroll innocent on the charge of robbery in the first degree." One wabbit down. It must be duck hunting season.

"And how do you find Kevin Carroll on the second count of the indictment of attempted murder?" Daffy Duck was standing at the edge of the pond and insisted it was still wabbit hunting season, but I'm the smartest hunter in the court room. Daffy stuck his fluffy little head inside my mighty cannon and smiled into the camera. "Your Honor, we find Kevin Carroll… " I held my finger firmly on the trigger and stared through the telescopic lens at the two bulging eyeballs staring back. "Innocent on the charge of attempted murder." Kablewie! Right between the ears.

The show was almost over, but Missus big mouth wasn't quite finished acting like a clown, and besides, she seemed to have an urgent need to choke my scrawny little neck like a chicken before they rolled the credits and closing Loony Toon theme song. "He tried to kill my husband! You hippie sonofabitch! I should—"

"Officer, escort that woman outside."

"Thank you," I mouthed to the jury. They all smiled back, but their smiles were nothing compared to the one I was already showing the toughest man in his own bathroom mirror. Stanley Madoff couldn't paint a black hole big enough to crawl through in a cartoon graveyard.

That's all folks!

I bet you can actually hear the music. I know I can.

25

Muhammad Ali became my second favorite athlete behind the great Yankee center fielder Mickey Mantle. I watched Muhammad Ali's career with great interest. All the poetic predictions. All the brilliant foot work. The many punishing jabs. I watched him lose to Joe Frazier in the fight of the century and return the favor the next time around. The Thriller in Manila showed a man possessed of a talent like no boxer before. When Smokin' Joe Frazier finally ran out of smoke he looked up at the self-proclaimed Greatest and realized, Ali was right all along.

I was close enough to Muhammad Ali to shake his hand when he walked from the third base dugout in Yankee Stadium before he stepped into the ring in his final battle with Kenny Norton. I watched Ali knock out the mighty George Foreman in a clash he was thought too old to win, but Ali's gift of speed was waning. The end was near, though not before Ali decided to fight a wrestler. I didn't think it was such a great idea, but when Ali did anything it was a spectacle like no other in sports. I love a good spectacle.

The fight was set. Muhammad Ali vs Antonio Inoki. The venue, Nippon Budokan Arena, Tokyo, Japan. The event to be televised live around the world via satellite hookup. My seat was much closer to home, Shea Stadium, Queens, New York. The live headline ticket was Chuck Wepner the boxer vs Andre the Giant skyscraper disguised as a human being.

The ring was set up on home plate. My brother and I had pretty good seats directly behind the plate one level up on the railing with nothing and nobody in front of us but a fifty foot drop into the box seats.

Chuck Wepner, 6' 5" looked like leprechaun next to the 7'5" giant. After Andre tossed Chuckie over the ring ropes the fight was pretty much over, except for the brawl between their two camps. It was finally time for the main event.

Tommy sat in the first seat on the aisle, I was on his right. The massive projection screen above the ring came to life. The crowd in the stadium was getting louder. Muhammad Ali finally entered the ring.

243

"Ali! You fucking niggaaa!" Thirty or forty rows up, sitting on the concrete steps between the sections, some fool had started yelling. "Ali! You fucking niggaaa!" I looked at Tommy. Tommy looked at me. We both turned and glared up at the asshole yelling from the top of the staircase. The entire section on both sides of the aisle began to stir. Obviously, this intoxicated fool didn't understand that Ali couldn't hear him screaming from Shea Stadium all the way in Japan. The smattering of black people not amused. The masses of white people getting aggravated. Slowly and steadily the unruly asshole came down the steps. "Ali! You fucking niggaaa!" The crowd getting louder. "Shut up, fool!"

"Asssshooole!" Three steps down. He cupped hands to mouth. "Ali! You fucking niggaaa!" The young idiot was pissing off a lot of people. "Quiet, jackass!"

"Shut up, moron!"

"Asssssshooole!"

Down he came, three and four steps at a time. Every time he sat he cupped hands to mouth and yelled the same dumb shit over and over. The young greaser in the white tee-shirt finally ran out of steps. And time. He squatted in the aisle next to my brother. The annoying dickhead grabbed the railing and pulled himself up so Ali could better hear him in the land of the rising sun. "Ali! You fucking niggaaa!" When he plopped down again he looked like me at six years old waiting for the start of the Lone Ranger, chin in hands, eyes big on the screen. Tommy turned. "I'm gonna clock this clown."

"I got this. Switch seats." Tommy stood up and stepped in front of me. I maneuvered my fat ass onto his aisle seat. The genius reeked of gin. After listening to this blabbering dickhead for five minutes the patience portion of my brain was pretty much tied into a very tight knot. I decided to let out a little slack. A thousand fight fans were yelling and screaming, nobody moving. Except me. "Ali! You fucking niggaaa!"

"Buddy, if you don't know howda fly, ya sittin' in the wrong seat. Shut up or move! I'm not gonna ask again." He finally looked me in the eye. "What the fuck you gonna do, hippie?" This was another one of those situations where it helped to look like a long haired, peace loving hippie. Not a threat. He was bigger by a little. So was Andre the giant.

My attack had to be lightening quick like an Ali jab, as effective as a Joe Frazier left hook with all that energy generated by my brain and released through the end of my foot. The loud idiot was totally focused on the heavy weight champ as I leaned as far as I could to my right over

244

Tommy's lap while drawing my left leg into my chest. My target was stationary except for his big mouth. "Ali! You fucking—"

His big yap was wide open when I uncorked my leg that was attached to my little boot and planted a very hard heel with a vicious anger that partially severed his ear. Blood spurting. Crowd applauding. I tried to do a little Andre the Giant by tossing the stunned fool over the railing into the netting above the box seats below, but the bloody fool held onto that rail like he was hanging from the 86th floor of the Empire State Building. The crowd behind me erupted. "Watch out!"

"Stop, buddy!"

"Cops coming!" A thousand fight fans saw the best fight of the night up close and personal and all seemed anxious to pay me back for the free exhibition. Ten of New York's biggest were already rumbling down the stairs in a hurry. I wasn't expecting such a quick reaction. The bleeding greaser was dripping all over his nice white tee-shirt and me. "Turn around and put ya hands behind ya back." I turned around towards home plate. "No! Not him! The other guy!" My new best friends erupted on both sides of the aisle. "No! Not him. The other guy!" I turned around towards my new fans. The dickhead staggered in place, the crowd manic to help the skinny hippie who quieted the annoying disruption.

"No! Not him! The other guy!" Twenty rows up on the aisle a young black woman was quietly speaking to a very large and very dark blue sergeant. The big man acknowledged the woman with a courteous tip of the hat, but his expression darkened quickly as he hurried down the aisle past his blue line of subordinates. "Take 'em off." I turned around. A nice light blue officer took 'em off. The drunken greaser coming unglued. "What the fuck are you idiots doing! Look what the fuck this hippie did to me!"

"Well, this nice gentleman—"

"This nice fucking hippie just kicked me in the fucking head." His bloody hand pressed to his leaking ear.

"Are ya gonna let me finish?" The light blue officer yanked the big mouth by the neck. "Is going home after the main event."

"That's bullshit!"

"Then my boys will take you to get stitched up at Flushing General. After that they'll be getting their overtime booking you into the one-o-nine. Any more questions, genius?" The entire crowd drawing closer for a few parting jabs. "Have a good night, asshole!"

245

"What are you locking me up for?"

"For bleeding all over my stadium."

"Fuck you, mother fucker." The crowd getting louder.

"They're gonna love you in lock-up, sweetie!"

"Ali! Ali!"

"Ya gonna miss a good fight asshole!"

"FUCK ALL YOU MOTHER FUCKERS!"

"Watch ya mouth and turn around," the officer ordered. The idiot stumbled around. The light blue officer hooked him up, dragged him up the aisle on his way to the emergency room and then hopefully a bullpen at the 109 and a cell full of dope sick angry black guys that don't like Italians.

What a great night. I watched Andre the Giant toss Chuck the Bayonne bleeder Wepner around Shea Stadium like a rag doll. I had a pretty nice victory myself, though not sanctioned by the New York State Boxing Commission. Got applauded like a rock star. Every crazy moment endorsed by my new best friends at the New York City Police Department.

Muhammad Ali finally started dancing around the ring to start the first round. "Ya wanna hot dog? Hey! Hot dog!"

"Nice kick, bro. I didn't know you were a southpaw."

"Pretty good shot, right. I bet he's got a headache."

26

On August 6th of 1977 we moved for the fourth time in nine years to a nice two-bedroom apartment in a well-kept two-family house on a quiet tree lined street in Throggs Neck. For two kids who grew up in the projects like Ellen and me, this beautiful area of the Bronx is how we pictured Hooterville.

Richie and Joe were seven and eight years old, and Logan Avenue full of boys the same age. I was sitting on the stoop in front of the house. Joe and his new friend Jimmy were playing catch with a hard ball and gloves in the middle of the street. Little Jimmy was telling Joe that his dad had just signed him up to play little league baseball in the spring. Little Jimmy also mentioned that the cutoff date for new kids to register was this coming Saturday.

My love of baseball and the need to impart it to Richie and Joe is exactly what the doctor ordered. I needed to be more involved with my boys and I needed to pull my head out of my fat ass. This was a great way to accomplish both objectives.

Tryouts to find the next Mickey Mantle were being held three blocks from our apartment at the beautiful facility operated by the Throggs Neck Little League. The manager of Family Used Cars Jim Gamble picked my son Joe to play for his team. Jim also asked if I was interested in coaching. I was grateful for the opportunity. Move over, Billy Martin.

Richie didn't have the opportunity to play in the league as an eight-year-old. New kids to the neighborhood and the league were placed on a waiting list, but I was already spending so much time practicing at the field with both of my sons that the people necessary to impress saw that the new kid was actually a better than average pitcher and a very good infielder. He caught behind the plate as did Joe and both of my sons switch hit. The most tenured manager in the league took Richie from the bottom of the list and put him on his team just before the start of the season. It was sort of irregular, but nobody seemed to question Lou Trimantano. Lou got a good all-around player and both of my boys would be playing organized baseball in the spring. I had nothing do with it. I wish I could take credit.

Within a few weeks of settling into our new neighborhood I began running for exercise, and except for running behind a garbage truck it quickly became my favorite form of relaxation. The only time I had enough energy for serious exercise was right after injecting the necessary daily requirement. Heroin elevates your energy level to run at peak efficiency for a very short period of time. Until I moved back to the Bronx, the only time I found myself doing any serious running was usually away from the cops. I was faster than most, but once they shout, stop or I'll shoot, it sort of takes away the excitement of competition.

♣

I was driving along Castle Hill Avenue on the way to cop my daily dose of energy when Donny Barello waved me down from the parking lot in front of Willie's luncheonette. I pulled over to the curb in front of the community center. Donny hurried across the avenue with a big smile. A smile on a junkie means he has money in his pocket.

The drug spot was well within walking distance for normal people, but for a dope sick junkie a half mile would seem like a trek to Africa. "Ya hear 'bout Coco's bag, yet?" asked Donny. "What the hell is a Coco, Dom?" Donny wasn't too sure about much, but the beautiful spring day got a whole lot prettier as Donny explained what he heard through the dope fiend grapevine about the new dealer and the best bag of heroin in years down by the Cozy Corner Bar and Grill.

The tactics for buying drugs from a new dealer can be tricky for both dealer and junkie. The innate ability for a dope pusher to smell cops as opposed to legitimate clients from a hundred yards away is essential for staying out of prison. For an addict, the possibility of purchasing a bag of milk sugar or pulverized aspirin or any number of look-alike substitutes is one of the many pitfalls of being a junkie shit head.

For ten years I coddled relationships with the runners, the younger kids whose job it is to steer potential customers to the dealer who would later compensate them for every bag they moved off the corner. So a runner's job is to talk real fast and convince every white guy from North Connecticut to South Jersey to buy what they were hawking. "If ya wanna get high, don't walk me by." But sometimes a twelve-year-old street hustler might have something more pressing on his mind: desperate need to get a quick fifty dollars so his mother can feed her own dope habit, and all the kid needed was an unsuspecting doper who he sends to his accomplice who in turn rips you off by selling you glassine bags filled with baking soda. You gotta know the players and lay of the land. I didn't just roll off the back of a freaking turnip truck. Getting straight is my job.

Every dealer has his own brand stamped on the glassine envelope, it's how addicts distinguish good dope from bad. If somebody bought a bag of Star Wars in the morning and it was less than stellar, the word went out, don't buy Star Wars. I never bought a bag of dope because the name sounded cool or macho. I bought Death Wish, Rocky and Jaws, and I would've bought a bag of Tinkerbelle if word on the street was that junkies were overdosing on Tinkerbelle. A few comatose addicts in an alley or roof top could put a new dealer on the map in twenty minutes.

The potency of any particular brand of drugs could never be counted on and usually changed day to day or even hour to hour. In the morning The Godfather will have me sucking my socks, while three hours later The Godfather will be making me an offer I can't refuse by selling me milk sugar stamped The Godfather, so it was prudent to be smart, not and idiot like Fredo and stay in the loop of local dope fiends in order to know what was happening on a regular basis.

Beamo was working with the Taxi Driver crew, but I was intent on getting whatever Coco was dealing. "A oh, Kev!" Beamo hurried across the street to greet me. "Who's Coco, B? I hear he's got somethin' nice." The smiling young hustler quickly explained everything I needed to know, so I casually slipped Beamo my last dollar bill. He nonchalantly eyeballed the two gangsters standing across the street by the Soundview projects. One was Coco. The other one wasn't. Beamo explained the need for caution as I slowly walked away. "They gunna wanna see tracks, (needle marks), Kev."

"Not a problem, B."

The suspicious duo was looking me up and down and sideways as I casually ambled across Rosedale Avenue. With my best non-threatening stance, I looked them both in the neck at the same time. One was tall, the other taller. One was ugly, the other uglier. I had no idea who was who. "Lemme get seven." The dark ugly thug on my right glared a hatred reserved for the man that would rape his mother. The other, like I wasn't there. Being ignored doesn't usually piss me off, but this wasn't one of those usual times. I was sick. I stared directly into the eyes of the thug on my right. I figured he was the boss. He was wearing a thick gold chain. "You, Coco?" He cocked his head and squinted as if questioning my sanity. "Step off, officer." It wasn't the first time I got that reaction buying drugs from criminals. Apparently somebody else didn't like my face or attitude or both. "I'm not gonna' tell ya again, pig!"

Every runner and dealer within ear shot called me by name to get my attention as I crossed the avenue, but apparently somebody didn't like my resemblance to law enforcement or the fact that we weren't formally introduced. Besides, if he really thought I was a narc they would've bolted the second I stepped from my car. I guess they decided to have a little fun. I can usually take a joke, sometimes, but not always, and sometimes I can be a real asshole.

Beamo had already walked to the corner to keep me in view. I turned a hundred and eighty degrees and nodded in the runner's direction. The runner nodded back. The two thugs didn't seem to notice. "You just saw me talkin' ta Beamo. Just gimme seven so I can get the fuck outta here." The simmering duo stood at parade rest, hands high behind their backs. "If I have ta tell you again you dumbass cracker." His baritone anger and twisted scowl would've scared a hardened criminal, but his ugly attitude turned my brain into three pounds of raging inferno.

I was being dismissed by an arrogant black drug pusher for being too white and I liked it as much as holding my kidneys until Sister Mary Monster was good and ready to let me go. I bit my lower lip and glared a pair of ice blue ball breakers through his thick skull.

Considering present company and proximity in the middle of the Soundview projects in the asshole end of the south Bronx, I should've left the Kevin the Troublemaker shit in the back of my head, but that rarely ever happens. "Fuck you, nigger." And that's what happens when dope sickness gets in the way of good common sense. I turned to leave…

Nobody noticed the four little blue birds flying around my head or the stars twinkling in my eyes except me as I lay on the ground in a pool of blood. As a matter of fact, I didn't even notice it myself because I was way too busy being unconscious. Whatever happened to sticks and freaking stones?

When I awoke two days later I managed a smile as Ellen rushed into the room. My wife would never be confused with a poker player. I was in a hospital bed with a massive headache when my stoic, unshakeable bride walked up to my side. Ellen stared down at her husband with a look of astonishment that scared even me and I don't scare easily. She put a hand to her mouth, "Oh my God!" I don't ever remember hearing oh my God! in situations that weren't about to get a whole lot worse, and I've heard quite a few oh my Gods! as a lifelong trouble-maker. "What?"

"What did they do to ya hair?" I was suddenly more alarmed for my beautiful curly locks than I was for my freaking head ache. "What?" Ellen took her little compact mirror from her bag and put it up to my face. "Fuck." One half of my head was as bald as an egg with a big dent and a six-inch crease of black stitches. The other half was covered with brown curls lying on the left side of my chest. I looked like something out of a bad haircut freak show. Ellen then explained why I happened to be lying in Jacobi Hospital with half a bald melon.

Beamo had run around the corner and alerted Donny the smiling junkie as soon as Coco cracked a home run off the side of my head with a baseball bat that I assumed was hidden behind his back. Hit me flush in my bad attitude that was luckily still encased in my thick skull.

Donny dragged my bleeding carcass into the front seat of my car and raced me to Jacobi Hospital. Donny finally called his best friend Tommy Jackson the next day. Tommy told Ellen that Donny was scared that she'd would poke him in the eye through the telephone if he told her that her husband had a big hole his head and that I got it while I was with him buying drugs. Donny doesn't even know Ellen, but I could imagine why he might be apprehensive. Donny knows me. That's all Ellen knew.

"What's today?"

"Monday."

"Fuck."

"I was scared, Kevin. I didn't know where you were."

"Where's the car?"

"In front of Tommy's building on Haviland Avenue."

Ellen had a lot of questions and asked none. I felt like my brain was exploding through the crack in the side of my head. "I had fifty dollars in my pocket."

"Where are your clothes?"

"How do I know where my clothes are, Ellen?"

I was still floating in and out of consciousness and awoke with a

251

thought as Ellen was about to leave. "Can you do me a favor?" Ellen was still kissing me on the lips as a tear was rolling down her cheek onto mine. "Ya think you can get somebody in here to straighten out my hair?" Ellen wiped her tears with her hand and smiled. "You do look pretty stupid."

"Thanks. I feel much better now."

I'd been operated on for a depressed skull fracture. I was told after the fact that the splintered skull fragments were pressing on the brain causing pressure that would eventually build up to the point of a massive hemorrhage and death within twenty-four hours. Ellen was never notified and only found out that I wasn't in jail the next morning when Tommy Jackson called with the good news.

I was out of the hospital in five days. None of the drugs they were giving me were called heroin, so by the time I was released I thought I might shit in my pants before they rolled me off the freaking elevator.

My ability to walk was limited and driving impossible. I refused to take the prescription drugs they gave me for pain and possible brain seizures. I certainly didn't have a good reason for not taking the drugs, but I did have a pretty good excuse. My bruised brain was still scrambled like an egg by that baseball bat. I'm not a brain surgeon, but an idiot can see the possibilities for severe stupidity.

Ellen pleaded always and often, "Just take one pill, Kevin. How could it hurt?" I gazed up from the couch with a perpetual squint to block the light of agonizing pain. "Ellen, if my head is gonna explode I wanna know about it in advance. When the pain goes away I know I'm better." It took four months. Sonofabitch! I hate cops. I mean doctors. I'm so confused.

♣

Except for my inner circle of very close friends, no one was told of the incident at the Cozy Corner. Anyone interested in knowing why I was bald and walking feebly with the help of a cane, including family was told I was mugged. I hate freaking muggers.

I found a new location to buy drugs. The Hunts Point area of the Bronx was growing a drug industry to rival Central America. When I drove through the area for the first time there seemed to be Central Americans standing on every other corner awaiting the next shipment from home. The entire area was a supermarket for the junkie community.

When I finally went back to the Cozy Corner approximately four years later I went with a different purpose. Coco had been residing on and off in my head and it was finally time for the eviction. After four painstakingly boring nights of surveillance I was ready. I think. I'm pretty sure.

MOVING DAY

Commonwealth Avenue is lined with massive oak trees. The canopy of green was made that much darker by the absence of street lights shot out years ago by thugs doing business on the corner. It was two o'clock in the morning. The block was dark enough at night to scare death into the living, but the scene in my head was much darker than that.

I was parked half way down the street. Crouched low in the front seat. Anxious, seething and praying the cops wouldn't fuck this up. I removed the tiny bulb from the overhead fixture, and with my car door slightly ajar my dark idea was still wisely veiled beneath a very black hoodie.

Coco finally staggered from the bar. It took a long minute before he finally gained his bearings. He started down the block. When he passed my car on his way to his new Lincoln I crossed the street and followed along like the shadow of a ninja. I could've tapped him on the shoulder. "A-oh, Coco. Ma man." He was too drunk to be startled. I was too close to miss.

I waited long years before returning to the Cozy. Beamo was now a degenerate crack head and still the first runner on the block to greet me. Half his face was melted away from an acid attack when he got caught robbing something out of somebody's car. "Yo, Kev. Ma man. How you be?" As usual Beamo was all smiles for the friendly addict with the same name as his. "Hey, B, what's going on? Who's got something good?" Beamo was directing me with a casual nod while I was pulling the usual dollar from my pocket. "You da man, Kev." As I walked across the street Beamo was facing me, shuffling backwards. "Smooch gots da bomb, Kev. Blue tape, Kev."

"What about Coco. He still runnin' here?" The homeless, bedraggled druggie probably couldn't remember what he did five minutes ago. What happened to me happens all the time around the Cozy Corner Bar and Grill. Not memorable on a block where shootouts, stick-ups and beat downs are a daily occurrence. "I guess you ain't herded, Kev.

Somebody fuckem up, Kev." That's all I needed to know. I was actually wondering if he was dead, but I played along like I give a shit. "What do you mean fucked up, B?" Like fucked up in a wheelchair. Fucked up in a nursing home? "I ain't sho whahappen. I bees in Rikers, Kev. He don't come roun here nomo, Kev. Jimmy Gee say they ugly his face wit a baseball bat."

"He was already ugly, B. What are you talking about? What did they do?"

"I ain't sho, Kev. Jimmy Gee say he all fucked up in the hay now. It like five sit year ago. Ma man Coco be cool wit me, Kev. Ya know I'm talkin' about? He usea tacare me, Kev. You know I'm talkin''bout?"

"I know what you're talkin' 'bout, B. That's terrible." Yeah, terrible. Good old Coco. I sure hope he's okay. You know what I'm talkin' 'bout?

27

We spent the night at my sister's house. A long afternoon of barbecuing and cold beers continued well past my capacity to breathe and mumble at the same time.

Kathleen and her husband Larry lived upstate in Middletown, about an hour and a half from the Bronx. Their three boys and ours got along like brothers. They annoy each other. The stay was great and the ride home the next afternoon was going as usual. The boys were sleeping in the back and Ellen was up front holding on for dear life. "Can ya slow down, please?"

"If you wanna drive, Ellen I can pull over." Ellen doesn't drive, won't learn and can't even be quiet.

We were nearly home. I was still cruising along in the middle lane in our big white Coupe DeVille when I suddenly realized that the Randall Avenue exit was about to show up in my rear view mirror. I quickly veered over a lane of traffic and inadvertently cut in front of another exiting car. The car behind me quickly swerved hard to the right. I watched in horror as his shiny new bumper practically kissed the guard rail.

I braked, slowed down and waved my hand as an apology, but apparently my apology was seen as a little less than a poor excuse for bad manners. Or maybe the driver of the late model Riviera thought I was showing off my favorite finger, but whatever his problem, the young guy was going berserk for an opportunity to speak his mind with his fist and his left hand already out the window cursing.

I was still slowing for the yellow traffic signal up ahead on Tremont Avenue when the irate driver raced up and screamed through the passenger window. He flew through the yellow. I braked for the red. "Kevin, don't." My peace loving wife had my next move figured out before I got it straight in my own brain and way before the highly agitated, screaming lunatic. "Don't worry. This won't take long."

The guy wasn't exactly a physical monster so I didn't understand what was fueling his confidence. I could only imagine what he saw: a skinny peace-loving, hippie with my little hippie clan on our way home from Grandma's house, but the guy couldn't possibly see the screw he loosened in my head as he raced by. I was about to illustrate with dramatic absurdity that the old axiom don't judge a book by its cover is something he might want to consider for future reference.

He turned hard left and squealed to a stop on the avenue. When I glanced over my shoulder he was already outside the car pulling a baseball bat from behind the front seat. Ya gotta like a guy that comes prepared. For baseball, and stuff.

The young greaser was dressed in the finest but nevertheless standard uniform for Throggs Neck area wannabe tough guys, dark green double knit shirt, superbly matching sharkskin slacks and emerald green alligator shoes shiny enough to give me a freaking headache, and he was about to get it all messed up because he was still there and already waving a frantic invitation to join him at the rear of his beautiful car. "Come on you fucking hippie faggot." I get this all the time. I must give a terrible first impression. "Kevin, please! Don't get out of the car! Please!"

The highly agitated big mouth with the beautifully coiffed John Travolta Saturday Night Fever hair doo was swinging that bat like he was standing in the on-deck circle at Yankee Stadium. My outward demeanor was as calm as a heart surgeon during heart surgery as I flipped the transmission into park, but what he set in motion in my brain quickly came to a boil. Ellen was hysterical as I opened the door and walked to the trunk. "KEVIN! PLEASE! I CAN'T TAKE THIS ANYMORE!" She really needs to calm down. I got this.

You never know when an act of God might force a tree across the road so my old Boy Scout motto was never far from my mind, be prepared. The razor sharp two headed log splitter was perfect for chopping down large trees, but it was actually a whole lot better for chopping up bad attitudes.

The young man was obviously feeling the moment, his mighty baseball bat connecting to the side of my curly brown head. "Come on you fuckin' hippie faggot. I'm gonna fuck you up." He sounded pretty convincing, too.

The brown paper bag in my hand was covering the business end of a four-pound neck adjuster. The long hickory handle practically scraping the asphalt as I casually ambled across the avenue. I was still thirty feet away from mister fancy shoes when I ripped the paper bag from the ax head, tossed it aside and slid the handle through my hand, dropping the shiny threat towards the ground. I never opened my mouth and he never said goodbye. Mister disco fever danced away so fast that I didn't even catch his license plate number. So, I guess my work here is done.

Ellen was not happy. I'm not sure about the kids. I had a smile in my head and it wasn't easy keeping it off my face, but I managed for the sake of peaceful coexistence, and I'm all about peace. I love freaking peace. You just have to give it a chance. I gave it a chance. It didn't work. Maybe next time.

♣

The Delusso Brothers were my latest employers. Lenny and Benny Delusso sub-contracted for Colonial Aluminum, a major siding company on Boston Road in the North Bronx. We installed aluminum siding all over lower Westchester County, the Bronx and Yonkers and the wages were enough to pay the bills with enough left over to feed my new best friend, Mighty Joe Young.

It was Christmas week. We just finished up a big job so Lenny and Benny collected a big check from a very satisfied homeowner and the brothers decided to spend a little on me.

The Delusso's seemed to be in an especially good mood. Lenny and Benny were taking turns telling amusing stories of their old neighbor Mister Angelino from the old neighborhood and the three pigeon coops he tended on the roof of their old building. Lenny told me that he and Benny would often sneak up to the roof as very young boys where the old pigeon keeper would teach them everything they needed to know about raising and racing birds, but Mister Angelino would eventually move a mile away into a private house with his oldest daughter.

Benny said that Mister Angelino would walk every day back and forth from his daughter's house to the building in order to feed and exercise his prized possessions. Lenny said that Mister Angelino eventually built himself a brand new shack. The spacious walk-through coop was adjacent to the junk yard on Boston Road by the expressway. Benny said that the old man sold Christmas trees to make a few extra dollars for the holidays. "Were gonna stop by before we head into the shop." So they could buy a little Christmas joy for me and the family.

Lenny thought that we might even go for Chinese after the visit if I was hungry. "I'm always hungry." He laughed and so did Joe. I figured they really like Chinese.

Benny was still cruising down I-95. The three of us were squeezed into the front of the old truck, actually I was squeezed in the middle. The Delusso's seemed to have plenty of room on either side. Younger brother Benny is six two and a good two-sixty with long curly red hair. His older brother Lenny looked like he might've had a few fights wrestling the last piece of lasagna away from his kid brother. Benny checked his watch. "We're gonna catch Chinaman."

"Not if ya keep drivin' like an old fuckin' lady."

Lenny explained that the Chinaman from the restaurant on Burke Avenue comes by every Friday evening at six on the nose. He said the Chinaman checks all cages for the sick birds. The ones with saggy heads. Then he snatches them one by one with a gloved hand and stuffs them in a burlap sack. "When he gets back to the restaurant," Benny noted with a sly grin, "he snaps the necks and turns them into chicken chow mein." I was shaking my head, laughing through the entire tale. "Ya know you guys really are fucking nuts?"

The Delusso brothers had been raising and racing homing pigeons since they were children and both sounded very knowledgeable on the subject. The crazy stuff about the sick birds was actually very funny, but only until the little Chinaman dressed in white pants and greasy apron came through the creaky wooden door at six on the nose. I looked at Lenny. Lenny smiled wide, eyes wider. "Told ya."

Lenny and Benny laughed along with the birdman of Boston Road as he casually strolled from cage to cage on his final inspection before heading home for the night. On the other hand, I was totally flabbergasted. My jaw hanging slack as the little Chinaman opened the nearest cage and plucked out the first of about ten sickly pigeons and stuffed it in his bag. Two minutes later the little man calmly walked out the same door without so much as a whisper. Not even an ancient Chinese proverb to settle my confusion.

The crazy Delusso's killed my appetite and Christmas in one ugly visit. My free Christmas tree from Lenny and Benny wasn't actually free. I still pay the price every time I pass a Chinese restaurant being circled by a flock of tired looking pigeons.

Chicken chow mien was my favorite until I realized that some Chinese people don't even know what a freaking chicken looks like. I haven't even thought about chicken chow mien since Christmas week, year of the tiger. Now that I think of it, where's my damn cat?

My job with the Delusso's only lasted a year. My final day only memorable because I fell off a ladder and hyper-extended my left knee, which had blown up to the size of three knees. I had no insurance and the genius at the city hospital who read the x-rays explained away my agonizing pain as a simple sprain. I was informed some years later that I actually obliterated the ACL (anterior cruciate ligament), tore the medial meniscus and blew out enough cartilage in the lateral meniscus that it appeared as a hole on the MRI. I hate doctors. And the other genius who repaired it twenty-two years later was no better than a carpenter. He told me I would run again. The man was an idiot. If I had to run from the cops I'd be limping all the way to jail. Sonofabitch. I hate freaking cops.

❧

The *Chief-Leader* is the weekly civil service newspaper and one that I read religiously. This week's headline: FIRE FIGHTER EXAM SCHEDULED. I knew the mental test would be tough because that was their history. The practical portion of the exam was set up to be the most physically challenging the city had ever put forward.

My grade on the academic part of the test was just good enough to move me on to the Brooklyn Navy Yard for the running around part. After a few weeks of actual testing, an average for passing was established and published in the *Daily News*. The sad reality was that a staggering one in eight candidates was moving on to the investigation phase of the process.

I barely made a passing grade on each exercise, agility, strength, balance and a few that focused on all three, but it was the mile run where I thought I might excel. The mile had to be completed in less than twelve minutes in order to get the full fifty points. Although I was never timed in a race I knew I was fast. It's mandatory for troublemakers. By the time I crossed the finish line I was so far ahead of the field that all eight timers were cheering me on. I was still catching my breath when my personal timer told me that I just completed the fastest mile in the first eighty-five hundred applicants.

Of the seven men I competed against all morning long I'm pretty sure I was the only one in my group that injected heroin in order to see straight. I was also the only candidate in my group that passed the running around portion of the exam.

Heroin is not a stimulant, but rather a depressant. Any doctor could tell you that a person with heroin in their system wouldn't be anything but compromised. Heroin didn't make me more agile and I wasn't any stronger and I certainly didn't run faster because of the effects of heroin. My daily injection simply enabled me to compete without crapping in my shorts. Addicts call it getting straight. Doctors call it normal sinus rhythm.

Move over Wheaties. Heroin, breakfast of freaking champions.

⚜

My acceptance as a recruit into the New York City Police Academy was thought by all my family and friends to be some kind of a joke, and if you weren't laughing after the words POLICE ACADEMY I got a bridge to sell ya. That was a pop quiz to see who was paying attention. SIT UP STRAIGHT!

No kidding around this time. In January of 1979 I was actually notified by the Department of General Services that I was being considered for hire as a New York City sanitation worker. All I had to do to get the job was to show up at the sanitation clinic for a complete medical examination. As a relatively healthy person, relatively speaking that is, the only portion of the exam of concern was blood work and urine analysis because both will surely reveal the presence of something I rather not have to explain.

At the present time my toxic whiz sample would probably explode before they placed the little bottle in the refrigerator. The medical exam was scheduled in two weeks. Thoughts of withdrawal from heroin were unnerving, but absolutely essential to gain employment with the city and a job with a great pension. With eight days to go I finally copped my last bag of dope. Should be a snap. Another joke. Try to keep up.

Well it was hardly a snap a crackle or even a pop, but the agonizing and very exhausting effort was worth every minute of self-control. My urine was now clean enough to pick up garbage for the City of New York at the rate of twelve thousand, five hundred dollars a year, and within an hour of producing the cleanest urine my kidneys had filtered in ten years I was at the Cozy Corner and ten minutes after that I was celebrating my new job. It would've been nice to stay clean, drug free, but I wasn't that smart, yet. For some people getting smart takes massive amounts of stupidity. I got a long way to go.

28

The attitude for authority that I brought into the Department of Sanitation was the same that I brought along to the first grade and look how that turned out. I worked as hard as the hardest workers, but my attitude for everything else pretty much sucked.

According to the senior guys it was imperative that I keep my nose clean and get through the one-year probation period without a formal complaint. If I manage that minor miracle, according to those same men the department wouldn't be able to fire me without an act of Congress, but that doesn't mean the city wouldn't try to impeach me for a slightly dirty nose.

Anthony Merlino and I started the job at the Randall's Island Training Center along with forty-eight other newly hired sanitation men. Anthony and I soon became close buddies because we quickly saw in the eyes of the other that we both had that same fascination with heroin. It would be the same as any two people looking for that kindred spirit. In our case it was in the eyes. The reflection of a dark secret.

After driving garbage trucks around and around in a big circle for two weeks, Anthony and I were both assigned to the same west side Bronx garage. I got through my first year on the job without serious incident, but not long after that every new worker assigned to the Bronx was reassigned to the borough of Queens on a temporary basis.

Anthony and I were also detached to the same district over in Queens. My new daily commute was a twenty minute drive beyond the toll on the Throggs Neck Bridge. The union said it would be at least a few months before we came back to the Bronx, but nobody was that optimistic.

I was anxious to get started in my new home away from home. Anthony was off on a regularly scheduled three-day weekend. The massive garage was a sea of unfamiliar faces.

The midnight-to-eight garage supervisor babbled through the general orders of the day, the do's and don'ts of the job. Done with that, the old grump with the long face and shaggy gray hair mumbled through the standard six AM roll call. After that he called each driver by name and handed out the dump tickets. "Carroll." It was only then that my two partners for the day knew who I was and casually walked up and introduced themselves.

After quick handshakes Jimmy Shea and Patrick Doherty took turns explaining what I should expect during the shift. As we walked out to the truck, Jimmy said that our route was over thirty minutes from the garage and we weren't in a hurry. "We might even get lucky and hit a little traffic." This way of working was quite different from the Bronx. Everybody in the Bronx was in a hurry. Run up the route. Dump the truck. Day over. Three hours of actual work even on a bad day was still a pretty good day in the Bronx. Patrick said it was another thirty-minute drive back to the garage for lunch and another thirty minutes back to finish the route in the afternoon. These Queens guys kill time like professionals. All I wanted to do is throw the garbage in the truck and take a nap. These guys preferred sleepwalking behind the hopper.

By late morning and definitely by noon my body would be craving the drug, and by the end of the work day I'd be so drained of energy that the need to reenergize my blood stream with my daily dose would be the only thought in my head. Trouble loomed in the form of anything out of the ordinary, so I needed my day to be as uncomplicated as possible. No drama. Lack of heroin can bring about all kinds of unnecessary stupidity.

Patrick, the union shop-steward for the 4-Section area we'd be working explained rather emphatically that after we take the ten-minute break in the afternoon we'll work for another five minutes and at exactly 12:45 we lock up the hopper, take our last slow journey back to the garage and arrive in time for our contractually guaranteed wash-up, and after that we sign out and go home.

The best way to learn about our union regulations is to work in a place like this. Morning break is fifteen minutes and begins two hours after the start of any shift. Lunch time is a half hour and starts two hours after break time. Getting the garbage in the truck seemed to be an afterthought. Every move made with precision with supervisors making sure we were paying attention. The afternoon break is taken on the route where the truck is at 12:30 and the truck must remain parked on the spot for ten minutes.

Thankfully, my very first day in Queens was uneventful, but as the saying goes, it's never quite over until the fat lady sings, and I'm almost positive I heard Big Bonnie warming up the old vocal chords, but definitely not singing. I think she was mumbling so I really couldn't hear.

At 12:30 PM the three of us were sitting up in the cab talking the usual garbage man trash and after a very quick ten minutes the shop-steward noted the time. "Let's go." I glanced in my side view mirror and watched as a supervisor drove up and parked behind the hopper. "We have company."

"Don't worry about Brubaker. We're good. Go to the corner and make a right and back into the flat (pile of garbage) in the cage." Patrick was checking the mirror on his side of the truck as I was pulling away from the curb. "We have more company." I figured I was working with two union radicals. I've never seen this much scrutiny. Even for me. A foreman, a superintendent and a boro chief. Way too much possibility for drama. Maybe somebody threatened somebody at lunch time. It wasn't me. I turned and looked them both in the eye without a flicker of recognition for a possible reason behind this highly irregular show of department resources.

Patrick directed me to a large flat of garbage in a city housing development less than a minute away. The enormous pile of smelly black bags was approximately fifty tons of compacted garbage and it was our job to take away as much of it as possible. Half the truck was still empty, which means we could easily take five tons off the pile and throw it into the hopper, but certainly not in five minutes, and Patrick was especially emphatic about the rules regarding travel times. 12:45 lock up the hopper.

The three of us jumped down from the truck and started throwing garbage. Our foreman, a large tough looking black man stood ram-rod straight and glared a laser through my brain He was sending a message: work faster, hippie. The big foreman was already pissing me off. I stopped throwing garbage, grabbed the hopper handles and sent up less than a hopper full.

The skinny bald headed superintendent and the tubby thin lipped assistant chief were both leaning against the super's car looking in our general vicinity. All three bosses watching the furious energy behind the hopper that lasted exactly four minutes.

I was still working the hopper handle, cycling the garbage up into the truck while keeping a close eye on my five-dollar watch. Almost, almost. At exactly 12:45 on the nose I locked up the hopper and took off my gloves. Like the captain of a ship the driver controls the truck. I'm the captain.

Ten yards away three very expensive babysitters came erect. The two union blabbermouths started crying. What are ya doing, Carroll?" moaned Patrick. "Get in the truck or I'll leave you here."

"We can't leave yet, Carroll," begged Doherty. From the moment we met all they talked about were their union rules. Apparently they were all talk.

The big supervisor marched over and gestured back towards his two superiors. "I got two hundred thousand dollars worth of supervision watching you clowns load this truck. Keep loading." I glared up and pointed at my skinny wrist. "My watch here is synchronized to the atomic clock in Colorado. The atomic clock is estimated to lose one half second every ten thousand years." The atomic clock doesn't even tell time, but I was certain this big genius didn't know that. "My watch says we're done." The big foreman was squinting sideways like I was speaking some alien tongue. "Don't talk, Carroll. Load the truck." My two nervous partners were still shrinking away from any possible confrontation. "Come on. Open the hopper, Carroll. Let's finish this." My body was sick, my brain exhausted, but my mouth was already doing warm-up calisthenics. Confrontation is my profession.

"I said get in the fucking truck or get a ride back with him." I pointed to the big angry supervisor, then strode alongside the truck and pulled myself up into the cab. The big foreman was hot on my heels and already smoldering outside my open window. "You just made a big mistake, Carroll. You're not gonna like it here anymore."

"I didn't even like crossing the Throggs Neck ridge this morning to get here and I'm not gonna like it again tomorrow." The two union blabbermouths sat next to me like freaking sheep. I pulled away from the smelly pile of garbage and a very agitated supervisor.

Mike Tyson has a saying, everybody's a tough guy, 'til they get punched in the face. My two partners talked a big game all day long, but the moment they stepped into the ring they tripped on their shoe laces and fell on their faces. I had euphemistically punched the neighborhood bully in the mouth while his mommy and daddy looked on with their mouths hanging slack.

I took their words for gospel and why not. Our union rules pertaining to travel times are firm directives and always different in each location because of geography. Foreman Brubaker decided to change the rules at the very end of the game and apparently I was the only one on the truck that got pissed.

By the time I signed out of the garage an hour later I heard more crazy stories from supposed concerned union sympathizers about Wild Bill Brubaker. Every one of them made it sound like I did battle with King Kong and was lucky to be alive. Wild Bill had a reputation to uphold and some little snot nose from the Bronx wasn't coming into his house to screw it all up.

I actually thought that I toed the union standard, stood firm in the face of 'The Man'. I suddenly felt like General George Custer pointing a water pistol at ten thousand screaming Indians standing behind Gatling Guns. It was time to rethink my thinking. This garage was full of lazy slouches who only wanted to work hard a few minutes a day and I'm sure my partners would've passed on the furious display at the end of the shift if they weren't being watched by two-hundred thousand dollars worth of sanitation babysitters. I needed to work hard and fast to end my day as soon as possibly in order to keep my bad attitude from appearing.

♣

Early the next morning as I parked my car at five minutes to morning roll call, Anthony from the Bronx immediately rushed up to my side. "What the fuck you do yesterday? Your name is all around the fucking garage." Anthony had a tendency towards being a little high strung. "Fuck everybody. I followed the union's instructions to the letter and nobody liked it, including the union."

"You're fucking nuts, Kevin. They're gonna get you. And they put me with you today. I'm fucked."

"Don't worry 'bout it, Anthony. I'm planning on a very short day."

Two minutes later I'm standing in the middle of the cavernous building with Anthony yapping in my ear when the big tough foreman slowly made his way across the floor to say good morning. Or maybe not. Anthony hurried away. "You made a big mistake yesterday, Carroll."

"Which one? I made a lot of mistakes yesterday."

"We heard you're a wise ass, Carroll. I love fucking wise asses."

"You mean that figuratively, right?"

"I'm gonna fuck you today, Carroll. Watch ya back. I'm gonna get ya by the end of the day."

"The end of the day? You better move faster than that, I think I had some bad sausages for breakfast." Okay, I'm a wise ass, but I love being a freaking wise ass. It's like being a troublemaker, only special.

The notorious Queens borough tough guy made an about face as steam whistled from flared nostrils. I strolled out to greet two very unhappy sanitation workers. "What was he saying, Kevin?" asked Anthony from the Bronx. "Yeah, Carroll," said Queens guy. I haven't even met my latest Queens victim yet, but I assumed Anthony clued him in to my tendencies. "I've seen Wild Bill mad before, but not like yesterday. After you signed out he flung a telephone through a window. What the fuck did you say to him, Carroll?"

"Every time I opened my mouth I think I said something he really didn't wanna hear."

"Ya think?" said Anthony.

"You fucked with the wrong guy, Carroll," said Queens guy. "Brubaker's fucking nuts. He eats guys like you for breakfast." The anxious Queens guy pulled away from the garage. I was seated by the other window with Anthony in the middle.

Anthony and I were calmly talking Bronx stuff while the foreigner from Queens was doing his best to break through the language barrier. I turned to Anthony. "I'm goin' LODI." (Line of duty injury).

"When?" asked Anthony.

"Very soon."

"Back injury?" wondered Anthony.

"What the hell you guys talkin' about?"

"Try to keep up. I'm talking about going LODI."

"Ya want me to drive ya to the hospital?"

"No, I'm not hurt yet, but when I am you'll know it. It's gonna be obvious."

"Whaddya mean, obvious?" probed Anthony.

We were working in the section closest to the garage. Within a few minutes Queens guy pulled over to the curb and stopped at the first private house on a whole block of private houses on a beautiful tree lined street. I was still gathering my nerve when I looked out the window and immediately recognized my ticket to the emergency room. "Don't even get out of the truck, Anthony." Three black bags, an old beat-up aluminum garbage can and leaning against the can, an old rotted wood frame window. "Whaddya thinking, ya crazy fucker?"

"I'm thinking stitches, Anthony." Anthony turned sideways into my face close enough to comb his hair in my eyes. "Are you fucking insane,

Kevin? Just go down with a bad back. Everybody goes down with a bad fucking back."

"Calculating, Anthony. I'm calculating nobody will think I could possibly do this to myself just to get away from this shit-hole district." The young Queens guy never said a word. He looked past Anthony with his jaw hanging open. "Think about this. You don't have to do this, Kevin." But my mind was set. Nobody downtown questions stitches. Everybody downtown questions a healthy looking worker claiming a bad back. There will no mistaking. Carroll went down with a nasty cut. "Stay up, Anthony. And don't move the truck, buddy." I didn't even learn the guy's name.

I had way too much shit in my head from the time I got out of bed. I needed to get out of this district permanently in a hurry. I made an enemy of a legendary sanitation tough guy on my very first day in my new district and Wild Bill Brubaker didn't appear the type a guy to lose interest anytime soon. Which means he'll soon be dipping into my wallet and I can't have that because I'm already on a pretty tight budget. I've been running the tolls on the Throggs Neck Bridge and I'll keep doing it until I hit the lottery and I can't hit the lottery because I can't afford an extra freaking dollar. Sonofabitch. I hate cops. I mean toll bridges. Actually, I hate cops and toll bridges.

It was still only six fifteen in the morning and the streets deserted. I jumped down and carefully placed the window flat on the sidewalk. I searched in the can and took out a large McDonald's bag filled with mushy McDonald's crap and placed it under one of the small squared sections of glass as a cushion to muffle the sound of cracking crystals. Then I stepped through the small pane without disturbing the early birds.

The biggest sliver of glass was six inches long, pointed like switch blade at one end and wide as the butt end of bowie knife at the other. I picked up the McDonald's cushion filled with broken glass and threw it in the garbage can and climbed back into the cab. Anthony was shaking his head. Queens boy was shaking his head. I was shaking my head as I unbuttoned my outer green shirt, pulled it off and wrapped it tightly around the thicker end of glass. "What the hell ya gonna do now?"

"Please, be quiet, Anthony." I didn't exactly have a plan until I saw the window. It wasn't one of my better ideas so I'm not sure why I was so calm. Of course I've had lots of experience sitting in holy ass whippin' chairs and that was stress. This was not. I straightened my right leg and placed the point of glass on the spot on my pants that would coincide where I'd soon be in dire need of medical attention and carefully pushed the pointy tip through the material and sliced a small diagonal hole in the cloth. You can't slice your leg without ripping your pants. My baggy pant leg was easily pulled up to my knee. I pushed the white sock down to my boot.

When I started the job at the training center the experienced sanitation workers and supervisors all explained the many dangers of picking up garbage. Broken glass protruding from plastic bags was noted as one hazard for slicing legs. And wouldn't you know.

The only thought in my head, except for the impending pain was to call the union and plead my case for an immediate extraction to a less stressful work environment, or at least a district with lots of troublemakers where I could easily blend in. I placed the razor sharp edge of glass on the side of my calf muscle with enough pressure to know it was gonna hurt. "Don't do it, Kevin." I was gazing out the windshield into outer space, just like the old days. Kevin the Surgeon suddenly sliced a gash deep and long enough to bleed sufficiently enough to make me nervous. "Take me to the damn hospital."

Blood was pouring down my leg into my boot. "You are fucking insane, Kevin." I quickly tied my shirt around the open wound. "You didn't see anything, Anthony. You only heard me yell." I leaned forward and looked directly into the wide eyes of Queens boy. "And you don't know nuthin'. You didn't see anything but blood." The young guy only knew me for ten minutes, but I figured he probably thought I was crazy, so I was certain his cooperation would be heartfelt. Everybody needs to be on the same page or the cover up could blow an ugly cut into a complete waste of blood.

I limped away from the hospital with fourteen of the greatest excuses for smiling since the invention of the whoopee cushion. I was still grinning while my front bumper was hugging the rear end of another unsuspecting car owner as he slowly made his way through the exact change toll booth on the Throggs Neck Bridge.

I was out of work a day and a half when the clinic called. The head nurse ordered me downtown the next morning. "I have fourteen stitches in my leg. Send an ambulance or a car big enough that I can stretch my leg out on the rear seat. If not, I'll see ya when the throbbing goes away."

"Mister Carroll. You have ta—"

"I don't have to do anything." CLICK! It was my first LODI, but I already knew enough to know exactly what I could get away with. I knew the clinic couldn't force me to walk in agonizing pain and possibly pop my stitches. OUCH. You have no idea of the agony. Oooh, the agony.

Right after I hung up on the clinic I called Tommy Hughes at the Union Hall. I brought Tommy up to speed on my verbal warfare with Foreman Brubaker. The fact that Brubaker threatened to get me by lunch time after I stood up to him for toeing the union line should be more than enough for my union advocate to back me up on both accounts. "We got the whole story already, Kevin. It sounds like you really pissed him off." Well it is my job. "Brubaker was heard saying he was going to be picking your pocket regularly so I'm gonna get you moved to another location. Remember, Kevin, the clinic can check you by phone or come to your door from eight AM to nine PM Don't get caught doing anything stupid until I can get ya moved." Does that mean I can't get my dope until nine o'clock at night? "I really appreciate it, Tommy."

Tommy's warning was right on the money. The clinic physician's assistant was at my door twice a day every day plus somebody from downtown called me three times a day. I guess it doesn't take much to piss some people off.

I was still at home two weeks later and still collecting a full paycheck when Tommy called from the union hall with news of my detachment to another district, Queens West four. I was already smiling as Tommy was telling me the good news. I hung up the phone and walked, I mean limped to my living room. Ellen was at work in the Key Food up on the avenue. The kids were in school. I flicked on the T.V. I tuned into Pinky and the Brain from the comfort of my couch until something much funnier caught my imagination. It was the fat lady and she was right there inside my television. She was hard to miss because she filled up the whole screen. In fact, she filled up the whole freaking living room. The fat lady was finally singing and she was belting out my favorite tune. "And the hoooome.... of the... Braaaaaaave!" I love it when the fat lady hits that high E.

29

After a year and a half in the borough of Queens I finally returned home to Bronx five, and with that much more experience. I learned if you're doing anything stupid, do it with a sense of urgency. I came back to the Bronx as The Flash in an ugly green uniform.

Accepting money from home owners or store owners for hauling away anything is illegal. The department calls it a contract and the city frowns on it. In fact, besides murder, the most serious infraction of department policy is getting caught taking money for contracts. Not exactly a test in geometry for motivated professionals. Don't get caught.

They say necessity is the mother of invention. My need was heroin, and like money it doesn't grow on trees. I created so many easy opportunities for making extra cash with my very own garbage truck that I could've sent my kids to Harvard with enough left over to feed the gorilla, or at least a small community college and a chimpanzee.

While most New Yorkers look upon our winter blizzards as major inconveniences, the wives of sanitation men view our snowstorms as a means of paying down the bills and longer, possibly exotic summer vacations. The back to back snow events a week apart in February of 1983 dumped a total of twenty-five inches of fluffy white money, and with all the overtime since November the bachelors were talking new cars by spring.

The first of the two storms deposited a foot of white overnight. I was pre-scheduled to work the seven PM shift. Prior to a major snowfall the department splits all personnel into two shifts, seven to seven. The senior guys stay days and the junior men get pushed to the night shift. It took me five hours to get from my home in Throggs Neck to my west side garage. I will not be trudging through the snow and riding the subway tomorrow.

The change over from day shift employees to night shift replacements was taking the supervisors an eternity to accomplish and nobody that signed the attendance sheet for the PM shift was complaining. We were sitting around on our fat asses doing nothing and getting paid. I love the snow.

As a relatively new employee with just a few years on the job and preparing for my first major snow storm, the seemingly chaotic atmosphere appeared as the normal way of doing business. Everything that could go wrong did go wrong. Vehicle and equipment breakdowns added to mental fatigue, plus white out conditions equaled what the senior guys called the sanitation circus. Supervisors called it paperwork, and the longer they did paperwork the longer we sat idle, and the longer we sat idle the crazier we talked. Before I knew it anything resembling sanity blew out the window, and that too appeared to be normal. It wasn't long before sanitation drug addicts of every imaginable substance were itching for comfort.

Heroin addicts got together and made a run to 183rd Street and the Grand Concourse. Coke freaks did the same to another location. Drinkers chipped in for beer and every pothead in the trailer put up for an ounce of weed. Three hours later the trailer was a rockin' with stupefied sanitation workers ready to party the night away. Unfortunately it was up to us to push the snow around, and every time I peeked out the freaking door the shit wasn't melting.

It was this very blizzard that branded Bronx five as a drug den. There were so many accidents later that shift that the city is probably still paying for the fallout. I was finally dispatched into the battle with a plowed-up garbage truck and headed for the most important street in the Bronx: mine.

The three and a half miles of Cross Bronx Expressway was barely passable through the middle lane. I finally exited at Randall Avenue. My neighborhood still resembled the frozen tundra of Siberia. I continued along the service road and plowed through two feet of virgin snow and made a cautious right onto Logan Avenue. Two minutes later my big white truck with its bright orange plow and my ingenious idea were all stuck two inches from old Mister O'Brien's ancient Chevy Nova. It was already one in the morning when I realized I could no longer move the truck without damaging the car. Curious silhouettes filled bedroom windows. A young car owner grateful for my efforts and anxious to move his own vehicle by morning heard the truck begging for traction and finally came out with a sturdy shovel. An hour later, Logan Avenue from Miles to Lawton was ready for roller skating. I was away from my route over three hours and nobody noticed, except for my very appreciative neighbors. I love the circus.

The midnight to eight garage supervisor Otto Stroop was spit-n-polish. I wasn't and we were banging heads as soon as I became the guy with the longest hair in the building.

According to Stroop I violated procedure when I called in late to go sick. One hour before the six AM shift is the general order. "It's too late, Carroll. You can't go sick at five fifteen in the morning." I abruptly informed Stroop that I didn't feel sick until a few minutes ago and banged the phone in his ear. When I showed up the following day, Stroop insisted that I sign a complaint form before signing the attendance sheet. I refused, scribbled my name and stood ready for roll call with everybody else on the other side of the chest high counter that separates the sanitation men from the office section or the room.

Two minutes later the tension was still palpable while Stroop was reading the general orders for the day. When he finished his daily babble he gave his daily uniform inspection. After eyeballing each driver he handed each the all-important dump ticket. Foreman Stroop was about to dispatch the day shift into the street when he turned back to his desk and picked up three portable communication radios. When he turned back again he placed the radios on top of the large manila envelopes that were already lying on the counter and told me to take the mail and two-way radios to the field supervisors in the section office on Sedgwick Avenue. I had to go to the section office anyway to pick up my two loaders, but this was still highly unusual. Stroop didn't trust me to take out the freaking garbage. "Be careful, Carroll. These radios are very expensive." Stroop was obviously trying to piss me off me and he did an excellent job in a professional manner.

A minute later I turned to leave the room but Jordan Steiner happened to be standing exactly where I needed to go. I bumped into Steiner. The three heavy radios slipped off the mail and crashed to the floor. How did that happen? "I just told you to be careful, didn't I, Carroll?" For a troublemaker with my level of expertise, being annoying on very short notice happens to be my specialty. "Didn't I, Carroll?" Supervisor Stroop was already leaning over the counter and watched as I slowly collected the radios. I could feel the radiation from his eyes behind me. I twisted my neck like an owl in order to glare a hole through his thick German skull. Our eyes were still locked in battle as I slowly walked from the office.

Steiner finally came down the flight of stairs a minute later. "Steiner, what did he say when I left the room?" The giant, muscular, bear of a man couldn't pass a single car or storefront window without flexing his biceps while sucking in his gut. Big Jordan Steiner was as sharp as a bowling ball with the attention span of a goldfish, and the big man avoided controversy by any means. "Come on, Carroll. I don't know." Steiner was walking away from me while shaking his giant head, but I knew I could wear him down. "Ask somebody else, Carroll." I continued pursuing his giant shadow. "What did he say, Steiner? I just wanna know. I'm not gonna do anything."

"You're a pain in the ass, Carroll."

"I know, Steiner, but what did he say?" Steiner was backpedaling towards the garage door. "I swear I'm not gonna do anything, Steiner. I just wanna know."

"If you do, Carroll, ya better forget where ya heard it."

"I forgot already, Steiner."

"He said you probably didn't get any last night." I was actually amazed that he remembered the freaking question.

Well, I still can't fly, but I had enough take-off speed to get me up the stairs so fast that most of the men were still in the office. It was probably an unfortunate defect of birth, or maybe supervisor Stroop was schooled by nuns, because his left handle stuck out far enough to catch radios waves from Jupiter and the other ear flat, like it was stapled to the side of his head.

For someone that grew up with crooked teeth I was all too familiar with the frailties of the human psyche that stared back from an ugly reflection. My teeth are no longer a problem, but Stroop seized on anything else to break my chops, and my long hair was a constant source of entertainment. "Missus Carroll, you need a haircut. Mister Carroll, you're out of uniform and you need a haircut." I ignored it all and smiled in his face. I knew how much my mere presence annoyed him, but I was about to turn the table and jam it in his freaking neck.

Stroop was still walking into the adjacent super's office when I crashed into the room. "You've been talking behind my back, Stroop. Do it again and you'll never sit in traffic on the LIE ever again." The man was way too vocal about his aggravating daily commute. "I'll bend your other ear out so far you'll be able to fly to the asshole end of Long Island for the rest of your career." Stroop charged and grabbed the edge of the counter like he was about to leap over. "Are you threatening me, Carroll?" Some might consider the blue radiation I was searing through his corneas as a threat, but how smart would I be to help him write my own complaint?

"No. Why do you ask?" The man was hyperventilating. "It sounded... like a.. threat." I walked away while Stroop was still stammering.

An hour later I was closing up the hopper to take the first load to the dump when the delegate for my union drove up in his car. "What happened this time, Kevin?" I explained my morning to the union. Tommy Hughes explained his. "Well, forget about all that, Kevin. Take the men back to the garage. You were suspended an hour ago." Sonofabitch.

That morning I was detached (moved) to another Bronx district, for the good of the department. Merely suggesting to help a superior fly over the Throggs Neck Bridge to the asshole end of Long Island will generally get this type of reaction from the main office.

I didn't actually start working at my new district for another thirty days, the limit for suspensions before trial, where the city took another five days' pay for stupidity. My bad attitude was attached to a bigger mouth and both were already costing me some really big bucks.

Detachment actually worked out pretty well because the city eliminated three and a half miles of Cross Bronx Expressway from my daily commute. I hate the Cross Bronx Expressway. My new district, Bronx nine was like most Bronx garages, the faster you worked the more time you had for finding trouble.

The self-inflicted anxiety at my old garage didn't actually follow me to the new one because Superintendent Straitback had his own way of running his house. No outside interference and no petty bull shit. I came into my new district with a reputation as a good worker with a hard edge and a nasty mouth, but Superintendent Roger Straitback still started me off with a clean slate, so for a short while I kept my head down and my mouth shut and did what I was told, throw garbage, not threats.

I was faster than most when it came to running up the route and better than everybody when it came to driving a very large garbage truck through difficult situations. Speed and accuracy are paramount when it comes to illegal activity and the money from those less than legal endeavors (contracts) was fueling my drug habit. Twenty dollars a day in side cash was considered a bad shift in Bronx nine.

My attitude was now being controlled by heroin. The loss of self-esteem was killing my ability to deal with normal everyday occurrences, so my capacity to comfort my family was hardly manageable because my life was hardly manageable. Insomnia was keeping me from my nightmares. Depression is a heightened state of mental fatigue and I was way beyond that. I showed the world the bright smile of an idiot with a black secret. A jail term would've been easier.

♣

When the Department of General Services sent notification about my medical examination at the Fire Department clinic I was in a state of euphoria. The possibility of being hired was exhilarating, while the medical part scared the crap out of me. The medical exam was scheduled in ten days. Short notice for applicants is meant to weed out the drug abusers and other assorted assholes. It took me eight days to clean up for the Sanitation exam. I went cold turkey. Right after the weekend.

The city's investigation into my background was probably more comprehensive than most other candidates. A misdemeanor conviction for stealing milk during the milk drivers' strike is one blunder I easily explained away. With two growing boys and no milk in the fridge or local stores I did what I usually do under stress, laugh, but this situation wasn't funny, so I drove a few blocks to the source, Hermany Farms. I was actually home free until my ancient Impala refused to start. I was parked in the very dark employee's lot across the street from the factory, the two cases of cold milk sitting next to me on the front seat. Two blue geniuses happening by the factory at two in the morning heard the engine sputtering. They thought I was stealing a car. They probably made detective.

The city investigator said I was quite resourceful. Except for the getting arrested part.

The bust for methamphetamine in the subway was dismissed after a year on probation. I explained away the drugs as a necessity for working different shifts at the Post Office plus the all-important need to stay awake on the always dangerous subway. It was a lie and a damn effective one if I say so myself, but the tale obviously satisfied my investigator. Prior to that I was arrested and charged with a misdemeanor for stealing little bitty tee-shirts and tiny BVD underwear in Korvette's. I didn't have a good excuse for that one, except that my boys needed underwear and I didn't have any money and I used the same excuse for getting busted for stealing tires in the police impound yard in Queens in order to replace the four baloney skins on my new '65 Impala. That one sounded pretty stupid even to me, but the investigator didn't seem to care. He actually thought it was pretty funny, stealing from the cops. My juvenile record for the Texaco gas station burglary is still sealed.

The department of sanitation merely presented me as a hard worker. I figured the department would rather Carroll be somebody else's headache. The neighbors saw me as they saw me. If I wasn't playing catch with one of my boys in front of the house, I was down at the little league field coaching the entire team. The face and demeanor I showed the world was as normal as Andy from Mayberry, and that's obviously what my neighbors told the investigator. But the icing on the cake was spread by Mister Robert Patterson, vice president of the Throggs Neck Little League. The retired fire captain called an old friend who obviously had enough influence in the process to push my investigation in the right direction, and I definitely needed a little shove over the finish line.

The day I was processed through the medical division I was the only candidate in the room. Because of the wider scope necessary to investigate my background I wasn't cleared in time to stand in line for blood work, chest x-rays, urine gathering for analysis and everything else the rest of the candidates did together as the next probationary fire fighter class.

A young nurse had already attempted to draw blood, three times. All the veins in both arms front and back had collapsed long ago. The nurse finally called the doctor, and not a moment too soon. The dark purple marks erupting on my forearms had me looking more like a junkie than what I did to myself in the last fifteen years. As the doctor searched for a viable source of blood he made small talk to calm my anxiety. "This is Tuesday, Kevin. I'll rush this sample through, as soon as I find it, that is. If I can get the results by Friday, you'll be able to make the class on Monday morning. They're expecting you." He eventually discovered blood. I was at the Cozy Corner before the large hole in my right hand closed up, and ten minutes after that I was sucking my socks and hanging off the back of a fire truck as dreams of my new job were dancing around my empty head.

☘

It was late Friday afternoon. I was watching Days of Our Lives when the phone rang. "Ring, ring, ring, riiiing, ring, riiiing, ring, ring, riiiii-ing, riiiiiing!"

"You wanna get that, please!" Ellen was in the damn bathroom. I had to get off my fat ass.

"Yeah." I hate answering the damn phone. "Mister Carroll?"

"Speaking."

"Mster Carroll, this is Nurse Burke from the medical division of the fire department."

"Good afternoon, Nurse Burke. What can I do for you?"

"Mister Carroll, some anomaly has appeared in your urine screen." Yeah, it's called heroin, genius. "We need you to return here Monday morning to give us another sample." Well, it's a little late for that ya freaking witch. I just got straight five minutes ago. "Thank you nurse, but I decided to stay with the sanitation department after all." Yeah, that's what I decided, alright.

Putting out fires didn't sound like much fun, anyway. Lighting fires, as I remember, that was actually pretty damn exhilarating. That's what I told myself, but I absolutely knew I'd blown a great opportunity. I think firefighter is the best and probably easiest civil service job in the city. Who wouldn't want to get paid for food shopping or working out and sleeping and possibly going to a fire, maybe once in a month? I'm a gambler. Every time I stick a needle in my arm I think I'll be high by the time I pull it out. And if I was getting paid to run into a burning building I would bet my life that I would not be the one left to die. How many recruits would ever take the job if that weren't the case?

Sometime after I started working for the city I read a Time magazine article that noted sanitation worker is the number two most dangerous occupation behind loggers. Number two. Every single day sanitation workers get crushed in accidents behind their own vehicles or have toxic liquids explode under pressure in their faces. The unusual not unusual, everything from a metal bed frame, a two by four and a thousand different objects that people put at the curb for removal that snap off at the blade and shoot out of the hopper and break a bone or make an ugly mush uglier.

It was very early in my career. I was working in that part of west Bronx where it looks like people throw their garbage out their apartment windows into big piles. On two occasions within a few weeks paint exploded in my face. The first time I went back to the garage and showered. The second I showered in an open fire hydrant, and both times I finished the route. I only got colored, but it could've been worse. I could've been hit with acid. I've seen guys slip and fall on everything from dog shit to pure white snow only to get up and finish the job. When they wake the next morning in serious pain they call in sick and eventually go downtown to the clinic, and by that time it's too late to say they were injured on the job. Weeks later they're walking into the garage with a cane because of a herniated disk. Every day all the time and nobody cares except for our loved ones because we're not 'heroes', just garbage men. That's the job. So yes, I was pissed that I couldn't get paid to sleep and shop and work out, and I'll remain pissed for a very long time. I know a lot of firemen. They all know they have a great job. Just ask one. If you can wake him up.

Let's see. How many people have I pissed off so far? Well, it is my job.

30

9:00 AM

"Kevin, is ya brother there? He didn't come home last night." From the time Bernadette hung up the phone and drove to my apartment in the Bronx from Queens my mind was racing and not a single thought was encouraging.

When it came to his responsibilities my brother was all family. Little Tommy was five, Aileen three and baby Caitlan six months. Bernadette was frantic because Tommy would always call home in the event of an unexpected delay.

Tommy's battle with heroin was a lot like my own. Heroin was winning. Although his ability to wean himself from the drug with methadone was making headway, progress with methadone is measured in baby steps, and intravenous heroin abusers are natural sprinters. The instantaneous surge of heroin through a body is a sensation surpassed only by orgasm. Maybe.

Once heroin grabs onto a soul, the body is simply incapable of readjusting to normalcy without major psychological intervention. It is the mind's effect on the body and not the reverse that keeps us from our dreams.

Bernadette was driving around in stunned silence as I was directing her to the various drug locations that I knew my brother frequented. I was also knocking on doors of Tommy's acquaintances with no indication whatsoever of a recent appearance. Bernadette finally pulled over to a phone in the shopping center on White Plains Road. Fear had already replaced my concern and Tommy's wife was way beyond that as I got out and dialed their apartment in Queens with hopes that Tommy might actually answer it himself. To this day I don't recall the voice or words at the other end of the line that informed me that my little brother was dead. Now I had to tell his wife.

Tommy was smarter than me. My little brother could recite batting averages and earned run averages of every New York Yankee since

Babe Ruth. Education took him as far as Iona College, but Tommy left school in junior year in order to work full time and marry his soul mate. His sense of honesty and goodness of heart were attached to a perpetual smile and both gifts from a loving dad.

His joy of life was most evident around his young children. My brother seemed happy, but unfortunately Tommy was also a gambler. You have to be one in order to shoot heroin. My little brother Tommy lost his gamble with drugs at the age of thirty. It is impossible to explain the loss.

Tommy was every bit my equal when it came to disguising his abuse. It is a carefully choreographed ballet as we slip through the shadows of the underworld and adapt to the insanity like a crazy man without actually being insane. Those addicts capable of juggling both balls at the same time usually stay addicted the longest, but the ability to juggle life and addiction is not something you aspire to. It is something to fear. The ability to blend into society without detection gives a drug addict the feeling of normalcy, so why change?

My parents had no idea of my brother's involvement with drugs. The devastation was so completely maddening for them it was impossible to watch. Unless you have personal experience or are familiar with the particular signs of abuse, it is impossible to imagine a seemingly normal looking person being so caught up. I myself have fooled many people for many years.

Tommy's two closest friends never made it to his funeral. Charlie Dineane and Jimmy Gleason were also gamblers and already dead by nineteen eighty-five.

Life as a heroin addict is so completely chaotic that it's impossible to fathom living without the daily turmoil and circus atmosphere that surrounds it. The constant insanity would drive normal people hairless, but when normal is shooting an unknown substance into a vein, how could life without it be anything but boring? I did not choose to be an addict. I'm a gambler. I chose to gamble. I'm certainly not winning and I've already lost so much. I will lose much more.

My dad was sitting at the edge of my bed and calmly asked if I had ever smoked marijuana. Dad said it was a topic of great concern at a recent Holy Name meeting. He said he was told teenagers were getting hopped up smoking drugs in the lots where I was hanging out with my friends. I wasn't quite thirteen years old. It was the first time I ever heard the word marijuana. I had no idea what dad was talking about. He didn't ask to accuse and believed my simple denial. My prior antics would've had any normal person looking for reasons for my stupidity, and drugs certainly would've been a plausible excuse. I could've used a good excuse.

Even after my brother's death my parents still had no idea about my addiction. They will stay in the dark. It's more comfortable in the dark. I know. I live there.

31

By 1986 I'd been arrested on seven occasions for various infractions ranging from petty larceny and hitchhiking to robbery and attempted murder. The failure to control my addiction was costing thousands, the cost to myself esteem by far the greater loss. My days were spent in fear of dying a junkie and leaving Ellen and the boys with nothing but bills and heartache. The nights were not short enough.

I was driving along Rosedale Avenue and slowed as I entered The Soundview Houses where I quickly made eye contact with the regular lookout at the usual place. Then I spotted little Mickey, the pitcher, holding up the telephone pole on the corner by the entrance to the building. One o'clock on a sunny Friday afternoon always brings out the crazies in bunches to the Cozy Corner: sick sweaty drug addicts scratching as far as the eye could see.

I parked away from the hustle and bustle of the drug supermarket and casually strolled back towards the action, my eyes on a steady search for the omnipresent danger, my sixth sense fully engaged as I sniffed the air for donuts. No self-respecting officer of the law travels without a bag full. The coast was clear.

Two minutes later I pulled away from the curb with four dime bags tight in my fist and the craziness in my rearview mirror. Just up the block I made a right turn onto Seward Avenue. The big sedan that blew the stop sign on Saint Lawrence Avenue startled me. The red flashing lights behind me scared the shit out of me, but the man running from the other side of Seward Avenue with a drawn nine millimeter and badge hanging around his neck dispelled any notion that my donut sniffer was in good working order. The scariness surrounding my car felt like a freaking bakery exploded in my face. "Show me your hands, mother fucker!" Sonofabitch. I guess I'm gonna be a little late for work. I wish I wasn't so damn hungry. Freaking cops.

I was arrested at two in the afternoon and finally allowed my one call at five in the evening, an hour into the four to twelve shift. I called Ellen, who notified my garage supervisor who said that he understood my dilemma and kindly asked my wife to remind me, as per department policy to bring in proof for my broken down car. Old Supervisor Gerardi bought the bull shit. The young shiny badges at 125 Worth Street didn't.

Within twenty-four hours the main office was notified by the Inspector General's office and downtown called uptown and uptown suspended me for failure to inform the department of my arrest. The freaking computerized network between agencies cost me another thirty days in the street. I hate freaking cops that use freaking computers.

♣

Being a New York City Sanitation Worker and picking up garbage for a living isn't all it's cracked up to be, but it does have a major benefit. They pay you like a college graduate. There isn't a uniformed civil servant in the city that makes more money, including cops, and it pisses them off to no end. Sanitation supervisor might be the best promotion up from the dirtiest job in the city.

Cops get stripes and do the same job with more responsibility. Firemen get promoted only to be first in the fire. Teachers become principals, court officers become sergeants of other court officers, and corrections officers get promoted and still get locked down for eight hours just like the criminals. On the other hand, sanitation workers get promoted from picking up garbage in smelly green pants and filthy canvas gloves to a clean dress uniform, complete with brass bars, a shiny badge and a ticket book that screams attitude without opening the flap. The job of supervisor in the department of sanitation is so completely different from picking up garbage that it hardly seems like a real job in comparison, but it is a real job and the pay is enough to piss off every other civil servant that happens to be keeping score.

The department gives a test for promotion every four years. The first one I applied for was in 1981. Everybody that knew anything said that if you didn't study, you wouldn't pass. As usual I didn't study. As usual I didn't pass. My next opportunity to obtain a shinier badge came in '86. Word went out again. This time the word was very encouraging. It said not to worry about studying, so I didn't study and I didn't worry because everything the nuns beat into the back of my head was still in the back of my head and there was no math. I love no math.

So I finally stopped going sick for a runny nose, diarrhea, a pimple and the multitude of maladies that came to mind as I reached for the phone to call the job. Running behind a garbage truck is at times a tough, dangerous occupation. Add to that the sometimes tortuous New York weather. Throw in my daily battle with dope sickness. I needed change and I needed to get off my fat ass and make it happen. My new best goal was to drive through the snow in a warm unmarked Chrysler K car with my own trusty two-way radio. Making supervisor is how sanitation workers go to heaven.

※

Working nights during the winter has its benefits. First of all, it's easier to do illegal stuff in the dark and I was usually doing something I needed to hide, plus the ten percent night differential goes a long way in paying the necessaries. All of them, including the dumb ones.

It was about seven o'clock in the evening. I was driving relays out of Bronx Eleven on Zerega Avenue, taking loaded trucks and dumping the garbage into the barges at the marine transfer station in Hunts Point. The usual deal from the supervisor is dump four trucks and the rest of the night is mine.

It was Thursday, pay day, and I cashed my check in the check cashing store on Hunts Point Avenue at the beginning of the shift. After I dump the last truck I'll drive back to the garage, jump in my own car and zip down to the Cozy Corner and treat myself to five bags of Death Wish Two.

The hill on Hunts Point Avenue was perfect for making up time. The trucks are governed (speed limited mechanically) at forty-five miles an hour, but put a heavy truck on a hill and throw it in neutral and that baby will fly like a fat guy on a surfboard down a mountain road coated with ice.

The light at the bottom of the hill was green and I passed it doing seventy. The depression in the middle of the roadway was normally a slight jaw rattler at thirty miles per, but when I rolled into it with the speeding colossus my front wheels came up flying and so did the eight wheels that followed. I was actually airborne before the front left tire hit the curb divider in the middle of the street with twenty tons of momentum and ricocheted the truck like a queue ball off the side pocket towards the other side of the road. My body exploded out of the seat into the windshield and back again. The white monster on wheels was totally out of control as it bounded across the street.

The sleazy Goats Bar was just to my right, but the truck quickly veered towards the two story structure of the US 1 Auto Wreckers junk yard on the other side of the small parking area that separated the two buildings. The car parked at the curb was a black Chevy El Camino. As I remember it was a glistening beauty until I rolled over it like a Sherman Tank and flattened it like a pneumatic car crusher. Four other car owners paid the price for stopping off at the Goats Bar as the sanitation monster continued eating metal and flattened everything in sight. The glow of fire in the fifty-five-gallon drum was next and the wall behind it loomed as twenty tons of rampage obliterated the building and continued on through the junk yard until the only thing left visible from the street were the warning lights flashing amber above the hopper.

As the truck was about strike the building I frantically leaned over and pressed myself down behind the stick shifter in the middle of the vehicle. The cinder block structure completely crushed the low entry cab and the heavy iron pipes that speared above my head would've impaled me if I was still upright. I couldn't move, but I wasn't hurt.

Smoke was already filling the cab. I thought sparks ignited a fire, but cleared my head enough to recognize the smell as burning wood that was rising up from the fifty-five-gallon drum that the junk yard employees used to warm their hands. I'd dragged the barrel under the truck, through the building and what was left inside was warming my fat ass as I contemplated my dilemma from under the wreckage, but that wasn't even the bad part. "You mother fucker!" Okay, the bad part just started. "You fucking sanitation mother fuckers speed through here every fucking night and day you fucking mother fuckers!" I knocked over his building like a barrel of Leggo's. "We're goin' kill you, you sanitation mother fucker." Apparently he was a bit upset.

Heavy duty pipes impaled my headrest and dozens of cinder blocks littered the entire cab, but the instinctive reaction to protect my face from the windshield left my body at a very awkward angle. I was still leaning on my side behind the shifter and couldn't move enough to maneuver my arms because of the weight pinning me down, but I managed to shoulder the closest blocks one by one up and over to the passenger side. The cab was completely crushed and both doors mangled. After a few frantic minutes of sweat and fear I finally saw that the glass at the bottom of my door had popped out.

I finessed myself upside down by contorting my body into a pretzel and still managed a hand on my fat ass to feel for my wallet as I inched my head ever closer and closer towards the hole in the bottom of the door. "You better be dead you fucking sanitation mother fucker!" The screaming never stopped as I finally wiggled free from the smoking wreckage of 25SH-166. The ninety-five-thousand-dollar garbage truck was garbage. I was about to start paying. "'Cause if you ain't were goin' kill ya when you get out here, you fucking mother fucker!"

The loaded truck cut a path deep into his junk yard, the destruction complete from one end to the other. Giant shelves constructed of fence pipe holding car bumpers, fenders and doors were demolished. Tons of shattered auto glass plagued the entire area.

I cautiously crawled through the smoking mess of tangled steel and glass plus the pitiful remains of a two story building, and when I finally found my way to the sidewalk I was still half in a daze. The junk yard owner and his big burley son quickly addressed the other half. The two fuming junk yard dogs yanked me back to reality by my scrawny little neck and started extracting the price of their once thriving enterprise from my dumb fat ass. I got more bumps and bruises from the beating than from the accident.

Sanitation worker Isaac Barkley was running relays from the Hunts Point Market to the dump when he saw the wreck and raced to witness the destruction up close. By the time he parked his dump truck the father and son tag team were probably exhausted from punching me around. Big Isaac handily pushed them off and dragged me away.

The Goats Bar quickly emptied into the street, where intoxicated patrons were left to figure out how many would be calling taxi cabs, and not because they were all shit-faced. The number was five. Their smashed and mangled vehicles littered the small parking area between the two properties.

Within minutes flashing lights illuminated the frigid night sky like a Las Vegas casino. Fire trucks, cop cars, ambulances, sanitation section cars and the department safety officer all converged on the area. Night Borough Superintendent Stanley Shitforbrains finally strolled onto the scene like a freaking F.B.I agent. The big boss asked me ten annoying questions before he asked if I was okay. I was ready to punch something and his stupid face definitely needed a new expression. From a distance I was watching a way too friendly conversation with the junk yard dogs and a uniformed police official. A big smug looking cop with a protruding chin and an outstretched, grabby hand made a bee line in my direction. "Give me ya license." I calmly told Dudley Dickhead that I was assaulted by the two men from the auto wreckers. "I want them arrested." He was smiling, holding back a laugh. "I don't believe you were assaulted." I was straining for patience and my attitude was still gaining balance as I pointed to my lumpy face. "What do you call this, genius?" His attitude for my higher pay grade was beginning to show. "How come all garbage men smell alike?" This is why I hate cops. "Probably because we all banged ya fat ugly mother." The asshole in blue was suddenly the idiot with the exploding red face. "You little piece a shit."

"Fuck you, asshole." Dudley Dickhead cuffed me and shoved me in the back of his squad car. "Sarge!" His thin blue skin was apparently being held together by a badge too heavy for his poor choice of tactics. I screamed through the closed window. "You're still an asshole!" Seconds later his sergeant invited me out, uncuffed me and told me to watch my filthy mouth. I told him my civil liberties were a birthright granted by the constitution and the other asshole didn't have a body or badge big enough to keep me quiet. He walked away more pissed off than the other donut sucking shit head.

The department safety officer finally took my statement. Ten minutes after that he was trailing the ambulance that drove me to Lincoln Hospital.

A man listening behind the curtain that separated our two gurneys in the emergency room pulled the drape to the side. "You the sanitation guy be driving that truck?" The young black man told me that he was working at the junk yard. He said he heard the loud crashing outside and started running for his life, but a falling cinderblock came down on the back of his leg. "Man, I thought you was landen a fucking 747 out there. Scared the shit out me."

"Wow, I'm really sorry you got hurt. How does it feel?"

"Feels fucked up." But the guy was smiling from ear to ear. "They say this mother fucker busted."

"Damn, I'm really sorry."

"Yo, don't be sorry, bro. Somebody gonna be writin' me a moefuggin' check." I think I made his day.

After registering my paper work with the triage nurse, the department safety officer finally appeared at the foot of my gurney. Officer Winters said he was in a hurry to get back to the office. He said downtown wanted his report completed by the end of the shift. The paperwork needed to detail all the damage to my truck, the five cars, the building and one smiling black man and me. Officer Winters looked like he was ready to choke my scrawny little neck like a chicken. "Downtown told me to convince you, Carroll that it's in your best interest to be at the clinic in the morning. They want a urine sample, Carroll. They mean business. Don't fuck around."

For the average drug addicted city sanitation worker, this complication would've been a very serious problem. For a professional with years of problem solving know-how it was a minor distraction. This latest dilemma obviously called for an ingenious plan and I happen to be talented enough to know somebody smart enough to have one. The moment I was released I walked to a phone in the lobby and dialed up the only other professional with practical experience in dealing with this very specific situation.

Paddy Crawford grew up in the Castle Hill Houses and we were good friends long before the job. The sarcastically comical troublemaker with the piercing blue eyes and outgoing personality was promoted to assistant supervisor for the department five years before I started working for the city. Paddy and I spent way too much time dodging the cops in our efforts to buy drugs, but once we drifted above the clouds in a heroin induced haze my friend would often amuse me with wild stories of his job as a supervisor and the trouble that he alone had caused his promising career. Ducking the consequences of his stupidity became Paddy's way of laughing at the system, and his hysterical descriptions of manipulating the urine collection process at the sanitation clinic were funny enough to be told on The Johnny Carson Show.

Some things are destined and others happen by dumb stupid luck. My son Joe was scheduled for a doctor's appointment in the morning in order to get medical clearance to play baseball for Lehman High School where he was a freshman. Ellen wasn't real keen on my brilliant idea, but my options were severely limited by the seven a.m. deadline, and besides that, she didn't have a better one. Ellen woke Joe as soon as I convinced her.

My groggy son moped into the bathroom with a drinking glass after I explained that his late night effort would save him time at the doctor's office. "I'll drop it off first in the morning." I knew the doctor wouldn't be requiring a urine sample. Joe didn't, but turning Joe's urine into my whiz would take a little more than parental arm twisting.

My nervous system was working overtime as I walked into the clinic on Hudson Street at seven o'clock sharp with a steaming container of tea purchased from the corner deli. Sick sanitation workers filled every seat in the very large room. I heard the green flu was running through sanitation garages like beans through a fat baby's ass. The Band-Aid on my left index finger wasn't covering a cut from last night's accident. It was securing a tiny sewing needle to the fleshy tip of the finger. The plastic baggie of Joe's pure unadulterated urine was tied off with a rubber band so the golden liquid bulged into a corner. The urine was still cooling down to acceptable body temperature as it floated under the lid of the tea container, but my golden savior needed to be given to the nurse before it cooled too much because cool to the touch would be totally unacceptable. My name at the top of Chief Osbourne's shit list pretty much assured that wouldn't happen, so it wasn't very long before a nurse holding a tiny plastic bottle called, "Carroll." I was off in a far corner, feigning sleep and casually sat upright at the sound of my name. I quickly plucked the baggie of whiz from the styrofoam cup and placed it strategically under my regular urine spout and calmly strolled towards the iron fist of the clinic. Little nurse Connie, barely five feet tall with a black pixie hairdo and a big attitude. "Do you have to go, Carroll?" Of course I have to go. The freaking boiling piss bag is practically poaching my nuts. "Yeah, I think so." Little nurse Connie walked down the hall to the men's room and pushed the door. "I don't think I need help. It's not that big."

"Keep walking, Carroll. I have to watch you. Orders from Osbourne."

"Not a problem." Sonofabitch. This is a freaking problem and as far as I'm aware, unprecedented.

Little nurse Connie started babbling the moment we stepped through the door. "I understand this is unusual, Carroll, but blah, blah, blah... blah, blah, blah." The little nurse stood to the side of the urinal facing me and willie, and considering that she and willie were practically at the same height was a little disturbing. It was imperative to whip out the tip of the bag and willie at the same time and little nurse Connie was only interested in seeing willie.

I tried to look her in the eye and distract her attention. Maybe gain a little sympathy. She seemed preoccupied. I slowly unzipped and nimbly pulled the corner of the baggie towards the tiny bottle while the index finger on the other hand carefully punctured the plastic bag with the cleverly placed sewing needle. "You're probably uncomfortable, Carroll, so try to relax and blah, blah, blah." She probably thought I was nervous about exposing willie because I was still fumbling behind the curtain. I tugged the corner of the baggie into the bottle. "If ya can't go, Carroll, we can try later and blah, blah, blah." The main event was then performed with the dexterity of a card cheat. I positioned my regular urine discharge spout over the baggie into the bottle and proceeded to squeeze the bulging baggie into the small container. It even sounded like I was taking a leak. "See, that wasn't so bad now, Carroll, was it?" I'll have to check with the union. I might be eligible for hazardous duty pay.

Little nurse Connie didn't see or suspect a thing. Paddy Crawford is a freaking genius.

32

If the young danger-seeking gamblers among us fully understood the stranglehold effects of that first shot of heroin, no intelligent risk taker would ever take the leap. An idiot could recognize the possibilities. Shooting heroin is akin to eating a potato chip. Eat one chip and before you know it you're staring bewildered into the bottom of an empty bag. Shoot heroin once and you're counting the days to get that beautiful feeling back. Heroin is like the comfort of a warm blanket on a chilly night because the brain snuggles up to a drifting cloud of passing visions that belong in somebody else's life. The good life and that great feeling lasts until King Kong comes banging on your freaking door.

During my early honeymoon with hard drugs, when I was still infatuated with constant thoughts of sucking my socks, the idea that I would ever wind up a strung out junkie never entered a single brain cell. In the beginning each encounter with heroin was exhilarating. I was doing the unthinkable, laughing at the devil and poking him in the eye, but the honeymoon was like most honeymoons, and once I was addicted, getting high was more like a stress-inducing, full time occupation. Withdrawal pain was the devil poking me in the eye.

The effort I exhausted conjuring different means of obtaining money to buy drugs on a daily basis was trivial compared to incessant thoughts of breaking free from my life of insanity. I knew it would take an eternity of separation from my fearful wife in order to detox, followed by rehab, where professional drug counselors would attempt to psycho-flush the dumb crap from my head. Thoughts of leaving Ellen to fend for herself were unnerving. Was it just another excuse? My thinking was obviously flawed because all calculations at this point of my addiction were being controlled by the sicker portion of my brain. The darker malignant part.

Unfortunately, the need to abuse my body was years from abating. For as long as I could find a vein I would also need the means to confuse the forces of evil at the department clinic. As the years passed, the department became more determined to catch junkies driving garbage trucks. By the time it was all over I became a urine sample bio-engineer. You simply have to love what you do.

♣

Other than work and coaching the kids in little league baseball I rarely ventured outdoors. My life had degenerated to little more than a peek out the living room window.

Ellen's job as a meat wrapper in the Key Food supermarket up on the avenue was keeping her mind off of me for a few hours a day, but the stress of living with a full-time drug addict was taking its toll. Ellen's easy smile and carefree optimism were no longer evident in every conversation.

Going to the movies and getting a slice of pizza afterwards is something we did regularly when we were going steady, but the last time we actually went to the movies Ellen was eight months pregnant with Richie. Rosemary's Baby was probably a dumb choice. It's about a woman having the devil's child. Maybe a little too close to reality for my petrified bride.

Ellen was never one for the big city lights. She doesn't even like jewelry and I'm still pretty thrilled about that. What she learned at home from her mom and pop is what she brought to our marriage. Ellen grew up with seven siblings, and love is a prerequisite for a peaceful coexistence in tight quarters.

My beautiful wife needed me to be something more than a crazy hair-brained drug addict, but she also seemed resigned to wait out the insanity. So far, Ellen's waited eighteen years. As the saying goes, time sure flies when you're having fun. Ha, ha. More jokes.

My friendships with both Chris Carpenter and Mark Madden were as solid as the day they were forged, almost twenty-five years ago. When I did venture outside it was usually to catch up with one of them. Every other waking minute was spent in front of the boob tube with the big redhead.

During their little league careers I spent hours at the field nurturing my sons, along with many other neighborhood boys. I coached baseball with an emphasis on fun. After a few years I was approached by a league official, Gene Meleci. Gene thought I would be a good candidate for trustee, but I turned him down because of the fear of closer scrutiny. I needed to be hidden away as much as possible, but with Gene's approach I realized my effort to look normal in public was not something I imagined.

At the end of each summer anxious mothers searched me out in the

296

hopes that I might recruit their sons on whatever team I'd be coaching the following season. Their boys were not the first team players, so I believed it was because of my approach to the game. I never raised my voice, except to encourage. Being down at the little league field was the only time I felt comfortable in public.

Winning baseball games as the manager was great, but walking away from the field without buying hot dogs and sodas for the team was horrifying. Every winning manager did it, but every other manager wasn't paying his last nickel to get straight on heroin.

Trophy day is a big deal around the Throggs Neck Little League field. My team, Dom's Bakery won the thirteen-year-old championship. Unfortunately, I wasn't there to pick up my own plaque as the winning manager. I was in bed, writhing in pain, dope sick and praying to the Almighty for a quick fix. The best player on my team, my son Joe handed me my plaque when he came home with his own first place trophy. The culmination of a great summer of winning… wasn't that great.

♣

"Mister Carroll. Get in here!" Superintendent Straitback was an old school, no nonsense boss. You didn't get summoned to his office unless you did something to piss him off. When I entered the inner sanctum the super was seated behind his desk. His crisp white short-sleeved shirt exposed muscled arms and a thick chest, both seemed to expand as I walked through the door. "Yeah, boss. Whaddya need?"

"Mister Carroll. I got a letter today." This can't be good. "I think you should read it before it goes downtown." The super casually tossed the single sheet of paper across the desk. The boss leaned back in his chair and laced his fingers behind a thick head of fashionably long salt and pepper hair while a stern uncompromising stare smoldered into my brain.

Dear Superintendent Straitback,

On Saturday June 3, I observed one of your trucks drive onto my sidewalk for the very last time. Truck number 25N-326 backed down from the corner and drove on my sidewalk for forty yards in reverse in order to pick up my garbage. When I attempted to address your driver he tried to run me over.

Over the years your trucks have misused my sidewalk on many occasions. I have three estimates to replace it and the lowest is ten thousand, three hundred dollars. Please send a check in that amount. If I don't receive financial compensation within ten business days, I will be forced to hand this matter over to my lawyers.

I placed the letter down and slowly pushed it all the way back across the desk so the boss wouldn't strain a tendon reaching. I turned up my palms, shrugged my shoulders halfway to my ears, pleading for the question the boss already knew the answer to. "So, Mister, if you write the man a check we can make like this never happened." The boss was making a funny, but he wasn't exactly laughing. Fortunately, this matter was already addressed except for the extortion part. I should've run the idiot over when I had the chance.

It happened on a Saturday, alright. The janitor of the building in question had placed a ton and a half of large black bags on the sidewalk for pick-up. The usual amount for a Saturday. What wasn't usual were the eight cars parked bumper to bumper in both directions extending from the neat pile of garbage.

My partner and I had a choice: either we heave the bulky black bags, the couch, two chairs and the nineteen-inch television set over the cars towards the rear of the truck or do exactly what the situation called for on numerous occasions at many different locations every day of the week. "Back it down, Carroll." Good choice, Michalese.

I drove up to the corner of Westchester Avenue and backed down the sidewalk right up to my partner's nose. When we finished loading the garbage Michalese went back to his seat. I jumped behind the wheel. As I placed my hand on the shifter I was suddenly staring out at a feisty bald headed old man standing on the corner blocking passage and smiling like he was holding a winning lottery ticket, but he wasn't. The crazy old goat was holding a Polaroid camera up to his eye. He yelled, "Gotcha!"

Sonofabitch! I hate getting my picture taken when my hair's all sweaty.

I was actually more anxious than mad. The boss was getting tired of all the paperwork I was generating and this guy was a shit storm of trouble. And paper work. I slapped the shifter into drive and slowly rolled towards the smiling obstruction. "Don't hit em' Carroll."

"Michalese. I'm not gonna hit em'." We were already close enough

298

to stare each other in the eye. I was measuring his conviction. He was gauging mine. He wasn't budging and I was still rolling towards the crazy old man in the middle of the only way off the sidewalk. "Stop, Carroll. Ya gonna' hit 'em."

"I'm gonna hit you, Michalese, if you don't shut the fuck up." After clicking away the old photographer placed his camera on the ground and gestured me onward with both hands. The truck was now crawling slow enough to get stuck in a crack as I inched it up and placed twenty tons of steel and garbage a millimeter from his creaky old knee. "Driving on the sidewalk is an automatic complaint, Carroll," cried my partner.

"You should've thought about that before you backed me down, Michalese." Pinhead.

There's usually never a cop around when you need one so I definitely wanted to kiss the young man in blue standing on the opposite side of the street. The barely adult sized, freckled faced officer was casually observing the show as my obviously annoyed antagonist grabbed onto the bumper and slid under the front of my truck. I got out and stood directly over his bald head. "What are you, stupid?" The crazy old man squinted straight up at the mid-morning sky and me. "Who do think you're calling stupid?" New York's youngest was already making his way towards a front row seat. "You're the only genius lying underneath a loaded garbage truck. So you're it."

"Excuse me, sir. Will you please come out from under this truck?" The unusually polite boy in blue peered down at the angry prone citizen lying on the sidewalk directly under my weekly paycheck. "I'm glad you're here officer. I just got hit by this guy. I think I need an ambulance."

"Sir, that's probably not going to happen today."

"Then you should probably call your supervisor, sonny boy. I know how this works."

"Sir, I observed you grab the bumper and slide under the truck. You better crawl out before I'm forced to arrest you." Now we're talking. "What are you going to arrest me for?" The cop hesitated. I didn't. "For being an idiot."

"I'm not talking to you, wise ass, and you better get a supervisor here, Opie if you don't know what you're doing." My favorite civil servant in blue was ready for action. I was ready for popcorn.

Well, the old photographer who actually owned the building and the sidewalk didn't get locked up for aggravated stupidity, but it still took an hour and a stern commanding voice by an adult looking sergeant to finally get him up to his feet.

Of course I got a complaint for driving on the sidewalk and another earful from Superintendent Straitback when I finally got back to the garage. I'm sure there was some financial arrangement for the years of constant abuse to his rocky, mutilated, weed choked sidewalk, but I personally didn't contribute a penny. Well, at least not directly.

The incident was just another in a long list of annoyances that were bulking up my personnel folder to the size of a file cabinet.

♣

It was just another Saturday evening. In the middle of just another summer. The Cozy Corner was doing its usual brisk business. Haggard junkies and dapper dealers intermingled in light of day and parted within seconds. Dealer cash in pocket, junkie with hope of a good bag of dope.

Big Bob was big. Six foot six if he was an inch. Big Bob was a big black junkie with a big time habit and he stood on the corner like a cigar store Indian. A big one. His presence always suggested the usual. "Yo, Kev. Lemmeholadollar." And as usual I let big Bob hold my dollar. I even let him keep it in his own pocket, and for as long as it stayed there I was insured against any potential vandalism to my vehicle. Probable flat tire if I didn't. Like every other junkie of normal height and weight I always had my premium ready for Big Bob, the Cozy Corner insurance adjuster.

I parked under the dark green shade of Commonwealth Avenue, a solid line of two family brick houses on the left. The Academy Gardens apartment complex the right. The dope money was tight in one fist as I slipped the insurance to Bob from the other. Without breaking stride I continued on towards the dealer I spotted when I drove into the block.

It wasn't ten seconds before I was walking away from Moochie with four bags of Rocky 2. If I needed credit, Moochie would be the dealer that wouldn't hesitate to extend it because I was as regular at the Cozy Corner as the cops.

When I strolled back around the corner Big Bob was suddenly glaring at my cupped hand like it was a sausage hero. He stepped off the curb into the middle of the street. The baseball bat in his hand was

300

unnerving, to say the least. Big Bob was sweating and not because it was summer. He was sweating because he was dope sick and I had the medicine he needed in my fist. "Yo, Kev. I gotta be having that."

"I can see that, Bob, but why don't you get the next guy because you ain't gettin' this."

My last forty dollars was going into my arm or I would be as sick as Big Bob. "Sorry, Kev. I can't wait."

"I'm sorry too, Bob." I was still a few yards away from my car. Keys in one hand, four bags of relief in the other. The giant junkie suddenly cracked the closest wrist with the bat. The pain shot straight to my eyes. My keys fell to the asphalt. Big Bob had my keys and my way out.

I was writhing in pain as I pleaded for understanding. "Come on. How many times do I have ta give you a fucking dollar, Bob. I don't have any more money and I'm not giving you my fucking dope." He pushed me against my own car and forced the bat against my neck. I'm thinking maybe a few jokes might lighten his disposition, but I couldn't think of one. Big Bob dropped the bat and pulled my arm up by the wrist over my head and pulled my hand backwards as I screamed for relief. The big asshole got my dope and I got my attitude back. "Fuck you, ya fucking nigger." He didn't even blink. Big Bob twisted a smile in a satanic knot around brown teeth and threw the keys by the front of my car. "Thanks, Kev." He already knew what I thought. Didn't care what I said. Big Bob was on his way to get straight with my last forty dollars.

The giant asshole calmly stepped on the sidewalk and walked towards the pizza place. The anger generated by the fear of being dope sick drove my car down the block like a lunatic. I made u-turn on Lacombe Avenue and very slowly managed the curb onto the deserted sidewalk and headed back to the pizza place. The odometer was reading thirty until big Bob walked out of the restaurant. He paused. I didn't. I practically stomped the gas pedal into the engine bloc and when the big dumb ass finally turned to meet his maker he frantically hopped over the hood of a parked car into the street.

Big Bob was sprawled in the middle of Commonwealth Avenue and my car was already drawing attention in the middle of the intersection like a naked woman singing the star spangled banner at a Boy Scout Jamboree.

My options were severely limited so I decided to play the crazy card. Black guys hate the crazy card. I jumped from the car and pointed at the giant, prone, heroin addict. "If that mother fucker doesn't give me back my fucking dope I'll park on this corner until the cops close it down." If I wasn't a regular contributor to every dealer on the block I would've been shot. It was a gamble. I knew Big Bob was an annoyance for all the dealers. No dealer wants to see his clientele being ripped off right under their noses. It lacks respect and black guys are big on respect. Besides, clients might not come back to The Cozy for their drugs. "What's going on, Kev. You gotta get the fuck outta here."

Denny B was the man. He had five dealers and ten runners doing his bidding and nobody did business on the corner unless Denny B gave his blessing. I personally slipped him bundles of cash, twenty, thirty and forty dollars at a time over many years, and from his tone, he wanted me back tomorrow. "Here, Kev, take this shit." Denny slipped me my regular four bags. "I'll take care of that stupid mother fucker personally. Now get the fuck off the corner, Kev." He was a bit harsh and didn't say please, but I left anyway.

Twenty minutes later big Bob was straight on my dope, but I couldn't see his big dumb ass from the other side of the Bronx as I nodded off.

Big who?

33

Being a drug addict is a fulltime job, like the man working a factory line. Every day I do the same things. Except for the occasional out of the ordinary drama, the monotony is enough to turn brain matter into mush.

The fear associated with addiction is all consuming from the time I wake in the morning. Where will I get the funding to feed the gorilla? The struggle to hold my head above water was achieved with the assistance of sharks circling the bloody trail of my financial incompetence.

Loan sharks are businessmen. If you have a job they will loan you enough to survive and still pay them back. Our bills always got paid, usually late. There was always food on the table so the kids weren't panhandling on the street corner, but there was never enough money for drugs, so I borrowed small amounts, enough to get straight, but not so much that I couldn't afford to pay back in a timely manner.

Ellen maintained my sanity, so the insanity of my addiction was only crazy until I got home. The love for my wife is something to study, but my ability to show it to her on a consistent basis was lacking to the point of stupidity. I lived for the day to give Ellen the kindness she's shown me for many years. My wife was always and still is my ground wire, and as long as I'm close enough to reach her I can filter the daily minutia through a transceiver of caring bravery you'd expect from battlefield nurses.

♣

It was about eight o'clock on a beautiful Saturday morning. The sky was clear and bright and so was I. Nothing in my empty head but sucking m socks. I made fifty dollars on the route. The clear bag on 138th Street was screaming my name.

I was driving a brand new low-entry collection truck up Lafayette Avenue just moments after dropping the loader off at the garage upon finishing the route. The red light on Castle Hill Avenue seemed long enough to eat my lunch. Summer traffic, one or two cars slowly passing by. When the light finally changed I turned left onto the main thoroughfare. The area was completely void of pedestrian traffic.

The big white diesel was still straightening out from the turn when the most startling image I had ever encountered was suddenly staring me in the face, and I've had a gun pointed at my head: the horrified expression of a little girl leading an old woman by the hand rushing across the front of my freaking bumper. There was no time to think or breathe. The new wheels stuck to pavement and the front of the vehicle snapped down with a Sussssss! from the air brakes. The little girl continued her frantic dash while grandma was doing her best until the fifth grader broke free when grandma got hit in the head and knocked to the ground by the accordion door folded out beyond my front bumper.

Grandma was on her back holding her head in the middle of the avenue while the little girl with the big brown eyes and colorful dress stood in stunned silence on the sidewalk in front of the Chemical Bank with her mouth hanging open, but it wasn't hanging more than mine. I was freaking thunderstruck.

I scrambled from the truck and placed a calming hand on grandma's forehead for comfort. I told Grandma not to move and hoped she understood panicky English. I sprinted across the street into the bank. The anxious young manager told me that he had witnessed grandma getting hit. "I was just about to call for an ambulance."

"I'll get it." The wide-eyed manager handed over the phone and sprinted outside to comfort the injured grandma. I called the accident into my garage and from there the supervisor called 911.

To make a long sad story even more depressing, the accident was actually an incident perpetrated by the old Puerto Rican grandma. She was pulling a stunt, an insurance scam to collect money from the city. Luckily, two different witnesses on two different sides of the avenue reported the same scenario. The little girl was crouching behind the mailbox by the corner and grandma was hugging the telephone pole as my truck slowly came through the turn. When the big white dollar sign straightened onto the avenue they grabbed hands and dashed into the street. I was lucky enough to be doing the speed minimum. Just another lucky day in the life of Kevin the Troublemaker.

What could've been a much bigger deal was greatly lessened in severity by the first cop on the scene, a female Puerto Rican. Officer Sanchez told Superintendent Straitback and Supervisor Lefty Solino that in Puerto Rican society this was business as usual for old people looking to leave money to lazy grandchildren. My Irish grandma was pretty tough but this old Puerto Rican grandma was downright scary.

Twelve years later I was summoned by city lawyers to the court house at 161st Street in order to review my testimony before trial. My attorney told me that an offer had been made by the city and rejected by grandma's lawyers. He also told me the opposing attorneys figured I'd be retired and therefore unwilling or unable to testify. The trial never happened.

I hope grandma made a lot of money. It was quite a shot in the cabeza.

And if I should someday be gifted with my own lazy grandchildren I will certainly wait until they are of the age of reason so they can fully appreciate my heartfelt distress. I will break it to them easy with a tear in my eye. I will explain that old grandpa Kevin wasn't born with that particular gene, that innate unconditional need to be jumping out in front of oncoming traffic in order to save them from having to get a freaking job. If you count first grade, which I most certainly do I've been working since I'm six. Get a freaking job. Sonofabitch!

♣

My route was complete, truck dumped, gassed up and parked inside the massive garage. I took a quick shower downstairs in the locker room, changed into civvies and jumped into my car.

The working masses were still headed to the Hunts Point subway station on their way to another day at the loading dock, warehouse, sweat shop. It was only eight o'clock in the morning and I was already driving towards St. Ann's Avenue and 141st Street. Two weeks earlier I'd walked onto the same street for the very first time.

The cops had the Cozy Corner closed down tight as a clam's ass. Ten squad cars with red and blue blinking lights flashing bright could be seen from the space station. The area directly in front of the bar was cordoned off with yellow tape. The long bump in the middle of a white sheet spread on the sidewalk appeared as the last in a long line of murder investigations. I didn't get close enough to be noticed because cops have an uncanny ability for sniffing out local bakeries and weary drug addicts. I didn't have a bag of donuts, but I was sick as a dog. I parked a few blocks away from the bar and casually strolled around the area like any other white guy in a very dangerous section of a mostly brown neighborhood. Carefully.

A friend on the job had been suggesting St. Ann's Avenue to widen my prospects for better drugs and this appeared as good a time as any to check out a new location. By the time I abandoned thoughts of waiting out the cops it was already ten o'clock in the morning. Patience in the face of overwhelming odds is a junkie's best friend. Sometimes not. Sometimes you have to think beyond desperation.

I parked two blocks from the spot and ambled down the hill. As I drew closer to the buzz on the street my heart was pounding and my nervous system screaming for calm. My face is always a red flag for anyone in the drug trade. Once again I was walking into the wonderful world of insanity. It's a good thing I'm a charter member. Too bad we don't have identification cards or a special call or whistle or something.

I was still strolling down 140th street. From half way up the block I could already see the passing carnival of drug transactions, but only until a shiny new face appeared from beyond the building line. Mine. Somebody, then everybody realized it didn't belong. Word went out. I never heard it: There's a cop on the block.

Young Spanish girls pushing babies in baby carriages with dope swollen diapers disappeared. Look-outs and dealers of cocaine, crack, pot and heroin headed to hallways and abandoned buildings or simply walked away until the next word went out. The one for all clear. Even the dumb potheads and the dumber crack heads were in the wind. The abrupt departure of everyday life was eerie. If there was a tree I could hear the birds chirping. Unfamiliar white guys walking the hood always get this reaction. I would've walked away from somebody that looks like me if I didn't know who I was, but I still wasn't leaving until I got what I came for.

I happen to have a pair waaay too big for a man my size, and besides I happen to have extraordinary patience when I'm dope sick. Some call it dope crazy. I call it calculating. I cautiously ambled into the block. Faces nowhere. Eyes everywhere peering from blackness at the determined stranger interrupting the normal flow of commerce. I was already a few steps beyond forever when a friendly face stepped from the shadows and greeted me with a toothy smile. "Yo, ma' man, Kev." It was crazy Carlos Sanchez from Castle Hill. **Thank You, Jesus!** The young Puerto Rican wiggled and jiggled while he shook my hand. The whole process seemed to last twenty minutes. "Listen, ma' man." Crazy Carlos was bobbin' his head, his hands a spastic pantomime of hilarity. "They think you a cop." I'd imagined Carlos was thinking the same as me, it's crazy Kevin Carroll my home-boy from Castle Hill lookin' like the damn po-lice and standing around pissin' off all my new peeps.

"Well listen, ma man, Carlos. If they still think I'm the man then you in more trouble than me, but you know I'm not, so why don't you get me four bags of the best shit on the block so I can get the fuck off this street before the real cops close it down."

Crazy Carlos quickly hooked me up with four good bags, and within two weeks I was as regular on St. Ann's Avenue as the young Spanish girls pushing babies in baby carriages with dope swollen diapers.

34

With the city FIAT (Field Inspection Audit Team) officers harassing our district, Superintendent Straitback was getting tired of being caught with his pants down. A plainclothes FIAT superintendent would drive into the building and announce a mid-day roll call and the entire garage full of sanitation men would be absent until the two PM sign out time. At six in the morning the entire district was warned, do not leave the garage after you finish the route under any circumstance. But of course I was a special needs sanitation worker and I needed to get to my new favorite drug spot on St. Ann's Avenue.

When I raced away from the garage on my motorcycle I failed to cover my aggression with a helmet, so when Superintendent Straitback turned onto Casanova Street he didn't even blink at the fugitive sanman speeding away in the opposite direction. The insult was the final straw in a whole pile of straw. The most annoying worker in his district was still failing to follow his very direct instructions. Do not leave the garage. So the super had his own roll call and guess who wasn't present?

The next morning the boss ordered the garage foreman to take me off of my garbage collection route as punishment. I was given a hand broom, a shovel and a sweeping route and the key to the Chevy Luv and told to watch my ass. My penance was an all-day sweep-a thon because according to all the general orders the superintendent wasn't allowed to take me behind the garage and shoot me.

The entire northeast was in the middle of a heat wave. It was a hundred and three degrees yesterday and headlines in this morning's *Daily News* and according to those same weather schmucks we're 'predicted' to be a little bit closer to the sun by lunch. I was pissed. This was the worst possible scenario for someone normally on the way home after two hours of work: stuck in a high profile area with a broom attached to my hand and a bad attitude growing like a tumor in my brain.

I was sweeping and sweating along Castle Hill Avenue when I finally reached the portion of the route that crosses over the Bruckner Expressway. The overpass is completely void of trees and water fountains, and the sizzling heat was already firing up my defiance. I couldn't imagine how I wouldn't screw this up.

When I finished sweeping to the corner I slipped in behind the wheel, whipped my brow, closed my eyes and it was that very moment the boogeyman drove up. "Mister Carroll." No, no, no, no, nooooooo! I opened my eyes and turned towards the window. "You're sleeping. Drive back to the garage and sign out. You're suspended." Well, that didn't take long. "Super, I only shut my eyes for a second." Unfortunately, this debate was over before I got out of bed in the morning. I've been a nightmare for the superintendent for five years, and when Straitback woke this morning I was certain to be somebody else's nightmare by the end of the shift. It wasn't even eight o'clock in the freaking morning.

The garage supervisor strongly suggested I call the union before leaving the building. I did. The union sort of advised that I pack my bags before Straitback started writing my complaints. The boss couldn't legally force me to vacate my assigned district, but the union also implied that if I stayed I might be going home with smaller pay checks. I inferred that the super probably indicated an urgent need to choke my scrawny little neck like a chicken. That's illegal, but he could write me up for everything and anything, and he might even start off with one for defiance. A good boss will know how to make defiance sound like attempted murder on a written complaint form. He already got me for sleeping on the job and I'll probably look like Rip Van Winkle when he finishes the paperwork. I cleaned out my locker and headed to Bronx twelve to avoid the wrath of a thoroughly pissed off hard-nosed superintendent.

♣

Of the twelve sanitation districts in the borough of the Bronx, only BX-12 was considered a pimple on the borough's ass and it was Vinny Gallo's job to make certain it was constantly irritating. As the most powerful of all the union shop stewards in the borough, Vinny insisted, even decreed that all workers under his umbrella stay behind the hopper all day long. Not necessarily throwing garbage, but faking it if necessary, which means working barely fast enough that a supervisor watching from a distance won't find a need to call for a respirator. Leave out work (garbage) if possible and give the city a relay (loaded truck) absolutely. The idea was to make overtime for the men in the district. Somebody in BX-12 had to pick up all the garbage left on the curb. Somebody else in the district had to dump all the loaded trucks. No other district in the Bronx was leaving out work. Every truck in every district was dumped on shift. Vinny Gallo was not invited to Bronx Boro Christmas parties.

I actually started the job two years before Vinny. We got along well, but my reputation for running up the route and disappearing until sign-out time was problematic for the strident union man. Vinny's job was to set my new agenda early and slow me the fuck down. His reputation was about to take a hit. "Listen, Carroll. I know you're a runner. Everybody in nine is a runner, but this is Bronx twelve. We don't run. It's an eight-hour day and my guys stay out until the very last minute." Vinny really didn't understand my personal take on the job. I really hate the smell of garbage, and the faster I run up the route the faster the smell goes away. I told Vinny his badge was no bigger than mine and that I had no intention of lying down for the union. There was nothing I said after that Vinny Gallo wanted to hear.

I was partnered up for the day with old Joe Langford. Old Lang is friendly old acquaintance from   who worked like a man twenty years younger, and somebody with a shinier badge than mine and Vinny's put us together for the shift. Old Lang departed BX-9 under a cloud of which I knew nothing about and he wound up in boogieland just like me. When I showed Langford the dump ticket with his name written under mine, the old guy was the happiest man in the district. His skills had been slowly rusting away, but at least for today old Lang would be finished before the morning coffee break.

Joe and I ran up and down both sides of all the streets and completed eight hours work in an hour and a half. "Listen, Joe. I don't want to step on any toes, especially yours, and I don't wanna cause you any trouble with the union, so what time ya think I should dump the load?" Joe gave a quizzical smile as he held the door of the truck on his way to the locker room and a well deserved shower. "Kevin, this is America. You can dump any time you damn well please." Exactly what I was thinking. I love America.

When I arrived back at Zerega Avenue I parked the truck in the yard behind the building. The eight to four garage supervisor was taking a smoke break. Supervisor Lawlor was gazing out towards the creek and called out when I stepped down from my vehicle. "What's wrong with your truck, Carroll?" Supervisor Lawlor obviously thought my truck was down with some mechanical failure because it was still only eight thirty in the morning. "I'm done." This is a completely new phenomenon in BX-12. "What do you mean done, Carroll?"

"I mean done. The route is clean and the truck dumped." I walked up and handed the supervisor the dump ticket with the scale weight stamped on the back and casually walked out towards my car. He called out. "We need more guys like you around here, Carroll!" The supervisor had no idea who I was except for my name and that I was really fast. In another week he might be looking to punch me in the face.

There actually were a few guys ready, willing and able to run up the route, and my new district superintendent knew exactly who they were. So every day going forward the boss made damn certain to piss off the union by placing those restless gazelles with the fastest new troublemaker roaming the asphalt jungle.

♣

Finding innovative ways of making money to feed the gorilla was a full-time job. Mongo is somebody else's garbage rescued from the hopper by enterprising sanitation men and sold for personal gain. Some guys chop the aluminum from discarded air conditioners with the powerful hopper blade. The copper yoke from old television tubes is also a source of cash. Aluminum siding, copper gutters and old brass plumbing parts and even dead car batteries were collected and stored until enough stuff was accumulated to make it worth an illegal stop at the metal scrap yards in the industrial, whore infested section of Hunts Point. But my need was money in bulk and not dribs and drabs of nickels and times. Dope dealers don't take change.

It was the beginning of winter. December. Four to twelve shift. About six-forty in the evening. The accident up ahead was the cause of dead stopped traffic on the Bruckner Expressway and it was pissing me off, but only until I recognized a great opportunity staring me in the face from the side of the road.

A milk truck had obviously skidded into a light pole on the soft shoulder after being rear ended by a yellow cement mixer. By the time I was passing the scene, the big mixer was parked in the right lane and the small milk truck was being hooked up to a wrecker, while twenty feet of aluminum light pole lay in the grass, unattended. Even dead light poles have a special place to go when they die and I was suddenly envisioning a very special place for the one calling me from the grave on the side of the road.

I parked my empty truck in the usual place behind the garage and went upstairs to the locker room, showered, changed into a clean uniform and planned my operation. It barely took a minute to work out all the details and as usual my latest money making scheme was freaking brilliant.

At ten o'clock I went downstairs to the truck and within five-minute I was driving the big white diesel over the entire length of the unfortunate light pole. I jumped out and hurried to the back and checked for a pulse. The wires at the base were all disconnected. Electrocution, not part of the plan. I lifted the top end of the pole attached to the big street light as if it were merely part of my job, leaned it on the rear of the truck and snapped it off like a chicken bone with the hopper blade and left it lying in the hopper. Then I picked up the main section of pole and placed it on the edge of the hopper, hurried to the thicker end by the severed base and shoved the entire pole into the body of the empty garbage truck slash covert light pole transporter.

The massive concrete anchor under the rising roadway of the Whitestone Bridge at Ferry Point Park was the perfect place for the next phase of the operation. It was dark and deserted. The constant cycling of the hopper is loud and annoying for home owners, but the nearest houses were miles away and Saint Raymond's Cemetery not a cause for concern. Unless I get caught. In that case I'll just hop the fence, lay in front of a tombstone and wait for somebody to throw dirt on me in the morning. I'll be breathing, but I'll still be dead.

I turned off the unlit roadway that circles directly under the bridge and quickly backed the truck up to the gigantic concrete abutment. I jumped out, ran to the back, opened the hopper, grabbed the giant street light and dropped it on the ground. I pulled the pole out of the truck and positioned the top end on the edge of the hopper. The next part of the operation enabled me to take the entire light pole to the scrap yard with a little red wagon. I chopped the entire pole and arm attachment with the hopper blade into pieces no longer than eighteen inches in length. Then I flattened each small piece to make it unrecognizable as a city light pole and placed the entire pole, one piece at a time back into the hopper.

When I arrived back at Zerega Avenue a few minutes later I parked the truck in a dark corner behind the garage. Then I backed my personal car up to the rear of the truck. A minute later the entire light pole was in the trunk of my Lincoln Mark VII. Bright and early the next morning I drove it to the metal scrap yard where I turned the light pole into a hundred and thirty-five dollars worth of gorilla food. This was the greatest idea for easy money since Edison invented aluminum. I mean light pole. Bulb, whatever. Or was it Tesla?

Of course I didn't get greedy. A hundred thirty-five bananas feeds the gorilla for three days. So every fourth night I was killing another innocent light pole, knocking it down with the truck and shoving it into the empty body. When the Bronx garages were ordered to dump at the North Shore marine transfer station out in Queens, I dumped the truck and killed another pole on my way back to the Bronx. I was supplying enough scrap aluminum for the city to buy new poles at a cut rate. They were standing them up, I was knocking them down. By the spring of 1989 the entire Bruckner Expressway, Hunts Point to the Interchange was in total darkness. I'm not sure how I didn't get busted. Maybe it was because it was so freaking dark. I love the freaking dark.

35

After ten grueling years of throwing garbage it was suddenly impossible to focus on the job without pulling my long curly hair out. My number on the list for promotion was finally within range of being called. That's right. Kevin the troublemaker will soon be getting a shiny new badge. You really gotta wonder who's steering the ship.

Having a day off from the job was not always a day off from work. The drenching rains of February were depressing enough, and my need to get high was pushing my exhausted brain for better ideas. The gorilla was now in charge and demanding answers.

It was about ten thirty at night. Everybody in the house was fast asleep but me. I wasn't even tired because my brain was way too busy working out the details of another brilliant plan. When I finally figured it out down to the most basic elements necessary for success I shut off the television and put my latest genius into action.

A clean uniform shirt hung over the bedroom door for the next evening. I slipped off the couch, buttoned it up over a black tee shirt, slipped into my dungarees, tied up my sneakers and drove to the garage. I parked in the yard by the collection trucks furthest from the lights along Westchester Creek.

For two long dark days and nights the cold driving rain was enough to depress those inclined to leap off the nearest building. I wasn't on prescription medication, but I definitely needed drugs. I slipped behind the wheel of the furthest truck in the shadows of the building and drove the big white monster through the open gate onto Lafayette Avenue. Within five minutes I was backing the truck over another unsuspecting light pole. Jumped out. Shoved the pole into the body of the stolen vehicle and raced my latest aluminum lifesaver to Ferry Point Park at the base of the Whitestone Bridge.

I was still driving towards the Park when I recalled the upper arm portion of a light pole lying in the grass at the base of the roadway. The clear plastic globe glistened under the glare of my headlights when I rounded the turn under the bridge the last time I drove through. I figured the arm snapped it off at the railing above from an accident and fell to the grass below. Probably a good forty pounds of aluminum. I wonder if it's still there.

I drove over the curb onto the soggy grass and engaged the emergency air brakes. After slogging about ten yards I spotted a glint of silver through windswept rain. I picked it up and cradled it in both arms and started back to the truck.

It was pitch dark and the monsoon type storm was whipping my face, so when it appeared that the rear end of truck was a little askew I had to wipe my eyes to clear my vision, but it wasn't my vision that was sucking the back of the truck into the soggy earth. Two days of torrential rain did. The rear of the big white diesel was slowly slipping away to a muddy grave. **You're killing me here, Lord.**

I dropped the street light and ran in a panic, jumped into the cab and hit the gas, but the wheels only spun me closer to hell. I jumped out for a quick look. Didn't look good. I was half in shock, but the other half of my brain instantly visited the place in my head where I store emergency plans, and within seconds I was pulling up the special of the day just moments before I was about to start screaming or crying. I got it!

The plan was ingenious as usual. Run back to the garage. Steal another truck. Push the first one out with the second. Park both under the bridge. Chop up the pole. Drive it back to the garage. Maybe take a little nap. Then sprint back to Ferry Point Park and retrieve the original disabled culprit. That's the plan.

The mile run back to the garage in the cold driving ran was torturous. No other junkie on earth could sprint that long and fast without a cop hot on his heels.

A quick twenty minutes later I drove back into Ferry Point Park with the rescue truck, but sometimes a quick twenty minutes isn't always quick enough. I was still sitting behind the wheel, staring out through the driving rain, the big white diesel slowly disappearing before my eyes. A scarce three inches of rubber visible above ground. I had to move like a cop in a bakery on his way to an emergency. No time for chit chat. In. Grab the bag. Out. Gotta go because in twenty more minutes some little Chinese kid might be driving a very dirty New York City Sanitation truck through the hustle and bustle of Hong Kong. Freaking Chinese troublemaker!

The flashing hazard lights on back of the first vehicle illuminated the gloomy night with an eerier amber glow. I inched the bumper ever so slowly towards the stuck truck. The sick feeling in the pit of my stomach was nothing compared with the god awful thoughts of losing the two hundred and fifty pounds of gorilla food hidden inside the body.

The vehicles were finally together, nose to hopper. I slowly pushed my foot on the gas, but the unthinkable was already happening so I mashed the gas pedal to the floor and stared out as mud under the rear eight wheels was shooting into the air, filling my side view mirrors with fear. The first truck never budged, the second a total miscalculation. Two very dirty sanitation trucks are now stuck in a muddy grave at Ferry Point Park. This could possibly hinder my prospects for promotion.

The forest green button-down shirt emblazoned with a bright orange stripe across the shoulder and front pocket was my cover to blend into the environment in order to steal the trucks. But if seen in uniform now somebody might get the right idea. I quickly ripped off the shirt, rolled it into a ball and threw it into the cab of the miserable excuse for a rescue truck. I was still gathering my thoughts. There goes one now, and another. I suddenly couldn't catch a good idea with an open parachute. I'm usually so good at this. Maybe I'm catching a cold. I really don't feel too well.

Now I'm standing in an open field in the shadow of the Whitestone Bridge in the middle of a torrential downpour at the edge of my latest disaster under a black sky devoid of heavenly bodies. My black tee shirt is soaked to my skin and my sneakers squishing into the muddy ground. I'm freezing my fat ass off and frantically looking for a loving Savior. The Lord is obviously very annoyed so He sends His earthly envoy, 'The Messenger' to do His bidding and to scare the living bejesus out of me. 'The Messenger', barely visible through the curtain of rain being slapped both ways by aggressive wipers is waving a hesitant hand at a familiar looking citizen and I can't be certain, but I believe 'The Messenger' might've actually noticed the two very large white elephants over my shoulder that somehow appeared to have gotten themselves stuck in the mud. They're not with me.

I waved back at night boro Superintendent Joe Blanchard. We lock stares. He slowly passes the scene. 𝕿𝖍𝖆𝖙 𝖜𝖆𝖘𝖓'𝖙 𝖛𝖊𝖗𝖞 𝖓𝖎𝖈𝖊, 𝕷𝖔𝖗𝖉. I keep staring in stupefied silence until the big boss rounded the turn under the Whitestone Bridge and disappeared into the gloom as fast as he came. This is very unfortunate. Nobody will be calling me lucky in the morning. This will take some world class storytelling to get out of this one. It's a good thing I haven't lost my professional status.

When a second city car arrived five minutes later with a friendlier face behind the wheel I started crying before he cracked the window. "Jack, you gotta keep my name offa this. I'm not even working tonight and I'm twenty-three names away from getting promoted." The four-to-twelve garage foremen from Bronx ten arrived with good news and bad news. "Carroll, not only is your name on it, but it's already downtown." Not good. Jack Gentile then presented the good news in the form of an option. "Just leave, Carroll, and come up with a good story." Not bad. Sounds like me and ole Jackie boy are on the same page.

The garage officer could've buried me next to his two trucks, but instead he gave me a way out. All I needed now was deniability, probably, maybe, hopefully my finest attribute. I don't even know what ya talkin' about. Why would I steal a garbage truck? I get them for free on the job.

A good work ethic was still a foreign concept for most of the men in my district, and because of their collective lack of effort, the Bronx Boro Commissioner was changing leadership in BX-12 with absurd regularity. The latest in a long line of superintendents given the job of straightening the place out had fallen on the very capable shoulders of Billy Dillard. Billy is close buddies with my old friend Paddy Crawford, urine counselor extraordinaire, and when I started the job, Paddy introduced me to Billy as his cousin. From that day forward Billy Dillard treated me like family.

When I walked into Billy's office in the early morning he was still getting an earful from the Bronx Boro Commissioner. Billy finally hung up the phone, so I sat in the chair next to his desk. Billy, always calm, merely shrugged with a sly grin. "Wow, sounds like you had an eventful evening. The boro said it took three and a half hours and two wreckers to pull those trucks out of the mud, and Blanchard said that he saw you at the scene. What's the story?" The boss flashed a little twinkle in his eye so my nervous grin turned to a prayerful smile. "You wanna know what actually happened?"

Billy's had more battles with downtown than any district super in the city. Billy fully understood the inner dynamics of the department of sanitation because his mom is the personal assistant to the Commissioner in the main office, and because of her connections she was able to pull her son's ass out of the flaming wreckage on more than one occasion. Billy was a troublemaker with a shinier badge. "Or, do ya wanna hear the story?"

"No, Kevin I don't want to know what happened. I just wanna hear the story and you better make it good." Piece a cake. After I told Eddie the whole story he smiled and walked me towards the door. "That's beautiful. Stick to it and don't change a thing. You're being transported downtown to the IG's office for an interview."

If world class story telling is ever given as a college course I should be the one handing out the diplomas at the end of the year.

THE BIG INVESTIGATION

I sat unshakable, even smug as I stared across the desk at the two black city investigators who seemed determined to arrest me before lunch time. Before they barked a single question they played bad cop crazy cop for my entertainment. I didn't dare laugh.

After I explained my entire evening in detail they both looked like they were ready to choke my scrawny little neck like a chicken. "Mister Carroll... You expect us to believe that?"

"I really don't care what you believe. That's what happened." Both investigators were livid. "Are you aware that it rained heavily all day yesterday?" This must be one of those trick questions.

"What's your point?"

"My point, as you say is that you said you were running through the park." Two can play this game. "You're right. That's exactly what I said." Stick to the story. "In the freezing rain? At night? In a black tee-shirt?" The irate investigator was shaking his head, mouth hanging open, eyes searching the depths of my commitment. "That's exactly what I said because that's exactly what I did."

The other man stood abruptly, stomped around to a chair opposite mine and pulled it close enough that I could smell the fried eggs and bacon he had for breakfast. His unblinking eyes fixed with cat-like intensity, trying to change my story by sheer will of concentration, but this city wizard had a better chance of marching down Fifth Avenue as Grand Marshall in the Saint Patrick's Day Parade. I planted my feet and pushed back. He bit his lower lip. He was practically shaking with rage, but merely smiled towards his partner. "Explain the entire night again... from the beginning."

In the very beginning God said let there be light. In the beginning of my story it was actually very dark so I turned up the lights and rendered a tale worthy of a Nobel prize for fantasy under hostile fire. "Like I said, I was running as I do every single day of the year. I run in

319

rain, fog and heat into the hundreds and frigid cold enough to snap off my nose, and as stupid as it sounds to you, I even run at night. So, last night I was running around the roadway under the bridge."

"What bridge is that again?" Another trick question. "I told you guys five times already. The Whitestone." The other guy was rattling his head. "Don't try to be a smart-ass, Mister Carroll." Even if I was a dumb-ass I could still pull the wool over on these two wizards. "Keep going." I sat straighter, grabbed the armrests and crossed my legs at the ankle. "As I said, when I got closer to the bridge I saw the two trucks from my district with the lights flashing, so I continued onto the grass and from there it was easy to see the problem. Both trucks were stuck in the mud, so I went to see the drivers, but both cabs were empty. When I turned back towards the roadway Superintendent Blanchard was driving by. He just waved and kept going. I figured everything was okay. I waved back and ran home." Dumbfounded does not even begin to explain their expressions. They were definitely ready to choke my scrawny neck like a chicken and arrest me for something, but they had no proof of anything, and this, as old Joe Langford can tell you, is America, and in my America you gotta have freaking proof.

Not very long after my interview with Heckle & Jeckle at the inspector general's office, the Department of Sanitation promoted me, Kevin John Carroll, AKA, Hippie Freak, Shit Head, Crazy Carroll, Lucky, Madman, Lunatic and The Legend… to Supervisor.

Only in America.

36

KEVIN THE TROUBLEMAKER GOES TO HEAVEN

Thanks to Superintendent Dillard and his well-connected mother in the commissioner's office, my first assignment as supervisor was as a roving officer back home in Bronx 9. The man in charge of the district, Superintendent Straitback, was still the same boss who banished me three years earlier for gross insubordination and for generally being a pain in his ass.

I was told by a friend that the super threw quite a shit fit when the teletype machine printed out my name assigned to his district, but Roger Straitback is the most evenhanded man I ever worked for, except for Crazy George. "Mister Carroll. I won't ask how you managed to get back here. I'm willing to give you one chance. Fuck it up and I'll break my wrist writing your complaints. Do I make myself clear, Mister?" The super was a man of his word. If I could look him in the eye and give a commitment he'd get amnesia on my past offenses and start me off with a clean slate like any new supervisor, and I knew that when I contracted with Billy Dillard to make it happen. "Thank you, super."

The idea of working in a district that I knew like the back of my hand for the best Super in the department and with fellow supervisors willing to take me under their wings was like walking through the lots behind Taylor Avenue and every day was my sixth birthday.

♣

Making the transition from sanitation worker to supervisor is a difficult chore for most men on the job, and most men getting promoted didn't have a past littered with transgressions. Three weeks ago I was throwing garbage cans and doing contracts with the same guys the department has now charged me with monitoring in order that they adhere to the same regulations I ignored for ten years on a regular basis.

Now I'm suddenly standing on the other side of the fence: the dark

side where I had every intention of being an asset for the city and showing myself in a different light. A good light with soft tones. My plan
was to act in a professional manner in accordance with all department
general orders pertaining to the actions of supervisors with one simple
exception. If I see a truck backed into an obvious contract, (side job
for $) make a left. I will not be the cause of two hard working civil ser-
vants to lose their pensions. The city didn't suffer loss because of their
actions, and another modest home owner had his five yards of concrete
removed for an affordable price. Every other infraction will be up for
spontaneous examination and the consequences, if any, might depend
on how I'm greeted by the guilty party when I arrive at the scene. I'm
not a moody person. Moody people piss me the fuck off, so I prepared
myself for a shit storm of sanitation stupidity that I will surely recognize when pushed up against my shiny new badge.

I had gotten away with more craziness than anybody I knew or even
heard about and getting caught doing dumb shit so many times that
the union sarcastically suggested I relocate my locker to the trial room.

Some of the contracts I did in one night could pay my rent, but I
always did my job, and faster than most. When I walked into the different districts throughout the Bronx for the very first time in my freshly pressed supervisor's uniform I got congratulations from some very
stunned sanitation workers. "How do ya like it, Carroll?" But what
they actually wanted to ask me was, how the hell did ya pull it off?
Well, I did graduate from eighth grade. Everything else I figured out on
the run and I didn't need a dumb cop on my fat ass to be a fast thinker.

I was taught to get the garbage in the truck as fast and efficiently as
possible. Dump it in the south Bronx M.T.S, (marine transfer station),
return to the garage, gas up the truck, day over. Everybody not willing
to work like me altered my mood. For the money the city pays sanitation workers we should mow people's lawns after we pick up their
garbage. And still, there are grown men barely able to read that cry
about this great job.

Sanitation supervisor was my first occupation that didn't require
physical labor. Talking and writing, that was the job. Severe weather
was no longer cause for concern or reason to go sick. If it was excessively hot outside I merely cranked up the air-conditioner, and even in the
freezing bleakness of winter I never needed, nor did I ever wear a coat.
I was once asked by Boro Commissioner Romano on a particularly
frigid day why I didn't have a coat. I was walking the street supervising

the snow pile removal operation along Tremont Avenue. "I have a coat, boss. It's called a Ford Taurus and I try to stay in it as much as possible."

I didn't mention that the heroin running through my system was like antifreeze for my fat ass because the chief didn't need my whole life story. Chief Romano was once a section supervisor in Bronx 12 during my time in the armpit of all Bronx districts, and if he said it once in that sand-paper, gravelly voice of his he said it a hundred times. "I'm glad to see you, Carroll. Yours will be the only truck I won't have to follow around all day long. You'll be done by break time." I got along great with supervisor Romano and thrived under his stewardship as the Bronx Boro Commissioner.

My constant difficulties were almost always the result of my own stupidity made ten times worse by people with shinier badges trying to build up their anemic reputations in order to move up the sanitation ladder. Those same weasels wielded ball point pens like assault rifles, which further added to their seeming need to show superiority with a belittling attitude that was probably the result of never having had a pair of balls until the city pinned then in gold on their chests. Not once was I ever verbally abused by a chief or written up for trivial nonsense. The complaints I did get were mandatory. I got a lot of those automatic complaints, like refusing an order to report to the clinic. Automatic complaint. Threatening a foreman with bodily harm that would enable him to fly over the Throggs Neck Bridge to the asshole end of long island. Automatic. And refusing a direct order to load a truck while two-hundred thousand dollars worth of sanitation baby sitters looked on, automatic. But I did get yelled at all the time by my district supers. I expected it because I deserved it. My immediate superiors also protected me because I never lied to them ever about anything and I've admitted to some very disturbing nonsense. I figured they can't shoot me.

I was once the target of a big Boro investigation. Actually, I was the target of quite a few investigations, but this was an especially big one. A young and very green sanitation worker with just a few years on the job was never introduced to my sunnier disposition because he was a big lazy lump and I was always forcing his big dumb ass to do his work. Sanitation worker Poopadopp made up some very serious accusations in retaliation, and he finally made enough of a case to his union who in turn attempted to get a pound of flesh from my fat ass, but I actually have a few pounds to spare and relished a formal confrontation.

Sanitation worker Poopadoop, his union rep, my union rep, two assistant chiefs and second in charge Louis the dick Testarosa and Bronx Boro Commissioner Romano were all in attendance to hear his allegations. This was a big deal. I was supposed to be worried. I was actually more nervous going to confession in fifth grade.

After an hour of very pointed questions from the Boro big shots, long rambling answers from my lying accuser and practical defenses for my actions I sensed a great deal of frustration in the tone and on the face of the second in charge. Louis the dick had pushed for this meeting. He was a constant thorn in my fat ass and he wanted me in trouble as much if not more than Mister Poopadoop, but Louis couldn't possibly know that when trouble is in the air I actually breathe and think better. Commissioner Romano finally heard enough. The boss glared at the large imposing sanitation worker. "Mister Poopadoop. I want you to look around this room." He did, rather defiantly because he still didn't understand where this was going. Freaking idiot. I did, because the Commissioner was more my advocate than my own union rep and the Commissioner was also a firm believer in the unorthodox motivational tactics that I used often on assholes. The commissioner leaned on his desk and slowly scanned the people he counted on most to be his eyes and ears on the street. "The only person in this room that I know for certain will tell me the truth is Supervisor Carroll." There was way too much irony in that statement for me. Way too much pain for everybody else.

I wasn't privy to the inner dynamics of Boro politics, so I didn't know exactly who the boss meant to embarrass, but it certainly wasn't supervisor Carroll. Everything the Commissioner said after that sounded like a declaration for the Congressional Medal of Honor. I thought Mister Poop-in-his-pants would choke on his fat tongue, and Louis the dick almost fell off his freaking chair onto his bald melon.

Saint Kevin the Troublemaker walked from the room with a brand new halo floating above a very large head.

Considering my lack of formal education I had a great job that came with a pay check big enough to be proud of, and if I wasn't a doper I could've laughed all the way to the check cashing store.

My drug addiction was now a raging three headed monster. The higher rate of pay and regular overtime was usually enough to pay the bills, but after twenty years of shooting heroin my drug habit was out of control. It was like having a fancy girlfriend. Every night of the week I was taking my arm on the town.

Since the mid-seventies I'd been on and off methadone programs as needed. Methadone is a powerful substitute for heroin and ten times more harmful, depleting the body of calcium, causing weakened bones and rotting teeth, but for the shivering drug addict methadone is a nice comfy blanket on a chilly night. A low enough dosage, below forty milligrams in my particular case ensured that I'd feel the heroin after ingesting the methadone, which I did on a regular basis because my biggest problem is the one I embraced the very first time I stuck a needle in my arm. The obsession of watching my red energy swirling through the clear liquid in the syringe had such an overwhelming psychological effect that even if I didn't feel the drugs, the stimulus or adrenaline rush was a temporary calming effect until I figured out my next move to get more money. But psychology doesn't fool the gorilla for very long. Gorillas aren't stupid. Psychology pisses them off.

Taking crazy chances on a daily basis is what separates intravenous drug abusers from the rest of society. Drug abusers are gamblers of the highest regard. I've placed money through holes in the cinder block walls in abandoned buildings in some of the most dangerous, god awful neighborhoods in the city and what came back through those holes I protected with my life. The drive back home was more like a leisurely flight to Utopia. When I landed inside my bathroom I carefully poured the contents of the tiny glassine bags onto a spoon, mixed it with water and heated it to a clear liquid. I drew the liquefied treasure through a cotton ball strainer up into my syringe and finally tied off a vein on one of the few remaining sources of blood, hand, foot, neck and prayed. That's what gamblers do. Pray. Pray we're about to shoot heroin and not something else because once a sick addict travels outside his regular comfort zone, particularly at night, watch out. Boogeymen are very resourceful and they're disguised as legitimate dealers. I've poured crushed aspirin onto a cooker, baking soda, milk sugar, powdered Nestles quick, vanilla cake mix and so many other sugary heroin look-a-likes I could've opened a freaking bakery.

The gamblers that play with heroin are not defective, stupid, sick or crazy. We are simply gamblers. We gamble on life and I bet mine every time I stuck a needle in my arm, hand, foot, neck and lived to carry the gorilla another day. Heroin is a loaded gun disguised as a white powder and if you gamble long enough or with the wrong dealer you will surely shoot yourself in the head as surely as devious dirt bags sell rat poison to heroin addicts. I once pulled that out of a hole in the wall, too, and I know it for certain because I'm the junkie who called the ambulance when my junkie friend injected strychnine and immediately went into convulsions.

As I became more confident in my abilities as a supervisor I also resorted to taking outrageous risks. My latest methadone program was way across town on 153rd Street and Third Avenue. I'd drive through two neighboring sanitation districts and park the unmarked city car by the little playground across the street where I quickly wrestled off my uniform shirt. Then I'd walk in the door and wait in the line in my black tee shirt like all the other sick methadoneans.

The clinic checked for dirty urine on a random weekly basis. Those still on drugs could stand in line for two long hours, six days a week, and on Saturday they'd give you a bottle for Sunday. But if the urine was completely unadulterated for an amount of time determined by the counselor you were granted a one day a week pick up and given six bottles for take home.

According to a friendly methadonean line buddy, warm black tea looks enough like urine and the counselors accepted it as such, so apparently did the geniuses at the testing laboratory. I believed the tale had merit because the junkie who told me the story also recommended a few convenient spots to get a good bag of heroin, and every Monday morning he was walking away with six bottles to take home. So I gave it a shot. Six months later I was on a one day pick up and selling half my bottles right outside the clinic door for seventy-five bananas.

When I was running behind the hopper I learned every trick in the book about how to get the job done, union regulations be damned. As a supervisor I had no problem asking subordinates to do the same, for the good of the district of course. As a field officer I was in a position to do favors for extended work effort, which was always a gamble. There were also other times I did favors for my guys because I felt like it.

Big Bobby Gentry got stuck on the night shift, and he was explaining his dilemma as he signed the attendance sheet at the start the evening. Then I explained mine. "You can tend bar all night, Bobby and

I will sign you out at midnight. You call me on the hour every hour in case someone shows up to hold a roll call. If you don't call me at sign out time, Bobby I will call the Boro and your big ass will be AWOL. I do not sign out dead guys or guys in jail. Am I clear, Bobby?" City employees are known for occasionally getting arrested on the clock. Some are even dumb enough to get dead during their criminal endeavors, only for some unwitting supervisor to sign them out at the end of the shift. Not me.

The big jolly Irishman looked like a big Irish wrestler. "I won't forget this, Hoss." Gentry called everybody Hoss, probably good with faces, bad with names. I looked up from my desk and smiled. "Neither will I, Bobby."

Gentry and his partner Adolph Heinrick completed their route in two and a half hours, dumped the truck and were back in the garage by seven PM Bobby brought me in a large pizza pie against my insistence as a thank-you for allowing him to work his part-time job while on the clock. A bag of dope would've been nice, but it's not something you ask somebody that wouldn't know a bag of heroin if he pulled it out of his own pocket. Big Bobby left the office to tend bar in a local establishment, and his good friend and partner Adolph Heinrick went along to watch. The burley, ex-semi pro running back and proud German head case could choke you with a pinky. Adolph is the strongest man I ever worked with behind the hopper. Adolph would toss two-hundred pound cans of wet ash from the sidewalk over the hoods of parked cars and into the hopper like he was flinging a bag of feathers. With big Bobby tending the customers and Adolph the German enforcer watching and possibly throwing a few back, this bar would not be the place to get rowdy tonight.

It was a bit warm for January. No possibility of snow. Just another boring night. The garage supervisor and I were talking the usual trash as he entered the truck weights into the computer. At nine fifteen and with all of his early work completed supervisor Johnny Rolland strolled next door to the Bronx ten lunch room on the other side of the office wall. The serious business of nightly poker was soon under way, and so it wasn't long before I could hear Rolland producing the nightly result, another contribution to the san-man welfare fund, but when Rolland suddenly rushed back through the office door I knew without words or eye contact who was hot on his heels. Night Boro superintendent James Dowdy strolled into the operations office and he wasn't here to

327

sit in on Rolland's nightly card game. Dowdy was here to announce a roll-call and be a pain in my fat ass. Don't watch my hands. Watch my lips. I'm about to make an asshole disappear.

My four trucks were done early as usual and their legal lunch break over, and according to department regulations, eight sanitation men should be somewhere inside the massive building. What are the chances?

Two week earlier the same boss gave me an order via telephone conversation just before the start of the shift. "Carroll, I want you to cut all your collection the first sign of snow." The highly unusual change of protocol was baffling, but as a good soldier I relented without question. "You got it, boss." I was told to order my men to return to the garage at the sight of the first snow flake and immediately dispatch them all on salt spreaders. The super didn't offer further explanation. I didn't ask. The general order pertaining to this very specific situation states that each officer is to determine his own needs at the start of a snow event and for a good reason. Brooklyn might get a blizzard. The Bronx light drizzle.

By eleven o'clock at night the man in charge of the Bronx was leaking brain matter from his ears because downtown was stepping all over his fat head. Every time I saw a snow flake I called the Boro over the radio. "Bronx nine to the Boro."

"Go, Bronx nine."

"George, I'm at White Plains Road at the intersection of Soundview Avenue and I have flurries falling at this time. I'm cutting my collection to snow removal, now."

"That's a ten-four, Carroll." Central called out from the main office in Manhattan. "Bronx nine. What do you got up there?"

"Central, I have light flurries falling at this time."

"That's a ten-four, supervisor."

Two minutes later I was back in the garage. Supervisor Rolland was straining to contain his excitement while he covered the transmitter of the phone with his palm. "Man, he is smoking." Rolland had his own running feud with the night Boro dickhead and was obviously enjoying my little dance with the devil. I grabbed the phone and covered the mouth piece. "John, by the time I hang up this phone he'll be on fire....Yeah, boss, what's up?"

"Carroll, what are you doing? Nobody else is calling for snow operations. What's it doing right now?

"Hold on, super. Lemme look out the window." Rolland was holding his mouth with one hand, his side with the other, doubled over, crying with laughter. When I called it in a few minutes ago there wasn't enough snow falling in the entire district to cover my head, but his order was very precise. First sign.... "It stopped, boss."

I could practically hear the tumor growing at the base of his spine through the eerier dead silence. "Carroll, what, where, what are youuuuu doing? Where are your four trucks?" All eight of my men were standing in front of me, smiling. "They're right here in the office, as per my orders."

"Well, whataya gonna do now, Carroll?"

"I'm gonna send 'em back out to get the garbage, super." Click. The man hates me. So when fatso strolled into my office and announced a roll call, Kevin the pizza man stepped up to the counter. "How's it going, super?" He was smiling, I was smiling, but the tension was palpable. The boss was still signing into the location across the room. "Everything's good, Carroll. Everybody here?" Without hesitation Kevin the gambler stepped up to the stove.

"Everybody's upstairs, super." He turned from the blotter. The steaming pizza box was practically melting a hole in the ozone layer. "You guys havin' pizza?" Gotcha, ya little bubble butt. "Actually, the guys brought in a few pies and gave this one to me because I'm such a sweetheart. I was going to split it with Rolland, but he already ate." This is the magic part. "You hungry, boss?"

The starving phony fucker eventually ate four slices because this phony fucker let him and we were still bull shitting each other forty minutes later when the phone rang. "Bronx nine. Carroll."

"Carroll, it's Gentry." Big Bobby was yelling over the crowd noise at the bar. "Everything alright, Hoss?"

"Sweetheart, hold on a minute. I got the Boro here. Well if it's that important." I held my palm over the phone. "Super, it's my wife. I gotta take this. You wanna have that roll now?"

"Na, it's okay, Carroll. I'm gonna go next door and surprise Bronx ten." Exactly what I was thinking, ya fat bastard. I knew the boss didn't have the balls to eat half my large pizza pie and write me a complaint before he had a chance to fart.

Dowdy was still signing out in the blotter when Gentry yelled again. "Listen, Hoss you can call me sweetheart as long as you sign me out at twelve o'clock." I stood up and closed the pizza box while the night boro superintendent waddled out the door. "Don't be a smart ass, Bobby. The Boro was here. Now call me in an hour and don't keep me waiting again."

"I owe you, Carroll."

"Adolph still conscious?"

"Still conscious. Talk to you in an hour."

The smile on Rolland's face wasn't even close to the one on mine. We looked like a pair of teenage chuckleheads staring at a 42nd Street peep show.

Don't watch my hands. Watch my mouth. Poof!

The next show, maybe tomorrow. I'm here five nights a week.

♣

Until Doug Thompson started his career as a new supervisor in my district all but a very few men were kept at a discrete distance because of my fear of being found out as a doper. For that same reason I never once went out for drinks with the guys after a shift. The fact that I couldn't afford to wander outside the financial obligation to my left arm was also a big reason to go directly home after work. I hate my left arm.

Doug's easy smile greeted everyone the same way. His skill as supervisor was derived from an inner strength to deal with every situation with a clear head and a firm hand. Doug was also the only college graduate working within the boro and he used his smarts, usually without being a smart ass. Usually.

When the eight to four garage foremen retired Doug transferred into that position, which afforded him a steady day shift. During the winter months I was the night district superintendent, which enabled me the pleasure of driving Doug home with the city vehicle after his shift. Not legally of course. It was a gamble. I was gambling I wouldn't have an accident on the worst stretch of highway in the tristate area, and I was also gambling that none of my eight men would need me for anything for at least an hour.

Doug's sense of humor was similar to mine and we tended to laugh the whole ride home in bumper to bumper traffic on the treacherous Cross Bronx Expressway. Doug was also color blind in his dealings with the varied shades of department personnel. Whites treated the same as blacks, blacks the same as Latinos and women the same as men. Every other nationality, sexual preference and religious denomination was treated with respect by supervisor Thompson. Just do your job. Color or gender didn't sway his judgment or ability to deal in a fair minded way. Doug and I are also similarly wired when it comes to dealing with laziness and bad attitudes, which usually required a foot in the ass, but the department frowns on that. The next best motivational tool was sarcasm and we were both pretty adept at pissing off any worker bold or stupid enough to challenge our well-developed skills.

The work experience program (WEP) was the Giuliani administration's initiative to force welfare recipients into being productive members of society. Those failing to show up for work in the various city agencies were immediately released from the programs and the welfare stopped. The program wasn't meant to demean or humiliate, but rather in our case, to clean the city with the help of a larger and cost efficient labor force.

Shinequa had been working around the garage for months, cleaning the men's rooms, sweeping the garage floor plus many other mundane chores. The young black woman's WEP status though was as a street cleaner. Everything a sanitation worker could sweep, she could.

The recent department scorecard rating for our district showed a downgrade in the cleanliness of our streets, so the main office assigned Bronx nine six additional WEP workers. The young black woman who spent the spring cleaning inside the massive building by herself was suddenly assigned to her proper duties outside in the hot smelly streets.

To say Shinequa was pissed would not do her anger justice. She refused to go outside until Supervisor Thompson showed up for work at seven thirty in the morning. Doug was apprised of the situation by the midnight to eight garage supervisor going off duty. Shinequa had been working herself into a frenzy and she was still cursing and pacing the outer office an hour after the rest of the WEP workers were dispatched. Doug was smiling at the distraught worker as he pulled a pink piece of paper from his filing cabinet. On the paper, the woman's status as a street cleaner.

"You can smile all you want, Thompson. I ain't goin' outside. I don't care what you say." The tall friendly officer with warm brown eyes grabbed the long broom handle. "Schinequa. Did you ever see Roots?" Shinequa put her hands on her hips and cocked her head waaay to the side. "What the fuck you talkin' bout, Thompson?" Doug's smile was still growing. "You know, Roots?" I wasn't sure where he was going, but he was definitely having fun getting there. "You know, Schinequa? The old seventies TV mini-series about Negros in the south during slavery. Well, did ya?"

"Yeah, Thompson, but what's ya mother fuckin' point?"

"Well, my point, miss lady is this here. You see, in Roots they taught us folks the difference between house niggers and field niggers." Shinequa's eyes flashed wide enough to see the explosive charge in her brain. Her mouth had flopped open wide enough to see her stomach. "And this here paper says you're a field nigger. So you either take this broom... " Doug handed the broom handle to the woman with a stern look. "Or I will take you off the clock and you can do the rest of your crying downtown. Do we understand each other, Schinequa?"

The angry woman snatched the broom, walked towards the door and threatened supervisor Thompson with all kinds of civil rights hell, but she never doubted his authority. "You ain't right, Thompson."

"Don't take it personal, Schinequa. My job is making other people do their job. Just business." Schinequa went to work while Doug Thompson signed the blotter to start his day. "You're fucking nuts, Doug."

"Yeah, Kev, but what is she gonna do, call the NAACP on a black man?"

Doug Thompson rose through the department ranks to become a two-star chief in charge of Brooklyn North. The pressure of added responsibility never changed his demeanor as his badges got shinier. The same smiling supervisor I drove home to his family in Washington Heights was the same guy who greeted me with a hug and two stars on his collar. His stay in the Bronx as deputy chief afforded me the status of welcome family member whenever I happened by the Boro office. When Doug was promoted to full chief and moved to Manhattan nobody missed him more than me because anything I needed Doug got it, vacation changes, emergency leaves and any problem that crossed his desk with my name on it, disappeared.

Doug Thompson proved to be quite a magician because I was still pissing off a lot of people with my big mouth. When I was accused of using a bad word towards an African American asshole, Doug questioned the validity of the accusation with a smile. "Kev. Did you call that man a nigger?" Doug Thompson knew me well enough to know I wouldn't lie, especially to him. "Sorry, Doug. The dickhead almost ran me over."

"Don't say you're sorry, Kev. From everything I heard it sounds like he deserved it." Doug Thompson called a spade a spade even if it was a black guy. It was the reason he was loved by his fellow officers and more so by the men he led.

37

My ability to do normal things without feeling like I'd rather be dead was the only normal I knew. Everything was a struggle. The depression and frustration of addicted life is all consuming, so visiting mom and dad was no longer a matter of just showing up. Listening to mom had become stress times aggravation.

My parents moved from the expansive Parkchester housing development years ago and they were presently renting a beautiful house in Silver Beach Gardens. The tiny picturesque enclave is situated high on a bluff with vistas of the entire Manhattan skyline, from south Battery Park to north Harlem. Silver Beach is a touch of the country on the shore of Eastchester Bay at the foot of the Throggs Neck Bridge on the border with Mayberry.

The house was well within walking distance, but I still hadn't managed a visit for at least a month. Probably more. I got straight after work and it was two hours after that when I walked in the front door unannounced. Mom was watching television, legs stretched out on the couch. Dad was due home momentarily. She sat upright, rather quickly, a puzzled, almost fearful look in her eyes. I kissed her on the cheek. "I just called you," she noted and hesitated, way too long. "I just hung up the phone with Michael Madden. Mark is dead."

The overwhelming anxiety for a life of failure was suddenly magnified by the horrifying panic of staring into a mirror and nobody staring back. The emptiness of my hollow existence drained of a prayer by the reality of death. I didn't know what to do or say as the words in my head stayed in my mouth. Tears of silvery blackness streamed onto a chest sunken in despair. I couldn't get away fast enough. Mom begged behind me as I made my escape, "I'm sorry, Kevin. Call your father and… happy birthday!"

There has only been one other instance in my entire life when someone said something so incredibly hurtful that the intensity of that notice will fester in my head until someone else in my family gets the very same notice, Kevin's dead. My brother was my brother and we were extremely close, but Mark Madden and I shared the same soul. We shared the same birthday and a love of each other's company since we were children.

Mark was as generous and kind hearted as he was good looking. In fact, Mark was better looking than most women. His extraordinary talent on guitar was his reason for breathing. Mark's earliest musical influences were the Beatles, but he was especially intrigued by the genius of John Lennon. My earliest musical influence was Mark. If my friend hadn't needed a bass player I would've never picked one up.

Mark met the love of his life while they were both young teenagers. Catherine had, and probably still has the face of a super model, and with his rock star looks and a mere two hundred yards of real estate between their respective homes, their eventual meeting was just a matter of time. It wasn't just the physical attraction that drew them together, both were thoughtful, generous and kind to a fault. It was probably their differences, not their similarities that provided their relationship with plenty to talk about. Catherine was fun loving and confident where Mark was introverted and not as self-assured. Their symbiotic partnership worked on many levels.

They married very young, but unfortunately were doomed from the start. Mark's drug use was known to his girlfriend, but not to its fullest extent. Within the confines of marriage not much can be concealed, at least not for very long. It was hardly the life she bargained for and Mark was hardly ready to stop. Without the encumbrances of children, Catherine was free to start over and Mark was left to regret her exit until the day he died.

Mark lived among the shadows of drug addiction for twenty-five years and died on his birthday of a broken heart. November the 29th still comes along once a year, and every year on my birthday I'm reminded of a great friendship that passed on to the great beyond from a lonely park on White Plains Road. Birthdays are reminders for as long as you can remember and nobody ever accused me of having a faulty memory. Usually a blessing, sometimes not.

❧

My personal take on the job never evolved from the day I was hired. We pick up garbage. We don't build missiles. It became my mantra. The men pick up the garbage, sweep the streets and plow the snow, and as a supervisor I made sure it happened in a timely efficient manner.

But there are some a bit higher up the food chain that think it's more important to salute and bow to the almighty brass after a day of throwing garbage or dealing with abusive citizens or lazy workers in our capacity as supervisors. Like any big business the grunts do the real work, middle management catches all the hell and the shiny badges will risk a herniated disk taking the bows.

Throughout my career I've watched quite a few men advance through the ranks. Some of the lesser of these individuals seemed nervous and even scared as they rose to the upper echelons of the department. I've also come across a few chiefs that couldn't give a simple command without spewing worthless general orders that mandate supervisors work in a very structured manner, and anyone circumventing their precious system was singled out for written complaint and possible loss of wages. I was never written up for a frivolous infraction of department policy, it was always a serious violation.

A fellow supervisor I considered a close friend was also an Emerald (Irish) Society official, and because of his position big Jack Babcock rubbed elbows with the very top of the department on a regular basis. Babcock once made a comment concerning something he gleaned over the years at various department functions. "Kevin, I think you make the brass nervous." I'm pretty sure big Jack thought he was giving me a heads up after my latest dust up with the Boro, but I already sensed apprehension and even uneasiness from some in charge on numerous occasions. I told Jack he was probably right. I said it was probably the reason I could tap dance around their general orders like Gene Kelly. Or maybe that particular ability was a gift from God, because nobody could get away with the crazy shit I was doing and still have a job without divine intervention.

The bosses unofficially classified supervisors by how we got the job done. It was the reason I was able to get into so much trouble and not have to look over my shoulder. I got the job done. As long as I didn't kill anybody they would look the other way for most transgressions most of the time, but most Bronx supervisors weren't as lucky. Most supervisors regarded the boro chiefs as ineffective hacks who preferred extracting blood for nonsense, and the not so effective supervisors were harassed and hemorrhaged money on a regular basis.

⚜

During the winter months the Department of Sanitation works around the clock because the department could never count on the snow falling between the hours eight and four. The winter schedule is referred to as snow plow, and both night shifts are staffed with just enough personnel to man the salt spreaders. In my district that number is eight, but a regular night without inclement conditions consists of the mundane chore of collecting garbage.

I was working my regular winter shift, four to twelve. My eight men were off the street and back in the building by seven pm. After checking their four routes for completion I returned to the garage to call the boro with my early report. The forecast was for up to six inches of snow, but until that happens my work was done, but I still had a job to do.

10:00 PM

The occasional streetlight along the main thoroughfare was mostly dim and barely yellow. Darkness: the perfect cover for muggers. I parked my black unmarked Chrysler K car at the curb where it simply melded among the shadows of Hunts Point Avenue.

A light February snow was just beginning to fall. My job was to notify the boro of this anticipated change in weather via radio transmission, but that would certainly put the kibosh on my immediate plans. I needed to get straight. I needed to cop four bags of dope and a new diabetic syringe. My regular source for cash at the garage was a little tardier than usual. I was sicker than usual.

I placed the two-way radio under the front seat, quickly stripped off my uniform shirt and folded the badge and collar brass inside for cover against curious thieves on the prowl for a fancy warm shirt. My entrance into the underworld was swift from long years of practice. First stop, the bodega on the corner of Garrison, where I purchased a new diabetic syringe handed to me in a tiny brown paper bag through a plexiglas partition by an unsmiling clerk with no more effort than it would take me to buy a stick of butter. Just up the block and around the corner I strolled past the regular lookout. I warily entered the building, hurried up five flights of very dark stairs and copped four dimes from the pitcher in the stairwell.

It was late, the cold sinister streets completely void of anything resembling human endeavor. I was alone with my dark thoughts as I approached Hunts Point Avenue. Two tubby men in blue suddenly waddled from behind the building line on the opposite side of the street. The only white guy walking the hood, freezing in the flurries, dressed in a black tee shirt caught their attention. "Hey, whitey! What are you doing here?" The only thing I could've done worse was curse them out, then run.

Twenty years of jogging on gimpy knees was about to bite me on the ass. My city car was twenty yards away, the city cops twenty yards further. Kevin the gambler took off at a sprint, and twenty yards later I lost the dumbest bet I ever laid. My damaged knee blew apart in the middle of Hunts Point Avenue where I collapsed in a heap of agonizing absurdity.

The two fat Irish slowpokes simply strolled up to the body. One started doing the Irish jig on my fat ass while the other was dragging me by the wrist across the avenue. They were like two angry nuns, with guns. I didn't expect sympathy and was hardly surprised by the ass kicking. Forced exercise on New York's Slowest is punishable anyway they feel like it. As long as nobody's around. Nobody was around.

My second arrest for possession of an opiate and paraphernalia was nothing compared to the embarrassment. It was snowing and the night district superintendent was shivering in a warm jail cell, dope sick and dumbfounded to come up with a viable excuse for criminal stupidity. I couldn't think of one. Sonofabitch.

♣

After thirty days on suspension without pay I was finally ordered downtown to the clinic. Of course I was still dirty (drug saturated), but walked confidently from the men's room and placed the sample on the nurses table. Three hours earlier that crystalline urine sample was produced exclusively for me by the man with the cleanest kidneys in the Bronx, the black man who was selling me heroin. Big Mike never smoked, didn't drink and never did an illicit drug in his life and I was buying his fresh, unadulterated whizz for ten dollars a glass full. When Big Mike couldn't give me his telephone number because he didn't have a telephone I had one installed in his apartment on Barrett Street and paid the bill for months. So when I needed that fresh clean sample at six in the morning I just gave big Mike a wakeup call. "Not a problem, Kev." Damn right, not a problem. With a few more desperate customers like me, big Mike could have a whole new career, pissing for dollars.

Three days later the city was finally forced to schedule my department trial at the Kevin John Carroll memorial wing at 150 Broadway in lower Manhattan because my urine sample came up clean enough to be used as mouth wash. Only kidding, but it was really, really clean because if it wasn't I would've been really, really fired and the trial a mere exclamation point on the end of my career.

DEPARTMENT TRIAL ROOM—MAIN AUDITORIUM
KEVIN THE TROUBLEMAKER DIVISION

It appeared that my union mouthpiece was doing his best to get me fired. Big hands Benny Botticelli seemed to know the judge advocate well enough to make jokes at my expense, or maybe the union was trying to scare me straight, but it was hardly necessary. I already knew I was in big trouble. It was the details I feared.

The judge was interrupted by his clerk, who walked in the room and whispered in his ear. I tugged on Benny's sleeve and whispered directly into his thick skull. "Listen, Benny say something nice. You're killing me here." Everything he said so far would cost me a month's salary. In another minute I could be signing away my pension. The advocate who was collecting my union dues should make me sound a little more like Saint Kevin. I was hoping for a little union razzle dazzle to make this thing sound a little less than a hanging offense, but unfortunately the hangman had already measured my scrawny little neck, and after ten exhausting minutes of listening to them building the gallows I was sure the city would be choking it like a chicken before I stumbled from the room.

Two minutes later the judge rendered his decision. "You're a very lucky man, Mister Carroll. You have a friend here in Mister Botticelli, and I suggest you shake his hand when you walk from this room." Those were the first uplifting words to reach my ears in thirty long days. Benny as usual gave me no clue that he had already secured a deal in my favor. "Commissioner Doherty suggested termination, Mister Carroll, but I'm merely demoting you to sanitation worker for the next six months. You will also be drug tested for two years." Okay, that's a little disturbing. "Clean up your act, Mister Carroll and you will be reinstated to supervisor with full seniority. The date for reinstatement is on the paper you will sign now." And all that good fortune was arranged as per standard operating procedure before I even walked in the freaking room.

My luck was still holding up the next day. It was a blustery fifteen degrees outside, but my first assignment back as sanitation worker was inside, and that's where all my luck ended.

The Bronx Boro Commissioner Angelo Spaghettiface obviously had a problem with drug abusers, because for the next two days and unheard of prior to my unceremonious demotion the big boss had me mopping the floors in the Bronx Boro office among all the same people I dealt with for five yearsas a supervisor. The cleaning is always done by janitorial staff, so the Boro Commissioner was either attempting to break my spirit or teach me how to mop, but the chief was about to be disappointed on both accounts. I learned to mop a floor in Crazy George's diner and I was damn good at it, and Crazy only paid me a dollar an hour. For three hundred dollars a day plus benefits I'll shine the commissioner's freaking shoes, so I mopped the floors with a smile. As for my spirits, well, I still had a great job and the judge advocate had assured me in writing that my shiny supervisor's badge was being held at 125 Worth Street for a mere six months. Armed with that knowledge I could do six months standing on my head with a mop in one hand and the chief holding the other, but what the whole messy experience did in my head was not pretty. In fact, it was damn freaking ugly.

With my back and pension up tight against the wall I figured the department was looking to crush my hopes of ever again wearing a supervisor's badge by pushing me further, but I never thought they'd be so enthusiastic on the first two days. I believe the department thought I'd revert back to my old habits, go sick or lash out at every man with a shinier badge than mine, and that was suddenly everybody. I was now the junior man in the entire Department of Sanitation. So I adjusted my attitude in a big hurry, and when I didn't do the expected the city still had the option of wearing out my urinary tract on a regular basis, but I had more tricks up my sleeve than a Las Vegas magician. I could now piss a glass of holy water in my sleep, so on August seventeenth the day before my twenty eighth wedding anniversary I was reinstated back to supervisor.

I strolled out the door of room 804 at 125 Worth Street with my badge and a smile bright enough to lighten the dark hearts that just handed it back to me. I shined that bad boy up in the elevator and headed for the subway.

They don't call me lucky for nothing. They call me lucky because I'm damn freaking lucky.

341

38

By the mid nineteen-nineties I was getting so much rest from my times on suspensions that my skin had a new glow, my gimpy knees were getting stronger and the trials and tribulations of the job were almost a distant memory.

Almost.

My regularly scheduled visits to the clinic were costing me more than gas money. Every few weeks the city would order me downtown to take a whiz, and before I drove into Manhattan I would make a quick stop in Hunts Point and hand Big Mike a ten-dollar bill for another glass of fresh clean urine. There were also a few discrete sanitation men willing to take a quick whiz for free in a hurry for my benefit. I had this routine down to a science. If I had a Bunsen burner in the men's room I could probably turn poop into pizza pie. All I needed was the right motivation. I love pizza pie.

I was now on the job fourteen and a half years and forced to piss so many times I could've filled a swimming pool, and not once was it ever found to be anything but yellow.

Guys on the job were now searching me out for counseling. "Carroll, can you help out? I gotta go downtown." I was fast becoming the junkie guru for beleaguered sanitation heroin addicts. The legend lives.

The criminal case was another complete sham. I was standing before the judge at the second and final arraignment proceeding in Bronx Criminal Court. The system of give and take went exactly as I expected. I did all the giving. My city appointed mouthpiece finally produced the arrest report with the arresting officer's statement at the very bottom. "Blah, blah, blah, when I saw the perpetrator and another man exchanging money." Their entire case against me was based on a lie to justify their reason for calling me in the first place, which is illegal, even in Hunts Point. "Hey, whitey! What are ya doing here?" I copped my dope around the corner in the stairwell on the fifth floor. I hope he's Catholic because my pathological blue accuser will be spending a lot of time in hell with his tongue on fire. And I'll be spending twenty-five hours picking up litter for the Parks Department in Pelham Bay Park as per my plea agreement.

I always loved running around that park. Never realized it was so damn filthy. Freaking pigs!

♣

Some of my greatest escapes in the dark underworld of addiction were done with supernatural composure under the type of pressure necessary for making gem stones, but not this time. This time I was merely Lucy taking the football away from Charlie Brown and his dumb brother Charlie Blue.

I parked my car in front of the check cashing store on 149th Street in The Hub, the massive shopping district one block east of Third Avenue. My glistening white Pontiac coupe stood out, white bucket seats and blue tri-color racing stripe that highlighted the pointed hood and continued along the door where it looped over the cab, giving the car the look of a California street racer. The dope spot was two blocks away in the shadows of an abandoned warehouse.

The dope was tight in my fist when I rounded the corner onto the main avenue. My eyeballs almost exploded out of my head. Two big bumblers in blue eyeballing my vehicle looked like the Beverly Hillbillies, scratching their heads while circling the pretty white chariot. "Lookie here, Jed. Deez cheer numbers looks a mite funny."

"Oooo wee, Jethro. I tinks we gots us a sitchiation here, boy."

One big cop was reading my plate number aloud off the windshield registration, the other was listening while staring at my front bumper. I couldn't actually hear their conversation as I slowly strolled through the crowd behind them, but they seemed as giddy as two brawny southern goobers on Sadie Hawkins day. "We definitely gots us a sitchiation, boy."

I calmly walked to the other side of 149th Street to wait out the investigation, but after another twenty minutes these two blue geniuses were really pissing me off. From 1959 until I got married in '68 I had spent enough time in the projects around Puerto Ricans to hold a Spanish passport and at the very least I learned the lingo. Not the Spanish lingo, but the English language mangled by every Puerto Rican this side of Miami Beach. To this day Chris Carpenter and I greet each other same as we did when we were kids. "How jew bing my frain." My expertise with fractured English is about to convince the police department, there's a killer on the run.

344

I walked around the corner and dropped a quarter in the phone on Third Avenue and 150th Street. "911 what's your emergency?"

"My Broda, he chot! Dismotorfooker he choot mybroda indahey! Oh my Ga!"

"Sir, please slow down and tell me where you are?"

"De bla! Oh my Gaa! I kell dismotorfooker!"

"Sir, sir. Please tell me where you are?"

"Thirdabenjew and one feety sreet. Hep! Oh my Ga! Juan! Open-u-eye! Please Gaaa!"

"Sir. Please stand by. I'm sending an ambulance and patrol car to Third Avenue and 150th street."

With an opportunity to apprehend a violent felon as opposed to a common license plate thief I was praying a fifty-yard dash wouldn't be too much to ask the bored civil servants now leaning against my gorgeous paint job. I better not find any blue scratches.

My estimated gamble paid off as soon as the police dispatcher put the call over the air. By the time I hung up the phone and strolled around the corner, Barney Fyfe and Sheriff Taylor were already racing across the street in an all-out sprint to aid the wounded citizen.

I should be teaching broken English at the police academy. I didn't even get a ticket. Not even a dirty look.

Ya'll come back real soon now… hair!

♣

It was a typically slate gray, blustery, cold late Sunday evening in January. All my usual drug spots were closed up for all the regular reasons: shot up by rival competition, no casual walk up business, or the not so regular, but always depressing, blue ballbreakers parked on the corner for an entire eight-hour shift while devouring the contents of a local bakery in an effort to close down a major drug location. Fortunately the spot in Harlem on 112th Street off Lenox Avenue was all the talk of those in the know.

The entire neighborhood was a blacked-out boarded-up desolate shit hole of abandoned buildings. I prayed to the god of all sick junkies as I drove into the unknown. **Just let it be open**. The emaciated Spanish kid with the bulging brown eyes seemed especially interested in meeting my weary blue soul searchers the second I turned into the block.

I drove up the street and parked the same shiny Pontiac with the same stolen plates by the corner. Going to a new drug spot without an introduction by a regular doper was never a good idea, but my regular guy and his regular loan came late. I was sick and out of options. Dusk was settling over black America and I couldn't get my stupid white ass out of Harlem fast enough.

The skinny kid was pacing in front of the wrought iron gate by the stairs leading down to the basement. I was still approaching and cautious when we locked eyes. I instantly recognized that the skinny kid was just another sick junkie and if he wasn't looking out, who is? My sixth sense told me go back, my sick body told me pursue matters. The squirrelly junkie was gazing over my shoulder towards the only car on the block. "Jew look like da man." He screwed up his face. I showed him the swollen tracks on my left hand. He finally sighed with relief. "Jew still look like da man."

"Where's the damn look-out?"

"I tink he go down stair."

"Why?" The kid shrugged. I didn't like the situation and the filthy junkie wasn't exactly thrilled, but after a quick negotiation we hurried down the stairs into the pitch-black basement.

I put his twenty dollars with my fifty and stuffed it through the hole in the cinder block wall. The nervous junkie kept a wary eye on the door at my back. A sudden call from the street above started the calamity. "Mahondo!" The Spanish alert means get the fuck outta here. A crash behind the wall came next. The dealers were in the wind and me and Flaco are about to catch hell.

I frantically slipped away from the doorway into the darkness while the skinny junkie disappeared into the ether. The hand searching in front of my face was nonexistent until I tripped and jabbed my fingers into a wall. I had no idea as to size or configuration of the area, but the sense of walking blind through an underground crypt was embraced like a hug from my grandma.

I ran my fingers along an unseen partition that suddenly led to a corner. I squatted facing the wall and made my body small, hopefully invisible with my head between my knees. Two or three heavy bodies quickly bounded down the wrought iron stairs. The sound of shuffling feet, a board knocked over and a beam of light suddenly found its way to the floor directly under my fat ass. I was about to start praying harder when a foot found pay dirt with enough leg to kick a football out of Giant Stadium. "Fuck!"

"Look what we got here, Sully." I thought Sully was coming over to help his partner pull his foot out of my fat ass. I couldn't sit for week. "Get up, stupid. What are you doing here?" Well let's see, I was coming by to visit my grandma and forgot the building burned down. There was absolutely nothing I could tell these narco dickheads that wouldn't sound stupid. "I was copping when you guys showed up. I got nuthin'." The other kid started praying in Spanish. "Turn out ya pockets." He quickly patted me down. "Who's he?" The dickhead pointed towards the trembling junkie being questioned by flashlight. "I don't know him, but he lost money, too." The cop smacked the kid, twice. It appeared the filthy junkie had a questionable reputation within the police community.

The entire incident in the basement took a minute, but what it took off my life expectancy can never be known, but I do know this, I'm glad I wasn't that skinny Puerto Rican kid.

They cuffed him and half dragged his skinny ass up the stairs and across the street and threw him into the back of a blue van. "This is your lucky day, junkie." I lost fifty freaking dollars so I didn't exactly feel like kicking up my heels. "Don't ever let me see you around here again. Ever." He didn't have to tell me twice. I hurried up the dark, deserted street to my illegal Pontiac and drove it home like an old grandma on her way home to grandpa.

The ache in my legs was already spreading to my brain. I was sweating like a freaking pig and it was barely twenty degrees. This will be a very uncomfortable night, but being dope sick over night was not an unusual occurrence. The main contributor was the lack of cash, but many other circumstances swirled about the business of buying and doing drugs, and many culminated with the same sorry ending.

One particular incident stands out like a giant highway billboard: JUST SAY NO—TO INSANITY. It was dead of winter. The freezing rain was pelting the living room window all day and into the night. Pay day was the next day and money came late from a regular source at the garage. My left leg was in a plaster cast, ankle to thigh, due to a spill on my motorcycle. The bike was intact, but when I slipped on oil in a sharp turn I went down, my foot lodged between the exhaust pipe and engine and flipped my body, buy the foot stayed wedged and sprained ligaments and tendons in my already damaged knee. But the bigger problem was my tiny standard shift Toyota Corolla. Even without the plaster cast I couldn't bend the left knee enough to depress the clutch petal. A motorcycle ride in the freezing rain wasn't exactly my idea of an alternative, but taking a cab wasn't in the budget.

I carefully cut through the hard outer shell of the cast with a keyhole saw and separated the cast from my leg. A motorcycle clutch is also on the left side, but the clutch is extended far enough to reach with a painful effort. I padded my entire body underneath my clothes with newspaper, ankle to neck, double socks up to my knees, heavy boots and a woolen head cover under a full-face helmet and my contribution to the drug trade kept dry in a plastic baggie. While I was ready for Siberia, I was hardly ready for the deep freeze of depression. Drug spot after spot after spot was closed up for the night. After three hours of flying around in the freezing rain I was ready for a warm dry rubber room in Bronx State Psychiatric.

When I finally found the regular look-out standing inside the doorway of the apartment building on 138th street and Cypress Avenue I thought I'd found Jesus. Doggedness didn't even enter the equation. I was dope sick and trying not to crap all over my motorcycle seat.

It took forty minutes to thaw out my fingers, but I didn't actually come back to life until I was watching my blood rising up into the syringe. I slowly pushed the plunger that finally circulated the antifreeze throughout my sick body.

Heroin addiction is not for the faint of heart. You don't have to be that smart either, obviously.

♣

It was ten-fifteen in the morning, lunch time, six AM shift. The heat was already steaming off the asphalt as I drove up to collect the last of the WEP workers on Morrison Avenue. This area of my district is underprivileged, over developed and drug infested. I could have twenty WEP workers sweeping these streets twenty-four hours a day and the blighted area would be littered again before we put the brooms back in the van.

Five sweaty welfare workers were anxiously waiting at the curb when I pulled to a stop. They hastily loaded their brooms and shovels into the back of the van. One by one they stumbled in the side door. The Spanish equivalent of this job sucks permeated the air. I turned up the air-conditioner to dry everybody off before heading into the garage.

I was checking my side view mirror before pulling away from the curb when a shiny red Mercedes coupe exiting the Bronx River Parkway drove alongside my vehicle and stopped. A drop dead gorgeous brunette lowered her passenger side window and leaned over, exposing two of the greatest distractions since the evolution of man's brain. I don't mean to say they were nicer than Ellen's. That would be stupid and self-defeating, but on a scale of... ..never mind, where was I?

"Officer, can you please... ."

A choir of angels was beginning to sing when the light turned green. Some rowdy idiot driving a forty-year-old gypsy cab pulled directly behind the Mercedes and leaned on his horn. BEEEEEEEP! BEEEEEEEP! BEEEEEEP! I waved him around the lost damsel in distress with the long shiny tresses and cheeky smile, but the unruly asshole was too close and stayed stuck. I glared through his windshield. BEEEEEEEEP! He gave me the finger. BEEEEEEEP! I blew him a kiss. I hope he's not gay. "I'm sorry. Where are you headed?"

"Tri-Boro Bridge?" BEEEEEEEEEEEEP!

After my way too brief directions the raven haired beauty pulled away. I quickly nudged in behind her shiny red bumper and cut off the annoying horn blowing cabbie like he was driving a lawn mower. This happens to be something I'm particularly good at: being equally annoying on very short notice.

I slowly turned onto the service road and watched as the mid-morning entertainment entered the Bruckner Expressway. The aggressive hack quickly pulled alongside my van and kept pace. I looked left. He looked right. The greasy forty year old cabbie suddenly cut me off like I was parked and forced me into the curb. I guess he wants to play.

The driver raced down the Bruckner service road waving his hand out the window, sort of a friendly invitation to follow along, but it was hardly necessary. I was already in hot pursuit when his ancient gypsy cab screeched to a stop in front of the bodega on the corner of Boynton Avenue.

The fuming, bleary-eyed Puerto Rican jumped out and waved me over. I wasn't sure if he really expected me to further our little exchange, especially in front of the ten Puerto Rican witnesses standing about the corner, but I wasn't about to blow an opportunity to council the man on the destructive dangers of road rage just because he had a few friends. It wouldn't be the first time I got my ass busted by a crowd. My piss poor attitude pretty much assures it from time to time.

I slammed the van into park. "Don't get out," I ordered the WEP's,

"I'll be right back." The guy was already leaning on the trunk of his car, screaming in Spanish. The crowd, all drinking and smoking were suddenly drawn to the excitement. The empty forty-ounce beer bottle in his hand was a threat and the long Motorola radio in my right hand was better than my left hook.

Downtown would consider my actions as a threat to public safety and totally against regulations, but I wasn't thinking beyond the anger. Luckily, he made the first move when he stumbled towards me and pushed a hand into my chest. This of course is illegal. I'm good to go. I shoved him back to arm's length and very suddenly cracked my trusty Motorola off the side of his cabeza. The radio split in half and so did his melon. He went down to his knees holding his head and already bleeding onto the asphalt. The stunned crowd drew closer to the heap.

My walk back to the van was actually swift, but seemed an eternity as the Spanish grumbling behind me was nonstop as I awaited a flying forty-ounce retaliation. I got away clean, except for the broken radio. I didn't even consider the broken head. The guy was driving drunk. I figured I did the city a public service. That's pretty much how I was thinking as I drove into the garage for lunch.

Fellow officers Tony Tantone, Wesley Lavelle and Gene Greatheart were standing about the garage office. I walked in with a smile holding back a laugh. "What did you do this time, lunatic?" wondered Tony. So I nonchalantly explained to my friends what happened. "Ya better get in there and tell Pat and ya know he's gonna go fucking berserk."

"That's why I'm not telling him. I'm having a good day and I want it to stay that way."

Keeping the super calm was Gene's job. "I don't know, Kev," cautioned Gene, "but if you do decide to tell him at least wait till I get his lunch. He might be in a better mood after he eats." The back and forth banter was forcing me to rethink my thinking. I try to do that on occasion to keep from getting dizzy, but I really had no intention of telling the super anything until Wesley offered a novel suggestion. "Why don't you just call Stevenson in the Boro. Tell John you left the radio on the roof of the van. Tell him it slipped off when you hit the gas and broke in half when it hit the ground. As long as the guy didn't file a complaint with the cops you can have a new radio without the super ever knowing anything."

I gritted my teeth, shrugged my shoulders and slowly shook my head. Wesley threw up his hands. "It's not great, but it's better than your story." Wesley is the union delegate and always the calmest man in the room. What would Wesley do is the motto we relied upon for situations that needed a remedy before further examination by higher officials. Nothing was a big deal to Wesley. Wesley viewed the shiny badges downtown as little people trying to be big shots by making a big deal out of every situation that didn't conform to their general orders. "You know, lunatic," offered Tony, "if you do decide to tell Pat he'll probably jump right over the desk. So let me know first so I can get a good seat in the office."

They were still laughing with thoughts of my latest effort driving the super over the edge. A small group of interested sanmen had gathered around the office. Keeping things lively was part of my job. Gene had another idea. "What if the guy saw dollar signs after you dented his skull? If he did go to the cops you'll be arrested. You should probably wait 'til after work, then check in with Lieutenant Russell."

Tony was probably right on the money. Wesley had a novel suggestion. Gene made a convincing point. I decided to go with my first thought and forgetaboutit, and that's exactly what I did until three hours later when I drove into the garage at the end of the shift.

"Listen, lunatic. We never asked you," wondered Tony. "Were there any witnesses?" My latest calamity was a big topic for the guys. Watching the super explode all over me was probably more fun than watching The Three Stooges, but as mad as he got, Pasquale Genovese never once wrote me a complaint. He's a screamer like Roger Straitback, only louder and bigger. "About ten," I noted, "not including the five WEP's." Wesley was still shaking his head. "You know you're fucking insane."

"Kevin, did ya have fun this morning?" wondered Gene. "I always have fun, Gene."

"That's good," chuckled Tony. "Why don't you just run in there and tell Pat how much fun you had this morning before this whole thing blows up in your face."

To say that our boss with the curly black hair and piercing green eyes had a boiling point, especially in dealing with me would grossly underestimate the anger generated by my constant craziness. It was more like an explosion rate. The boss was usually set to blow as soon as he heard somebody calling my name. If he's walking and talking he's up to something.

It was fifteen minutes before the end of the day. Reality finally set in. "Listen, Pat. I had a little situation this morning." By the time I finished telling the boss about my morning I thought he was gonna shake his big curly head right off his very thick neck. "No you didn't! No, no, no you didn't! Are you fucking crazy? This morning! This morning! Do you know what time it is, you fucking lunatic? How am I supposed to call the boro with this now? You fucking asshole! This morning?" Everybody else thought it was funny. The man's got no sense of humor.

I gave the super a few more minutes to blow up and cool down before I took a chance between breaths. "What if I run down to the precinct, Pat, and see if he made a complaint. Maybe the guy didn't even file a complaint." The boss was still shaking with rage as he blasted away with both barrels. "What the hell are you smiling about, you fucking idiot?" I really didn't think it was such a big deal. I broke my radio in the act of preserving the honor of every sanitation supervisor in the Bronx. The guy touched me. "Whaddaya wa'me to do, Pat, cry?" The super was leaning way across his desk, looking me up and down like he was sizing me up for a strait jacket. "There is something seriously wrong with you, you fucking sicko lunatic." Mom had that figured out by the time I was eleven. "Let's just see what happens, Pat. I'm thinking the guy was drunk. It'll take me three minutes to run down to the precinct."

"You talk to Lieutenant Russell and you'll be lucky if he don't arrest your dumb ass as soon as you walk in the door, you fucking sicko."

43RD PRECINCT

"Good afternoon, Lieutenant Russell. I had a little situation this morning."

Just call me lucky. Everybody else does.

☘

I've never met a supervisor who didn't hate working with the big mechanical sweepers. We write tickets to cars that don't move and everybody wants to beat you up. "Whoa, whoa, whoa. I was right here."

"No you weren't. I was right here. You were right over there." Everybody was right here and if they were, the city streets would be spotless and I'd be issuing very few summons, but in the world of Kevin the Troublemaker, situations constantly arise that require my other skills:

the charming talents to disarm an idiot and turn a bad deed into a teaching moment. I love teaching. Makes me feel smart.

It was a typical, blustery late November morning. I was driving just ahead of the big sweeper down Castle Hill Avenue on the early segment of the route, seven-thirty to eight. I beeped the little guy peering out from the end of the line inside the Seven Eleven. He ran out without his early morning coffee and donut but in time to save himself thirty-five big ones. I continued down the avenue and beeped three people who all waved frantically from the ATM's inside the City Bank on the next corner. This is against department policy. Don't beep. Write the summons. But if I wave the broom around the illegally parked cars and write the summons I don't clean the filthy street. Supervisors are rated on the cleanliness of the streets, and my super would rather the streets be clean. I like my super and try to keep my immediate boss happy because sooner or later some asshole will piss me off and I'll tell him where to go, so I'll need a superintendent in a relatively good mood to help me fight the Boro when the shit hits the fan. Maybe today. You never know.

We still were moving down the avenue towards the restaurant on the corner of Gleason Avenue. The driver in the old beat up Eldorado idling in the bus stop shouldn't be a problem, but sometimes I find problems where other supervisors merely find summonses. The broom operator in my rearview pulled up to my car as I awaited the light. Mister Eldorado stuck his arm out the window, pinched the bottom of a small plastic grocery bag and shook the entire contents of balled up tissues onto my street into the breeze. The light turned green. I turned red. I pulled in front of the early morning entertainment, got out and walked up to his open window. My regular operator Johnson knows my tendencies, so she drove her broom right up to his rear bumper. No way out. Johnson would always climb down from the machine in order to get my back in heated confrontations, but how can I look like a tough guy with a pretty young woman standing at my side. The balled-up tissues were already blowing down the avenue. "Back in the broom, Johnson!" Now let's get this party started.

"Excuse me, sir. You do know that that's illegal, don't ya?" The young tall skinny driver with the overly expressive eyes and pouty mouth decided that this was a good time to be a wise-ass. "Oh, you mean the tissues. Yeah, I know. I got a bad cold." He admitted to littering and spreading germs. I no longer felt the need to tell this pig you can only have one wise-ass at a time in these situations. I'm now legally empowered to show him how I've advanced that particular skill to an art form.

"Okay, I see you're a real funny guy, but I hope ya fast, too, because if you can't catch all those tissues before they hop on the Cross Bronx Expressway, I'll be the only one laughing. So you either hand me ya driver's license or a bag full of dirty tissues."

"Ya mean I can pick 'em up?" Fun, fun, fun. "If ya can catch 'em." The tissues were blowing along the avenue towards the expressway. The very athletic looking litter pig in the two hundred dollar sneakers jumped out and took off in hot pursuit. "I'll watch ya car!"

As usual, Johnson was all smiles as she watched the show from atop the broom. "Ya crazy, Carroll."

"But fun, Johnson. I'm always fun."

"Every day, Carroll."

"Well it is my job, Eileen."

"I told my daughter about you, Carroll. I wish she could see this."

Mister Eldorado's young dark eyed girlfriend walked from the restaurant with breakfast and a quizzical look. She leaned her head into her boyfriend's passenger window. "Where's Hector?" I pointed down the avenue towards the octopus of arms and purple velvet legs on the next corner. Two minutes later the very exhausted litter pig returned to the scene while waving the barely bulging plastic bag above his head. "I got 'em all."

"Not quite, but I appreciate the effort. Now move this car. We got a route to complete. Back in the machine, Johnson."

It's all about keeping the streets clean. And fun. I'm just a fun-loving sanitation supervisor with a need to teach. Just ask Johnson. If she ever stops laughing.

39

The random drug tests at the sanitation clinic were actually scheduled with some regularity. Every five weeks it was like getting a day off. Concerned friends at the Bronx Boro office would almost always give me a heads up the day before a piss test, but every once in a while the orders from downtown would be transmitted later in the evening and my friends in the boro would be gone for the day, leaving me with a Pearl Harbor in the morning. In that case, the super's clerk would inform me of my appointment the moment I stepped into the operations office at the start of my shift.

First thing, call Ellen. "Start boiling water and get the thermos bottle ready and take the bag out of the closet. I'll be there in five minutes." Then I call big Mike in Hunts Point and tell him to start drinking. "I'll be there in fifteen minutes."

"Not a problem, Kev." Twenty minutes later I was in big Mike's apartment in Hunts Point transferring the drug dealer's urine from a plastic cup to a much smaller and easier to conceal methadone bottle. When I filled the tiny methadone bottle with water from the sink in my bathroom it appeared to hold just enough liquid for an actual test. I think. I'm pretty sure. We'll have to see.

A soft rubber ear syringe is used to squirt water into handles, I mean ears, in order to blow out the wax. An ear syringe is shaped like a big tear drop and the rubber bulb was my latest covert means for discharging Mike's clean urine into the clinic's little plastic bottle.

At the last possible moment I'll remove the tiny methadone bottle floating in the thermos of boiling water. Then I insert the tip of the ear syringe into the methadone bottle, suck up clean urine and cap the open end with half a Q-tip. All stealthily managed inside my black canvas knapsack and away from clinic personnel and nosey sanmen. Then I place the warm ear syringe strategically under willie and anxiously wait to be called...

"Carroll!"

The young black male assistant wrote all my personal and job related information. When he finished the paper work he handed me the official container. Then he followed me down the hall into the men's room. Close scrutiny was still in order, but the men's room monitor wasn't nearly close enough because I quickly managed another miracle by turning Mike the drug dealer's urine into the cleanest sample this side of Vatican City holy water.

I carefully placed the little plastic bottle on the sink next to the cap in order to zip up. "It's not enough." The black devil grabbed the tiny container and suddenly poured Mike's yellow gold into the toilet. My freaking eyeballs almost exploded as I watched my prayer getting flushed into the Atlantic Ocean. I had to remain calm, but I was ready to stuff his freaking head in the freaking toilet. "What the hell ya do that for?"

"I said it's not enough. It has to come up to the line." I was already leaking misery from every pore in my body. "It was up to the line."

"It was just under the line. It has to be on or over the line."

"I can't believe this."

"It's alright," he consoled, "just drink some water and do it again." And just do it again was screaming inside my head for the next six hours, but it still wasn't alright.

The throbbing ache of panic was still pounding behind my eyes when the head nurse walked up and pushed an ice pick into my ear. Okay, maybe it wasn't really an ice pick, but her voice was pitched high enough to emit light bright enough to split the atom, so when Miss Squeaky voice told me that the clinic was closing in fifteen minutes and that I'd be suspended if I didn't give her another sample it felt like my ears exploded from getting stabbed with a freaking ice pick.

What the hell was I thinking? Well, I wasn't exactly thinking. My sick brain was praying that I'd be sent home and ordered back to the clinic on Monday morning. I mean, if I can't go, I can't go, right?

It was already three forty-five in the afternoon. I was alone in the clinic for at least two hours. I was seated away from prying eyes and my brain is racing.

Leaving the floor is an automatic complaint, and considering my special relationship with Chief Einstein Osbourne I'd probably be suspended a month.

The stairwell was just beyond the elevator. I quietly crept from the room and frantically hurried down the two flights of stairs to the ground floor. In the lobby an attendant standing behind the small podium was first to get the offer of a life time. "Listen, buddy. I got sixteen dollars in my pocket. It's yours if you can fill this bottle with clean urine." He appeared sympathetic and honest. "Sorry, Pal. I smoked a joint at lunch time." With sorry I was half way out the door. Freaking pothead. A messenger rushing past the front of the building was next: two beers at lunch. Can anybody around here pass a damn drug screen? The late afternoon sun was simmering off the asphalt as I hobbled across Hudson Street to the delicatessen. The store was empty of customers so I pressed the man behind the counter. "Buddy, I hope you can help me out. I'm about to lose my job with sanitation for smoking pot. I have sixteen dollars. It's yours for clean urine."

"Oh, man I'm sorry." The young owner never gave a reason, but he did have a great suggestion. "But I have two Mexicans working in the back and they don't do anything. You can ask them."

The little tiny Mexican didn't even take the money.

I sucked the Mexican urine from a styrofoam coffee cup with the ear syringe and ran back across the street and up the stairs with five minutes to spare. My body was still shaking with fear as I stuck my head in the office door way.

"I thought you signed out."

"I was in the bathroom drinking water. I think I can go now."

"It's a good thing. We're about to close."

The Mexican urine was still warm. Ay Chihuahua, I love Mexico.

♣

The summer was once again in full swelter. I was working as always with the big mechanical broom. The daily sweeping of the metered parking in my district ends at nine o'clock in the morning, but never soon enough for me.

I was waiting impatiently just behind the taillights of the only car on the entire block in a very commercial area, Castle Hill, Newbold to Westchester Avenue. The small Toyota of concern was parked just off the corner outside the Subway sandwich shop. The busy elevated train station over Westchester Avenue was one of many reasons making the avenue a filthy mess on both sides of the street, and then there were other reasons: pigs, not cops, just the regular kind: filthy litter pigs. In my entire life I've never thrown anything on the ground, so litter pigs really piss me off.

The big mechanical street sweeper in my rear view mirror had just crossed Newbold Avenue. The flashing lights atop my car was already a warning, and the no-parking signs at either end of the block should've been enough to keep this genius from blocking my broom in the first place, but some people always seem to need that little extra kick in the ass. Or maybe he just can't read. This could be another one of those special teaching moments. I tooted my horn. My sixth sense suggested that this particular student was determined to piss me off, while my seventh sense told we were just about there. He glared into his side view mirror. We momentarily locked eyes, but he quickly turned back to the woman on the passenger seat. We're there.

Kevin the teacher exited the car in a huff, slammed the door behind when a half a foot long ham and America cheese hero came flying out the driver side window. This must be my lucky day. Not because I'm hungry. I'm always hungry. Actually, I was just excited to show off the new curriculum. "Excuse me, but I know you seen me. Are you trying to piss me off?" Here I am looking all official in my fancy green uniform with my shiny gold badge and captain's bars, ticket book in hand. The question was rhetorical in nature, but the pig didn't look smart enough to keep his mouth shut, or maybe he had a problem with authority. That I can understand.

"Excuse me ma man." The idiot paused for dramatic effect as he pointed to his highly irregular disposal. "But that there shit is bio-degradable." There ya go. Not smart. His big round face and large brown afro were already hanging out the window, so I gave him my best, who the fuck you think ya talkin' to expression as I pointed to his personal insult on my personal avenue. "Well listen, ma man. I'll tell ya what. If that there shit bio-degrades before I finish writing you this one-hundred-dollar ticket, I'll eat the sandwich and the ticket."

"Damn, sanitation. You ain't right." I already sensed resignation in tone and slumped posture, but a little verbal reinforcement never hurts. Besides, I couldn't help myself. It's what professionals do. I pointed back towards Johnson. "If I order that broom around this car and that sandwich it'll cost a hundred and thirty-five dollars total. I've been pretty patient so far, but you're running out of time."

He huffed and puffed as he very slowly extricated himself from his tiny Toyota Celica. It's a good thing he didn't finish that sandwich. He barely made it out the door and moped his big dumb ass to the corner, where he grabbed two pieces of cardboard from the city basket. Then he moped back and scraped up the two pieces of bread, the ham, the American cheese and every shred of lettuce and strode back and slammed into the basket. "Now move your car." Asshole!

I win. How can you not love a job that lets you teach without a degree and win just by showing up?

♣

It was still pretty early in the morning on just another day in my exciting world as a New York City Sanitation supervisor. I was checking one of five garbage collection routes to make sure everything on the curb was going into the hopper, and as always as usual my guys never disappoint. The part of the job that few supervisors enjoy is the issuance of an ECB (environmental control board) summons. The requirement is one a day. The city doesn't call it a quota, but try giving your AM report without one dirty area or failure to properly recycle summons and see how that works out. The city will have you handing tickets to seagulls at the Staten Island Landfill.

I very slowly made my way up Virgil Place towards Castle Hill Avenue while glancing at both sides of the street for something left on the curb that was left on purpose, a possible summons. Coming up on my right was my favorite and most frequented establishment in the entire district and the reason for my fat ass. The Carvel Ice-Cream store. On my left, the gas station. As a very young teenager it was called Texaco. I still get a warm fuzzy feeling for the old days, until I remember that this place cost me three days in camp hell and a horrifying crew cut. If Baby was just a wee bit faster than that Texaco wrecker I could've gone to the World's Fair with my friends instead of my parents and escaped hell on Earth in the summer of sixty-four.

Just up ahead a man with an absurd looking black rug covering his bald melon was walking a large German Shepherd on a leash. The dog stopped suddenly in the middle of the sidewalk adjacent to the gas station. The poor dog appeared to have a little stomach issue because he was already draining his intestines like a soft ice-cream machine. His disheveled, brown bearded owner dressed in filthy purple sweat pants, tattered red plaid shirt and old dirty Converse sneakers patiently waited. And waited. I should've written him a summons for making me see this at nine o'clock in the morning, but no little plastic bag or piece of newspaper in hand to clean up after his pet was all the excuse I needed to start the entertainment portion of my day. I drove up alongside and stopped. The startled dog walker with the bulbous red nose quickly sniffed me out. The blood drained from his face, except the nose. We locked eyes. Not me and the dog. The dog didn't appear to give a shit. Actually, the dog was still giving quite a shit, but the idiot holding his leash and I were staring each other down and as usual, I was winning.

In my rear view mirror a car was driving up the block. I waved him around. He drove around. I threw the transmission into park and hit the flashers. If the fuming dog owner hadn't figured it out by now he was either dumb, blind or both. I wasn't leaving. Rudolph the pig-nosed dick head was now in the penalty phase of the morning.

Rudolph was now staring down at the large mound of poop smoldering in the middle of the sidewalk. To say the man was pissed about getting caught would not begin to tell the story. I thought his nose would explode. Catching a poop leaver about to leave the scene of the crime is so much better than catching litter pigs, and for the record, I've never once written a summons to a litter pig or poop leaver. My way was so much more enjoyable, and for the casual observer I was also demonstrating the art of sanitation enforcement without opening my big mouth.

Rudolph held his mangy looking animal down tight with one hand. Not the shepherd. Shepherd was beautiful and wasn't moving, but the strange thing occupying his bald head looked like it could eat his face if he wasn't careful as he bent into the fifty-five-gallon drum. The big green barrel was placed alongside the wall by the gas station owner for people doing oil changes and other various jobs that could litter his property. Nope. No doogie bag in there. His face turned red, nose glowed and ears smoked as he patted his pants pockets. What's this. A possibility? The bright-eyed Shepherd suddenly looked up with his tongue hanging, maybe he's looking for a cookie. Gimme a cookie. I feel much better already.

The big Shepard was wagging his tail while his thoughtless handler slipped his fingers into two very flat pockets, and lo and behold, wouldn't you know, he miraculously pulled up a teeny tiny tissue. He was still glaring at me. I was determined not to smile, and it wasn't easy because this was big time professional fun. This was like going to the circus for sanitation supervisors, but I returned his glare with a determined stare as he slowly unfolded the prayer that needed to be a miracle if he ever expected to pick his nose right-handed in the foreseeable future.

Our eyes remained locked as he placed the flimsy tissue in the middle of his palm. He was still glaring evil intentions at the annoying sanitation supervisor. I was patiently waiting to see this through to a satisfying conclusion. The dog lover was about to show me exactly how much he loved his big Shepherd, or maybe that he was on a fixed income. Desperate times, desperate measures. The frustrated dog lover bent at the knees and lowered straight down so as to not disturb the furry creature on his head and anxiously shoveled the smoldering pile of poop that quickly enveloped the tissue and very average sized five fingered pooper scooper. The fuming pig then flipped his hand and slammed it on the side of the barrel and dragged his fingers on the edge to wipe the shit off. That took a lotta balls. I would've taken a ticket.

My job is keeping the city clean. There was still quite a mess on the sidewalk, but I was actually quite pleased with the extraordinary effort. My work here is done. "Have a good day."

"Fuck you asshole." Obviously, a dog lover of few words.

I still needed a summons and I'll never find one if I keep being so magnanimous with my time.

I drove up to the corner. Ooh, ice-cream!

40

Pennies from Heaven. It's the money that falls from the sky for the benefit of sanitation workers. Everybody else calls it snow.

I heard about it from the time I started with the department, the great blizzard of '69'. Every old timer worked it and every one of them had a story. It was the snowstorm that buried the outer boroughs and Mayor Lindsay for weeks in seventeen inches of money, but it wasn't even close to the big blizzard of '96'. In the northern most borough of the Bronx we had thirty inches of heavy dense snow, and by the time it was all gone I had instigated enough drama to supply the department with crazy new stories that will linger in locker rooms 'til the next generation.

The severity of a storm determines whether or not the department piles snow. The city gathers the snow into very large piles on commercial strips only. Front-end loaders first pull the snow off the sidewalks and into the avenues. Then we push the mounds that were plowed to the curb into massive piles for later removal to predesignated parks and parking lots throughout the boroughs. Metered areas are afforded the greatest amount of resources because the stores there generate tax revenue that pays for stuff like expensive sanitation workers.

This storm dumped so much snow that the city was forced to hire outside equipment and drivers, gigantic tractor trailer-sized dump trucks that hold a hundred yards of material and front-end loaders with enormous three yard buckets. What the city pays them for a day, regular people don't make in a month, and it was up to me to make sure city got their money's worth.

The piles were two stories high and the twenty-six we were taking away were located on one of the most heavily traveled commercial strips in this part of the Bronx, White Plains Road, Lafayette Avenue to Westchester.

Three hours into the shift a large private front-end loader was leaking the hoist oil that's needed to maneuver the massive bucket. The giant earth mover was raising and lowering its bucket so slowly I could've loaded my trucks faster with a little plastic shovel. The general order pertaining to this situation states that the minute a hired piece of equipment goes down, it's off the clock, but of course I afforded myself a great deal of discretion. After all, I am the freaking man in charge here.

From the comfort of my heated car I was watching as the young driver climbed down from the massive machine. I drove closer to give him a verbal nudge in the other direction. He explained his dilemma the moment his foot hit the ground. Then I explained mine. "You're killing me, here. Right now you owe me dinner. If you can't get this thing fixed soon I'm taking you off the clock." The baby-faced operator was practically crying. "No, no please. Just let me call my boss. Give me an hour."

"An hour? Do you know how much the city is paying your boss for an hour? I'll give you another twenty minutes. After that your boss will be taking me to Disneyland or you and this machine will be off the clock."

"Don't worry, the wallet will be here soon."

"Believe me, buddy, I'm not worried."

After three more conversations with the nervous front end loader guy and three more ballooning price quotes, his boss finally showed up with a mechanic. The damage was extensive. They removed a two-foot length of pipe that had to be welded back at the shop in freaking Long Island City.

Timmy Hurley was rumbling down White Plains Road on his way to the garage for lunch and he was driving the answer to my prayers: a big orange front end loader with DSNY printed on the cab. "I have a problem Timmy. I need these trucks loaded before you go in." Timmy never hesitated because I never hesitated when Timmy needed to leave early and needed me to sign him out at the end of the shift. I took care of him so often I could've signed his freaking pay checks.

I was still driving towards the next corner when the operator of a private hundred-yard dumper (tractor trailer) was waving me down. And now he's waving me out of my heated car. I don't like this guy already. "Listen, Carroll. We have a problem."

"Listen, pal, you're gonna have to make this much more personal. Say I have a problem."

"Okay, okay I have a problem. I have a frozen load. By the time they punched my ticket at the dump the load froze and it's still on the truck."

"That's definitely a personal problem." We'd loaded his truck an hour ago and I personally punched his ticket and sent him to the Orchard Beach parking lot where he was supposed to dump the snow, but twenty tons of snow and ice lying in a massive aluminum truck for an hour will harden under the right conditions and nothing will budge it but a few hours parked in the California sunshine.

"Do you have a shovel?" The big driver was as large as his rig. He seemed a bit confused and more than a bit agitated. "No, I don't have a shovel." Now the giant genius is giving me attitude. "That's okay, because I actually have another option."

His expression went from annoyed to dumbfounded stupefaction. "Excuse me?" Causing anger and confusion is one of my great assets. "All my trucks have shovels." I pointed to a garbage truck blocking traffic on Story Avenue. "You can borrow one off that truck. Then drive up to that corner and shovel the entire load onto the pile. When the truck is empty, get back on line." See ya in July. The big angry driver was shaking his head as I pointed up White Plains Road towards the line of trucks waiting to get loaded by two city front end loaders. "Or, you can hand me two hundred dollars and I will send you to the dump with the same load for the rest of the shift." The smile came first... then the twinkle in his eyes. "Lemme make a call." Obviously, nothing was obvious to this idiot, but the big Frankenstein looking dummy finally figured it out. "I'll be right back." Big Frank lumbered into the restaurant on the corner. Three minutes later he walked back with a paper bag and a smile. A giant scary one. He plucked a coffee container and a rather nice looking chocolate glazed donut from the bag and handed the bag to me, another coffee and the donut screaming my name at the bottom. "Thanks." My fat ass really needs this. "The boss said he can go for half that."

"Half is fine." I thought two hundred bucks was a stretch, anyway.

"First thing in the morning, okay?"

"First thing or you'll be watching the game from the dugout." Nobody makes an empty threat with a baseball metaphor with the passion of a psychopathic lunatic like a junkie with a need. I had no authority to keep his truck on the side lines, but the big idiot with the deep set eyes didn't know that.

My main concern was still the disabled front end loader. If a very shiny badge shows up from the main office to inspect my operation he'll quickly notice the big machine loitering on the sidelines. I have a

PhD in giving plausible excuses. I just needed to stay close enough to give it. Piece a cake.

The only time that the big chiefs climb down from their ivory tower in lower Manhattan and mingle with the lowly sanitation minions is during major snow operations. Every department head is responsible for evaluating specific bridges and highways for drivability, plus they oversee all other department functions pertaining to the blizzard and the aftermath. No boss ever questioned my ability or how I conducted business during snow operations. I was given more compliments in the snow because I got the job done, one way or the other. Usually the other. Only the bottom line counts. I make the snow go away.

SNOW PILE REMOVAL

Two massive front end loaders scooping off two different mountains of snow, then quickly backing up to load the never ending line of tractor trailers and department cut downs constantly pulling up to the piles and racing away to the dump. The blur of activity not unfamiliar to those professionals acquainted with the task. The only traffic allowed through a snow pile removal operation is emergency vehicles and city busses. All other traffic is waved off and detoured by traffic enforcement or fellow supervisors. Cars sneaking into the dangerous fast moving work area behind busses or fire trucks have no way out. Sanitation trucks with plows are positioned at both ends of a street and my drivers only dare move when ordered. If a foolish driver enters the dead zone there is only one way out, hand over your driver's license, whereupon I enforce the exit fee, the one hundred dollar ticket for pissing me off and impeding a DS operation.

My pockets were bulging with the generous contributions from private funders, so I was actually in a pretty good mood, considering I was standing in the middle of managed chaos, but my sunny disposition quickly darkened when some idiot came speeding through the work area from behind an ambulance. I quickly motioned the two plow trucks together at the far end of the block, then I called over the radio for supervisor Arroyo to lock down the other end of the street. To paraphrase a great line from *A Bronx Tale*, now he can't get out.

If there is one supervisor with a shorter fuse for annoying dick heads than me it was Willie Arroyo. When Willie transferred into Bronx 9 I immediately thanked him. "You're gonna take a lot of heat off me, Willie."

"I know, and you're welcome, Carroll." Until the bosses let Willie down one too many times he was just like me: do whatever it takes to get the job done. A little headstrong with a little attitude and when pushed to his limit, a little crazy, but Willie got the job done because he knew the damn job.

Willie closed up Story Avenue with two plowed up collection trucks nose to nose, plus a large imposing enforcement agent. Then he drove to me at the corner of Lafayette. In the few seconds it took him to drive up the block the young and very anxious Puerto Rican daredevil was losing his mind. The young porker was doing his best to roar like Godzilla. "I'm in hurry. Move dose trucks, mother fucker." The twenty-year old fat ass was shaking the steering wheel like he was trying to rip it out. My biggest and brightest smile was glistening through his windshield. He stuck his head out the window. "I said move those trucks, mother fucker before I run your dumb ass over." I didn't even have to open my mouth. This is why I love this job.

"Listen good, genius, 'cause I'm only gonna say it once. I'm gonna be on this street for another nine hours, so if I don't see ya license soon you'll be jumping up and down enough to lose weight, ya dumb fucker." He ejected from his beat up Honda. Willie gave me a weary glance. I smiled and stepped forward. The porker stepped up. We were nose to nose, which means he was way too short. "I'll kick your ass, you dumb mother fucker. I'll be back here with the cops." This is actually my favorite part of the job. There is nobody I've come across in my entire life with a better arsenal shot from two lips.

"The cops a' gonna be awhile 'cause you ain't leaving to tell nobody. White Plains Road is closed down and the only way those trucks separate is with magic. I'm the senior supervisor on the scene and unfortunately for you, the only one holding the magic wand." My index finger circled in front of my nose. "The cops can kiss my fat ass, too." Willie couldn't stop laughing. "You're killing me here, Carroll." The entertainment hurried back into his car, revved the engine a few times and inched his angry Honda up to my leg. So far this was the best part of the storm.

"Okay," I said, "If Willie says you can leave, you can leave." My smiling sarcasm was the only signal Willie needed. The guy started babbling in Spanish and Willie put both hand up to stop him. "Whoa, whoa, whoa, hombre. Englaze, englaze. My favorite Puerto Rican supervisor hates annoying slime-balls in a hurry as much as I do. His Puerto Ricaness was not an asset and I knew it before I passed it off to my laughing partner.

I'm usually as friendly as Mister Rogers in my daily encounters with the public, but once a citizen opens the door to verbal assault, I rip off my sweater and velcro up my bullet proof vest and start firing my mouth like a Marine with an M-16.

After a few more minutes of amusing myself at the expense of the enraged loudmouth in a hurry, the inevitable finally sunk in. Willie finished writing his discharge papers. I took the pink copy and delivered it myself. "Have a good day, Mister Salizar." He snatched the ticket out of my fingers. "Move those trucks, you fucking bato." I should probably know what that means, but never cared enough to ask. "Come back soon. The city needs the money." Young Mister Salizar stuck half a peace sign out the window while I parted the two garbage trucks with a mere wave of my magic finger. The two bored sanitation workers parked nose to nose had been watching the entire show and couldn't stop laughing. The men were still beep, beep, beeping their trucks away from each other when the angry asshole suddenly floored the gas and raced through the two plows and spun out onto Lafayette Avenue where he almost got creamed by a passing bus. And the city actually pays me to do this.

By the middle of February I'd pissed off enough angry assholes in a hurry during snow removal operations to keep me in complaints for the rest of my career, but nobody ever made one. At least not formally.

After one of the heaviest snowstorms ever in the city, the department decided to test the urine of all sanitation enforcement agents (ticket writers) previously found to have a problem with drugs, and since I was on the officer's hot sheet I was summoned downtown to keep order in a very crowded room.

The job of obtaining and testing3333333333333 urine samples was now in the hands of a completely different concern. The office was located in our new clinic on Beaver Street in lower Manhattan and they had their own standards, with special scrutiny only as warranted.

My clinic appointments were always stressful, so my magic bag of tricks containing the clean whiz was more like an extension of my right arm. I carried the small canvas bag into the men's room and quietly took out the thermos bottle of boiling water and placed it carefully on the back of the sink. I unscrewed the top of the thermos and cautiously plucked the tiny glass jar containing the urine and wiped it dry with toilet paper. Then I placed the tiny jar of fresh clean urine strategically inside my underwear. Ouch! A few minutes later I was summoned to the counter and told to report upstairs.

I was a wee bit warmer and actually pretty calm until I sat facing a large blond woman with the cold hard stare of a German teletype operator transmitting crucial orders from Berlin to the Russian front, hair knotted up in a tight bun and tighter lips expressed her resolve which froze me in place. "Picture identification." I took out my job ID and placed it on the desk. The woman efficiently completed the standard paper work. Two minutes later the big-boned man-girl administered the new mandatory breathalyzer. I blew triple zeros and signed off on the results. Helga took a small plastic cup from a big box on the floor, placed it on the desk and pointed to the men's room. Once inside the men's room and away from the prying eyes of Helga the Horrible I took the clean urine from inside my underpants and placed it on the sink. So far this was the easiest operation until I plucked the glass thermometer from my shirt pocket and fumbled it to the floor. Smash! Sonofabitch! Houston, we have a freaking problem here.

If I still had a thermometer I could've placed it inside my tiny glass jar of fresh clean urine and checked the heat. The acceptable temperature levels are printed on the paperwork, between ninety-five and ninety-eight point six degrees. Mike's urine was always heated way above that and easily cooled down in the toilet bowl using the thermometer to gage the exact temperature. The newest wrinkle in the collection process was a thermometer strip attached to the side of the sample cup, so once you pissed in that cup your fate was sealed. Being that my thermometer was in three pieces with the highly poisonous liquid mercury running between the floor tiles, I used the old hand feely test. It felt good. I'm thinking, ninety-seven, maybe ninety-eight degrees, so I very carefully poured Mike's urine into the official cup.

If the temperature strip on the side of the plastic cup had a red ball of mercury on top it would've exploded all over the freaking men's room. It was still a hundred and three degrees when I placed the cup on the desk in front of the large imposing clerk. By the time I told Frau Helga I was feeling a little sick with a fever it rose two more degrees. I should've said malaria and she should've called a goddamn ambulance, but instead the big girl hit the alarm for general quarters to assemble a firing squad. I mean summoned a freaking supervisor. I was lucky she didn't punch me in the face.

Two minutes later the old boss walked from the men's room with my toxic urine still glowing in the plastic cup and registering a very normal 98.3 degrees. Big Helga stood at parade rest as the supervisor sat at her station where the old goat made a first-rate observation and a worthwhile suggestion. "I'm going to assume this is dirty." Freaking genius. "And if it is you'll be suspended in a few days. Fucking asshole. Get your act together, Mister Carroll." Piss off.

My job was on the line, suspension the first step in the process towards termination. I was suddenly in a black fog of fear and well on my way towards desperation.

Two minutes later I was riding down in the elevator when I thought I heard a crash from above. Maybe my toxic sample exploded in the refrigerator or maybe a tumor exploded at the base of my skull. I hate freaking tumors. The fear of losing my job was as overwhelming a thought as I've ever processed.

How the hell did I get here? Fuck if I know.

♣

Three days later the main office called my garage and ordered me back to the clinic. I didn't actually think the evidence exploded in the refrigerator, so I was actually pretty excited by the notion of getting another chance to pull a rabbit out of my magic bag of tricks.

Up to this point if the city intended to suspend somebody they simply called the garage and informed the superintendent who broke the bad news. So this call came as a nice surprise. I figured I was getting a second chance to make a better impression. My first thought, call big Mike in Hunts Point and arrange for another early morning rendezvous, but I was still adjusting my thinking and decided to prepare for a possible sneak attack. If forced to give my own urine it needed to be disguised. Vinegar. It's not just for salad, anymore.

The night before my re-examination I drank a full bottle, eight ounces of straight white vinegar like a drunk with an ice cold Budweiser. The recommendation from those in the know is an ounce, maybe two should be enough to confuse the results, but I wasn't taking any chances.

If there ever comes a time, say later in life when my intestines clog and it becomes necessary for waste matter to find a new exit, this is a sure fire secondary shit hole maker. One more drop of vinegar and my next meal could've landed in a plastic bag attached to my hip. I was still doubled up in pain and exhaling vinegar through my fat ass the next morning as I sat in the clinic with my magic bag of tricks clamped tight in my fist. I was in a doctor's office with the head nurse, Miss Squeaky voice. She was writing from the time I sat. My little bottle of clean urine was ready to flex its muscle and my own whiz was clean enough to flavor a nice Caesar salad, but she simply pulled the plug on the show. "You're being suspended, Mister Carroll. I suggest you get help from the EAU Donald Tierney will be a big help if you let him." My stomach was still doing calisthenics and my brain simply closed up shop. I went home to break the bad news to Ellen.

Even after all of my many disasters, it was still amazing to see how Ellen can receive devastating news and still turn it into Caesar salad. I mean lemonade. I mean something less than diarrhea. There has never been a situation yet where my wife couldn't see beyond desperation to the next sunrise, and I still couldn't crawl out of the dark corner in the back of my head.

Employee suspensions for violation of PAP 85-05 (drug testing protocols) were now being executed in a sterile clinic environment and far removed from any garage or work site. The change in location was supposed to eliminate the opportunity for the unstable employee to beat the shit out of his boss if the suspended worker foolishly viewed his boss as the creator or instigator of his problems. That was not my problem. I wish I had somebody to blame.

Freaking cops.

Looking back on this massive black hole of addiction that sucked the life out of me for the past twenty-seven years was more like staring into the Grand Canyon of lost dreams, but it wasn't even close in my muddled mind to a wakeup call. This situation was more like waking up in a sweat because somebody turned off the air conditioner. A wake-up call after shooting heroin for twenty-seven years is when somebody finally drops an air conditioner on my head, the proverbial back against the wall. I'm thinking I still got a little wiggle room here.

I wiggled around Donald Tierney at the EAU (employee assistance unit) on Monday morning. I was already suspended pending another urine test and department trial. The depression that engulfed my every thought was impossible to deal with, but I stumbled through the voluntary process as prescribed by my union.

Donald strongly suggested that I consider immediate long-term rehabilitation to save my life and hopefully mitigate the penalty from the department. I strongly suggested that my situation was under control. My less than honest assessment to my advocate, a man who actually cared, was received with controlled anger. I knew my problem was grave, but I wasn't yet willing to admit it to the world. Donald was hardly impressed with my accounting. He reminded me of our first encounter in 1986 when I explained away my arrest for possessions as a minor incident with no long term effect. His prophetic recounting was hardly an air conditioner on the head. He brought up Ellen, her sanity, what it was doing to my body, my mental state and the probability for losing my job. I was at the Cozy Corner within the hour.

My capacity for tempting fate in the face overwhelming odds was no different all those many years ago in first grade. Urgency is a state of mind and lavatory time is still any time I feel like taking a damn whiz. Threatening to shoot me is not actually the same as shooting me. Nobody likes to be threatened, even with common sense. At least Sister Mary Monster was teaching lessons with learning tools, and a smack in the head is a learning tool. When I finally left the first grade after a two year hitch, the only thing I brought into the second grade was my bad attitude, and now thirty-nine years later it's equipped with a giant pneumatic air compressor for quick activation.

My addiction was now a full-blown rage of fury. Every penny coming into the household that didn't pay a bill or significant family needs was going into my arm, and there was never enough. The cycle of insanity was all consuming. Thoughts of seeing myself as normal, doing normal things without the enhancement of drugs was the furthest thing from my clouded mind. No thought ever wondered in fantasy. Aspirations are for dreamers, and my only dreams are wrapped in a small glassine envelope. I am now mentally and physically incapable of dealing with life without heroin.

41

Over the last twenty-seven years I've investigated dozens of different locations in my quest for the best bag of dope in New York. The building on Barrette Street was by no means the place with the best bag of heroin, but it was the most convenient. Barrette Street runs directly behind my old sanitation garage in Hunts Point. The twenty-four-hour service was great for the hard working junkie on the go.

During the seventies, eighties and into the nineties, this area of six story tenements and two story houses was burning. The newspapers called it Jewish lightning. The desperately poor with no means of escape called it hopelessness.

The run down, mostly minority community is situated just north of the industrial junk yards, west of the massive Hunts Point Produce Market and east of where the whores did their half-naked stroll on Spofford Avenue. Gangs and drug dealers infested the neighborhood like cockroaches. I roamed this and other godforsaken places just like it daily because I had to. This area, like every other blighted neighborhood in every major city in the United States, is where police departments prefer to turn a blind eye to the drug trade. The good eye has a different purpose. "Louie, where's that new bakery everybody's talkin' about?"

I've stood in drug lines in broad daylight long enough to be seen from the space shuttle.

Once inside an abandoned building, fifteen-year-old Spanish thugs banging baseball bats on handrails were shouting orders, maintaining well-established protocols. "No chorts! No single! No talk! Keep you motor fucking cholder on dee fucking wall!" This was no place for Kevin the Troublemaker. This is the place where Kevin the junkie paid strict attention. If those dumb ass kids told me to piss in my pants in order to get my drugs, not a problem, how much, what color, hot or lukewarm?

I signed out of work at eleven forty-five PM My car was parked inside the massive garage and already heated against the February chill. I slowly drove out the door and past the crack house on the other side of the street. I continued down the block and waved back at the two regular prostitutes on the corner. I turned into the next block and passed the drug spot, but instantly recognized a serious impediment to my regularly scheduled business. No look-out. In the shadowy underworld of drug dealing, no look-out casually strolling up and down the sidewalk or pacing the dark deserted courtyard is highly unusual if a spot is open to customers. My apprehension heightened, but not enough to thwart the gambler because this spot was my only hope for getting straight at this late hour.

I warily pushed the door and stepped inside the filthy unlit lobby and freaked when a rat the size of a greyhound scampered over my boot. Sonofabitch! The vacant ground floor apartment is where I first encountered Mike the dealer, who was still selling me his fresh unadulterated whizz. Mike is the boss, but three regular pitchers were dealing his product twenty-four hours a day. Any number of situations could arise to close down the spot. The peep hole slid open. Click! Click! The door pulled in.

I was quickly yanked by my coat sleeve across the threshold by the same skinny thug normally posted outside the building on the watchout for the next blue invasion. "Be quiet, mother fucker." He's never very talkative, but he's never nasty, either. He appeared to have a bug up his dumb skinny ass.

The ever present candle flickering on the kitchen counter was casting long shadows that danced in the night like the start of a silent movie. I hugged the wall and awaited permission to speak. Tension in the empty room was thick. The god awful smell of urine and desiccated feces, thicker. The pitcher, a big ugly moose of a woman was quietly pacing the litter strewn shit hole like a rabid animal. The skinny lookout with the oversized coat secured the front door and suddenly kicked a ratty old step stool that almost hit the big girl in the back before it crashed the wall. The fuming teen rushed up to the smoldering mountain of a woman because passion is best expressed upside your face. Or neck. "I said gimme ma' damn PC, bitch."

The little look-out said that the bitch shorted him on his personal cut for the last ten bags she sold and the young entrepreneur wasn't going back outside to freeze his skinny ass off until he got it, which of course had nothing to do with me. She remained calm, but firm. "I'm not gonna tell ya again, Flaco. Get yo dumb skinny ass outside." Speaking out of turn in the middle of this dispute for wages was the easiest way to get tossed out in the cold. I prayed for a quick end to hostilities. The big pitcher finally graced my presence. "Whaddya need handsome?" She quickly turned again to the annoying flea grumbling loudly under his breath. "You gonna' look real stupit wit ma mother fuckin' foot hangin' out yo dumb ass, Flaco. Now get outside!" The big girl turned back again, now anxious for my purchase order. "Well?"

"Four."

"I only got two leff."

"Fuck."

"If ya take 'em I can go upstairs and re-up. Or you can wait."

There are defining moments in one's life. Decisions made or not made that seem so mundane at the time, but actually have potential to change life for the better or worse and the outcome to astound the senses. My life is about to turn on my inability to think beyond the paralysis of addiction. There is no lookout in front of the building. If I buy her last two bags, I have to wait for two more. Every instinct from twenty-seven years of experience was screaming, no, don't, because once I take possession, I'm dirty.

My sickness placed twenty dollars in the pitcher's hand. The pitcher placed two dime bags in mine. The crash that exploded the front door sounded like a torrent from the other side of hell. "Everybody on the fucking floor! DOWN! DOWN! ON THE FUCKING FLOOR!"

There were so many undercover dick heads charging into the darkened room that I thought I was standing behind the counter at Dunkin Donuts at closing time. "Let me see hands, hands, hands! Lemme see fucking hands!"

How did I get here?

❧

It was a year almost to the date since my last arrest. Union advocates saw little hope for saving my job this time around. Big hands Benny Botticelli, vice president of Sanitation Officer's Local 444 explained the situation, and even somebody left behind a few times in grammar school could grasp the need for fear. "They want your job, Kevin." I couldn't even imagine dismissal from the Department of Sanitation after fourteen and a half years.

The director of the Employees Assistance Unit, Chief Donald Tierney, stared impassively across his desk. When Donald finally opened his mouth, he asked only one question as I sat, still disoriented and still squirming with the fear that Donald might actually say that I can't go to the lavatory. "What do you wanna do, Kevin?" It was the same question that Donald asked me in 1986. It was the same question he asked me last year, so I guess it only took me ten years to figure out the right answer. Tears welled as the pain of twenty-seven years of addiction stuck in my throat. "I have to go away, Donald. You have to send me away." Donald nodded his head, eyes fixed on mine in wide surprise. "Well it's about time, Kevin."

"I can't do this to Ellen anymore, Donald." Donald pounded the desk and shook his head in anger. "No, Kevin. You're out of time. You have to do it for you, because if you don't you will surely die and you will kill your wife before they put you in the ground."

The sudden high-pitched whistling sounded like a bomb falling from thirty thousand feet. The sound was coming louder and louder because it was falling faster and faster through the dark clouds in my head. My teary gaze affixed to the ceiling of Donald Tierney's office to avert my eyes as thoughts of my dad released a flood of pain as a giant air conditioner crashed into my thick skull, opening a hole, illuminating the first signs of my new existence. It was the first time in my adult life that I didn't feel lost or confused or scared. And who would've thought that I could actually walk away from getting hit in the head with a message that weighed the same as an air conditioner? My dad showed me love, so he taught me to love myself. I finally figured it out with a little help from someone who actually cared enough to get angry.

♣

"Heroin addiction is a disease" was a very popular refrain around the Medical Arts detox hospital in midtown Manhattan. "Addiction is not your fault, it's in your genes." It's the crutch they hand me as soon as I staggered through the front door at the Daytop rehab facility in upstate New York, and if I believed a single word of their incessant psychological babble I'd probably still be addicted.

Heroin addiction is not a disease. It is a choice. It is the choice I had between boredom and escape. Every single person in rehab had an opinion. Maybe my Father's parents were drunks, or possibly my mother's parents were pill-heads, and maybe drug abuse goes back in my family tree a hundred years. "I don't know about any of people, but I have mirrors in my apartment. Maybe you should all take a look into the one in the bathroom at the end of the hall." I fought every councilor, struggling pothead, pill-popper, coke sniffer and every stressed out dope shooter in rehab with my personal take on my personal addiction every step of the way, every day, every evening and every sleepless night for three very long months.

In the very beginning heroin was the outlet for my adventurous spirit. To escape on the wings of fantasy from a life of average drudgery is page one of the gambler's handbook. I am a gambler. When you stick a needle in your arm and shoot a substance you bought on a street corner, that's a gamble. If you stumble away to do it again you win. If you die you lose. Consequences are for those who attend the funeral.

I refused to excuse my heroin addiction as if it were cancer or high blood pressure. It is the stupidity of youth that draws those inclined to challenge the norms of society. Heroin was my challenge and a risk I embraced with eyes wide open. I'm actually quite thrilled that I only lost twenty-seven years to the folly.

My time away in rehab was hardly therapeutic. I was separated from my wife for the first time in twenty-eight years. The sadness and ache of depression was overwhelming. I couldn't even call Ellen for thirty days. The clock in my head refused to tick. Early morning meeting, late morning conferences, before lunch get-togethers, mid-afternoon talk arounds, late afternoon psycho-babble and early evening happy-time. Hour after hour, day after day, month after month. I learned more about the addicted brain in Daytop in three months, than I did by shooting poison for twenty-seven years in the streets. I learned it was simple, stop shooting drugs. Ellen was counting on me. I was counting on me. My job was on the line. My life in jeopardy. Nobody was stronger walking away from rehab than me. I will not crawl back.

I didn't seem to have the same anxiety as any of the other patients in Daytop. My mission was clear. I needed separation from the street and a vision for the future. I especially needed time to remember the boy whose only dream was to fly.

Without prospects, addiction is paralysis. With hope, anything is possible. I'm living proof.

I insisted that my Ellen not visit me in upstate Rhinebeck, so after a little over three months away I finally returned home to my loving wife. Though few words were spoken, I immediately recognized the teenage friend I fell in love with thirty years ago, but Ellen hadn't actually changed. Seeing Ellen through blind eyes was always a thrill. Seeing my wife now with clear eyes, transformative. Ellen's been by my side since I was sixteen years old. Thoughts of my wife during rehab was like rocket fuel for spaceships: without it, they can't fly. Without Ellen, I would've crashed and burned many years ago.

Ellen had the patience of a saint and the tolerance of my dad. My life had been a lie that she kept secret. When my whole story was revealed to the world, she never blinked. The first thing we did was go to lunch. I really missed freaking lunch.

I'm still a gambler, but the penalty for a bad wager is no longer calculated in terms of life and death. Every once in a while I'll try a different pizza place closer to home as opposed to Ronnie's all the way down Tremont Avenue, and it's never a satisfying gamble. Sometimes I'll gamble on a vegetable instead of the french fries. Only kidding, I hate freaking vegetables. But I did change my barber a few times, and anyone with good hair who's gotten a bad cut from an average barber knows the devastation. My attitude is still sharp, but I keep my sharp tongue locked behind my teeth because I will no longer gamble with my life. When I fully opened my eyes after twenty-seven years of blindness, I was staring back on a streak of insanity that was scary even to me. Thirty friends and acquaintances will never get that same opportunity. Unfortunately, they all succumbed to the streets long before the age when they might've developed a wrinkle or a few gray hairs.

Within a week of my release from Daytop I was back on the job. A few weeks after that I was driving through the district with a fellow supervisor and good friend Tony Tantone. I was telling Tony all the ugly details of my dark and unhealthy past. At one point my partner paused for reflection. "You know, Kevin, you don't even have the same personality." The change from a dour introvert to a smiling work partner with a new persona was particularly gratifying, especially for me.

The Cozy Corner Bar and Grill is no longer a tavern, but Commonwealth and Randall Avenue is still a corner and it still located conveniently in the 9-1 section of my district. Beamo was back on the loose after his latest winter retreat at Rikers Island Correctional Facility. His sister Tanya had put him out on the street a few years back, and Beamo preferred to be indoors during the harsher New York weather.

Beamo was no longer trusted or even tolerated by the dealers, so after my departure from rehab I took a daily ride through the hood in order to look for the hapless addict, and with a little patience I usually managed to find the emaciated crackhead with the half-burnt face and fully fried brain with the same name as mine. "You hungry, Kevin?" Beamo would stop in his tracks and point a very excited finger. "That's what I'm talkin' 'bout, Capin' Kev!" Beamo would scream it to the heavens. "Youda man, Capin', Kev!" Beamo was friends with a uniformed city official and proud of it. His smile as big and broken as a Halloween pumpkin.

I quickly pulled the city car to the curb and walked the homeless neighborhood crazy into the greasy take-out only restaurant on Randall Avenue where I paid for a meal that wasn't the cost of a half a bag of dope, but the smile on the starving homeless survivor was worth my patience and my money.

Beamo was now that familiar smiling bubble-head found around many neighborhoods, that one unfortunate hop-a-long that wouldn't hurt a bug. He'd walk old ladies home with their groceries for a quarter, and yes, he would break car windows at night and sell the car seat in the morning to a young pregnant girl for breakfast. I still remember the smiling third grader with the street sense and cunning of a Las Vegas strip hustler, but the long years of working the back alleys of his tiny universe around the Cozy Corner Bar and Grill would eventually turn Beamo into a stumblebum shunned by everyone, including family.

I watched as the years tore at his smile because the streets ripped the man raw to unrecognizable in his own reflection. According to the *Daily News*, Kevin Bethea was shot to death in nineteen ninety-nine on the same street corner he directed hundreds of thousands of drug transactions that made the neighborhood gangsters rich and the neighborhood homeless beggar a dollar.

The little guy never had a chance. The man never had a prayer.

♣

The supervisors of Bronx nine ate breakfast together every morning for years. Every morning I wasn't hungry until I could finally afford it. Tony Tantone, Gene Greatheart and John Lavalle would sit in the Hill Top Diner on Castle Hill Avenue and talk about life and the best job in the city, and now the luckiest supervisor in the department could join the conversation. When it came my turn I could pay the check. I love breakfast.

My life was in constant turmoil from very early on, but nothing I couldn't manage until the insanity of heroin addiction. I simply couldn't handle the insanity thing. Three overdoses left me unresponsive. The most severe landed me in Jacobi Hospital. An unprovoked attack with a tire iron left an ugly mark on my face, and the crack on the melon with a baseball bat left me with a fractured skull and a very bad haircut. Stanley Madoff took a gamble when he pulled a gun, and after shooting my daily dose of gorilla food I was dumb enough to call his bluff. I stumbled onto the subway tracks in Quaalude-induced stupor and picked on guys twice my size on way too many occasions and paid in blood.

Driving a garbage truck through a junkyard was scary, but walking away from two spectacular Hollywood type crashes on my way to buy dope should've been enough to reinforce a dwindling faith in a higher power. Eleven arrests for an array of stupidity that might blemish somebody else's reputation, but I simply don't care what others think and I don't lose sleep over things I can't change. The people closest to me know who I am and I really don't give a fiddler's fuck what the talking assholes say behind my back.

The tales written here don't begin to tell the story of a life in constant chaos. I'm not sure why I'm not dead because I've had so many wonderful opportunities, but I do have a theory. I actually think I'm smarter than the average bear. Maybe not, but I did shoot heroin for twenty-seven years and I'm still here and collecting a rather nice pension check from the city, so I might actually be a freaking genius. I'm just saying. So what do ya think? Only kidding. Still don't give a rat's ass.

Some swear I was born with a horseshoe up my ass. Others are convinced of divine intervention. Those very few people familiar with the dark places I've traveled tell me I'm a walking miracle. I simply nod my head, smile and agree. Donald Tierney spread the deck in front of me over twenty-two years ago and I picked the only card that could save my life. I picked the joker. My smiling face on the flip side.

I've calculated my financial contributions to the heroin trade at over nine hundred thousand dollars. The loss is substantial, but nothing compared to the carnage of human companionship that shattered my spirit for many, many years. My brother Tommy and my best friend Mark Madden were supposed to grow old with me. 'Were' still haunts me every day.

Life after drugs is so completely different that it's impossible to wake up every morning without smiling. By the time I got home from rehab Ellen had fifteen hundred dollars on deposit in our very first checking account from the pay I was still entitled to from the job. When I returned to work I immediately enrolled in the tax deferred program and had the maximum deducted from my checks. Over the years those investments have accumulated beyond my wildest dreams. So I'm finally able to smile about my finances. Unfortunately there is nothing funny about hepatitis C.

The blood borne virus was bluntly revealed to me in March of 1996 by the head nurse in Daytop after my initial blood work. "Of course you know you have hepatitis." Of course I didn't know nuthin' because I was never tested, but I wasn't scared either, because I didn't know exactly what it was. The virus was probably contracted over forty-five years ago by sharing needles with an infected carrier, and I'm sure somebody else got it from me.

Not long after my return to life as a very deflated troublemaker I had the first of what became yearly medical examinations. The first blood work revealed a distressing spike in liver enzymes which soon led to my first liver biopsy. The procedure itself was like being knifed, but it proved that my body wasn't stressed enough that I would need to put it through the debilitating three medication protocol. Still, the fifteen years that followed weren't nearly as kind to my innards. After my third biopsy in September of 2012 I was given a choice, live or die. My viral load had exploded through the roof which caused my liver to degenerate to the point that it was now imperative to medicate, and from everything I've heard about interferon, the prospect of the cure scared me more than dope sickness. With dope sickness all I needed was money, but all the money in the world can't buy me a healthy liver. Sonofabitch. I hate freaking liver… disease.

In May of 2013 I completed a six-month protocol on three highly potent drugs, and I should probably note that they were all regulated by the FDA. Not that I put any more faith in the FDA than I would Beamo, but at least Kevin Bathea was trustworthy, at least with me. One of the three drugs had to be ingested with twenty grams of fat in order to be effectively absorbed into the body, so from five-thirty in the morning and every eight hours until eleven-thirty at night I was eating grilled cheese and cream cheese and jelly sandwiches, which eventually added eighteen pounds to my already fat ass. The combination of drugs laid me out for six months and caused two urinary tract infections, the second of which rendered me so weak that I fell unconscious in my dining area while talking to my son Joe and Ellen, who thought I was dead. I came out of a distant fog while Joe was still on the phone with the 911 operator and Ellen yelling frantically inside my brain to wake me up. I came to in the nick of time because I think my very anxious wife was about to punch me in the face. The ambulance came quickly and took us to Jacobi Hospital where I stayed overnight for observation.

According to my latest blood work, the virus is still undetectable in my blood stream. My luck is still holding up.

The language I've used in the streets as a young troublemaker and a not so young drug abuser can easily be viewed as racism. I could've fudged the wording to sound more in tune with societal norms, but it wouldn't be an accounting worthy of paper and ink. I've used derogatory language out of frustration and anger, but I am neither racist nor intolerant of blacks. Okay, probably intolerant. I once had a much longer list of things that pissed me off about black people, but over the years I scaled it back as I learned to better see beyond my lack of education. I can hardly imagine a culture brought to America in chains and enslaved by our forefathers, but I try harder to see their pain, and after many years of reading our history I better understand their anger.

I was strolling through Alexander's department store in mid-town Manhattan, just strolling around the men's apparel section, minding everybody else's business, until I spotted the white undercover security guard who was warily eye-balling a young, well-dressed black man who was also strolling around. The year was 1971, so my hair was long and my dungaree jacket casually draped over my black tee-shirt until I found a rather nice looking, thirty-six regular brown wool Nehru suit. I folded the suit into my jacket while the guard was feeding his racism and strolled onto 59th Street with a smile like a model in a million dollar commercial. I will always believe that blacks are far more resentful than whites and for good reason. A well-dressed black man will always get more attention from a white security guard than a white long-haired hippie. If our roles were reversed it would piss me off to no end.

The first words in every angry confrontation with a black person was always a reference to my lack of pigment, but how do you make fun of a white guy who loves being white by calling me honkey or a cracker? What's wrong with asshole, dick-head or schmuck? We live in a white dominated society, and from my perspective blacks don't seem to like it. I viewed black anger against me as their overwhelming sensitivity to injustice. Besides, I look like a cop.

Being pissed off at somebody is not the same as racism. I happen to be comfortable around anybody that doesn't piss me off, regardless of color.

Commonality is the mortar that keeps us together, but all too often it keeps us apart. It's why there's always a black table at mixed formal gatherings. My excuse is that I'm simply more comfortable around people with similar life experiences, not necessarily old ex-junkies, but my very closest friends have a tendency to look better with a good tan.

My ability to deal with black men in a fair way in my capacity as a supervisor was brought into question on two occasions. It's what lazy slugs do in a last ditch effort to save their pensions, play the old race card hocus pocus, don't watch me, watch that cracker. Two cases went downtown. Neither worker accused me of using derogatory language, but rather that I was prejudiced in my actions. They said I treated whites better than blacks. Every black worker that went downtown testified as to my impartially, and both cases were adjudicated in my favor. Every once in a blue moon the system dazzles me. Actually, those were the only two times.

My job as a supervisor was dealing with both good workers and the lazy slouches and not one color as opposed to another. There were white slouches that hated my guts and black slouches that said I was prejudiced and one Puerto Rican witch who insisted I was insane because I was the only supervisor in the Bronx that didn't put up with her prissy female bullshit. The witch told the Bronx Boro Commissioner I was crazy. I said she was a lazy scheming do nothing and he believed me. Because of me, the ranting loudmouth was banished from driving a sweeper or even walking her very fat ass through my district. I love winning. This one was especially satisfying. The legend lives.

In October of 2009 the supervisors of Bronx 9 threw a retirement party in my honor, but it was the sixty-five sanitation workers, black, white and female that made it memorable. The cherry wood plaque commemorating thirty years' service hangs proudly in a place of honor. There are chiefs at 125 Worth Street astounded by the accomplishment. I'm actually pretty astounded myself.

When I first dwelled on thoughts of retiring I fully expected a Boro Commissioner at the event. Doug Thompson was a true friend, and his sudden death at the age of forty-nine from a massive stroke shakes my faith that much more. My address to the men and woman during my prepared remarks was a lot of fun, but the room fell silent as I reminisced about the missing man in charge of Brooklyn North. Good men going to early graves is no way to fill the bleachers in heaven, and I couldn't leave the job without a final salute to Douglas Thompson.

My two boys had been living on their own for many years, so it took only a little misdirection from their mother to keep them in the dark regarding my whereabouts. Consequently, neither Richie nor Joe had any idea that I was away for a hundred and three days between detox and rehab.

My sons were told of my addiction at different times and both expressed the same sentiment in pretty much the same way. Both realized something wasn't quite normal about their early home life, but neither recognized that their father was addicted to heroin before Joe could crawl. As I illuminated specifics concerning their upbringing, the knowledge seemed to overwhelm them both. The family unit is still intact and my relationship with both my sons has remained rewarding for me and hopefully fruitful for them.

I was about a month into rehab. We were in an open forum when the senior female counselor made what I thought was an astute observation. Missus Allison said that I seem to have a lot of anger. I'm never loud and try never to draw attention to myself, so she probably picked up on the smoldering undercurrent of hostility in my brain. "That's very intuitive," I noted. "Let's see. I mentioned that I was forced to whiz in my pants by the nuns, and at home I was forced to listen to my crazy mother. 'I'll knock those goddamn buck teeth right down ya damn throat, mister.'" My mother would stick her teeth out and scrunch her nose up to characterize what she thought of my face.

Mom's new way of pissing me off changed our relationship forever. Dad never knew and I never told. "Oh, and I'm pretty sure that I mentioned the little thing about shooting heroin for my entire adult life. Yeah, I guess you can say I'm a little pissed off. You hit it right on the nose. You must've finished high school to get that smart." I was still learning to be less aggressive and hadn't quite made it to the top of the learning curve.

When the group ended, Missus Allison took me aside. "You should give serious thought to writing about it." She said putting it down on paper might alleviate some of my anger and from there I might even gain perspective. Up until this point in my life I'd never written more than a birthday card. It was also the first time I was paying attention to somebody standing in front of the room. I came to rehab to learn, so I gave it a shot. When I was released from Daytop I went home with four black and white composition note books filled with Kevin the Troublemaker.

The woman I originally thought of as an irritant smart ass actually armed me with the one tool I needed to keep my dumb ass clean and sober—a hobby, writing, and it kept my hyperactive brain hyperactive for up to sixteen hours a day when I was most vulnerable after leaving the cocoon of rehab.

My entire story had been written in a voice and from the prospective of who I was at the time. I am no longer Kevin the Troublemaker. Kevin the Troublemaker didn't like cops. Troublemakers rarely do. How I thought about cops then is not how I think about cops now. America has become an angry nation in my sixty-seven years. Our leaders have failed us. The police separate us from anarchy. We don't pay them enough.

What I said about firemen after failing the medical exam is exactly what I thought at the time. I can't even explain how pissed off I was. It wasn't until I was promoted to supervisor that I finally became satisfied with my station in life. Firemen, like policemen have extremely dangerous jobs. You couldn't pay me enough to do either.

But I would like to fly down one of those shiny brass poles.

42

My mother was born the day Charles Lindberg landed *The Spirit of Saint Louis* in France after the first transatlantic flight, May 21, 1927. She was named Evangeline after Lindberg's mother. My very earliest memories are that of a loving but usually strained union. The tension I believe was the fault of two seminal components. Of course I didn't know it then, but my mother had already been diagnosed with depression, so when Sister Mary Monster diagnosed me as a crazy hooligan, she unknowingly did her best to convince my mother that she wasn't the only one in the Carroll family that needed medication. The mixture mom and I produced was combustible, like natural gas and a flame. We could both be in the same room, but I always managed to cause a spark.

Dad was the only medicine mom ever needed. Dad would walk into the middle of mom's latest meltdown inflamed by my latest adventure and quickly calmed her shattered nerves with the cunning of an old psychiatrist. A smack in the head with a soggy lasagna slipper was dad's way of showing mom that he was teaching me a lesson. It was hardly a physical beating because dad seemed more concerned with the soothing effect it had on his highly agitated wife. Dad's preference for addressing my hyperactive brain function was to talk my ears into submission. I should be able to fly. His attempts at corporal punishment always lacked the necessary oomph, so dad never actually convinced mom that I wasn't in dire need of regular psychiatric counseling.

As a young teen I was getting more aggressive and my mother was keeping up with me step for step, but our relationship slid out of bounds forever the moment she made fun of my crooked teeth.

My mother's failings weren't described earlier because I had no intention of ever doing so. The anger I've held for my mother since childhood and the specific cause wasn't described earlier in order to keep the narrative light. By illuminating her miserable parenting skills I would've darkened the early years of my story. But after more than twenty-two years of daily reflection and incessant editing in an effort to accomplish my dream of being published, I realized not writing about my mother would be a major failing. My complete story could only be told when I finally shovel the crusted shit from the dark places in the back of my head, but I couldn't find a shovel. I used my fingernail. Worked like a charm.

I feel much better already.

I've always felt the self-hatred my mother instilled in me as a young child completely altered the course of my life. The anger and frustration festering in my head since my second set of teeth grew in backwards was like a tumor choking off normal brain function. When I looked in the mirror I never saw anything above my top lip. Never saw the straight nose, high cheek bones and blue eyes. I only saw what my mother saw and I didn't like my ugly new smile, either. I confused straight teeth with confidence, and the lack of both affected my attitude in a way I wouldn't fully understand until I was forty-five years old walking away from rehab where they finally unscrambled the psychological mess that was once a very young child with an embarrassing smile trying desperately not to whiz in his pants. Although my crooked teeth were yanked out of my head not long after my marriage to Ellen, I still see the exact same reflection: my mother sticking her teeth out, laughing in disgust at the ugly face she dragged into this world. "I will knock those goddamn buck teeth right down ya damn throat, mister." My mother didn't stick a needle in my arm, but she did help to keep it there. A psychiatrist would have a field day in my head, but I hate freaking psychiatrists.

The same senior counselor who suggested I write about the mental anguish to alleviate my anger also made an observation, but fashioned her remark as a mere thought to ponder. "You only know your mother as your mother. You will never know of any pain inflicted upon her as a young child that may be the cause of her anger towards you. What happened to your mother before she was your mother?" And that is the sixty-four-thousand-dollar question.

My mother finally died at the age of eighty-eight on the same date as my father, twenty-four years later. She was still very aware and unfortunately still very depressed, so it's a good thing, she still couldn't catch me.

My father talked often and always in glowing terms of his loving parents and I thank them often for his friendly smile and giving way. It's hard to miss what you never had. Unfortunately I never had that affectionate pat on my droopy diaper from Grandma Barbara or

Grandpa John because they both passed on and went straight to the open arms of a loving Savior two years before my grand entrance, but I miss them anyway.

My dad never boasted, but with a twinkle in his eyes he did often remind Kathleen, Tommy and me of his mother's special affection for him. "You're the best of nine, Buddy." Even with two future nuns in the family my dad was the best. My German grandma knew it while dad was still a young boy. You're best of nine, Buddy. Everybody should have a dad they could count on no matter what. My dad's the best of nine times nine, and I don't even know how much that is, but I bet it's a real lot. That, I know for sure.

♣

The odds-makers up at Willie's Luncheonette could never have imagined our disastrous marriage lasting even through Labor Day weekend of 1968, but Ellen and I beat the odds and all the talkers. But luck and longevity alone will not sustain love. Love is a job, like work. If you don't love your job, people notice. I could easily explain the love for my job, but if I tried to explain the love for the big redhead I'd have to kill a few more trees. Ellen is the reason for my next breath. Without my wife, my life and purpose would be empty of joy and I'm glad I've lived long enough to prove it with actions and not meaningless words to my best friend, lover and champion of my spirit.

We laugh at familiarity. Maybe you recall some annoying little kid doing the same irritating, dumb shit described here in my story. Maybe it was a brother, a friend or that impish smiling menace that lived upstairs or down the block or around the corner. Every neighborhood gets a few Kevin's. There's probably one taking the air out of your front tire right now and if you hurry and look out the window you'll see, it's not me.

I recall little friends as far back as Taylor Avenue and then bigger friends and even young teenage friends who said that their moms would not allow them to play with me anymore. "My mom says you're a troublemaker, or, mom says stay away from that Kevin. He's nothing but trouble." And for as long as I could remember I had more friends than the ice-cream man.

I've often wondered how different my early education could've been if given an opportunity to grow a brain in an environment sympathetic towards children with my particular malady, a daydreamer. In today's insanity I would be diagnosed with attention deficit disorder and drugged into oblivion, and then if I whizzed in my pants I probably wouldn't have cared. But I believe I was simply immature and not capable of concentrating on anything not already in my own little universe, and definitely not ready for the monster dressed like a nun.

I do not concentrate the slightest bit of energy on what I've lost due to my addiction. My every waking minute is spent re-attaining the principles of the little boy that grew up at the knee of the greatest dad in the world. What I saw and heard I never forgot. I simply lost my bearings for an eternity and a half, and finding those values in the back of my head is now my greatest pleasure.

I truly enjoyed writing about little Kevin. Bigger Kevin was not funny and my antics and their consequences pretty much changed the tenor of the tale. I would not be offended to hear that a reader has perceived me as a head case. I have an inquisitive nature and the nerve of an astronaut, and I smile way too much when I should fear for my life. It's these characteristics that might make me annoying, but definitely not crazy. And somewhere in a closet buried under fifty-five years of dust I have proof of that in writing from Doctor Edelman, psychiatrist and friend to juvenile firebugs with tendencies towards aggravated barbecuing. No, really. Why would I lie? I have proof.

For those who might remember me as a child and watched me develop into an extraordinarily annoying neighborhood menace, this accounting might reinforce the old whispered notion of my mental instability, but I implore those same individuals to look beyond the curtain of moral judgment, that place in our heads where we hide our secrets from the world. My secrets kept me locked away for twenty-seven years. No one looked or was invited beyond the curtain. When I finally turned my heart and soul inside out at rehab and revealed my blackest indiscretions, I evolved beyond the depths of despair and emerged as person that somewhat resembled my dad. He was in there all the time, I just didn't know.

Other than the torturous days spent in school, my early life was full of adventure and great joy, but as I grew older I began to take an accounting of my prospects for the future and realized my failings, which led me through prolonged stretches of anxiety. I attempted to cover my lack of education with smiles and jokes, but my teeth weren't that straight and I was no longer funny, which led to a vicious cycle of introspection and perverted logic that eventually led me down a hole that always started in the blacker regions of my head. But even on my darkest days the thoughts of my dad enabled my spirits to soar to those special places among the spaceships where even bald eagles and B-52's dare not fly.

I quite often lay awake in a flood of tears and visit the smiling face that belonged to the son of a postal worker and a loving affectionate mom. My dad gifted me the ability and intestinal fortitude to write this story after long years of struggle and personal neglect. My combative personality was earned in the trenches of childhood, but the inner strength and intelligence is another gift from my dad.

My dad handed out love like Bulldog Tanks on a daily basis for the son he cherished as much as his love of Jesus. I hope the readers of this tome can empathize with that kind of unconditional caring, if only in a small way.

My dad is always my inspiration and the beacon I always manage to find during my darker moments. I never heard the man say a bad word until I was thirty-five years old, and it wasn't that bad, but when I suddenly heard 'shit' after a few beers during a failed attempt at his regular Friday night card game, I thought I was in a parallel universe on a bad TV show.

Not long after my first arrest for possession of heroin, way back in 1986, I informed my dad of my many years of addiction. My honest intention was to clean up because the possibility of losing my job with the Department of Sanitation was gaining a certain momentum. Dad was heartbroken for my internal struggle and found it difficult to fathom the longevity of my compulsion, but he also said he was proud of me and he always told me he loved me.

My dad was stricken with cancer. I was stricken with the possibility of losing my dearest friend, my greatest supporter, my hero and the man I still struggle to emulate my every waking hour.

My dad was growing weaker, the chemotherapy straining his heart. My daily visits would brighten his spirits and he struggled to be positive. "The doctor said I might be able to leave soon." His sickness was killing me. My dad was withering away in a hospital bed, and every evening I was dragging myself away to leave him alone, with only his rosary beads to keep him company.

What god would betray this beautiful soul? I had no more faith to pray. I hugged and kissed him as always. "See ya tomorrow, dad." And as always he managed a smile through the pain. "See ya tomorrow, Luke."

It was late at night. The family was summoned to the hospital after a fatal heart attack. Dad was revived and coherent when he signed a DNR. We hurried his side to say good-bye to a brother, a father-in-law, a dad and a husband, and when those who loved my dad the most went home, I returned to his side to hold his hand, to cry alone and tell him how much I loved him. He never reopened his trusting eyes. I hoped he was listening, but his breathing was so shallow. My dad died as he lived, peacefully holding his son's hand as his Lord pulled him up by the other.

I always smile when I think of my dad. I always cry when I look upon my empty hand.

My dad was a paratrooper and proud member of the 82nd Airborne. Gerry Carroll dad was a veteran of the Battle of the Bulge during World War II, and I never knew it until my Aunt Helen, dad's oldest sister informed me of his service five years after his burial in Calverton National Cemetery.

My dad was the humblest and kindest of men and never preached, but rather lived what he believed, that all men are created equal in the eyes of the Almighty. The words I've expressed here can never articulate the incredible pain for the loss of the loving man that gave me my special name, and I still miss the gentle voice that sang it through a perpetually smiling face.

I inhale a little deeper now for I also breathe for the man that resides in my heart. My dad lives in me every day and Gerry Carroll will only truly die when they bury his oldest son, Luke.

How did I get here? Well, I still can't fly, but my dad did teach me to soar.

♣

This book is a loving tribute for my dad,

Gerard James 'Buddy' Carroll

❧

In 2009 Kevin John Carroll retired as a supervisor after thirty years' service to the New York City Department of Sanitation. Kevin grew up in and still lives in New York. He married the love of his life and they raised two sons, Richie and Joe. Kevin's introduction to heroin soon became what could have been a ticket to hell. His addiction lasted an agonizing twenty-seven years. He is now clean over twenty-two years. Kevin still has his beautiful Ellen by his side. *I Still Can't Fly* was Kevin's catharsis. Kevin does not look at his writing or his story as a learning tool. As the publisher, I say different: Kevin's survival is a lesson for the struggling masses. Find someone to love and live for them.

TITLES FROM HARD BALL PRESS

A Great Vision: A Militant Family's Journey Through the Twentieth Century
Richard March

Caring: 1199 Nursing Home Workers Tell Their Story

Fight For Your Long Day
Classroom Edition, by Alex Kudera

I Still Can't Fly: Confessions of a Lifelong Troublemaker
Kevin John Carroll

Love Dies – Thriller, Timothy Sheard

The Man Who Fell From the Sky – Bill Fletcher Jr. (Winter 2018-19)

Murder of a Post Office Manager – Legal Thriller, Paul Felton

New York Hustle: Pool Rooms, School Rooms and Street Corners
Memoir, Stan Maron

Passion's Pride: Return to the Dawning – Cathie Wright- Lewis

The Secrets of the Snow –Poetry, Hiva Panahi

Sixteen Tons – Novel, Kevin Corley

Throw Out the Water – Sequel to Sixteen Tons, Kevin Corley

We Are One: Stories of Work, Life & Love – Elizabeth Gottieb, ed.

What Did You Learn at Work Today? The Forbidden Lessons of Labor Education
Helena Worthen

With Our Loving Hands: 1199 Nursing Home Workers Tell Their Story

Winning Richmond: How a Progressive Alliance Won City Hall – Gayle McLaughlin

Woman Missing – A Mill Town Mystery, Linda Nordquist

The Lenny Moss Mysteries – Timothy Sheard
This Won't Hurt A Bit
Some Cuts Never Heal
A Race Against Death
No Place To Be Sick
Slim To None
A Bitter Pill
Someone Has To Die

CPSIA information can be obtained
at www.ICGtesting.com
Printed in the USA
BVHW031804060719
552764BV00002B/258/P